ENGLISH G

HEADLIGHT

6

Vokabel Trainer

Cornelsen

Vokabeltrainer-App

Verfügbar für: iOS, Android und Windows Phone

Cornelsen

English G · Headlight · Band 6

Im Auftrag des Verlages herausgegeben von
Wolfgang Biederstädt, Köln

Konzepterarbeitung von
Susan Abbey, Nenagh, Irland
Wolfgang Biederstädt, Köln
Frank Donoghue, Nenagh, Irland

Erarbeitet von
Marc Proulx, Berlin
Susan Abbey, Nenagh, Irland
Frank Donoghue, Nenagh, Irland

unter Mitarbeit von
Joachim Blombach, Herford
Annette Bondzio-Abbit, Bielefeld
Hartmut Bondzio, Bielefeld
Uta Franke, Leipzig
Martina Schroeder, Stedtlingen
Udo Wagner, Voerde
Herbert Willms, Herford

in Zusammenarbeit mit der Englischredaktion
Klaus Unger (Projektleitung); Jutta Seuren (koordinierende Redakteurin); Cornelia Frisse, Irja Fröhling, Undine Griebel, Annegret Hauser, Mara Leibowitz, Kathrin Spiegelberg, Silvia Wiedemann, Olivia Wintgens; Franziska Gross (bildrechtliche Unterstützung)

Vokabelanhänge
Ingrid Raspe, Düsseldorf; Uwe Tröger

Beratende Mitwirkung
Simone Beattie, Aalen; Eugen Blumenstock, Loßburg; Peer Brändel, Gütersloh; Uwe Chormann, Einselthum; Matthew George, Frankfurt a. M.; Bernhard Hunger, Dettingen; Anke Husmann-Niemann, Osnabrück; Prof. Dr. Jörg-U. Keßler, Ludwigsburg; Sylvia Krautstein, Köln; Christina McCrum, Köln; Jörg Rademacher, Mannheim; Ulrike Rath, Aachen; Mirjam Schrade, Böblingen; Udo Wagner, Voerde

Layoutkonzept und technische Umsetzung
Klein & Halm Grafikdesign, Berlin

Umschlaggestaltung
Cornelsen Verlag Design unter Verwendung der Entwürfe von Klein & Halm Grafikdesign, Berlin, und kleiner & bold, Berlin

www.cornelsen.de

Druck: Firmengruppe APPL, aprinta Druck, Wemding

1. Auflage, 4. Druck 2021
ISBN 978-3-06-033094-2 – broschiert

1. Auflage, 4. Druck 2021
ISBN 978-3-06-032656-3 – gebunden

ISBN 978-3-06-032678-5 – E-Book

PEFC
PEFC/04-32-0928

PEFC zertifiziert
Dieses Produkt stammt aus nachhaltig bewirtschafteten Wäldern und kontrollierten Quellen.

www.pefc.de

Dein Englischbuch enthält folgende Teile:

Unit 1–3	Die drei Kapitel des Buches
Exam file	Aufgaben zur Vorbereitung auf die Abschlussprüfung
Diff-Bank	Weitere Aufgaben – unterschiedlich schwer
Wordbank	Zusätzliche Wörter und Wendungen zu bestimmten Themen
Text file	Interessante Texte, passend zu den Units
Skills file	Beschreibung wichtiger Lern- und Arbeitstechniken
Language file	Zusammenfassung wichtiger Sprachregeln
Vocabulary	Wörterverzeichnis zum Lernen der neuen Wörter
Dictionary	Alphabetisches Wörterverzeichnis (*English-German*)

Die Units bestehen aus diesen Teilen:

Lead-in	Einstieg in die neue Unit
Theme 1 / Theme 2	Neue Themen mit vielen Aktivitäten und Übungen
Focus on language	Entdecken von Regeln und Üben wichtiger Strukturen
Text	Eine Geschichte zum Lesen
Skills training	*Listening – Reading – Speaking – Writing – Mediation – Viewing*
More challenge	Aufgaben mit höherem Schwierigkeitsgrad
Stop! Check! Go!	Üben, Vertiefen, Lernfortschritte feststellen (Von der Lehrperson kannst du ein Lösungsblatt erhalten. Hörtexte findest du auf der Audio-CD im Workbook.)

In den Units findest du diese Symbole:

	Partnerarbeit / Gruppenarbeit
	Nur auf CD / Auf CD und im Schülerbuch
	Filme auf der DVD
	Leichtere Übungen / schwierigere Übungen
MK	Aufgaben zur Schulung von Medienkompetenz
// p. 108	Parallelaufgaben: die leichtere in der Unit – die schwierigere in der Diff-Bank
More help p. 106	Hilfen zu einer Aufgabe in der Diff-Bank
More practice 3 p. 109	Weitere Übungen in der Diff-Bank
More challenge 4 p. 110	Weitere Übungen mit höherem Schwierigkeitsgrad

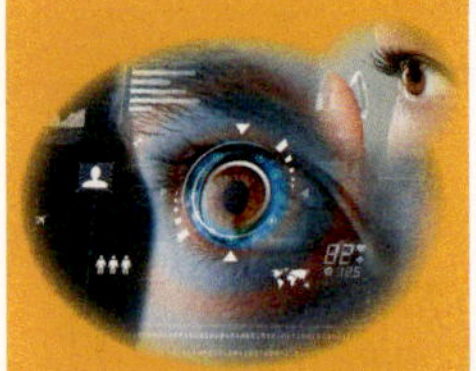

Anhang

Die Angebote des Schülerbuches sind nicht obligatorisch abzuarbeiten. Die Auswahl richtet sich nach dem schulinternen Curriculum.

(*) = optionale Angebote

English connects

1 You and languages

Talk with a partner:

- What's your first language? What's your second language?
- What advantages does your second language give you?
- How might English be useful after you finish school?

A

B

health

arts

sport

travel

architecture

technology

science

education

2 People in the world

a) Describe the five pictures (A–E). Then match each picture with at least one of the areas of life shown in the middle.

b) Listen to the five people. Check your answers to a) and add to them if you can.

c) Listen again and complete the table. Compare your answers.

name	work / activity	How many languages?	Where/Why is English used?
...	...	...	...

entertainment

politics

business & trade

engineering

► *Text file 1, pp. 130–133*

Unit 1

A diverse nation

1 Different faces of South Africa

a) Each partner chooses one text from p. 10 and one text from p. 11. Read your texts and collect facts about South Africa in a table.

Multicultural South Africa

South Africa is known as the *Rainbow Nation* because of the great diversity of people who live there. The first people came from different parts of Africa. In in the 1600s the Dutch colonized South Africa, followed by the British in the 1800s. When diamonds and gold were discovered in the 1850s, people came from lots of places, especially Asia (e.g. India and China). Today South Africa has a big mix of cultures, skin colours, languages, religions and food. There are eleven official languages, including African languages like isiZulu and isiXhosa, English and Afrikaans, and lots of South Africans are multilingual – they speak two or more languages. South Africa is as colourful as a rainbow.

A world in one country

South Africa has many different landscapes – huge corn fields, grasslands, desert, high mountains and thousands of kilometres of coast – a world in one country. Some people say that a good time to visit is between May and August, when there isn't too much rain and it isn't too hot. It's winter in South Africa then and there isn't so much vegetation, so you can better see the diverse wildlife in the country's many national parks. Travel prices are also lower at this time of year. ▸ *Text file 2, pp. 134–135*

b) Share your information. Summarize each chosen text in one or two sentences and name one fact that you find interesting.

2 Find out more

Choose two questions (1–4) and do research on the internet. Add your findings to your table. Then share and compare in class.

1 What language did the Dutch people bring to South Africa? What's it called today?
2 What's the biggest city in South Africa?
3 How long did Nelson Mandela serve as president?
4 What big sporting event took place in South Africa in 2010?

Students protesting against apartheid, Johannesburg 1987

Nelson Mandela

Apartheid and the road to freedom

Until 1994 people were segregated in South Africa. Non-white people had to live in townships – poor areas outside the towns and cities – and people were segregated in places like stadiums, parks, public toilets, and on buses and trains. They also had to go to different schools. It was difficult for non-white people to get good jobs and many were poor. This racist system was called apartheid. Many people protested against it and some, like Nelson Mandela, a leader of the anti-apartheid movement, were sent to prison. Mandela became a worldwide symbol for the fight against apartheid during the 27 years that he spent in prison. After he and others were freed in 1990, Mandela worked with President F. W. de Klerk to end apartheid. In 1994 the first democratic elections took place and Mandela became the first freely elected president of South Africa. He became known as the "Father of the Nation". He died in 2013.

Sport and culture in South Africa

Sport plays a huge role in bringing South Africans of different races and languages together. Football (generally called soccer), is enjoyed by most South Africans, while cricket and rugby, the two biggest sports after football, are traditionally followed and played by white and (in the case of cricket) Indian South Africans. This is changing, however, as more black South Africans get interested in these sports. South Africa's cultural life is as diverse as its peoples and languages. From the country's popular music scene to traditional folk art like tribal beadwork and the colourful house-painting of the Ndebele people, both of which are enjoying commercial success. But these and other areas of the arts have lost a lot of private and public support as the country's social and economic problems have become worse.

3 "Embrace diversity – embrace our differences"

This is a popular slogan in South Africa. It means that we should see diversity in a positive way. Why do you think this is important in South Africa? How important is it in Europe? Write a short text explaining your view. Swap your text with other students. More challenge 1 p. 106

▸ *Workbook 1, p. 3*

Born Free

1 South Africa – then and now

With the end of apartheid came a new generation of South Africans. Today young people who were born after 1994 are called *Born Frees* because they never experienced apartheid.

a) Look at these pictures of two *Born Frees*. Describe what you see and speculate about the two people and their lives. More help p.106

b) Copy the table below. Listen to the two young people talking about life under apartheid and their lives now. Complete the table.

	then	now
Asandiswa	…	…
Brode	…	…

Compare your results. How are they similar to or different from your ideas from 1a)?

c) Akhia and Lindokuhle are also *Born Frees*. Read and add their information to the table.

Akhia was born to parents of different races. Her father is white and her mother is black. During apartheid their relationship would have been illegal. "Under apartheid I wouldn't have been born and I would never have met my boyfriend, who is white. Now I think we have a lot of freedom." Akhia lives with her parents in a suburb of Johannesburg. In a few months she will be going to the US to study performing arts.

Lindokuhle lives in a township outside Johannesburg. He takes photos of life there. "I have been documenting the drug problems in my township. We have a lot of drugs and violence here. Of course I feel free, but there are lots of challenges. I see that we don't have total freedom because of inequality. To me freedom means being able to do anything or everything and taking responsibility for what you do."

2 Working with the text

a) Look again at the texts in 1c). Find words or phrases that mean more or less the same as:

1 the political system in which people of different races were segregated
2 a connection between two people who are in love
3 against the law
4 a poor area where people live
5 fighting
6 problems

b) Complete these sentences.

1 During apartheid Asandiswa's mum ...
2 Asandiswa is happy now because ...
3 Brode is the only one who says that ...
4 Brode likes ...
5 Akhia's parents couldn't have ...
6 Lindokuhle worries about ...

c) Answer these questions about the texts.

1 What features of apartheid do the teenagers mention? Describe at least three.
2 Not everything has improved since apartheid. Describe two things that are still the same or worse.

More practice 1 p.106

3 VIEWING Apartheid – a short history

a) You're going to watch a slide show. First look at these images from the slide show. Describe the pictures and talk about what they tell you about life under apartheid.

b) Before you watch, read these sentence beginnings. Then watch the slide show and complete the sentences.

1 Under apartheid non-whites lost all their ...
2 In the 1950s protests for equal rights were ...
3 In 1960 in Sharpeville many protesters ...
4 In the 1980s apartheid slowly ...

c) The slide show gives a very short history of apartheid. What techniques make it effective? Talk in small groups. Present your results to the class.

▸ Skills file 13, p. 180

d) What did you learn about apartheid from the slide show that you didn't know before? Write a short text.

▸ Workbook 2–3, p. 4

Transforming South Africa

1 Sport and social change

"Transformation" is what South Africans call the process of making the country more equal and fair. Many say this process is happening too slowly in the area of sport.

a) Most of the rugby players in South Africa are white. Speculate about the reasons for this.

b) What is the blogger Siseko excited about and why? Read and find out.

Siseko's transformation blog

Bringing positive change to South Africa

Connect Sports Academy – Progress at the basic level

Isn't it crazy that rugby is one of our biggest sports, but so few blacks play it at the professional level? Some say blacks in South Africa aren't interested in the game, but it's not true. We just don't have enough access. If rugby is only played in white areas, how should black kids learn it?

Rugby in the township

The coaches at Connect Sports Academy in Khayelitsha understand this. I had heard about Connect so I went to check it out. They teach rugby to disadvantaged kids from the township and give them the chance to compete with other teams in the Cape Town area. To me this is exciting because it's where real transformation begins – at the most basic level! The academy has a junior team, a senior team and a girls' team. They start out playing touch rugby and later they move on to full contact rugby. Let me tell you: a lot of these kids are GOOD! And both the boys' and girls' teams did really well last season.

The biggest challenge

But the Khayelitsha kids need support on all levels – from gear to food to transport. Murray Ingram, the director at Connect, told me the problems their kids have are frustratingly basic. They have to feed the kids at every match and training because, for many of them, it's the only meal they get all day. Murray says this support is the most important part of their work.

I think if we're serious about transformation we need to have more programmes like this. Places like Khayelitsha are full of talent! Imagine if every kid had an equal chance to train and play!

2 In the blogger's view

Complete the sentences in your own words. Compare your answers.

1 Very few blacks play rugby because ...

2 It's clear that the coaches are good because ...

3 Next to training, Connect's work includes ...

4 If South Africans want to transform sport, ...

3 YOUR TASK Celebrating sports in South Africa

a) Read Siseko's comment in an online forum. Do you agree with what Mandela said? Talk in groups. Then read the replies. How do the opinions compare with your own?

Siseko: Sport and Culture Day
I had fun yesterday at the *Nelson Mandela Sport and Culture Day* in Johannesburg. A very cool event. Mandela said that sport can bring us together! What a shame most South Africans haven't understood this.

Replies:

Nate: Mandela was right. Youth sport is important for reducing fighting in the townships. In sport we see how we're all the same. And people have learned this. I don't agree with you, Siseko. We're doing okay!

jozigirl: Sport CAN bring us together, but it doesn't if we're not open to change. You're right, Siseko, we could do a lot better. But I think that professional sports attract too much money that could be used to help poor people.

Bafana: I play sports with lots of different people. Race and culture are so UNimportant! We girls know this best. Women's sports need more support!

Siseko: Yeah, it's tough for women athletes and athletes of colour in this country. That's why they're my biggest sports heroes!

Replies:

jozigirl: You said it. Marsha Cox – my role model. She is a great field hockey player who has shown what women of colour in South Africa can do.

Bafana: Pule "Ace" Ntsoelengoe was a soccer god! Unbeatable!

Nate: Who runs faster and hits harder than rugby player Bryan Habana? Nobody. He was on the winning World Cup team in 1997. He has done so much for the sport and the nation.

Suri: Don't forget runner Zola Budd and swimmer Penny Heyns. But, hey, we have amazing white male sport heroes too. What about cricketer Allan Donald?

b) Give a short talk (at least two minutes) about
- one of the athletes mentioned above **OR**
- your favourite sports hero.

c) Sports blog Write a blog for the school online newspaper about sport in your area. Talk about the importance of sport for you and others you know.

▸ *Workbook 4–6, pp. 5–6*

1 English in South Africa

a) Before you read the article, look at the pie chart. What information does it show?

b) Read the article. Then complete tasks 1–4 below.

South African English is lekker!

South African English has some colourful words and phrases. For example, when you meet someone, they might say "Howzit!", instead of "Hello, how's it going?" Traffic lights in South Africa are called "robots", and "lekker" means nice. English speakers from other countries are sometimes confused when a South African says "I'll do it just now". That doesn't mean that they'll do it now, or even soon. It actually means they might do it sometime in the future.

Languages of South Africa

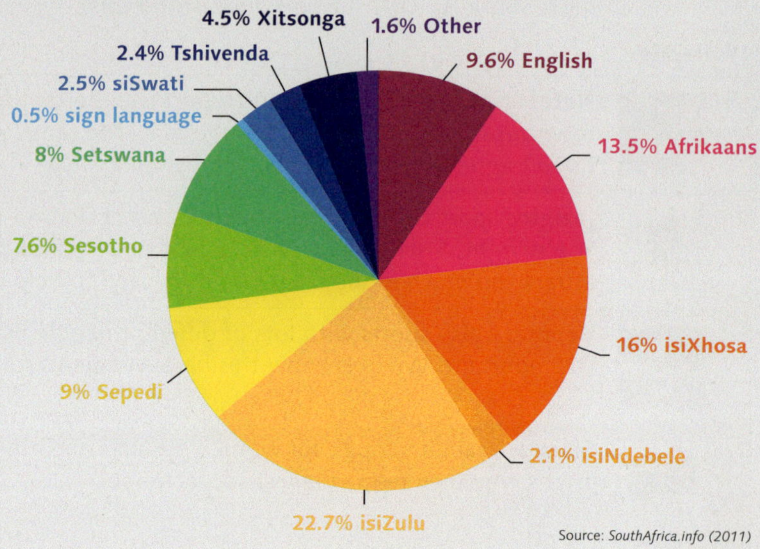

Source: *SouthAfrica.info (2011)*

As the chart shows, most South Africans don't speak English as their first (or home) language. However, the number of English speakers is growing, and more people are learning English. Because so many languages are spoken in South Africa, people need a lingua franca – in other words, one language that most people can communicate in. English has filled this role. It's the lingua franca in education, the media, business and also the government. As a result, more and more young people are choosing English as their second language.

1 Give three or more examples of South African English and explain their use.
2 Why do you think South Africans prefer to use English as a lingua franca?
3 Explain the difference between a first language and a second language.

▸ *Skills files 7.4, p. 162; 11.3, p. 177*

4 Fill the gaps with information from the chart.

English is the first language of only ... (1) per cent of South Africans. Three home languages are spoken more widely than English: ... (2), ... (3) and ... (4). And there are nearly as many home speakers of ... (5) as there are of English. ... (6) is the most widely spoken first language. Afrikaans, which is spoken by ... (7) per cent of South Africans, is the language brought by white settlers from Holland in the 17th century.

2 Using present tenses

FOCUS

1 You use the ***simple present*** to talk about
- things that usually (always, often, sometimes, never) happen or
- simple statements of fact. Example: "Lekker!" means "nice". ▸ *Language file 1, p. 181*

2 You use the ***present progressive*** to say what is happening at the moment and to describe pictures or cartoons. Example: The number of English speakers is growing. ▸ *Language file 2, p. 182*

3 **NEW** Some verbs (state verbs and verbs of perception) are **not** usually used in the **progressive** form.
Example: ~~I'm understanding~~ → I understand ▸ *Language file 2, p. 182*
Similar verbs: be, believe, hear, know, like, mean, need, see, seem, want

More challenge 2 p. 107

Find examples of the *simple present* and the *present progressive* in the article on p. 16.

3 A South African cartoon

Complete the sentences with the correct form of the verbs in brackets.

1 In this cartoon a boy *is asking* (ask) a man for directions while his parents ... (wait) in their car.
2 They ... (be) probably from England because the boy ... (wear) a T-shirt with the British flag.
3 There ... (be) a sign for the Lion Park on the left, and that's what the tourists ... (look for).
4 The boy ... (look) confused and question marks show that he ... (not understand) what the man ... (say).
5 The cartoon is only funny if you ... (know) that some South African English words ... (be) different to British English.
6 The British boy ... (not know) that in South Africa when people ... (talk) about a robot, they ... (mean) a traffic light.

4 Describing a cartoon

Write about this cartoon.
Then share your description and your ideas.

More help p. 107

1 Describe what you can see in the cartoon: first the picture, then the words (if there are any).
2 Explain what you think the artist wants to say.
3 Draw conclusions about the cartoon: What do you think of the illustration and the humour?
▸ *Skills file 11.2, p. 176*

▸ *Workbook 7–10, pp. 7–8*

5 Improve your English: typical mistakes

a) Read the tips and correct the text. Compare.

1 German 'Es gibt' is ... in English. Check in a dictionary.

3 German 'mehr als' is ... in English. Check in a dictionary.

6 'Also' in German doesn't mean the same as *also* in English. It's a *false friend.*

English – a world language

English is spoken as a first language by most people in the US, the UK, Canada, Australia, Ireland and New Zealand. ~~It gives~~ also many other countries around the world where English an important second language ~~is~~.
Examples are South Africa and India. In fact more people speak English in India ~~as~~ in any other country in the world.
In Europe more and more people ~~learn~~ English. For example in Sweden 80 % of the people say that they speak English ~~good~~, and in Germany 50 % say the same. ~~Also~~ it's very important to improve your English.

2 Remember the correct word order in English sentences (s-v-o).
▸ Language files 15–16, p. 188

4 To describe things that are happening at the moment you use the ...(→ p. 17, task 2)

5 Instead of an adjective you need an adverb here. Why?
▸ Language file 20, p. 191

b) Collect your own typical mistakes in a list like this. ▸ Skills files 1 and 3, pp. 156 and 158

typical vocabulary mistakes	*typical grammar mistakes*
1) different phrases in German and English, e.g. "Es gibt" → There is/are "mehr als" → more than	*1) word order → S-V-O in English statements e.g. There are many countries where English is important.*
2) false friends Some words are similar in English and German, but mean something different, e.g. also (= "auch"), become (= "werden"), ...	*2) Use adverbs for describing verbs, adjectives and participles, e.g. They speak English well. I like well-spoken English.*

More challenge 3 p. 108

c) Choose the right word for each sentence and put it into the correct form.

become • get • hear • interested • interesting • learn • listen to • mean • meaning • opinion • remember • remind • strict • strong • study • think

1 Our English exam is tomorrow, so I need to ... tonight.
2 I'm glad you ... me – I nearly forgot!
3 In his class we have to sit up straight and do lots of homework. He's so ...!
4 I don't agree. In my ... he's a good teacher.
5 I ... that learning English is fun.
6 It's important to ... good marks in English.
7 Today's lesson wasn't very ...
8 I like to ... British music on the internet.

▸ Workbook 11–12, p. 9

1 The blurb

First look at the blurb from the back cover. What do you learn about …
- the main character?
- the setting?
- the plot?

Now read the text and find out more.

Buyisiwe (Buyi) feels like a stranger in London, where he grew up. Then he gets some terrible news: his mother can't take care of him any more. He has to join the father he has never met, in Africa. What is his new life in Africa going to be like? How will he feel in his new home?

Returned (adapted from the novel *Scarred Lions* by Fanie Viljoen)

1 There was trouble in the air. I just knew it. For days I could feel it – in the crowded trains in the London Underground, in the school classrooms, in the streets. And it made me scared.

I felt hunted …

It was late in the afternoon. Friday. I took the escalator and finally stepped out of the musty underground tunnels. The morning rain lined the streets. Everybody wanted to get home as soon as possible. Grey clouds covered the sky. It would rain again very soon.
Trouble, I thought again. There was trouble in the air. So I walked quicker – I felt hunted like an animal.

I caught a sudden glimpse of myself in a shop window. Black face, frightened eyes, the cut on my lip. And I felt like a stranger. How could this be? I had lived in London all my life. I lived here with my mum in a two-bedroomed council flat above the street. I went to a state school here. But somehow I was a stranger. Was that my problem?

Buyisiwe. My name echoed in my head. A stranger's name. Why not James, Chris or Peter? Or even Jonathan? Why not any other name, like most of the boys in school? Buyisiwe. That is what they called me. A Zulu name that meant – 'returned'.

---

2 The rain was coming down as I got nearer to our flat. I hurried home. My clothes were cold and wet when I reached the front door. Inside it felt warm. Safe. I pushed back my cap and took the stairs to the second floor. Shouting voices came from one of the flats. I ignored it like I always did. I didn't know any of the people living around us. I saw their faces every now and again. But I didn't know their names. They certainly didn't know mine. They didn't care, and neither did I.

Mum wasn't home yet. I switched on the TV on my way to the kitchen. In the kitchen I gulped down some milk straight from the carton. If mum could see me now … "How many times do I have to tell you to use a glass?" That's what she would say. Sometimes I do it just to piss her off.

There was some leftover pizza in the fridge. The cheese had turned a dull yellow in a sea of olives, pineapple and some kind of meat. I heated it in the microwave and went back into the living room. I made myself comfortable on the couch. My mind drifted back to the fight I'd had at school with Jonathan.

"Zulu!" his voice still rang in my ear. "What are you doing here, Zulu? Why don't you go live with your people?"

Your people! This is my home. I don't know any other place.

3_ Mum sighed as she came in through the front door. Her eyes had dark rings under them, her face was paler than usual, her blond hair was a mess.

"Don't just lie there, Buyi, come and help me."

"What, pizza again? We had pizza last night."

"I'm tired. I'm not going to cook. Besides, you like pizza."

"Yeah, but not every day."

"You could have cleaned up a bit, you know."

I looked at the dirty dishes, the full dustbin, the untidy flat …

"I'm also tired. It's Friday. Who works on a Friday evening?"

Mum sighed again. There were tears in her eyes.

"You don't make life any easier for me, you know, Buyi. You don't help me in the house. I struggle to keep food on the table, to keep a roof over our heads. I'm tired of it all! So I've made a decision."

"What decision?" The fear returned. Something was different about mum. She was like an animal trapped in a cage, trying to get out. She turned away. Tears were streaming down her face now. Her shoulders were shaking. I wanted to put my arms around her, but I couldn't. There was a wall between us.

"This is probably the most difficult decision I have ever made."

"Mum?" I now whispered.

"After what happened at school today, I know what I have to do."

"So you found out about it?"

"The school phoned me, Buyi." Her face was sad. "Mrs Fletcher told me about the fight. It wasn't your first fight … And now I know that the time has finally come."

Mum fell silent for a moment. Things were about to change, I knew it.

"You are fourteen now, Buyi. It's time for you to meet your father. I've phoned him a couple of times. I told him about our financial difficulties. We talked things over …"

"Mum?"

"I know he hasn't been here for you when you were growing up. But that will change now. He … he has agreed to look after you from now on."

"What?" I cried. Terror filled my voice.

Mum nodded. "Buyi, you're going to live with your father in South Africa."

4_ I couldn't sleep for days after my talk with Mum. Africa? Where the hell is Africa, anyway? Why do I have to go to Africa? Just because I got into a fight? For not fitting in? For being different?

I couldn't sleep …

I really didn't know if I wanted to meet my dad. Why should I suddenly want to meet this man who has been ignoring me all my life?

Mum had planned everything. She got me a passport, got my father to pay for the ticket, packed my bags … and one day off we went to Heathrow Airport.

South Africa, I thought, what would it be like living there? I have seen bits on television. Not much, though. It's the place where Nelson Mandela comes from. And they've got wild animals down there. Would the animals be walking in the streets? Do they even have streets and shopping malls? Do people there live like people in London?

"I love you, Mum," I said before I went to the departure hall. I don't think I had ever said that before.
"And I love you too, Buyi," she said and hugged me. I wished I could have stayed with Mum forever. But the time had come to leave.

2 The story so far p. 108

Put the sentences 1–7 in the right order to summarize what has happened so far in the story.

1 His dad lives in Africa, but he has never met him.
2 Buyi isn't happy about this, but he has to go.
3 But this isn't his first fight. He often has problems and he feels like a stranger.
4 Buyi lives in a small flat in London with his mum.
5 She decides that it's best if her son goes to South Africa to live with his dad.
6 One Friday, Buyi has a fight at school.
7 Buyi's mum hears about the fights and she's worried.

More practice 2 p. 109

3 Headings

Look again at the text. Think of a good heading for each of the four parts (1–4). Make notes.
Compare your results.

4 The story goes on

Imagine you're Buyi on the plane, talking to the passenger next to him.
Talk about what you're thinking and feeling. Swap roles. Then read the next part of the story.

Returned – part 2

The land of my father

"Ladies and gentlemen, we are getting ready to land at O R Tambo International Airport. Please ensure that your tray tables are stowed, that all laptops and electronic devices are switched off and that your seat belt is fastened."
This was it. The moment I had been dreading. There was no turning back now. Nervously I looked through the small window of the plane. The city of Johannesburg was below us – grey, with splashes of green. Buildings as far as the eye could see, but it was different from London. There weren't many skyscrapers. As we dropped lower I began to see more clearly: trees, houses, swimming pools. Lots of swimming pools. And cars. Thousands of them on the highways.
Then suddenly the scenery below us changed. Instead of large houses, there were smaller houses. Grey, with silver roofs. Then again it changed to land with tiny shacks – simple little houses that looked so poor.

As my feet touched the ground of Africa for the first time, I expected to feel something special – a feeling of coming home to the land of my father. But there was nothing. I knew that I didn't belong here either.

▸ Workbook 13, p. 10

Disappointed

I walked into the arrivals hall where there was a sea of faces – people waiting for their loved ones, tour operators waiting for the tourists, chauffeurs waiting for business people. Who would be waiting for me?
"Your dad will pick you up." That's what Mum said to me. I didn't really know what he looked like. I had seen his face on an old picture ...
I looked at all the people. My heart was thumping. My mouth was dry. What if he hadn't come? It was a scary thought. I'd be here all alone. Then I saw a sign. It had my name on it. Buyisiwe. The man carrying the sign looked around worriedly. But as soon as he saw me, he smiled. My dad had come for me. So this was him.
"Sawubona!" he said and held his hand out to me. "Hello!"
"Uh, hi," I said. My heart was still thumping. Meeting your father for the first time was a mind-blowing experience.
"You're my dad." I don't know why I said that.
"No!" the man said. "I'm Lwazi. I work with your dad."
"So where is my dad then?"
"He had some work to do, so he asked me to come and pick you up."
Lwazi smiled again and patted me on the shoulder.
I didn't like that at all. I expected my dad to come.

New friends?

Then a white boy and a black girl came running. They were about my age. Fourteen. They were smiling too. The boy shook my hand and put his arm around my shoulder.
"My name is Andre," he said excitedly.
The girl smiled gently. Her dark brown eyes were kind as she introduced herself.
"And I'm Simoshile."

Lwazi took my trolley. Now I felt more at ease.
"I'm sure you're tired, Buyisiwe. We have to get going. There is still a long road ahead."
I saw Simoshile stealing quick glances in my direction. Was something wrong? I looked down to make sure my fly was done up.
It was. I shook my head. It was probably nothing.

Andre talked a lot. He spoke English with a strange accent.
"I'm Afrikaans," he explained. "It is my home language. But I speak English as well. And a little bit of isiZulu."
Three languages! How is that possible?
"That's nothing," said Simoshile. "I speak isiZulu and English. And a bit of Afrikaans, isiXhosa and siSwati."
She too had a strange accent, different from Andre.
"How many languages do you have in South Africa?" I asked.
"Eleven official languages," said Simoshile.
I only spoke English.

On the road

We were in the car, a 4x4 off-road vehicle.
I suddenly felt very tired – and afraid. Afraid of the unknown. But I felt an excitement too.

We drove on the left side of the road, like we do in England. I saw 'townhouse complexes'. Simoshile explained that people lived in apartments with big walls around them. She said that people here were crazy about security. They had security cameras, fences, walls, security guards, security gates, security doors and alarms. Shocking!

Minibus taxis whizzed by us. They were crowded with lots of people in them. They didn't seem to care about the rules of the road here. We were driving north. The scenery changed when we left the city and we drove through big open spaces – grasslands.
Then we drove past some poor shacks.
"It's a squatter camp," Simoshile explained.
They were little huts built with pieces of metal and wood. There was plastic over the windows. Some shacks didn't have windows. There were rocks on the roofs. It seemed terrible to me. How could people live like this?

Welcome to your new home

After a long time on the highway we turned onto a dirt road. Now I knew why we needed an off-road vehicle.
“Do you see there?” Andre asked, pointing to some mountains in the distance. “It’s the Waterberg Mountain.”

We came to a beautiful wooden gate. A security guard opened it. He knew Lwazi, Andre and Simoshile. He waved at us, smiling.
“Ngiyabonga,” Lwazi shouted. It probably meant ‘thank you’.
We drove a bit further. There was a buzz in the air. I didn’t know what it was, but it seemed to come from the trees.

At last we arrived at some buildings with trees and gardens around them. It looked very nice.
“Welcome to your new home,” Lwazi said.
“What is this place?” I asked.

My new home

“Don’t you know?” he smiled. “It’s a game reserve.”
“Do you like it?” Andre asked.
“Of course he does!” Simoshile said.
I nodded, trying to look brave, but I was as scared as hell.

5 Buyi's arrival

Complete these sentences.

1 Buyi’s first feeling when he arrives is …
2 When he learns that his father isn’t there, …
3 Buyi feels better when …
4 On the road, Buyi is shocked to hear that …
5 Seeing the squatter camp, he wonders …
6 Buyi’s response to the game reserve is …

6 Characterization

a) Copy the table and add categories like ***age***, ***home***, ***personality***, ***appearance***, ***feelings***, ***relationships***, … Then scan the text for information about Buyi and write it in the table.

category	quote or line number(s)	what it says about Buyi
age	…	…
…	…	

b) Compare your information.

7 Your response to the text

Choose task a) or b).

a) Imagine you're Buyi and you've just arrived in your new home. Write an email to your mum. Tell her about your journey, your first impressions, how you are feeling, what you are looking forward to, …

b) Growing up between two cultures has advantages and disadvantages.
What do you think they are? Write a comment. Give reasons and examples.

► Skills file 10.2, p. 170 More practice 3+4 p. 109 More challenge 4 p. 110

FIT FOR EXAMS

1 LISTENING Travel talk

a) Travel plans Simon is telling his friend Sienna about his plans.
Complete the sentences while you are listening. You'll hear the text twice.

1 Simon has won ...
2 He wants to go at Christmas because it will be ... in South Africa.
3 At Kruger National Park he especially wants to ...
4 He has heard that in Cape Town they ...
5 Robben Island is famous because ...
6 Sienna is disappointed because ...

FIT FOR EXAMS

Before you start, read the task:
- What exactly do you have to do?
- How many times will you hear the text?
- What is the text about? Look at the title.
- What other information do you get on the page? ► *Skills file 6, p. 161*

b) Phoning a hostel Listen twice to the phone call and fill in the missing information.

Hostel name?	Blue Moon Hostel
City?	...
Type/size of room?	...
Price for the room?	...
What kind of breakfast? How much is it?	...
Is there Wi-fi? Where?	...
Check-in time?	...
Other facilities at the hostel? Name three.	
Nearest public transport?	

c) At a station You'll hear three announcements only once.
Look at the questions below, then listen and answer the questions.

1 How many stops does the Stansted Express make on the way to Stansted Airport?
2 What time does it get to Stansted Airport?
3 What time was the train to Cambridge scheduled to leave?
4 When is the train leaving? Why is it late?
5 What does the announcer suggest to the passengers? Why?
6 Name two things that passengers can do if they see a suspicious person.

2 SPEAKING **Famous people**

Prepare and give a presentation (at least three minutes) about a well-known person from the English-speaking world – for example a sportsman or -woman, a pop star, an actor or a politician.

a) Choose a famous person who you want to talk about. Collect ideas, e.g. with a mind map.

b) Gather information from different sources (e.g. the internet, books, etc.). Collect pictures and/or other visual materials to support the information.

c) Structure your information, e.g. in a fact file.

d) Give your presentation in class. Then listen to feedback from your class.

e) Give others feedback about their presentations. ▸ *Skills file 9.1, p. 166; Presentation phrases p. 271*

Daniel Radcliffe

Queen Elizabeth

Serena Williams

Barack Obama

3 SPEAKING **Holiday plans**

Partner B: Go to p. 102.

Partner A:

a) You're planning your summer holidays.
You've found this idea – Interrail. Read the ad and answer your partner's questions.

b) Then ask your partner about his / her idea. Ask questions like:
- What kind of holiday?
- Where?
- How long?
- Cost / Pay?
- What job / duties?
- Live where?
- Languages?

c) Agree with your partner which of the two holidays you should go on and why.

Discover Europe with an Interrail Pass

Want to find out everything Europe has to offer? With an Interrail pass you have the freedom to go wherever you want. This is a fun way to explore Europe's best places. You can travel by train to 30 countries.

Special prices if you buy now!

Duration	***Youth***
5 days	190 euros
10 days	280 euros

Start where you like, stop where you like, finish where you like. You can see all the sights of Europe.

Here's a beach tour you can do:
Go from Portugal to northern Spain along the south coast of France into Italy, to Croatia and then to Greece.

4 MEDIATION COURSE (1) I need to learn German

Partner B: Go to p. 103.

Partner A:

a) A teenager who is new in Germany has been sent to your school to do a language course. There is information about the course on a flyer, but the flyer is in German. He or she asks you in English for help. Read the information. Then answer your partner's questions.

Sophie-Scholl-Schule • Gartenstraße • 27571 Bremerhaven

DEUTSCH LERNEN

Willkommenskurs für Jugendliche: Deutschlernen und vieles mehr

Was ist ein Willkommenskurs?
Der Willkommenskurs ist ein Sprach- und Orientierungskurs. Deutsch zu lernen ist wichtig, wenn du zur Schule gehst, wenn du Arbeit suchst, wenn du Anträge ausfüllen musst, oder wenn du einfach neue Menschen kennen lernen möchtest. Außerdem solltest du einige Dinge über Deutschland wissen, zum Beispiel über die Geschichte, die Kultur, die Gesetze und das alltägliche Leben. All das lernst du im Willkommenskurs.

Für wen ist der Kurs?
Die Willkommenskurse sind für alle, die neu nach Deutschland kommen und sich mit ihrem Deutsch noch nicht problemlos im Alltag zurechtfinden.

Es gibt Willkommenskurse für jede Altersgruppe. Der Kurs hier an der Sophie-Scholl-Schule ist speziell für Jugendliche im Alter von 12 bis 17 Jahren, die zur Schule gehen und sich dort so schnell wie möglich zurechtfinden müssen.

Wie lange dauert der Kurs?
Der Willkommenskurs dauert normalerweise 660 Unterrichtsstunden. Für Schulkinder bedeutet das mehr oder weniger ein Schuljahr. Am Ende des Kurses gibt es eine Abschlussprüfung für alle Teilnehmer. Solltest du das Kursmaterial schneller beherrschen, kannst du die Prüfung schon früher machen.

b) Swap roles and ask your partner these questions.

1 Will this be my new school after I finish the welcome course?
2 How many hours a day is the course? Does class start when all the other kids start?
3 I don't have any materials. I guess I'll have to buy some things, right?
4 I'm not sure that my parents can pay for the course. How much does it cost?
5 Does it say on the flyer which classroom I have to go to? Maybe you could give me some directions.

FIT FOR EXAMS
- Think about who you are mediating for, what they need to know, and why.
- Choose the information that you need – don't translate everything.
- Don't translate word for word.

▸ *Skills file 12, pp. 178–179*

▸ *Workbook 19–20, pp. 13–14*

5 VIEWING Amar (all great achievements require time)

a) Before you watch

The short documentary film you're going to watch is a simple journey with an Indian boy, Amar, through his daily routine.

If a film-maker decided to make a ten-minute film about your daily routine, what do you think he or she would want to film? Discuss.

b) Your first reactions

Watch the film. Then talk about your first reactions to it in class.

- What surprised / impressed / shocked / moved you about Amar's day? Why?
- Which scenes stick in your mind? Why?

c) Viewing log

Go to p. 180. Read the information on viewing logs and copy the table. Then watch the film again and fill in the table as much as you can. ► *Skills file 13, p. 180*

d) The film-maker's technique

Watch the film again and make notes in your viewing log about these things:

1 What do you hear (e.g. music, dialogue, voice-over, sounds, an interviewer)?
2 What do you see Amar doing?
3 What kind of places do you see in the film?
4 When do you hear Amar talking?
5 Where does the title come from?

e)

Make groups. Choose one of the following questions and discuss it. Make notes and present your result in class.

1 Many documentary films have a voice-over. This one doesn't. Why do you think the film-maker has chosen not to have a voice-over?
2 Think of the film as a story. How does the story begin and end? What events in between move the story along? Are some events more or less important than others? Describe the mood of the story.

More practice 5 p. 110 More challenge 5 p. 110

6 WRITING About the film

Describe your day in detail and compare it to Amar's day.

- Think about your daily routine, your home, your school and other places you go on a normal day.
- Would you like to swap places with Amar for a day? Why (not)?

Write about 150 words. You can put your text in your DOSSIER. More practice 6 p. 110

Hunting the hunters

You'll find the new words from these pages listed on p. 230.

1 What's it all about?

Skim the text 'The Lion Queens' and guess what it's about. Talk about your ideas.

The Lion Queens

by Kate Wills, *The Independent*

Poaching in South Africa's national parks is at record levels. As a consequence, certain animals, notably rhinos, are at risk of extinction.

However, a new anti-poaching unit, known as the Black Mambas, are now hunting the hunters.

A full moon over the Balule Game Reserve in South Africa means two things – poachers are out on the hunt, as are the Black Mambas. No, not the fastest and deadliest snakes in the world, but a specially trained team of rangers – nearly all of them young women – who police the parks night and day to protect the animals from illegal hunting. And they are very successful.

Photographer Julia Gunther spent a week documenting the Black Mambas as part of her project – 'Proud Women of Africa'. This unit is made up of twenty-four women and two men from villages surrounding the park. The women, who are all in their twenties and early thirties, spend long days tracking humans and animals. However, since they are unarmed, they don't confront the poachers. Instead, they call in the armed unit.

The Balule Game Reserve is home to leopards, lions, cheetahs, hippos, elephants and rhinos. Although these are protected animals, a huge number of rhinos are killed every year in South Africa, as their horns are sold for use in traditional Asian medicine.

The Black Mambas started patrolling in 2013 and as a result the number of rhinos killed in Balule since then has dropped to only three. For Lukie, 26, that's three too many. As well as tackling the poachers, these women are also challenging gender stereotypes in South Africa. "I'm proud to be a Black Mamba," says Winnie, 22. "Many people don't know that women can do this job. We will show them that we can do it." As Leitah, also 22, puts it, "I am strong, I am a woman – and I bite like a mamba!"

The Black Mambas

There is a lot of unemployment in this part of South Africa. Therefore, these young women are happy to have jobs. They work in the park for three weeks at a time. Then they return to their families for ten days. Of course, the life of a Black Mamba is dangerous. But despite this danger, they really like their work.

2 Working with the text

a) Text type:

1 Is 'The Lion Queens' a fictional or a non-fictional text? Give reasons.
2 Find out more about these types of non-fictional texts:
news story, ***magazine article***, ***travel feature***, ***interview***.
3 Now identify the text type of 'The Lion Queens' and give reasons for your choice.

b) Attitude: Attitude means what the writer thinks about a subject.

1 Describe the writer's attitude to the Black Mambas and their work. Support your view with quotes from the text.
2 The writer quotes what some Black Mambas say. What do the quotes tell you about the writer's attitude to these women?

Quolile, a proud Black Mamba

c) Purpose: What do you think is the main purpose (aim) of the text? Pick the best statement and explain your choice.

1 It supports wildlife in the Balule Game Reserve.
2 It criticizes poaching in national parks in South Africa.
3 It promotes the role that women can play in South African society.

d) Argument: The writer uses ***discourse markers*** that help you to understand the points and arguments of the article. For example, *As a consequence* (line 3) and *However* (line 6).

1 Find more words and phrases like this in the text.
2 What do these phrases mean in German?

▸ *Wordbank 1, p. 128*

3 Improve your style

a) Use the discourse markers in brackets and make these sentences clearer.

> ! With these ***discourse markers***, do you need to use one sentence or two? Check how the markers are used in the text.

1 There's a lot of poaching in the national parks of South Africa. Some animals might soon be extinct. (as a consequence)
2 The job of the Black Mambas is dangerous. They are unarmed. (although)
3 Many of the Black Mambas have young families. They spend three weeks away from home – in the park. (however)
4 Jobs like this are seen by many people as men's work. The Black Mambas are challenging such stereotypes. (therefore)
5 New Mambas are being hired. They have been so successful. (since)

b) Finish these sentences about the text in any way you like.

1 As well as the danger of meeting wild animals, the Black Mambas have to ...
2 Despite the great heat, these rangers ...
3 Instead of staying unemployed, women like Lukie, Winnie, Leitah and Qolile prefer to ...
4 The armed unit is often called in as the poachers ...

4 A radio comment

Listen to a South African social worker talking about the connection between game reserves and nearby rural communities.

a) Choose the statement that best describes the speaker's position.

1 Game reserves are a danger to local communities.
2 The wildlife tourism industry hasn't done enough for poor local communities.
3 Game reserves have been the solution to poverty in surrounding communities.

b) The speaker supports his argument by giving reasons. Listen again and take notes on at least two reasons that he gives.

c) The speaker also uses discourse markers when making his arguments. Which of the discourse markers from task 3a does he use? You might want to listen again.

5 Take a stand

Collect ideas for a written discussion about one of these statements or about a similar issue:

1 Poachers are often poor and desperate people. We should be helping them instead of hunting them.
2 Sometimes there are good reasons to kill animals in the name of conservation.
3 Women are the future in countries like South Africa.

▸ *Skills file 10.7, p. 173*

Step 1: Research your topic and prepare your text.

Step 2: Write your first draft. Use discourse markers where possible.

Step 3: Check your work with a partner or in small groups.
- Pass your text to your partner or the person on your right.
- When correcting someone's text, think about a) grammar, b) structure, c) content and d) style. Write your comments and corrections tidily in the margins.
- When you're finished, pass the text on.

Step 4: Rewrite your text. Use the comments and corrections from your partner or group to rewrite your text.

Step 5: Read out your finished text. Ask for further feedback.

1 LANGUAGE Shark spotters

a) Complete the text. Use the ***simple present*** or the ***present progressive***.

It's a warm, sunny day at False Bay, Cape Town. Tourists ... (1 love) to come here, and today lots of them ... (2 enjoy) the beach. A shark spotter ... (3 stand) on the hill behind the beach and another one is on the beach. They ... (4 have) an important job – they ... (5 look for) sharks. The people on the beach ... (6 know) that it is safe for them to go swimming because a green flag ... (7 fly).

What do the flags mean?

Green flag: Spotters ... (8 watch) the bay and there are no sharks.

Red flag: A shark has been seen, but it is a long way from people and it ... (10 move) away from the area.

Black flag: The weather ... (9 make) it difficult for the spotters to see sharks.

White flag: Sharks ... (11 swim) near to the beach and the beach is closed.

b) Complete the text. Use the ***simple present*** or the ***present progressive***.

1 Three sharks ... around a surfer, but he ... them. (swim, not see)
2 People ... at the surfer because they ... to warn him. (wave, want)
3 A girl ... up a white flag that ... a black shark on it. (put, have)
4 Swimmers ... out of the water because they ... the meaning of the flag and they ... to be attacked. (run, know, not want)
5 A man ... at the flag and it ... that he ... what it means. (look, seem, not understand)
6 Some surfers ... on the beach with their boards. They ... to go back into the sea because they ... that sharks usually ... in the bay for long. (stand, wait, know, not stay)

▸ *Language file 1–2, pp. 181–182*

2 WORDS False friends

a) Choose the correct words. Use a dictionary if necessary.

1 Mrs Diel is a ... (strong / strict) teacher. What's your ... (meaning / opinion) of her?
2 Can I use your ... (handy / mobile)? I need to phone my ... (bank / bench).
3 Let's rest on that ... (bench / bank) for a minute.
4 My friend has a great ... (receipt / recipe) for healthy cupcakes.
5 Here's your change. Would you like a ... (receipt / recipe)?
6 You'll get bad ... (notes / marks) if you don't take ... (notes / marks) when you're reading.
7 He has worked as a ... (chef / boss) in lots of restaurants, but he has never been the ... (chef / boss) of any of them.

b) Make sentences for your partner like the ones in a). Use the same false friends or others that you know.

More practice 7 p. 111 | More challenge 6 p. 111

3 MEDIATION Tourist attractions

a) You're visiting Vancouver, Canada, with your grandparents. They want to know about the Capilano Suspension Bridge Park. Read the text and answer their questions.

Capilano Suspension Bridge Park

Discover Vancouver's must-see attraction. Visitors can enjoy thrilling canyon views, breathtaking lookouts and unforgettable adventures. Here are some of the park's attractions:

- The Capilano Suspension Bridge has thrilled travellers from all over the world since 1889. For many, it is an act of courage just to walk the 450 feet (137 m) across the bridge, which stretches 230 feet (70 m) above the Capilano River.
- One of the newer attractions is the cliff walk, a special walkway connected to the side of a granite cliff high above Capilano Canyon. It's a heart-stopper – but completely safe!
- The amazing Treetop Adventure is a series of suspension bridges that take you up into the evergreen trees as high as 110 feet (33 m) above the forest floor.
- Then there's the Living Forest, a system of paths along the rainforest floor with information about the rainforest ecosystem along the way.

Explore the park on your own or join a free tour to learn the secrets of the rainforest.

1 Läuft man einfach über die Brücke und zurück?

2 Wie hoch ist die Brücke und was ist darunter?

3 Gibt es nur die eine Brücke oder auch andere?

4 Es steht da *cliff walk*. Was ist das denn?

5 Und wenn wir einfach durch den Wald laufen wollen?

b) Explain the park rules to your grandparents.

ATTENTION

- Stay on the walkways.
- Walkways may be slippery when wet.
- Parents / Guardians must take care of their children.
- If you drop something, do not try to get it back yourself. Tell a member of staff.

ON THE BRIDGE, TREETOPS ADVENTURE AND CLIFF WALK

- No running or jumping!
- Do not try to make the bridges swing from side to side!
- Not suitable for wheelchairs or crutches.
- Hold small children by the hand.

4 LISTENING Two young volunteers

Listen to the two young people who both volunteered abroad.
Take notes about their experiences in a table like the one below.

	Shane	Tess
1 Place		
2 For how long?		
3 Kind of project		
4 What activities? (at least three)		
5 Best things and reasons why		
6 Difficulties		
7 Reasons for volunteering (at least three)		

5 WRITING and SPEAKING A volunteer project for me?

a) Imagine you're interested in volunteering abroad. Research a few international volunteer programmes on the internet and make notes about a project that interests you.
Write an email to a friend in England and describe your project. Think about these questions:

- What is the project about?
- Where is it?
- How long does it last?
- What's special about the work or the place?
- What kind of activities do volunteers do?
- Is there anything that might be difficult?
- Why does the project interest you?
- What do you think you might get out of it?

b) Ask a partner questions about the volunteer project that he or she has chosen.
Find out as much as you can. The questions in a) will help you. Then answer your partner's questions. Finally, compare the two projects and your reasons for choosing them.

Unit 2

Take a stand!

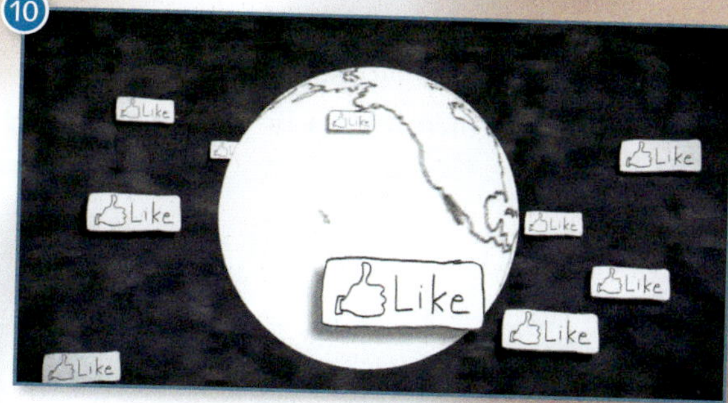

1 VIEWING Digital citizens

a) Work out the story in the pictures. What do the kids want to do? What's the problem? What solution do they find? Use your imagination. More help p.112

This story is about three teenagers ...

Yes, I think they live in a warm country ...

I think you're right – maybe somewhere in Africa ...

They're sitting ...

b) The end of the story isn't shown. Speculate about what happens next. Make notes.

c) Now watch the film or listen to the conversation. Compare the end with your results from b). Which end do you like more? Why? Which is more realistic? Explain.

d) Talk in class about the message that people should take from the (real) story.

More practice 1 p.112 More challenge 1 p.112

2 Taking a stand

a) This unit is about taking a stand on important questions or problems. In groups of four, talk about how the kids and the woman in the film take a stand.

b) PLACEMAT Think of ways that people can take a stand. Make notes. Then talk as a group about your ideas. Decide on one way that is best. Share your results in class.

▸ Workbook 1–2, p. 21 ▸ Skills file 13, p. 180

Make a difference

1 READING Digital activism

a) What issues are worth taking a stand on? How can the internet help?

b) Read the article from a British website and find out how teens are getting digitally active.

Youth make their voices heard – the digital way

Julia Bluhm (middle) with other activists at a *Seventeen* magazine protest

airbrushing a photo

1 In the past people went on demonstrations and protests if they were unhappy about something. These days young people turn to the internet first.

2 Julia Bluhm from Maine in the US was 14 when she decided that she didn't like the way teen magazines airbrush photos of girls. She created an online petition on *Change.org*, and she soon had over 80,000 signatures. She and a group of other teens then took the petition to *Seventeen* magazine in New York, and the magazine very quickly agreed to change their policy. Result!

3 This is just one example of young people using the power of the internet. It's estimated that two in five young adults use the internet in this way. They get involved in social issues using tweets, reblogs, *likes*, status updates, memes and photo series.

4 People of older generations aren't as quick to use some of these digital tools, which for them are relatively new forms of communication. But older activists argue also that they can't replace the effect of people on the streets.

5 Online activists point out that they also go on protests – Julia actually went to the offices of Seventeen with her petition. Young activists like Julia argue that raising your voice both on the streets and online can have a bigger effect. And while protests are local, on the internet you can contact the world.

SIGN PETITION

Comments

> **AJ** Don't think all you have to do is *like* something online to feel good about yourself. Clicking a box isn't the same as going out and doing something!

> **Tryx16** I respect people who put their views online. But I'd be careful. There are internet trolls and other people who make horrible and hurtful comments.

> **NinaH** I agree, AJ! There are loads of ideas at *DoSomething.org* – if you want to, well, do something. And Tryx16, don't let the trolls stop you. That's what they want!

► *Skills file 7.3, p. 162*

2 Working with the text

a) Match the headings with paragraphs 1–5. There are two more than you need. p. 112

A Different types of online activity
B Older people and social media tools
C 20% of young people aren't interested in social issues
D *Seventeen* magazine online
E An example of a teen activist
F One advantage of online activism
G Young people have new ways of protesting

b) Explain the following words in complete sentences.

1 demonstration (paragraph 1)
2 airbrush photos (paragraph 2)
3 petition (paragraph 2)
4 internet trolls (comments)

c) Talk about Julia Bluhm's online campaign. Explain what she was protesting against.
What do you think were the reasons? Make notes.
Compare your ideas in class. Would you support this campaign? Why (not)? More practice 2 p. 112

3 LISTENING A school campaign

You're going to hear an interview with two students who organised a campaign to keep students safe.

a) What are some possible dangers at your school? Collect ideas.
Listen to the interview and find out if the situation is like at your school.

b) Listen again and complete the sentences:

1 The problem at the boys' school was ...
2 First they collected ideas ...
3 Some drama students ...
4 They also had a competition to ...
5 One student had a great idea to ...
6 Two positive results were:
- The police and the town council ...
- The students ...

4 WRITING Now you

Choose a) or b) and write a text (at least 100 words).

a) Write an article about the students' campaign (see task 3) for the local newspaper.
Answer as many *wh*-questions as you can, e.g.
- Who started the campaign?

More help p. 112

b) "Young people need to be very careful when they post their views online."
What do you think about this statement?
Describe the kind of things that people should think about before they get involved in an online campaign so that they stay safe.

More challenge 2 p. 113

Do you care?

1 Does anybody care?

a) Talk in class about these questions:

- How interesting or important is the local / national / international news to you? Why?
- What are some topics or issues in the news that you think about?
- How much do you care about politics on a scale of 1 to 10 (1 = not at all; 10 = absolutely)? Explain.

b) Read this extract from Gary Turk's poem. Who does it address? Describe the poem's message.

Gary Turk

IT'S YOUR FUTURE

It's the young that pay tuition, it's the young that fight the wars,
It's the young who need jobs, or could end up living outdoors.
It's the young who adopt the planet, it's the young who clean up the mess,
It's the young who care for the old, so why do the young vote less?

You have a say, that needs to be respected,
People are dying for the right to have a leader that's elected.
So register to vote, be a part of democracy,
Doing nothing and complaining is outright hypocrisy.

You don't have to be a whisper, your voices are real,
You can be the generation that creates a better deal.
If you want to make a difference, you have to grow up,
Our country's fate is decided by those who show up.

2 Working with the text

a) Read the text again, then answer these questions.

1 What does Gary Turk think young people should do? Find two things.
2 What does he think people shouldn't do? Find two things.
3 Why does he feel it's important that young people vote? Give at least three reasons.

b) True, false or not in the text?

1 Gary Turk feels it's important that young people have an influence on politics.
2 He tells us that some people have to fight for the right to vote.
3 In his view, everybody should support democracy.
4 He says that it's OK if people don't vote.
5 He thinks that most young people just complain about everything.

c) Gary Turk says, "Doing nothing and complaining is outright hypocrisy." (verse 2, line 8). Explain what he means.

More practice 3 p. 113

3 YOUR TASK Young people and politics

What do young people think about politics and politicians? A group of students in Ireland did a survey of young people between 15 and 19 years and published their results online.
The majority of the young people said that politics is very important. And 57 per cent think young people should have more say in politics and in decisions made by the government. These pie charts show a few more interesting results.

A
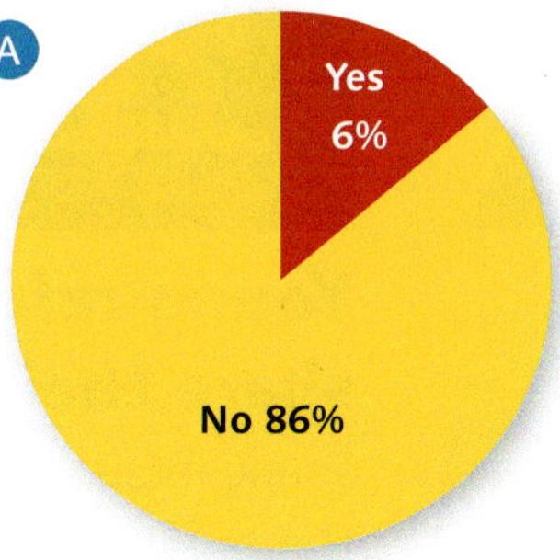

Do you trust politicians?

B
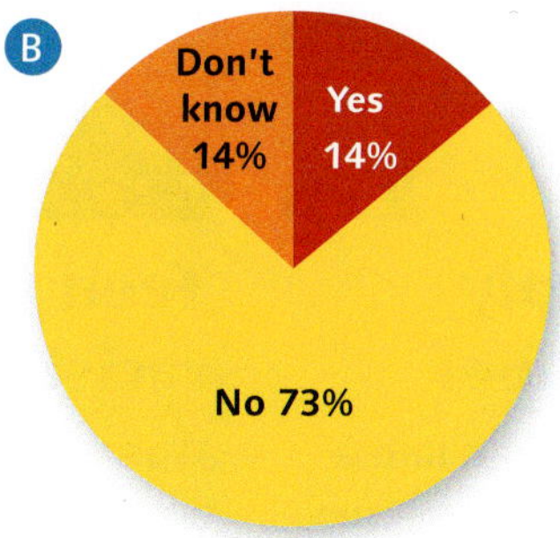

Do you think politicians really care about young people?

1 Look at the two pie charts. Describe the results to a partner. Take turns.

2 How do you think the survey results compare with what young people in your school think?

So what do young people in Germany think about politics and politicians?
Do a survey and find out. Work in small groups (3–4 students).

Step 1: Prepare. Think of questions that you want to ask. Below are some questions from the Irish survey. You can choose from these and make up your own. Agree on 8–10 questions.

- Are you A male or B female?
- What age are you?
  A 15 B 16 C 17 D 18 E 19
- How often do you watch / read / listen to the news?
- Do you think that politics is important for your day-to-day life?
  A yes B no C don't know
- Have you ever spoken to a politician?
  A yes B no

Step 2: Do the survey. You can ask your teacher for a survey table for collecting your results. Ask as many people as you can and note down their answers.

Step 3: Analyse the results. Write down how many people said what.
... per cent of the people said / (don't) think / (don't) believe / ...

Step 4: Present your results to the class. Give a short talk – about two minutes. More help p.114 ► *Skills file 9.1, p. 166*

Step 5: Write a report about your survey (100–160 words). More help p.114

1 Teens in the news

Read the short news blurbs. Then listen to the full reports and choose the right statements below.

Teens simply ignore robber

When a man walked into a store and demanded money, the young shop assistants ignored him until he went away. Police have praised the teens, but they have also given them a warning.

Teen changes racist graffiti

When a Birmingham teenager came across graffiti at his local bus stop, he decided that he had to do something about it.

Young refugees share their stories

Young refugees, students at a Sydney high school, told their stories of survival in a remarkable stage performance.

News item 1

1 When the man walked into the store, the two young shop assistants ...
- A had just finished their shift.
- B were chatting together.
- C were both getting ready to go home.

2 The police have told the shop assistants ...
- A that they should have caught the man.
- B that it's important to stay safe.
- C that the man could come back.

News item 2

3 Luke was worried that someone might ...
- A be hurt by the graffiti.
- B think he wrote the graffiti.
- C spot him at the bus stop.

4 After Luke had added to the graffiti, ...
- A somebody reported him to the police.
- B he cleaned off the graffiti.
- C he reported the graffiti.

News item 3

5 Many of the performers ...
- A have been living in Sydney for years.
- B haven't been in Australia for long.
- C were born in Australia.

6 The performance was ...
- A very depressing.
- B very successful.
- C very scary.

2 REVISION Talking about the past

FOCUS

1 The **simple past** is the verb form you use most to talk or write about the past.
It's often used with words like *yesterday*, *last week*, *two years ago*,
Example: At about 6 o'clock yesterday a robber walked into the shop.

▸ *Language file 3, p. 183* More practice 4 p. 115

2 The **present perfect** is mostly used if the time when something happened isn't important.
It's often used with words like *just*, *already*, *ever*, *never*, *not ... yet*, *recently*, *since then*, *so far*, ...
Example: The police haven't found the robber yet.

▸ *Language file 5, p. 184*

3 There are other ways you can talk about the past too.

a) The **past progressive** shows that an action or event was in progress and then something interrupted it.
Example: The two teens were chatting when the robber walked in.

▸ *Language file 4, p. 183*

b) The **past perfect** shows that one action happened before the other.
Example: One of the teens had just finished his shift when the robber walked in.

▸ *Language file 7, p. 185* More practice 5 p. 115

3 From the local news

Complete the report. Use the *simple past* or the *present perfect*. In some sentences signal words can help you.

John Young was one of thousands of young people who ... (1 come) into town last night to enjoy the big concert. He ... (2 start) the evening with a group of friends, but he ... (3 not stay) with them. His friends last ... (4 see) him outside the concert arena. His parents are now worried because their son ... (5 not come) home yet.

They ... (6 speak) to all his friends, but nobody knows where he is. Since then John's friends ... (7 use) social media to find out anything they can. They ... (8 post) a photo of John and several people ... (9 already, report) that they remember seeing him. However, their post ... (10 not lead) to concrete information about John yet.

4 Have you ever ...?

Walk around: Ask other students questions from the orange box. When someone answers yes, ask follow-up questions like the ones in the blue box.

Have you ever ...
- done something really brave?
- had a part-time job?
- been to a foreign country?
- taken part in a performance?
- seen a live pop concert?
- lived somewhere different?
- ...

When did you ...? How did you feel? How much ...? What ...? Where ...? Why ...?

More challenge 3 p. 116

! Pay attention to the change of tense between the orange box and the blue box.

▸ *Workbook 7–9, pp. 25–26*

5 Improve your English: typical mistakes

a) Read the comments and improve this student's report.

Cakes, cakes and more cakes!

I have never seen so many yummy cakes in one place! Last Friday morning we ~~have~~ organized our Monster Cake Competition at school. Students and teachers brought cakes that they had made ~~himself~~. All the cakes were very good, but Miriam from class 7 won first prize. She made a ~~very~~ wonderful house out of gingerbread. Mr Schmidt's chocolate cake was also amazing. His cake wasn't [as] beautiful ~~like~~ Miriam's cake, but ~~he~~ was really delicious and he ~~became~~ second prize. After the competition we sold the cakes and made over €400 for a local homeless charity. A big thank you to everybody who ~~taked~~ part!

1 ▸ *Focus box, p. 41*

2 ▸ *Language file 31, p. 199*

3 'Wonderful' means 'very good'.

4 ▸ *Language file 19, p. 190*

5 Which pronoun do you use for things in English?

6 Check in a dictionary.

7 ▸ *Irregular verbs, pp. 272–273*

b) Complete the report with the best answers from the table.

Teen hero in pyjamas

Two days ... (1) 19-year-old Martin Smith was ... (2) to music in his bedroom when he ... (3) a noise. Martin said, "When I went downstairs, ... (4) two men in the kitchen. They didn't see me because they had ... (5) backs to the door. One guy had my mobile in ... (6) hand. I wanted to frighten them, ... (7), I shouted, and they both ran out of the house." ... (8) Martin was only wearing his pyjamas, he followed them. However, the robbers were faster ... (9) Martin, and he didn't ... (10) them. Afterwards Martin said, "It was a stupid idea to ... (11) them. But the guy dropped my phone, so I ... (12) my phone back. That was ... (13) brilliant!"

	A	B	C
1	before	ago	later
2	hearing	listening	playing
3	heard	has heard	hears
4	were	there were	there was
5	their	there	they're
6	my	their	his
7	but	also	so
8	However	Although	But
9	than	as	how
10	caught	got	catch
11	chase	chased	escape
12	became	become	got
13	very	really	a bit

▸ *Workbook 10–11, p. 27*

1 The background

In Benjamin Zephaniah's novel *Face* it's the school holidays and Martin and his two friends Mark and Matthew go out looking for fun in their area of London. Martin is the leader. He's cool, funny and he has a girlfriend. He seems to have it all. Until something happens.

a) Does this description make you want to read the story? Why (not)?
b) What do you learn about the main character?
Talk about your ideas.

Now read the text.

No turning back (adapted from the novel *Face* by Benjamin Zephaniah)

1 Martin, Mark, Matthew and Natalie headed down the street in silence. When they arrived at the top of Natalie's street, Mark and Matthew waited at the corner while Martin walked her to her door. He had to make sure she got home safe, but he also had to make sure he got his good night kiss.

The Gang of Three decided to cut through a housing estate. It used to be a nice place to live, but it wasn't any more. One of the high-rise buildings had no doors on the front or the back, so the gang just walked through. Inside the back door, there were used needles everywhere on the floor.

---

2 As they walked through the estate, they could hear the sound of screeching tyres, the sound of a car being raced. The sound was coming their way. Out of the dark they saw headlights approaching. The lights were on full beam, so they couldn't see the car or the driver, and it was coming fast. The car went past them, then turned back towards them. It pulled up beside the Gang of Three. A shout came from the front passenger seat,
"Martin, man. It's me, Pete."

It was Peter Mosley. He used to go to Martin's school. But now he was a member of a gang, known for their crazy activities. The car was a red Ford. Martin didn't know the driver, who looked older.
Pete shouted, "Come on, let's go riding."
"Nah, we're going home," Martin replied.
"Come on, man," Pete tried to persuade the three to get into the car. "We'll just take you home."
"So you'll just give us a lift home," Martin said as he opened the back door of the car.
Matthew was furious. "Are you really going? You're mad!" He walked away.
Martin and Mark got into the car.
Matthew shouted to his two friends in the car, "What kind of friends are you two? I thought we were supposed to stick together."
He turned and headed home.

---

3 Martin and Mark were excited. They had never been in a fast car like this before. They were speeding over speed humps, driving on the wrong side of the road, going on the pavement. They went down one big road – the wrong way! When Martin realized this, he shouted, "Pete, let's go back, man! What's your mate's name?"
The driver looked about twenty. He had long black hair, four teeth were missing and he had a scar on his face.
"My name's Apache," he said.
"How long have you had the wheels?" Martin asked.
Apache began to laugh. "Twenty minutes, man. I got this car twenty minutes ago."
"What do you mean, you nicked it?" Martin asked.

Both Pete and Apache laughed. Martin and Mark looked at each other. They were scared. "Just leave us here," Mark said.

---

4 Pete shouted, "Cops behind us."
The police flashed their headlights to get the boys to stop. But Apache put his foot down, speeding forward. The police car stayed right behind them.
Martin shouted angrily, "You bastards, STOP!"
Apache wasn't listening. His plan was to drive to East Ham, a part of the city that he knew best, where he could lose the police in the back streets. Pete threw a small packet out of the window.
"What's that?" Martin shouted.
"I'll show you in five minutes. When we get rid of the cops, we'll come back for it," Pete answered.
The police put on their sirens and flashing lights. Apache and Pete seemed to love the excitement. They sped through a red traffic light.
"Let us out," Martin said. "STOP THE BLOODY CAR!" he shouted.
Apache and Pete only looked at each other and laughed.

---

5 As they approached a junction, they could see more police cars, crossing the road. Then they crashed into one of the police cars. The red Ford rolled over, throwing Pete out of the front window. The car landed on the other side of the road, upside down. There was a moment of silence.
The police came over. Apache climbed out of the front window and tried to run, straight into the arms of a police officer.
Mark climbed out of his side window and screamed, "Help, Martin's in there! My mate's in there!"
He tried to open Martin's door, but it was too damaged. Martin was unconscious. His head was bloody. A police officer grabbed Mark and began to take him away.
"That's my mate. I'm trying to help my mate," he protested.
"We'll deal with him," the officer said and put Mark in the back of a police car, next to Apache.
Ambulances, more police cars and a fire engine arrived. Then there was a loud explosion and there was fire in the car. Martin was quickly pulled out through the broken side window. The paramedics put him on a stretcher, into an ambulance and rushed him away.
From the back of the police car Mark shouted, "That's my mate Martin! I want to go with him!"
But nobody listened to him.

---

6 Twenty-four hours later Martin's parents were sitting on chairs on each side of the bed. They had both had a sleepless night. They were silent. They sat looking at Martin. Martin had been given a small room in the Burns Unit of the hospital, the same hospital where he had been born fifteen years before. He began to wake up and he opened his eyes very slowly. He began to feel the pains of the accident. His body felt hot. He tried to move.
"Martin, love, take it easy," his mother said. "Don't try to move too much."
His father left the room. His mother couldn't find words.
"Don't worry, love, the doctor will be here soon and she'll explain everything to you. Just lie back and relax."
When his father came back, a nurse and a doctor were with him. The doctor looked at Martin.
"Hello, Martin," she said. "You have had a very serious accident, you know. You have some cuts, lots of bruises, but no broken bones. That's good. But you have some burns on your face. Sooner or later you will see these burns, so you must prepare yourself for this. But don't be too alarmed. Over time we can improve things. Have you any questions?"
Martin didn't reply. The doctor continued.
"A hospital counsellor will come to visit you soon. He is here to help you – you can talk to him about anything. We are all here for you if you need us."
Martin could only say "Thank you" to the doctor. For the first time in his life he wanted to cry, but he didn't have any tears.

2 Understanding the text

a) Find the story parts (1–6) that match the following descriptions.

description	part
A In this part Martin and Mark realize that they have made a mistake.	
B In this part we get an idea of the area where the teenagers live.	
C In this part we learn that Martin's life has changed – probably forever.	
D Here we find out that Matthew is a strong character.	
E In this part we see the dangers of 'joyriding'.	
F Here we learn that Pete and his friend aren't afraid of the police.	

b) Think of a heading for each part. Compare your headings and agree on the best ones.

3 Working with the text

Part 1: Scan this part and find quotes that tell you what this part of London is like.

Part 2: Find a quote that shows you what time of day it happened.

Part 3: Find examples that describe how Martin and Mark feel about being in the car.

Part 4: How do Apache and Pete act towards Martin and Mark?

Part 5: Find the mistakes in these sentences and correct them:
When the car crashed, Apache tried to help Mark.
He pulled him from the car before the explosion.
Then an officer put Martin in a police car.

Part 6: Describe Martin's situation in your own words. How do you think he was feeling?

4 WRITING A comment

Choose a), b) or c) and write a comment (80–120 words).

a) We can learn a lot from Martin's story.
b) Good friends should stick together.
c) You should always be able to say 'no'.

More practice 6 p. 116 More challenge 4 p. 116

1 MEDIATION COURSE (2) At the market

a) **Part 1:** Vanessa is showing a visitor, Adana, around her home town. Listen to part 1 of their conversation and find out:

1 Where is Vanessa from?
2 Where is Adana from?
3 Why are they speaking English?
4 What does Adana want to find out?
5 What differences between their two countries do the girls discover?

b) **Part 2:** Adana sees this poster. What do you think it's about? Talk about it with a partner in English. Then listen to part 2 and compare.

c) Listen to **part 2** again and think about these questions:

1 Does Vanessa mediate everything? Explain.
2 What does Vanessa do when she doesn't know the English word for *Minimalist*?

FIT FOR EXAMS

Decide **what information** your partner needs. Only mediate the **most important information**. If you don't know a word, **paraphrase**.

▸ *Skills file 12, pp. 178–179*

d) **Part 3:** How would you mediate here? Practise with a partner. Then listen to Vanessa and compare.

Adana: Can you tell us more about the *Kauf-Nix-Tag*? What other activities do people do?

Vanessa: ...

Man: Ach, man kann vieles tun. Zum Beispiel rausgehen und die Natur genießen. Weit weg von den Läden, in den Park oder raus aus der Stadt, aufs Land.

Vanessa: ...

Man: Oder einfach zu Hause bleiben, mit Freunden oder mit der Familie, zum Beispiel zusammen kochen – nur nichts kaufen.

Vanessa: ...

Adana: OK, but what about fun activities? Can you do anything exciting on *Buy-nothing-day*?

Vanessa: ...

Man: Oh ja – es gibt den *Zombie walk*. Also, man schminkt sich wie ein Zombie ... ihr wisst schon ... weiß im Gesicht, rot oder schwarz um die Augen. Und man geht in die großen Läden und läuft herum, ganz ruhig und friedlich, wie ein Zombie. Du kaufst nichts, läufst nur herum, und die Leute sprechen dich an. Dann kannst du erklären, warum du nichts kaufst. So kommst du gut ins Gespräch.

Vanessa: ...

Adana: Sounds interesting – but maybe not for everybody! Hey, thanks for talking to us.

More practice 7+8 p. 116

▸ *Workbook 16, p. 29*

2 LISTENING Fashion Revolution

a) **A news report:** Listen. Which phrases complete the sentences best? p. 116

1 In the Rana Plaza disaster ...
- A nearly one thousand people were killed.
- B more than one thousand people died.
- C nearly one thousand people were hurt.
- D 1133 people were hurt.

2 *Fashion Revolution* wants ...
- A better wages for British workers.
- B cheaper clothes for shoppers in the West.
- C better quality clothes for everybody.
- D better working conditions in the clothes industry.

3 Shoppers should think more about ...
- A how much they spend.
- B what they wear.
- C who makes their clothes.
- D if they need more clothes.

FIT FOR EXAMS
You may not understand everything. That's okay. While you're listening, **keep an eye on the tasks**.

b) **A discussion:** You will hear a discussion between four teenagers: Anita, Jeff, Shiva and Alex. While listening, decide which of the statements are true or false.

1 The new department store sells mostly expensive, high quality clothes.
2 Sweatshops are factories where the employees work very hard and don't get a lot of money.
3 It's impossible to find out where clothes are made and who makes them.
4 By wearing your clothes inside out for a day, you show that you're against sweatshops.
5 The four teenagers decide to take part in *Inside Out*.

More practice 9 p. 117 More challenge 5 p. 117

3 SPEAKING Picking the right present

It's your friend Jake's birthday soon. He's interested in fashion, films and music. He also likes reading. But he isn't a very active person. You want to buy him a present.

a) Make a list of five possible presents for Jake. Below are a few ideas. Make notes about why the presents on your list are suitable.

b) Compare lists with a partner and discuss the pros and cons of your ideas. ► Skills file 9.4, p. 168

c) Agree on one present for Jake. Think about these things:
- Which present do you think he'd like best and why?
- How much money do you want to spend?

► Workbook 15, p. 29

FIT FOR EXAMS

4 READING and WRITING #ILookLikeAnEngineer

a) What are some typical job stereotypes? Talk with a partner. Then read the article.

These billboards were part of a recruitment campaign run by a software company in San Francisco. The company was looking for new workers and asked members of staff to say how they felt about working for them. Their quotes were put up beside their photos in San Francisco underground stations. There was a huge reaction to the ads – but not one that was expected. The young female software engineer who was featured in the ad campaign received a lot of comments, some positive, but some very negative. Some people just didn't believe that she could be an engineer because – to them – she didn't look like one.

So what does an engineer look like? The software engineer I.A. Wenger started a hashtag *#ILookLikeAnEngineer*, and encouraged other engineers to post photos of themselves to answer that question. The idea was a big hit and thousands of people posted pictures, and they are all so different!

Their photos prove that engineers are definitely not just young white males in hoodies. That's just a stereotype. Although women and people of colour are still in the minority in STEM (science, technology, engineering, maths) careers, Wenger's campaign shows that engineers can be any gender or race and just about any age. The question is: Can campaigns like this change the stereotypes?

b) According to the article, which of the people A–D is most like the stereotype of an engineer? And which of them could actually be an engineer? Explain. You can use words from the text.
Example:
The article says that the stereotype of an engineer is … (lines 24–25). So that means that the person in picture … is most like that stereotype. However, …

c) Do you think that hashtag campaigns like Wenger's are a good idea? Why (not)? Write a comment – at least 80 words.

FIT FOR EXAMS

First find the relevant information.
It might be in different places in the text.
Then draw your own conclusions.
▸ *Skills files 7.3, p. 162 and 10.2, p. 170*

▸ *Workbook 18, p. 32*

5 VIEWING Walk or fly

a) Watch the film and discuss these questions.

1 What do you learn about the life of the main character?
- What's his name?
- Where does he live?
- Friends?
- Family?
- Personality?
- What makes him special?

2 What do you think is the turning point of the film?

3 Is it a happy or sad film? Give reasons.

b) Make four expert groups. Read the instructions for your group and watch the film again. Then talk about your results in your expert groups.

Group A – location

The **location** is where a film is made.

1 What different locations do you see in this film? List them.

2 What do the locations tell you about Mark and his life?

Group B – characters

1 What characters have speaking roles in this film? List them.

2 Describe each of their relationships with Mark.

Group C – plot (storyline)

1 Summarize the plot of the film.

2 There are some flashbacks when the film goes back in time. What do they add to the story?

Group D – script

1 Who says these things in the film?
- *What are you supposed to be?*
- *He doesn't bite. He may try to rescue you from a burning building!*
- *Just be cool. I'm wearing tights. How can I be cool?*
- *Do good!*
- *How do you wee?*
- *It was daddy's job to keep people safe from bombs.*
- *How do you want to get to this party – walk or fly?*

2 Are these lines important? Why (not)?

3 What do they tell us about Mark's story?

4 Identify other lines in the film that you think are important. Explain why.

c) Now make new groups of four with one expert (A, B, C and D) in each group. Tell your new group what you've learned.

d) In *Walk or fly* Hannah says, "Most people want to be the same as everyone else." Do you agree or disagree? Comment on this idea. Give examples. What happens if you aren't the same as everyone else?

More challenge 6 p. 117

Doing the right thing

You'll find the new words from these pages listed on p. 231.

Jon Snow riding his bicycle in London

1 What happened?

Jon Snow is a well-known British journalist and television presenter.
He is best known in Britain as a presenter of TV news.
He was cycling to work one day when something happened. He wrote about it in his blog.

a) Read Jon Snow's post and find out what happened.

My shameful dilemma

Cycling along a reasonably well-heeled street in the Camden area of north London, my attention is drawn to an argument between a young man and a young woman on my left. Then I suddenly see him hitting her in the face.

I hear her screams and the man's shouts, and by the time my bicycle is abreast of them, she is in tears, her face badly marked.

I instinctively intervene and ask if she needs help. The man is in a hyper-paranoid, violent state, and turns fast and menacingly on me, shouting and cursing, and I take to my bike in flight.

I pause further down the road and look back, and there seem to be more people about. I cycle back towards the group, seriously concerned for the young woman's welfare. And it seems to me the man is standing close to a motorcycle.

The road is straight and somehow enclosed, with few escape points, and I conclude very quickly that if he were to give chase, he'd get me. I retreat, and I think about calling the police. But for some inexplicable reason, I don't.

Even now, I don't really know why not. Somehow I feel that they wouldn't have taken me seriously and that by the time it was all explained, the incident would have passed and there would only be my account of it.

I don't often see that sort of thing, and it's left me with a lot of misgivings.

b) Describe Jon Snow's dilemma.
Summarize the main events in the text in a few sentences.
Compare your summary with other students' summaries. ► *Skills file 10.4, p. 171*

c) Discuss: If you had been Jon Snow, how would you have acted?
Would you have done something? What? Or would you have just kept going? Give reasons.

2 Looking at the language

a) The language in Jon Snow's post is rich and interesting. Let's find out why.
Find the words and phrases that Jon Snow uses for the underlined words below.

1 I'm cycling along a street in a rich part of London. (line 1)
2 I notice that a young man and woman are having an argument. (line 2)
3 She's crying. (line 6)
4 I stop for a minute. (line 10)
5 I'm very worried about the young woman. (line 11)
6 ... I quickly see that ... (line 13)
7 I move back. (line 14)
8 For a reason I can't explain ... (line 15)

> **!** You can improve and enrich your style by collecting interesting phrases. Find out what they mean and how formal they are.
> Start by collecting good alternatives for the common word *say* in Jon Snow's post.

b) Use verbs from the box to enrich the language of these sentences.

1 "Get out of my house now," the woman said.
2 "I'm sorry I hurt you. I won't do that again," the boy said.
3 "I love you," he said, and left the room quietly.
4 "Let's go for a nice walk," her dad said.
5 "I don't feel well, please don't make me go to school," he said.
6 "We also think she's very nice," they said.
7 "Germany has a good team. But the English team is better," she said.
8 "It's very cold in this classroom," the teacher said.

> add • agree • answer • call • complain • cry • demand • joke • laugh • promise • remember • shout • smile • suggest • warn • whisper • wonder

c) Compare your sentences with different partners.
How do the different verbs (synonyms) change the sentences?

3 WRITING More dilemmas

Pick one of these scenarios (A or B) and continue the text to describe a dilemma.
Did you intervene, or just keep going? **Or**: Write about another situation with a dilemma.

A

I was on my way home from school one day when I saw something terrible. My best friend Alice was talking to a man. I could hear them talking. "How much?" Alice asked. "£25," the man answered. Then Alice gave him some money and the man gave her something. I was very worried. At first I didn't know what to do. But I felt I had to do something, so I ...

B

"Don't talk to Andrew," Beth whispered. "Don't message him, don't look at him ... or there'll be trouble," she warned. I had a problem. You see Andrew was a good friend. But Beth was one of the most popular girls in the class. Everybody admired her, me too! Some people were even afraid of her! First I was confused. Then I pulled myself together and ...

4 Brexit – a family dilemma

a) Brexit, the UK referendum that took place in June 2016, divided the country – and many families as well. Read about how Sharon K. of London experienced it.

When I heard the news that Britain had voted to leave the EU, I couldn't believe it. My parents celebrated in the next room and my shock turned to anger. I couldn't even look at them. These people who had raised me to be open-minded, tolerant and worldly had voted to shut Britain off from the rest of Europe. Didn't they care about my future? Could I ever forgive them?

I had known before how they would vote. The mood in our house had been getting worse for weeks. The referendum campaign had been on everyone's mind, and although I had formed my opinion, I hadn't been talking about it much with my parents.

I had listened to them complain about how the EU was costing Britain too much and how there were too many immigrants in Britain. I had been trying gently to make them see that there were good reasons for Britain to stay in the EU. But I guess I was foolish to think that I could change their minds.

My older brother, Nate, who's a builder, hadn't made it any easier. He was against the politicians and big business people who wanted Britain to stay in the EU. "I'll show them what I think of them," he had said. Nate had been coming to the house a lot and talking to my parents. At the same time Uncle John, who shares my views, had also been talking a lot to my dad. But their talks had become more and more bitter.

Since the referendum our family hasn't been the same. My dad and my uncle don't speak to each other. And my brother and I don't speak any more either. I don't know what to do about my parents. We don't say much, but I still live in their house and eat their food. It's a very uncomfortable situation.

b) Describe the views of the different family members.

c) Describe Sharon's dilemma.

5 The past perfect progressive

a) Look at the FOCUS box.

FOCUS

Complete these sentences from the article:

The mood in our house ... worse for weeks. / I ... about it much with my parents.

The ***past perfect progressive*** is formed with **had been + *-ing*-form**.

Examples: I had been writing ... / She had been saving ... / We had been talking ...

We use the ***past perfect progressive*** when an action or event had begun before a point of time in the past (e.g. the referendum) and had continued up to (or almost up to) that time.

Example: (Before the referendum) uncle John had been talking a lot to my dad. ► *Language file 8, p. 185*

b) Think of possible endings to these sentences using the *past perfect progressive*.

1 Before the Brexit vote, people who voted to leave the EU ...
2 On both sides of the campaign, the media ...
3 Many people were shocked by the result because they ...

1 LANGUAGE The European Parliament

Complete this chat between Ralf, a German student on a class trip in Brussels, and Cathy, his Australian friend. Use the ***simple past*** or ***present perfect***. ► *Language file 5, p. 184*

! Look out for the signal words.

Ralf I'm in Brussels. My friends and I ... (1 just leave) the European Parliament. What an interesting place!

Cathy Really? I ... (2 not visit) Brussels yet but I'd like to go there one day. I'm interested in European politics.

Ralf I think politics is important. My class ... (3 do) a survey last year and we ... (4 find) that most young people didn't vote in the last European elections. I think that's terrible.

Cathy Maybe people don't know about the advantages of the EU – like the euro. That makes it easier for people to travel, doesn't it? How long have you had the euro?

Ralf In Germany we ... (5 have) the euro since 2002.

Cathy Does the EU make a difference to your life in other ways?

Ralf Yes, it does. For example, the EU Parliament ... (6 recently pass) a law to make mobile calls to other EU countries cheaper.

Cathy So you think the EU is a good thing?

Ralf I do. But this morning I ... (7 go) to a discussion about "Rules against misuse of trade secrets". I ... (8 never listen to) to such a boring discussion!

Cathy OK, so politics is important, but sometimes it isn't very interesting.

2 LANGUAGE A week to remember

Complete this report about a Year 10 trip. Use the ***past progressive*** or ***past perfect***.

► *Language files 4, p. 183; 7, p. 185*

We started to plan our class trip about a year ago. After we ... (1 discuss) lots of different destinations, our teacher suggested Jersey, one of the small islands between France and the UK. We ... (2 not think) of going there until he told us about it. When we ... (3 do) some research, we found out that it is a good place for a holiday.
Everything went well until we arrived in Jersey. Just as we ... (4 leave) the airport, the bus drivers started a four-hour strike. The next day when we ... (5 have) breakfast in our hostel, the electricity went off. On day two it rained all day, but luckily we ... (6 plan) some indoor activities. While we ... (7 watch) the rain, some of us began to have doubts about the holiday. But after the rain ... (8 stop), we met some other students and had fun on the beach with them. We even had problems on the journey home: While we ... (9 wait) for take-off, an announcement said that our flight would be late because they ... (10 not finish) loading our bags yet.
In the end, although a lot of things went wrong, we all enjoyed ourselves on our trip to Jersey.

3 READING *Earth Hour:* Shine a light on climate action

! Use a dictionary if you need help with the text and tasks.

Every year, hundreds of millions of people around the world switch off their lights for one particular hour to demonstrate their support for fighting climate change. *Earth Hour* takes place every year near the end of March at 8:30 pm local time. During this time individuals, businesses and world leaders join together in a symbolic lights-out event.

Earth Hour was launched in Sydney, Australia in 2007, with more than 2 million homes and businesses. Today the event engages more than 172 countries and territories and millions of people around the world.

Taking part in *Earth Hour* is easy:

- See the *Earth Hour* website for the precise date of the next *Earth Hour.*
- Turn off all non-essential lights at 8:30 pm local time and let us know you are taking part.
- Stand up for the planet and celebrate with your friends, family, community, or at school. You could host an indoor candlelit dinner party with friends, have an outdoor picnic, create a lantern flashmob, or post photos of darkened landmarks on social media using *#earthhour.*
- Tell all your friends that *Earth Hour* is on its way to becoming the world's largest movement for climate change action ever. Let's change climate change together!

a) Choose the summary that fits the text best (A, B, C or D).

A The text explains how people can take part in an environmental project in Australia.
B The text explains how people can save money by switching off lights.
C The text explains how millions of people waste electricity.
D The text is about how people can easily take a stand for the environment.

b) Decide whether the statements are right, wrong, or not in the text.

1 The first *Earth Hour* took place in Sydney.
2 The event takes place in spring every year.
3 People switch off their lights at half past nine.
4 Even famous politicians take part in the event.

c) Complete each sentence with a suitable word from the text.

1 During *Earth Hour* millions of people show their ... for stopping climate change.
2 You can find the ... date on the internet.
3 Some people take photos of ... sights and post them on the internet.

d) Replace the word in orange with a word from the text.

1 a special hour   2 unnecessary lights   3 to organize a candlelit dinner

► *Skills files 7.3 and 7.4, p. 162*

4 WRITING Switch off your light, and switch on your social power!

Choose A, B or C and write a blog entry. Write about 80 words.

A Imagine you have just taken part in *Earth Hour* with your best friends. What did you do? How did you feel? Write about it.

B Do you care about the future of the planet? How can you make a difference? Write about your ideas and suggestions.

C Some people criticize the symbolic character of *Earth Hour*. They say instead of celebrating one special hour in a year, we should care about the planet every day. What do you think about social actions like *Earth Hour*? Are they effective and helpful? Why (not)?

5 MEDIATION Announcements at the station and the airport

a) Listen to the five train station announcements in German. Help the tourists in English.

Tourist	Excuse me. Can you help me, please? I'm going to Cologne. Is there a problem with the train?
You	*Yes, there is. The train to Cologne will be ...*
Tourist	...
You	...
...	

b) Listen to the five airport announcements in English and help the tourists in German.

Tourist	Entschuldigung, was wurde gerade gesagt? Betrifft das den Flug nach München?
You	*Ja. Der Flug hat zwei Stunden Verspätung, weil ...*
Tourist	...
You	...
...	

6 SPEAKING Typically German

a) Partner B: Go to p. 104.

Partner A: Describe these things to your partner without using the German word. Then listen to your partner. Which typically German things is he or she describing?

1

Schultüte

2

Strandkorb

3

Rosenmontagsumzug

b) Think of more examples of typically German things. Describe them to your partner without saying the German words. Can he or she guess what they are?

More challenge 7 p. 118

Unit 3 Future visions

A Active contact lenses

With these 3-D contact lenses you can read text messages and watch TV and movies using your eyes as a screen. You also can take photos of what you see simply by blinking your eyes. Most importantly, with active contact lenses you can check your body temperature, heart rate, blood pressure and other health signs.

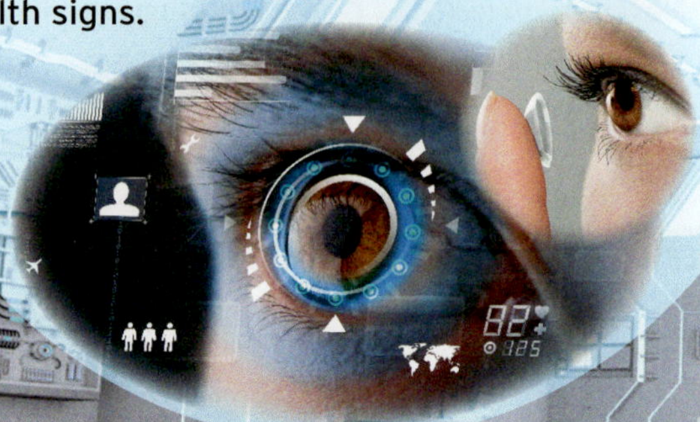

B Exoskeletons

These mechanical outfits give support and strength to the legs, back and arms. They can help people who have lost the use of their arms or legs. They can be used by firefighters or rescue workers in dangerous situations. For builders, e.g. shipbuilders, they can make the work of lifting and moving heavy objects easier and quicker.

C Piezoelectric power

The players make the power for the electric lights when they run on this football field in Brazil. The Greek word *piezo* means "push" or "press". The weight and movement of the players puts pressure on special materials under the playing field which generate electricity. In the same way, roads with heavy traffic and public spaces with lots of pedestrians can also generate power.

1 For a better life

a) Look at the headlines, texts and pictures and answer this question: Which of these technologies could improve your daily life the most? Why? Make notes.

b) Talk about your ideas with a partner. Agree on one technology that would have the most positive effect on your life.

More practice 1 p. 118

E

Driverless trucks

These trucks have special cameras and radar technology and can communicate with each other. A truck with a human driver can lead several driverless trucks in a technique known as "platooning". The wireless communication allows the trucks to maneuver together in traffic. This not only reduces traffic. Platooning saves on fuel and transport costs. And those savings are passed on to consumers.

D

Hi-tech pillow

This pillow reads your dreams, sends them to a computer, shows the dreams on a screen and then helps you to understand them. It comes with a book that explains the psychology behind your dreams.

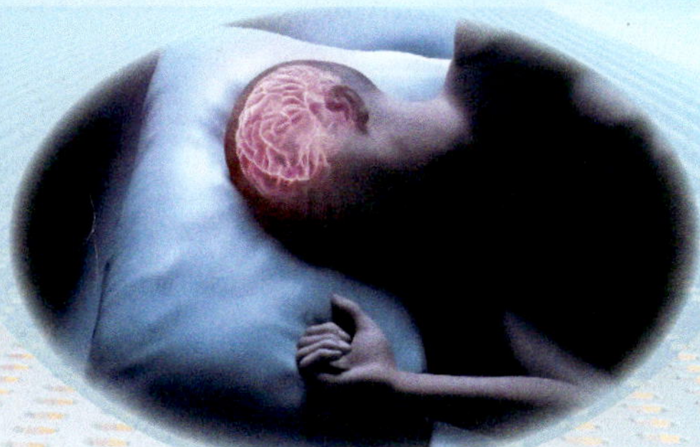

F

Weather control

Scientists can control the weather using the technology of "cloud seeding". Experts increase levels of rain and snow and reduce fog and hail by dropping or shooting chemicals into clouds. The technique helps increase water supplies in dry agricultural regions and improves weather conditions around airports. It is also effective in stopping hurricanes.

2 The opinions of a futurologist

a) Are the products dreams or reality? Listen to the programme and take notes.

b) Listen again and take notes on the advantages and disadvantages of the products.
Partner A: Listen for the products on p. 56.
Partner B: Listen for the products on p. 57.
Then talk about your notes.

c) Discuss these questions in small groups.
- Which of these products do you think would be most useful and least useful? Why?
- Which of these ideas or products, if any, are risky or dangerous? Explain.
- What other new ideas or products could change our world in the future?

d) Choose one person in your group to present your results in class.

A better world?

1 READING Emma's world

a) Look at the smart watch in the picture. What can it do? Which of its functions can make your life easier?

b) Read the story and find out how technology affects Emma in her daily life.

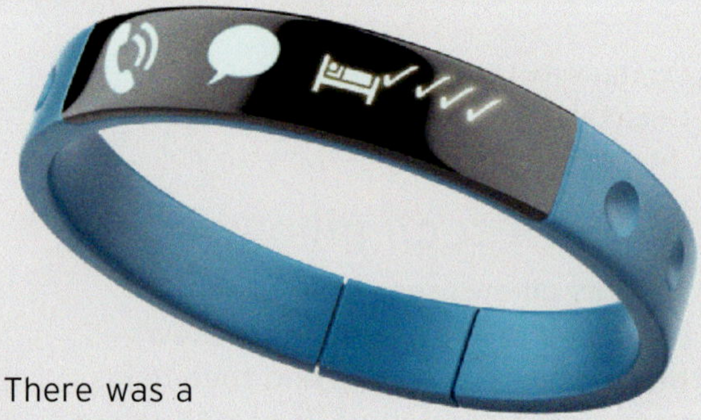

Emma opened her eyes and checked her smart watch. It told her that she had just had a perfect night (four hours of light sleep and nearly four hours of deep sleep). So she felt fit and ready for the day. She touched the glass screen on her desk.

"Good morning, Emma," it greeted her. "You slept well." Her school timetable for the day came up. There was a flashing message beside German: "Emma, you finished most of your homework. But remember to study for your German vocabulary test." "Oh yes, I nearly forgot," she said to herself. "I'll do it on the way to school."

Downstairs a fruit smoothie was waiting for her on the table. Her dad had received a report on the fridge computer that Emma needed to eat more fruit. She hadn't had her 'seven a day' yesterday. "Good old dad," Emma thought. He had already gone to work.

The journey to school was quicker now. People's wearable devices sent messages about where the traffic was bad and the driverless school bus could take a different route. So Emma had just enough time to learn her German words. She put on her wireless headphones and listened to her German vocabulary from the school network.

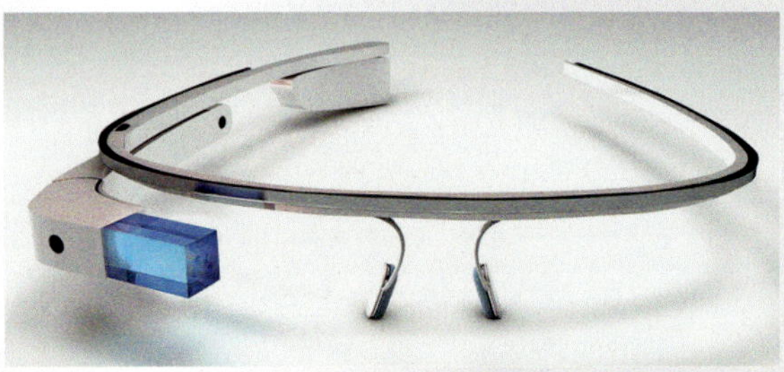

Emma moved quickly from class to class. Lessons were only 20 minutes long, because students didn't need time to open their bags, get their books out, etc. Emma remembered the bad old days when she had had to carry her heavy bag everywhere. Now she just put on her smart glasses. They saved the information that the teachers put on the smart boards. After school, she could study it all again on her computer at home. She could even watch the lesson again if she wanted to. But she didn't often do that.

After school Emma went to the home gym for an hour. Her PE teacher had checked Emma's data on his computer and he told her that she wasn't getting enough exercise. He also warned her not to eat any more fast food this week. He saw that she had eaten a burger on Saturday. So this evening Emma would only have a healthy salad for her dinner.

2 The next day Emma sat with her friends in their favourite cafe in town. They sent messages to each other and looked at people coming and going. Emma liked people-watching. And she liked the donuts here too - especially with caramel smoothies! The alarm of Emma's fitness tracker buzzed. She checked the display. "Oh no. It says I have too much glucose in my blood. I shouldn't finish this donut," she said to her friends. But nobody was listening.

Emma's tablet buzzed. There was a message from her mum: "You've been in the Pink Elephant cafe for almost three hours. You said you were going to play football!" Emma groaned - she knew that she was in trouble.

On the way home, the girls passed the *Johnny Rocket Club*. There was a big red sign outside: **Cocktails half price from 5 to 7 pm.** "Let's go in," one of the girls said. But as they passed the door, there was a loud buzzing noise and a scanner flashed:

UNDER 18! NO ENTRY! - UNDER 18! NO ENTRY! - UNDER 18! NO ENTRY!

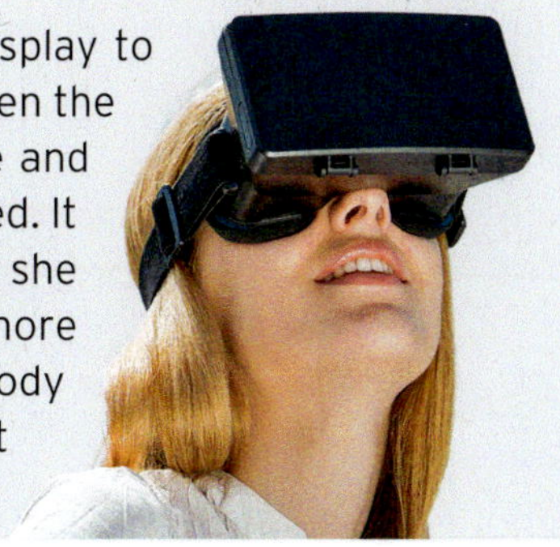

At home in her bedroom Emma put on her head-mounted display to watch a film. For a moment she thought about the old days when the whole family watched TV together. But now the TV was gone and the living room was the home gym. Emma's smart phone buzzed. It told her that she still had a lot of homework to do and that she hadn't had enough exercise today - she still had to do 6742 more steps before she went to bed. Emma's face became hot. Her body tensed and, without thinking, she threw the phone hard against the wall, shattering the display.

2 Working with the text

a) Which part of the story is more positive about the role of technology? Give line numbers and reasons for your answer.

b) Describe in your own words what happens at the end of the story. Explain why Emma reacts this way.

c) Find examples in the story that support these statements and write the line numbers.

1 New technologies can help us use our time more efficiently.

2 As a result of some new technologies, people don't spend as much time together.

3 Some new devices work to improve your health.

4 People can check or spy on you more easily with new technologies. More practice 2 p. 119

3 WRITING Wearable technology and me

Choose a) or b).

a) ● What do you think of wearable technology?
Write a written discussion about the pros and cons (about 150 words). ▸ *Skills file 10.7, p. 173*

b) Write a story (about 150 words). Start like this: *When I opened my birthday present, I got a great surprise. It was a ... My world was about to change forever ...*

▸ *Workbook 2–5, pp. 40–41*

Can we keep on like this?

1 LISTENING A student's talk on sustainable living

a) What do you think 'sustainable living' means? Share your ideas.

b) Look at the slides A–E. What do you think each one shows? Is it a photo, a chart, a drawing, a logo, ...? Make notes. Compare with a partner.

c) Listen to the talk. Then compare your answers to a) and b).

d) Write a provocative heading for each slide. Compare your headings in class.

A

B

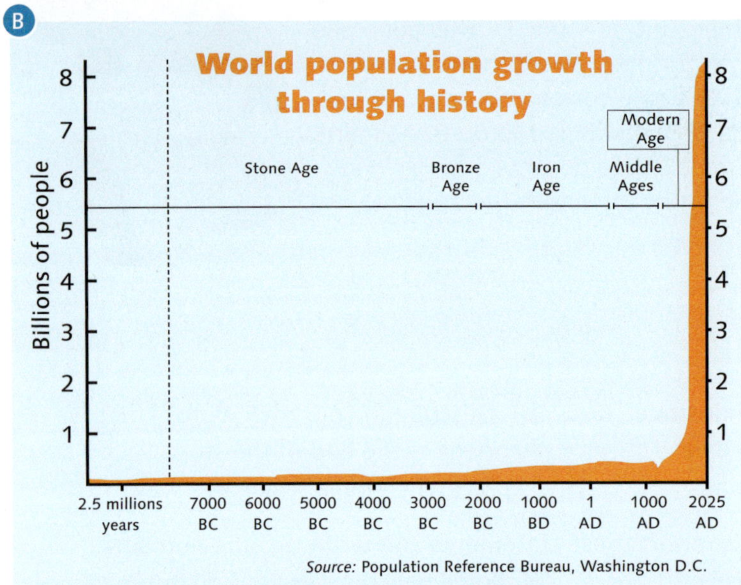

C

D

E

e) Read the questions. Then listen again and take notes. Now answer the questions.

1 Why does the speaker think that sustainable living has become a big topic?
2 Describe what the speaker finds most interesting about the graph.
3 Name at least two ways that people have changed the earth.
4 Find out why the speaker isn't pessimistic about the future.

f) Choose your own picture on the topic "Challenges for our environment" and prepare a short talk for the class. First describe the picture. Then give a personal comment on it.

▸ *Wordbank 2, p. 129* ▸ *Skills file 11, p. 175* More help p.119

2 VIEWING *Sorry*

MK

a) Watch this video by activist Prince Ea. Then explain the videos's message. How does it make you feel?

b) The video got over one million clicks on YouTube. Discuss possible reasons.

c) Watch again and make notes about these things. Compare notes in your group.

1 Find out who Prince Ea is saying sorry to.
2 He lists mistakes that his generation has made. Note down at least three.
3 Who can correct the mistakes, according to Prince Ea?
4 Name the most important issue according to Prince Ea. Do you agree? Explain.

More practice 3 p. 119 f

3 YOUR TASK Take action

More help p. 120

a) **Placemat:** In groups of four, choose a campaign, activity, petition, etc. to address an issue at your school or in your community.

b) Plan your project (aims, tasks, time plan, etc.). Choose one group member to document the project in a diary or blog. Then begin.

c) When you've completed your project, present your results in class.

▸ *Workbook 6, p. 42*

1 New frontiers

a) Read the article. Find out a) when people could go to Mars and b) the problems with living there. Then read the comments. Who are you like – DrSpock or Spacecadet? Explain your answer.

Will we ever live on Mars?

Humans have always been fascinated by Mars, and we still are, according to the success of the film *The Martian*. In this film a mission to Mars goes wrong and the main character is left behind on the red planet.

So will humans really go to Mars? This is a controversial question, but there are predictions that the first spacecraft could arrive there by 2030 at the latest.

So what will life on Mars be like? Remember that the average temperature is -63°C; gravity is only about 38 per cent as strong as the earth's; and there is almost no oxygen there. The optimists don't think this will be a problem. In spite of all the difficulties, they expect that the space pioneers will create an environment where they will be able to live and grow food.

There is another problem though. We might be able to get to Mars, but it's very unlikely we'll be able to get home again. However, this won't stop the real enthusiasts. Hundreds of would-be settlers signed up for a programme called *Mars One* even though the organizers clearly said that they could only offer one-way tickets.

Replies:

DrSpock: I recommend the film. But I'm not going to sign up for a one-way ticket to Mars!

Spacecadet: I'm definitely going to watch the film. I'd love to be a space pioneer. When I'm older, I'm going to sign up for a Mars mission. I'll send you a postcard from Mars! ☺

DrSpock: You're crazy! ☺ I'm going to concentrate on improving life on earth.

b) Make appointments with at least two partners and talk about some of these questions:

1 Do you like this kind of science fiction film? Why (not)?
2 Can you imagine being a space pioneer? What would you find most difficult?
3 Why do you think people want to get to Mars? How interesting is space to you personally?
4 How important is space travel? Should we be more worried about other things on earth? Explain.

c) Report the most interesting answers that you heard to the class.

2 REVISION Using future tenses

FOCUS

1 You use the ***will*-future** to talk about predictions.
It's often used with phrases *like I'm sure ..., I think..., I believe ..., I expect that, It's likely / unlikely that ..., It's possible / probable that ...*
Example: I'm sure that humans will live on Mars sometime in the future. But I don't think that it will happen by 2030. Will I go to Mars? No, I definitely won't!

2 You also use the ***will*-future** for quick decisions, offers of help and promises.
Example: You've never seen Mars? I'll show you some photos. – OK, I'll get my glasses! More practice 4 p. 121

3 You use the ***going to*-future** for plans.
Example: I've heard that the film *The Martian* is good. I'm going to watch it tonight.

► *Language files 9–10, p. 186*

3 Make predictions for your partner

a) Think: What do you think your partner's life will be like in ten years' time? Make predictions – as many as you can.
- Where do you think he or she will be?
- What job do you think he or she will have?
- Do you think he or she will have a car? What kind? (big / small / electric / ...)
- Do you think he or she will be married or have a partner? Will he or she have children? How many?
- ...

b) Pair: Listen to your partner's predictions and comment on them.
I think it's likely / unlikely that I will ...
I'm sure that I will ...
I don't think that I will ...
I definitely will / won't ...

c) Share: Tell the class one prediction that you hope will come true and one that you hope won't come true for you. More practice 5 p. 121

4 Talking about plans

a) Complete the answers. Use the ***going to*-future**. Then say what your plans are.

1 Have you thought about what job you're going to do in the future?

Amy: Yes, I know exactly what I ... (do). I ... (train) as an engineer and I ... (apply) to work for NASA in Huntsville, Alabama.
Jamilia: I don't know what job I ... (have). I ... (not study) science. I'm not interested in it.
You: ...

2 What are your plans for the weekend?

Amy: On Saturday I ... (finish) my homework. On Sunday ... (prepare) for my exams.
Jamilia: I ... (be) busy! It's my mum's birthday, so on Saturday we ... (have) a lovely breakfast together. On Sunday I ... (perform) in a concert with my choir.
You: ...

b) Continue these sentences. Write as much as you can. Use the ***going to*-future**.

1 It's my birthday next week, so ...
2 We don't have homework tonight, so ...
3 We have exams soon, so ...
4 I have some plans for the holidays. I ...

More practice 6 p. 122 | More challenge 1 p. 122 f

► *Workbook 7–10, pp. 43–44*

5 Dealing with new words

a) The underlined words are all new.
What similar words do you already know?

b) Guess what these words mean.

1 The end of the film was very predictable.
2 Many parts of the world will become over-populated.
3 Some people have a fascination with Mars.
4 I don't want to settle on Mars.
5 This film shows some very futuristic technology.
6 Until recently most experts rubbished the idea that humans could live on Mars.
7 Scientists see far more possibilities now than just ten years ago.
8 Humans will never live on another planet. That's just wishful thinking.

> **!** You know the word *prediction*, and you know other words that end in *-able*. That can help you understand the new word *predictable*.
> ► *Skills file 1, p. 156*

6 Improve your English: typical mistakes // ● p.123

a) Read the comments and improve this student's text.

Space – the new tourist destination?

I hope that space is the new tourist destination. I'd love to be a space tourist! I don't expect that I'll have the chance to go. But if I ~~will be~~ lucky, I'll go. I don't really believe it will happen because it simply so expensive ~~is~~ and I'm not sure that it will ever be cheap enough for normal people like me. But as soon as prices come down, I will on the first spacecraft. I'd really love to go into space for several reasons. First, I'd love to look down on the Earth from up there. Secondly, I'd love to explore new planets. A space pioneer's life must be so ~~excited~~! ~~So~~ I hope that space will be a tourist destination in the future. But unfortunately it's unlikely that I'll ever be a space tourist. ~~A shame~~!

1 Better with a linking phrase. ► *Skills file 10.1 b, p. 169*

2 ► *Language file 25, p. 195*

3 Word order! ► *Language file 15, p. 192*

4 Something is missing.

5 Wrong word.

6 A better phrase for your conclusion? ► *Skills file 10.7, p. 173*

7 Not quite right. Look up *shame* in a dictionary.

b) ● Space – the new tourist destination? Write a comment (80–100 words) on the question.

► Workbook 11–12, p. 45

1 O The blurb

a) First read the blurb from the back cover of the book. Answer these questions:
- Explain in your own words what 'global warming' is.
- Do you think this story could really happen?
- When does it take place – in the past, the present or the future? Explain.

b) Now read the text below.

Global warming has caused the seas to rise and now a lot of Britain is under water. Some cities, like Norwich, have become islands. Zoe Black has been left behind on Norwich by accident, when her parents escaped in the last ship. There is little food and water on the island and people are starting to panic. They are looking for ways to escape from the island. Zoe wants to escape too and get to the mainland to find her parents.

Floodland (adapted from the novel by Marcus Sedgwick)

1 _ Zoe ran. Harder than she had ever run in her life. She ran through deserted streets, past derelict buildings. Somewhere, not far behind, she could hear the gang coming after her. It felt as if her heart would burst, but she didn't slow down. She'd been planning to leave the island for a long time, but had been putting it off. It was a big decision to leave the island in a tiny rowing boat. Now she had no choice.

2 _ Zoe was a loner. Most of the people left on Norwich hung around together in groups, but she preferred to be on her own. It was safer that way, because you never knew whom you could trust.
Someone had found out about the boat she'd been hiding. A boat was an escape route, a way to get away from Norwich, which got smaller every year, as the sea kept rising. Now a mob of about fifteen people was following her. There was only one way out: to get to her boat before they got to her. So she ran on.
"Get back here!" someone shouted angrily at her, though they couldn't see her.
It wasn't far to the little shed where she'd hidden *Lyca*, her boat. Just before she went round a corner, she heard more shouts from behind. They had seen her.
"There!"
"Come on!" shouted another voice. "Get her!"

3 _ Scared, she went round the corner, but her foot slipped on the wet ground. She fell in the mud. She started to panic badly. She had dropped her bag as she fell, but there was no time to pick it up.
The sound of running feet came closer. Another two seconds and they would be round the corner. She got up and threw herself over a wall. She was in a graveyard. It went down a hill to where a small shed stood, near the water. Once it had contained all the equipment for looking after the graveyard, but now it contained Zoe's boat.
"*Lyca*," Zoe panted as she opened the shed door, "please be here, *Lyca*."
It was all right. The boat was still there.

4 _ Pulling it across the grass, and then into the water, she looked behind her for the first time. The gang was storming down the hill between the gravestones. Zoe moved faster. They were at the water now, and though one or two stopped, the rest came splashing madly after her.

"Take me with you!"

"Come back! We won't hurt you. Just take us with you!"

Zoe could see their eyes, clearly. She saw fear. But she couldn't trust them. Since she'd lost her parents, she'd made it a rule not to trust anyone.

She looked at the crowd in the water again. If she went back, there'd be a fight over her boat, and she wouldn't have a chance of escaping. Slowly, she watched as the people dragged themselves out of the water and back to the shore. Natasha was there too. That hurt most of all. Natasha had been her only friend. Zoe used to see her when the supply ships came, before they stopped coming. They used to have a little chat. Zoe suddenly remembered their conversation the last time they'd met. She had wanted to tell Natasha about her boat, and her plans to escape, but had decided not to. Maybe Natasha had guessed? It didn't matter now.

The crowd stood quietly, watching her as she rowed away.

Zoe didn't feel scared of them any more.

"Sorry," she said quietly. She began to cry, but she didn't stop rowing. Her uncut hair fell across her eyes, but she didn't stop to push it away. Her thin body rowed on until finally she had to pause for breath.

5 _ Feeling around in her pocket she took out her compass. It was the last thing she owned that had belonged to her parents. For that reason she had kept it in a pocket. If she hadn't, she'd have lost it when she dropped her bag.

She pointed herself south-west, and rowed. She knew that the big bit of Britain was somewhere in that direction.

6 _ She was rowing away from all that she had ever known. It was a strange thing. Before now, she had never rowed a real boat.

Her dad had taught her.

"You'll need to know how to do this one day," he told her.

He'd taught her how to use the compass, as well as lots of stuff about survival. Just in case the time came when she was on her own. Sometimes, when they weren't busy, they would sit in an old bath and pretend to row. It seemed like a game to Zoe at the time, but her dad made sure she was doing it right.

"Why don't you look where you're going?" she'd asked her dad.

"When you're rowing, you mean?" he said.

"Yes, why do you sit looking backwards?"

"It's the way you do it," he said. "You couldn't row as well facing forwards."

It had always seemed strange to her.

Norwich was getting smaller and smaller. She was heading into the unknown, without even looking where she was going.

7 _ She rowed and rowed, until her small supply of food had gone. She had put the compass on

the floor of the boat in front of her, and every few seconds she checked her direction. There was no sign of land now and she became more afraid. She looked at the compass all the time, it was her only chance now. Like magic, its tiny hand kept pointing in the same direction. It knew where she was going, even if she didn't.

The following tasks are on three different levels. Pick and complete one task for each level.

2 The characters

Make three true sentences about the characters in the text.

1 Zoe Black ... 2 Zoe's parents ... 3 Natasha ...

3 Headings

Write a heading for each paragraph (1–7) of the text.

Compare your headings and agree on the best one for each paragraph.

paragraphs:	1	2	3	4	5	6	7
lines:	1–10	11–30	31–46	47–82	83–90	91–113	114–122

4 The plot

Complete these sentences with phrases from the text.

1 Zoe wanted to leave ... (lines 1–10).
2 She thought that it was better to be alone because ... (lines 11–30).
3 When Zoe went into the shed, she was happy because ... (lines 31–46).
4 We know that Zoe was sorry about leaving Natasha because ... (lines 47–82).
5 Zoe rowed south-west because ... (lines 83–90).
6 Zoe knew how to row the boat because ... (lines 91–113).
7 In the boat Zoe felt very scared because ... (lines 114–122).

5 The mood

Describe the mood of this story. How does the story make you feel? Why?

– I think it's exciting / scary / sad / ... when ...

6 The narrator

Is the story told by a first-person narrator or a third-person narrator? Explain your answer and give examples. More practice 7 p. 124

A **first-person narrator** tells us what happened and how he or she felt. (***I*** is used a lot.)
A **third-person narrator** knows everything about one or sometimes about all the characters. (***He***, ***she***, ***it***, ***they*** are used a lot.)

7 WRITING What's next?

Tell the next part of the story.
Choose either a first-person or third-person narrator. Write about 120 words. More challenge 2 p. 124

FIT FOR EXAMS

1 LISTENING Shopping for a robot

Three visitors at ROBOTECH, a technology exhibition, are looking at robots.

Paula is looking for something fun that's child-friendly and doesn't cost too much.

Tariq is a tech geek who likes to collect the coolest new gadgets, no matter what they cost.

Iris would like a house pet, but she's allergic to most animals. She's looking for an alternative.

a) The three visitors watch four different presentations. Copy the table, then listen to the presentations and complete the table.

	1 	2 	3 	4 
What can it do? (at least 3 things)				
price?				

b) Decide which robot each visitor chooses. Explain your answers.

FIT FOR EXAMS

Taking notes while listening:
- Listen for **key words**. They're usually nouns, verbs or numbers.
- Don't write full sentences – just the key words.
- Use **symbols** and **short forms**:

=	'the same as'
≠	'not the same as'
+	'and'
etc.	'and so on'
e.g.	'for example'
!!!	'very important'
X	'not / no'

► *Skills file 6, p. 161*

2 SPEAKING A gadget that I must have

a) Prepare a short talk about a gadget that you'd really like to have. More help p.124
- Describe the gadget.
- Explain why it's special.
- Explain how it will improve your life.
- Describe when and how you use it.
- Where can you get it and how much does it cost?
- ...

b) Make notes for your talk.

c) Give your talk to the class (max. 2–3 minutes). Give each other feedback.

► *Skills file 9.1, p. 166*

► *Workbook 20–21, p. 50*

3 WRITING How to complain effectively

a) Read the email and say briefly what the writer wants and why.

Dear Sir / Madam

I am writing to you because I am having problems with a fitness tracker that I bought from your shop two months ago.

1) It is very uncomfortable to wear. The idea of these trackers is to wear them all the time, but my skin gets irritated after a few hours, so I often have to take the device off.

2) The battery life is so poor that I have to recharge it every two hours. In addition, it takes a very long time to charge the battery, so that's more time when I can't wear it.

3) The device is supposed to count my steps – but it isn't accurate. I know because I counted them one day and it told me that I had done 1000 more steps than I really had.

Because of these problems I took the device back to your shop last week since I hoped that your staff would be able to solve the problem, but I was told that they could not help me. After that I sent two emails explaining the problem, but I have received no reply from you.

Under the circumstances I'd like a full refund because this device doesn't work as it should. I attach a copy of the receipt. I look forward to hearing from you within 14 days.

Yours faithfully
Nazma Begum

b) Look again at the email. Describe briefly what the writer does in each paragraph.

More help p. 124

Then put the words and phrases that the writer uses into these categories:

1 greeting
2 explaining the reason
3 introducing the complaint
4 introducing further complaints
5 demanding action
6 ending

c) You're not happy with your new mobile phone. Write an email of complaint (about 120 words) to the online shop that you ordered it from. Say what's wrong with the phone (at least two things) and what you want the shop to do.
Write to: info@thephoneshop.co.uk

FIT FOR EXAMS

Complaints to businesses are usually made in **formal** letters or emails. Write politely and accurately. ▸ *Skills file 10.3, p. 170*

4 MEDIATION COURSE (3) Passing on information

a) A drone advert Your friend Andrea has found an advert for a drone on a British website. But she can't understand it properly. Read the advert and answer her questions.
Be careful: The advert doesn't provide everything Andrea wants to know.

Fly-Hi 100 Drone

The latest evolution in drone technology.
Train your flying skills with the Fly-Hi 100.
Lightweight and easy to use.
The perfect drone for all experience levels.

- 0.3 megapixel camera with live feed to the remote control
- Light enough to fly indoors (500 g)
- Rubber feet for easy landing
- Four LEDs for night flights
- 30 minutes charging time

Don't forget to find out the rules for flying in your area. And always follow the rules.
This model is available from ***Chatwin Drones***.

Hi! Hab gerade eine Anzeige aus GB für eine Drohne gefunden (Link hier). Kannst du mir mit dem Englisch helfen? Was bedeutet das mit den 30 Minuten? Kann ich nur so lange damit fliegen? A. 17:23

You: …

Super, danke! Wie ist die Reichweite der Fernbedienung? Wie hoch und weit fliegt *Fly-Hi* denn überhaupt? 17:25

You: …

Sagen sie, ob ich damit Fotos machen kann? Hat das Gerät eine Beleuchtung? 17:27

You: …

Was soll das Ganze kosten, mit Versand nach Deutschland? 17:30

You: …

Steht sonst noch was Wichtiges in der Anzeige? 17:32

You: …

b) An email to the company
You've gone to the website of *Chatwin Drones* and found the "contact" page. Write an email in English and ask the company for the information that you didn't find in the advert.

More practice 8 p.125 More challenge 3 p.125

FIT FOR EXAMS

When you mediate, think of **who** you're communicating with. If it's someone you know, use an **informal** style.
If it's a company, use a **formal** style.
▸ *Skills file 12, pp. 178–179*

▸ *Workbook 18, p. 47*

5 VIEWING The Red Thunder

a) Look at these stills from the short film *The Red Thunder*. Put them in an order that you think might tell the story. Share your ideas.

A

B

C

D

E

F

b) Then watch the film and compare. How different were your ideas from the actual story?

c) Your response to the film: Discuss these questions. ▸ *Skills file 13, p. 180*

- What did you find funny / sad / surprising / silly / well done / ...?
- What did you like or not like in the film?
- Did you notice the music in the film? If yes, in which scenes? How did it make you feel?
- Would you recommend this film? Explain why (not).

d) The camera work in the film helps to tell the story. Look at these two shots from the same scene. Identify what kind of shots they are (long shot/medium shot/close-up).
Talk about why the film director used these two different shots. How do they help tell the story?

A

B

e) Compare and contrast this film with other superhero films that you have seen (e.g. the film *Walk or fly* in Unit 2).

More practice 9 | p. 126   More challenge 4 | p. 126

6 WRITING You and superheroes

You've just read an online article that talks about why we need superheroes. The article asks readers for their thoughts about superheroes. Write a text of about 150–180 words.

More help | p. 126

Goodbye and good luck

You'll find the new words from these pages listed on p. 233.

1 Making a graduation speech

When students graduate from high school in the US, it is common for one student to make a speech to say goodbye to classmates and celebrate their time together. The suggestions below come from a website giving advice on what to include in a graduation speech.

Things you could include in a graduation speech:
- thanks (e.g. to teachers, fellow students, parents, coaches, ...)
- stories about classmates, teachers, trips, ...
- personal memories of time with the class
- what you have learned at this school
- where you and others will be in the future
- your advice to classmates
- a song, a poem, a joke, ...

a) Listen to Maya's speech. Which things on the list did she include?

b) Good speakers use different techniques to make their speeches more effective. Two popular speaking techniques are **rhetorical question** and **repetition**.

A **rhetorical question** is asked without expecting an answer (usually because the answer is clear or because the question has no answer).
It is often used to provoke, stress or argue.

Decide which of these questions from Maya's speech is a rhetorical question.
Explain your choice.
1 Didn't we find time to laugh and have fun?
2 Do you remember this?

Repetition can take different forms. In public speaking it means repeating a word or a phrase successively.
This gives more weight to a fact or an idea, helps clarify a point, or adds drama.

Which of these passages from Maya's speech uses repetition?
Explain your choice.
1 He's the guy who founded Microsoft and he's one of the richest people in the world.
2 Thanks for all your patience. Thanks for believing in us, even when it seemed hopeless. And thanks for making us work hard.

Listen to Maya's speech again. Write down one more example of each of these techniques.
Compare with a partner and talk about the effects of the examples you heard.

c) How would you rate the speech? Explain your opinion. Refer to the advice below.

Simple rules for a successful speech
- **Keep it short.** Don't bore people.
- **Say nice things.** Don't embarrass or be hurtful in your comments.
- **Make it personal.** Include everybody. Don't make it about you and your friends!
- **Include some humour.** People love funny speeches.
- **Use short sentences.** They're easier to understand.
- **Repeat key words and phrases.**

d) **Discuss:** How is a speech different to a presentation?

▸ *Skills file 9.1, p. 166*

2 NOW YOU A speech for your class

a) If you were preparing a speech like this for your class, what kind of things would you include? Discuss your ideas.
Then, working on your own, write a speech for your class, celebrating the end of year 10. Follow the advice above. Include also at least one rhetorical question and one example of repetition.

b) Practise your speech, and then deliver it to your class or group. Ask for feedback.

3 LANGUAGE More on the passive

a) Complete the FOCUS box.

FOCUS

1 Here are some examples of ***passives*** from the speech.
- I'**ve been told** that ...
- I **was shown** this class photo.
- I **hadn't been shown** it before.
- Your problems **will not be solved** in 30 minutes.

a) Make these into ***active*** sentences. Begin with *Someone* ... or *No one* ...

b) Compare. What are the main differences between the ***passive*** and ***active*** sentences?

▸ *Language file 33, pp. 201–202*

2 In German you don't always use the ***passive*** in the same way as in English. How could you put the four ***passive*** sentences in **1** into German?

b) The school principal gave Maya's graduating class some advice for the future. Complete his sentences using the *will*-future – *active* or *passive*.

1 Sometimes life ... (get) you down. That's okay. Just remember to pick yourself back up.
2 The road to success ... (fill) with lots of attractive rest stops. Ignore them!
3 That same road ... (have) bumps too. That's just part of the journey.
4 Work hard and learn to pay your own way. You ... (not offer) any free rides.
5 If you don't respect yourself, you ... (not respect) by others.
6 You ... (make) lots of new friends, but don't forget the friends you made here.
7 You ... (give) a lot of advice by different people. Remember: mine is the best!

c) Complete the sentences. Use the ***simple past*** or ***past perfect*** (**active** or **passive** forms).

1 When Maya first ... (start) at the school two years ago she ... (welcome) by the other students.
2 They ... (impress) her with their friendliness.
3 At the beginning of this year Maya ... (elected) senior class president.
4 When she ... (ask) to give a graduation speech, she was very nervous.
5 She ... (prepare) by looking at examples of speeches that ... (given) by other students.
6 She wanted a fun way to start her speech, so she ... (show) an old photo of the class.
7 After Maya ... (finished) her speech, everybody ... (cheer) loudly.
8 Then another speech ... (give) by the school principal, Mr Connolly.
9 At the end Mr Connolly ... (invite) to come back to the stage.
10 He ... (give) a big card and a huge box of his favourite chocolates from all the students.

4 WORDS Useful expressions

a) Translate the underlined phrases from Maya's speech into German.

- You're expected to do so much homework in year 10!
- You're supposed to be so serious.
- Here's an important lesson for life:
  Don't have your nails done before rock climbing!
- Our teachers make us work hard, but we don't mind.
- On Fridays they let us eat fries.

b) Maya is looking back on her graduation day. Complete the sentences with *have*, *let* or *make*.

1 The organizers ... the sports hall decorated for the graduation ceremony. That was special.
2 I don't know why they ... us wear those graduation gowns. We looked so silly!
3 At least they ... us wear whatever we wanted under the gown.
4 Some kids ... their hair coloured the school colours before the ceremony. Crazy!
5 After the ceremony we ... a group photo taken.
6 For the graduation party my parents ... me use their car.
7 But they ... me promise not to drink any alcohol. I kept my promise, and I had a great time.

c) Complete the sentences for yourself.

1 At school we're expected to ... because we're in year 10.
2 At home I'm supposed to ..., but I usually don't.
3 I'm going to have my hair cut because ...
4 My mum (dad / sister / brother / friend) makes me ..., but I don't mind.
5 It's great when our teachers let us ...

1 LANGUAGE Waterworld

Complete the blog with the correct form of the verbs in brackets *(simple past, present perfect, will-future, simple present, present progressive)*.

All my life, science teachers ... (1 tell) me that the planet is getting warmer and the sea is rising. But I ... (2 not think) seriously about climate change. Then, last week I ... (3 watch) a science fiction movie called *Waterworld*. It was set in the future and it ... (4 tell) the story of a terrible flood. Since then, I ... (5 do) some research and I ... (6 find out) that things are really serious.

Experts believe that by 2060 more than a billion people in the world ... (7 live) in cities near the coast. They also predict that coastal cities – including London where I live – ... (8 disappear) under water because of flooding. This means that in the future, more than a billion people in the world ... (9 lose) their homes.

So what can we do about it? Today governments ... (10 spend) a lot of money on better flood systems, but I ... (11 not think) this is the best solution. It ... (12 sound) a bit crazy, but some people ... (13 talk) about building cities on the water. This picture ... (14 show) an interesting design by an architect called Vincent Callebaut. He ... (15 call) it the *Lilypad City*. ... it ... (16 not look) awesome? What a great idea!

2 LANGUAGE Rubbish island

Complete the article using the correct form of the verbs – ***passive*** or ***active***.

Richart Sowa

Nowadays plastic waste ... (1 see) as a big problem.
In Mexico the artist Richart Sowa likes creating things from rubbish. Years ago he ... (2 start) collecting bags of empty plastic jars and bottles.
Then he ... (3 use) the rubbish to build an island on a lake, called *Joyxee Island*. More and more plastic bottles ... (4 add). Today his island ... (5 make) of more than 150,000 containers. Trees and bushes ... (6 plant) on the island to keep Richart's house cool. This is Richart's third island. His previous two islands ... (7 destroy) by hurricanes. ▸ *Language file 33, p. 201*

3 WORDS The right word

a) Find a suitable English word for *Platz* in these sentences.

1 Wird es in Zukunft ausreichend *Platz* auf unserem Planeten geben?
2 Nach dem Sturm war nichts mehr an seinem *Platz*.
3 Der FC Liverpool ist auf *Platz* drei.
4 Bitte machen Sie *Platz* für den Krankenwagen.
5 Unsere Schule hat einen Tennis*platz* und einen Fußball*platz*.
6 Nehmen Sie bitte *Platz*.

Platz *Substantiv*
1 *(freier Raum)* room, space
2 *(Sitzplatz)* seat **~nehmen** to take a seat
3 *(Ort, Stelle)* place **an seinem ~** in its ~
4 *(Spielfeld)* field, beim Volleyball; Tennis **court**
5 **für jemanden/etwas ~ machen** make room for sb./sth.
6 **auf dem ersten/zweiten/… ~** in first/second/… place

b) Use a dictionary to find suitable English words for *einfach* and *schwer* in these sentences.

EINFACH
1 Diese Zukunftsaufgabe ist für die Menschheit nicht *einfach*.
2 Eine *einfache* Fahrt nach Hannover, bitte.
3 Seine Idee ist *einfach* toll.

SCHWER
4 Was für eine *schwere* Tasche!
5 Die Aufgabe war sehr *schwer (schwierig)*.
6 Manchmal ist das Leben *hart*.

More challenge 5 p. 127

4 READING Don't end it, mend it!

Read the text. Then complete the gaps with the correct option.

People all over the world are organising repair cafes and repairing thousands of things every month. Have you … (1) of this initiative? Repair cafes are free and they are all about repairing things instead of throwing them … (2). In a repair cafe tools and materials are … (3) to help you repair electrical appliances, bicycles, furniture, toys, etc. You'll also find expert volunteers, with all kinds of repair skills. Visitors bring … (4) broken items. The specialists help them to get started with their repairs. If you have nothing to repair, you can enjoy a cup of tea or coffee. Or you can help someone else … (5) their repair job. For sustainable living, repairing things is … (6) reusing things. But most of all, repair cafes show how … (7) fun and how easy repairing things can be.

a repair cafe

	A	B	C	D
1	ever gone	ever heard	ever listened	ever seen
2	in	away	across	up
3	sold	selling	provided	provide
4	their	there	her	they're
5	which	where	when	with
6	so important	as important as	most important	important
7	lots of	lot	many	much

5 LISTENING and WRITING My generation makes a difference

a) Hannah, a 16-year-old high school student in Melbourne, interviews three friends for her blog. They talk about young people making a difference. Which themes are discussed?

1 Own web campaigns
2 Dangers of social media
3 One meatless weekday
4 Making better technology
5 Sustainable clothes
6 Personal worries
7 Car sharing
8 Becoming vegetarian

b) Listen again and complete the sentences with 1–6 words.

1 Elizabeth suggests a lifestyle change that can save ...
2 Naomi wants people to donate their ...
3 Naomi is proud to be a member of a ...
4 Cooper thinks that things like music, movies and fashion are ...
5 Cooper is sure that teenagers can have a real impact on ...
6 Hannah wants young people to share their worries and hopes with ...

c) Now you: Do you feel you can make a difference? What's important to you? Write a comment for Hannah's blog. Write about 80–100 words.

6 SPEAKING Is it better to recycle or buy new?

You're going to discuss if it's better to buy new things or to buy second-hand things and repair things. Read your role cards and prepare your arguments.
Think of your own ideas and examples to support your arguments.
Partner B: Go to p. 104.

Partner A:
You feel it's better to repair things or buy second-hand things.
Here are some of your arguments:

- cost (cheaper than new things)
- fun, creative
- more unusual and individual
- feel proud / good about yourself
- learn about how things work
- use less energy and reduce pollution

Students who are getting ready for their final exams (level B1, **Mittlerer Schulabschluss**) will find extra practice here.
(For level A2/A2+, **Hauptschulabschluss**, go to pp. 94 ff.)

1 The environment and me

You will hear three short dialogues. You will hear them twice. Choose the correct picture – A, B or C – for each question.

1 What's the problem?

A 

B 

C 

2 What's the right slogan?

A 

B 

C 

3 Which shoes are they talking about?

A 

B 

C 

2 The interview

You will hear a job interview. Read the eight statements below first, then listen to the interview. You will hear it twice. Are the statements true or false?

1 Daryl is still at school.
2 Daryl's dad does all the cooking at home.
3 Daryl has never worked in a restaurant before.
4 His favourite job is making salads.
5 He's good at working with other people.
6 The new job is a full-time job.
7 It's in a busy restaurant.
8 Daryl can start today.

▸ Workbook Exam Preparation, pp. 58–74

3 That's a nice car!

Three young people meet at a youth hostel in Germany – Stefan from Bielefeld, Taylor from Los Angeles and Julie from Liverpool. Taylor is showing the others some photos on her tablet. Listen and pick the right ending. There is only one possible answer per statement.

1 Taylor has had her car ...
- A for twenty years.
- B for fourteen years.
- C for at least three years.

2 With a hardship license in California ...
- A you can drive everywhere when you're 14.
- B you can only drive five miles.
- C you can only drive to school.

3 With a provisional licence in the UK ...
- A you can drive alone.
- B you have to drive with an adult.
- C you can't drive if you're 17.

4 With a provisional license in California ...
- A you must drive with someone over 21.
- B you can't take any passengers.
- C you can't drive between 11 p.m. and 5 a.m.

5 The way people get around in Germany is similar to the way they get around ...
- A in California.
- B in the UK.
- C in the US.

6 In the US most people ...
- A don't go to the shops.
- B go by bus to the shops.
- C drive to the shops.

4 Language change

Listen to the talk about how much the English language has changed.
Then copy the table and complete the information below. You can listen to the talk twice.

1 Who was Shakespeare?	a famous writer
2 When did he live?	about ... years ago
3 Number of English speakers in 1600:	...
4 Number of native English speakers today:	...
5 Where native English speakers live today:	...
6 Modern words that Shakespeare wouldn't understand at all (two examples):	... ...
7 Words that Shakespeare used, but we use differently today (two examples):	... ...
8 Shakespeare probably wouldn't be against language change because (one reason):	...

5 Teens and their parents

Listen to these people talking about what teens and their parents fight about.
You will hear the recording twice.
Who thinks what? Match the people (1–6) and the statements (A–G).
Be careful – there is one more statement than you need.

A Most fights happen when I'm in a bad mood.

B My parents are always checking on me.

C I want to find a compromise, but my parents won't even discuss my ideas.

D The problem is that my parents try too hard to understand me.

E There's just no communication between me and my parents.

F There are no big issues between me and my parents.

G My parents treat me like a child.

1 Jess	2 Malik	3 Molly	4 Ethan	5 Kelly	6 Robbie

6 Just imagine – a refugee's journey

a) Part 1 *Leaving home*: First read the sentences 1–7. Then listen to part 1 and complete the sentences with a few words for each gap.

1 At the start of the story, the speaker's life seems ...
2 However, things change when one night soldiers take ...
3 When the teenager comes home from work, his mother is crying because ...
4 The teenager meets ...
5 The journey across the desert is extremely hard because the weather ...
6 The truck hits something on the road and ...
7 The journey across the sea is dangerous because ...

b) Part 2 *In Europe*: First read the tasks 1–6. Then listen to part 2 and answer the questions in one to five words.

1 When the teenager gets to Italy, his life is very hard. Give two reasons.
2 Who helps the teenager on his journey to Calais (two examples)?
3 How do people in the camp help? Name two things that they give the teenager.
4 What parts of his body does the teenager hurt when he's trying to get to England (3 answers)?
5 How long does the teenager spend in the refugee camp in France?
6 Why does the teenager think he was lucky in the end?

1 "I'm a European"

This text appeared on youthreporter, *a website for young Europeans who are studying or working in other countries.*

Europe. Here in Italy the word makes people think about the continent, and of course the economic crisis. People don't really think about a big community. Even I, an 18-year-old girl, have always felt Italian and not European. Well, this was true until last October when I had the chance to go to Berlin and spend three weeks learning German. This gave me the chance to cross physical and psychological boundaries.

At first I was a little unsure. For me Berlin was just the German capital, a cold city, a place where the German politicians complain about Italy's economic politics. And in the beginning I was worried about living with a host family, away from my friends.

But I was completely wrong. My journey turned into a wonderful experience. I discovered a modern and beautiful city full of young people from all over Europe. And I lost my prejudices about German people. Here in Italy people are warm and passionate, but I expected people from the north of Europe to be cold and detached. How wrong I was! My host family welcomed me, made me feel comfortable, showed me places where real Berlin people go, prepared my breakfast every morning, treated me like a daughter, helped me when I felt a little homesick because I was so far from my family.

I changed my opinion about German. I had thought that it was a rough-sounding language. Now I know it can be as romantic as the Eiffel Tower at night. This was the best experience ever as I met new people and I lost the narrow-minded way of thinking of my little town in the south of Italy. I learned to be a European.

a) In which paragraph (1–4) can you find the following information?

A The writer wasn't very enthusiastic about going to Berlin.
B Berlin is an international city.
C The writer thinks differently now about the German language.
D Why the writer went to Berlin.
E In the past, the writer's image of northern Europeans wasn't so positive.

b) Decide whether the following statements are true or false.
Give the line(s) in which you find the information.

1 The European identity is strong in Italy.
2 The writer is Italian.
3 She stayed in a Berlin hotel.
4 The writer enjoyed her time in Berlin.
5 She changed her opinion about German people.
6 She never missed home.
7 She feels differently about being European now.

2 **The Bracelet** by Ann Angel

1 Trevor never said hello when he came into my house. He just made himself comfortable on one of the kitchen stools. Today was no different, only when I sat down beside him, he pressed warm metal into my palm[1] and closed my hand around it.

"Here," he said. Trevor was a guy of few words. I opened my palm to reveal[2] a silver charm bracelet. There was a silver heart locket at the centre. The bracelet was beautiful.

"Happy birthday," Trevor said. I looked from the bracelet to him, guessing what it might signify[3].

"It's your birthday, right?"

"Yeah, it's my birthday." I closed my hand around the bracelet, feeling its weight. The bracelet seemed like something you'd give a girl you thought you loved. Trevor and I had only been on two dates so far. His eyes searched my face to read my reaction.

"Thank you," I said, unsure what to think. I slid a fingernail under the heart locket and popped it open. Someone had put a piece of pink paper in each half of the heart. One side said, "Worth Loving." The handwriting looked girlish, nothing like Trevor's handwriting. I looked again to see if my best friend Kat had written these words, but they were too nice for Kat's handwriting. The bracelet must have cost a lot.

2 Trevor cleared his throat[4] and said, "Which birthday is it?"

"Sixteen. My family doesn't do parties," I explained before he could ask. "My mom usually makes a dinner for our birthdays. I think Kat's invited." He would already know Kat was coming. They shared about four classes and talked a lot. In fact, I had always thought those two would make a good couple and was surprised when Trevor asked me out. I looked at the bracelet. Had Trevor searched through the lockets to make sure his said "Worth Loving"? If he had gone to the trouble[5] of asking someone with nice handwriting to write the message for me, it meant something. I wasn't sure how I felt about him though.

"This bracelet is really pretty," I said. But I couldn't accept it. I didn't like Trevor enough to call him "Worth Loving".

"I gotta go to track practice[6] or coach will kill me." He was off the stool, brushing a kiss on my cheek as he passed, and almost at the back door before he turned and added, "Maybe I'll come over later. After dinner." He was gone before I had a chance to answer.

3 My mother came in with the twins – they were arguing. She put groceries down on the table and turned to Will and Josh. "Boys, I told you to knock it off[7] in the grocery store. And in the bakery. Now I'm telling you to knock it off in this house!"

---

[1]palm [pɑːm] *Hand(fläche)* [2]reveal [rɪˈviːl] *zeigen, zum Vorschein bringen* [3]signify [ˈsɪgnɪfaɪ] *bedeuten, signalisieren* [4]clear one's throat *sich räuspern* [5]go to the trouble *sich die Mühe machen* [6]track practice *Leichtathletiktraining* [7]knock it off *(infml) aufhören*

Josh punched[8] Will in the shoulder. "Yeah, jackass[9]."

"Josh and Will! Get Kelly's birthday cake out of the van!"

I warned, "That cake will be in pieces if you let one of them get it." I stood and put the bracelet on the table. "I'll get it."

"What's that?" Mom asked.

"A gift[10] from Trevor."

She picked it up. "Are you and Trevor serious?"

"I didn't think so. But he's coming over later. He knows he's not invited for dinner."

I went upstairs. I wondered just what the value of this bracelet was.

4 Kat turned up later. As she lined her eyes she told me she was with Trevor when he stole the bracelet.

"The note was inside. It doesn't mean anything," she said. "The bracelets were near the door when we walked out of the store."

My stomach turned sour[11]. "So the bracelet is stolen?" I stared at the bracelet. "It means nothing."

I dropped the bracelet. Kat looked at it.

"Do you want the bracelet?" I asked.

"Of course not. He gave it to you," she answered.

"I don't really like it," I said.

Actually I didn't really like Kat all that much right now. And I didn't think I could stand[12] Trevor.

"Go ahead. Take the bracelet. It's yours," I told her.

---

[8]punch [pʌntʃ] *jn. boxen, mit den Fäusten schlagen* [9]jackass [ˈdʒækæs] *(AE, infml) Idiot* [10]gift [gɪft] *Geschenk*
[11]my stomach turned sour [ˈsaʊə] *Mir wurde schlecht.* [12]stand sb./sth. *jn./etwas aushalten, ertragen*

a) Match the correct heading (A – F) to each paragraph (**1**–**4**).
Be careful – there are two headings more than you need.

A **The family comes home**
B **Feeling disappointed**
C **A nice cake**
D **A birthday present**
E **The birthday party**
F **Boyfriend and girlfriend or not?**

b) Finish the sentences using words and phrases from the text.

1 When the writer looked at the present, she thought that the bracelet ...
2 She didn't know Trevor very well because they ...
3 When she opened the locket, the handwriting didn't look ...
4 Trevor and Kat knew each other quite well because ...
5 Trevor planned to come back after ...
6 The two brothers were arguing everywhere, for example ...
7 The bracelet was easy to steal from the store because ...
8 In the end we know that the writer doesn't want the bracelet because she says, "..."

c) Find the information in the text. Give the line numbers.

1 The birthday present from Trevor surprised the writer. Give two reasons from the text.
2 The writer is an honest person. Prove this from the text.
3 Trevor doesn't know a lot about the writer. Find an example in the text to show this.
4 By the end of the story we know that the writer is disappointed. Give two reasons.

d) Answer the questions in complete sentences.

1 What do we learn about the narrator and her family?
2 What do we learn about Trevor's personality? (Name at least two things.)
3 Why doesn't the narrator like Kat in the end?

3 School in different places

1 Schooling on the move

Kelsie's family are fairground people[1]. So from about April to October the family is on the move around the UK. That makes going to school difficult. "We move every week or fortnight[2] to a new funfair. So I go to a school near our yard in the winter and in the summer I use 'distance learning' while we are travelling," explains Kelsie. "I get a work pack from school and I send my work in by email."

In fairground families, everyone helps out. "I do all sorts, I help with the machines – replacing light bulbs[3] and fixing things if they break. And I help out on our burger stand too." With these distractions[4] it isn't always easy to find the time to do school work. But Kelsie's parents make sure she keeps up with her school work. "I find that because my address says 'caravan site' some people expect I will be uninterested in my education. It's true that it's sometimes difficult for me to do my school work because of the way that I live. But I think I am actually more organized than most students, and I am very good at solving problems."

2 A day in the life of a homeschool student in Canada

We start school around 10 am. I get my planner, tablet, and computer and set to work. I don't work on all subjects every day. My mom lets me choose how to get my work done in the week. I just have to have it done by Sunday. My mom normally helps my brother and sister, but she is always available to answer any questions that I might have. If she can't figure something out[5], she looks it up on the internet. I work until lunchtime. I eat my lunch and then go back to work. I normally stop school around 2 – 3.

I think I'm lucky to be homeschooled. I didn't like 'normal school' – bells telling me when and where to go, wearing the same clothes as everyone else. I am very happy with the freedom that homeschooling gives me. I don't have to wait for others once I have understood a lesson. This allows me to spend time on things I enjoy, such as reading history books or being involved in extra-curricular[6] activities.

3 Boat schools in Bangladesh

During the monsoon[7] season in Bangladesh a third of the country floods as the continuous rainfall causes rivers to overflow. In some areas, roads are closed from July to October, when rivers rise as much as 12 feet. When the rain comes, thousands of schools have to close because of flooding and children's schooling is interrupted. Now an organization is bringing floating[8] schools to flood-prone[9] areas of the country. Their boats are outfitted with solar panels that power computers, lights and other equipment.

The floating schools collect children from their homes, teach them on board and return them at the end of the session. Then the school-boat moves on to the next village. Each boat has a classroom for 30 students and internet-linked computers and electronic resources.

[1]fairground people ['feəgraʊnd] *Schausteller/innen* [2]fortnight ['fɔːtnaɪt] *zwei Wochen* [3]light bulb [bʌlb] *Glühbirne* [4]distraction [dɪ'strækʃn] *Ablenkung* [5]figure sth. out *etwas herausbekommen* [6]extra-curricular [kə'rɪkjələ] *außerschulisch, außerhalb des Lehrplans* [7]monsoon [mɒn'suːn] *Monsun, Regenzeit* [8]float [fləʊt] *schwimmen* [9]...-prone [prəʊn] *...-anfällig*

a) Find the texts (1–3) that match the following descriptions:

A In this text you learn about a project to help students who can't go to school because of bad weather conditions.

B This text tells you about the personal experience of someone who never spends time in a regular school classroom.

C This text is about someone whose schooling is affected by the work that her family does.

b) Decide if these statements are true or false, then complete the sentences. You can quote from the text.

1 Kelsie has learned to be an independent learner.
This statement is (A) *true* (B) *false because the text says ...*

2 Kelsie's family don't think that education is important.
This statement is (A) *true* (B) *false because the text says ...*

3 The homeschool student works independently.
This statement is (A) *true* (B) *false because the text says ...*

4 The Bangladeshi boat schools can create their own electricity.
This statement is (A) *true* (B) *false because the text says ...*

c) Choose the correct solution.

1 In the summer months Kelsie doesn't
(A) find time for her school work.
(B) contact her teachers.
(C) go to school.
(D) stay interested in her school work.

2 The homeschool student
(A) misses being at a normal school.
(B) doesn't have time for extra-curricular activities.
(C) wishes there were more opportunities for sports.
(D) likes working at his own tempo.

3 All three types of schooling
(A) make use of the internet.
(B) are very common.
(C) use distance learning.
(D) are designed for kids who don't like normal school.

d) Scan text 1. Give two reasons why it's hard for fairground children to concentrate on their school work in the summer.

e) Scan text 2. Give two reasons why this student prefers homeschooling to normal school.

f) In text 3 the floating school boats are a combination of school bus and school house. Explain.

1 An interesting weekend

Du möchtest zum *Climate Change Challenge Weekend* nach Irland. Du hast den Flyer ausgedruckt und möchtest einige Mitschülerinnen und Mitschüler dafür begeistern mitzukommen. Beantworte ihre Fragen. Schreibe die Antworten in Stichpunkten auf.

a) Worum geht es?
b) Wo und wann findet das statt?
c) Welche Aktivitäten werden angeboten?
d) Wie ist die Verpflegung organisiert?
e) Wie ist die Unterbringung?
f) Was kostet sie?
g) Wie läuft die Anmeldung?
h) Wann ist Anmeldeschluss?

Trocaire

Working for a just world

CLIMATE CHANGE
Challenge Weekend

Date: 1st – 3rd July
Location: Maynooth University, Ireland

Are you 15 – 17 years old?

Are you ready to act on climate change?

Do you want to:
- learn about the causes of climate change?
- experience the effects of climate change?
- become part of the fight for climate justice[1]?

What's involved?
Throughout the weekend you will examine the causes, effects and possible ways to tackle climate change. You will:
- take part in workshops.
- listen to guest speakers.
- do a climate change disaster simulation.
- watch documentary films.

We will also have a variety of entertainment in the evening to help participants, team leaders and staff unwind and relax.

Accommodation and catering details:
- All meals will be catered for, including special dietary requirements[2].
- Accommodation is provided in dormitories on the university campus.

To apply:
- Cost for the weekend: £25 / EUR 30
- For more information and application forms, please contact the Trocaire office.
- Closing date: 18th June

**Your planet needs YOU!
Will you act?**

[1]justice ['dʒʌstɪs] *Gerechtigkeit* [2]dietary requirements *(pl)* ['daɪətəri rɪ'kwaɪəmənts] *Ernährungsbedürfnisse*

2 Let's go in-line skating

Amira is new in Cologne. She has just come to Germany and has started to learn German, but she doesn't speak it very well yet. However, she speaks English well. Amira wants to go in-line skating, but she has never done it before. You have a friend, Luisa, who loves skating. But her English isn't very good. Help Amira to get the information that she needs.

Amira Skating looks fun, I'd love to try it. Can you ask Luisa if there's an in-line skating club here in Cologne?

You ...

Luisa Ja, es gibt mehrere. Ich bin beim *Speed Team* – ein super Verein! Amira kann zum nächsten Treffen am Freitag mitkommen, wenn sie will.

You ...

Amira That's great. Please tell Luisa that I'm a beginner. Ask her if I can learn to skate at the club.

You ...

Luisa Ja, sicher. Ich kann es ihr beibringen. Ist ja leicht zu lernen. Amira hat wahrscheinlich keine Ausrüstung, oder?

You ...

Amira No, I have nothing. What do I need – just the in-line skates?

You ...

Luisa Ja, natürlich die Skates zuerst. Meine Schwester hat welche, Amira kann sie ausleihen. Die beiden haben etwa die gleiche Schuhgröße. Und dann braucht sie auch einen Helm und Gelenkschützer für Handgelenke, Knie und Ellenbogen – die sind besonders wichtig.

You ...

Amira That's great, thanks. I'm really excited about trying. Where should we meet on Friday?

You ...

Luisa Am Freitag ab 17 Uhr sind wir am Fühlinger See. Hier ist eine kleine Karte, mit einigen Hinweisen. Kannst du bitte Amira das Wichtigste erklären?

You *(For example: Where can you skate? How many kilometres? Is there any traffic there? Where do you begin? How can you get there? Do you have to be good at skating?)*

Amira I'm really looking forward to Friday. Please say a big thanks to Luisa.

You ...

Skating am Fühlinger See

Wo: Fühlinger See, Köln-Seeberg

Länge: Länge: 8,5km (einmal um die Regattastrecke und wieder zurück)

Belag: feiner Asphalt

Hinweis: Die Strecke wird auch von Spaziergängern und Sportlern genutzt.

Start: Parkplatz P1 (Oranjehofstraße)

Schwierigkeit: für Anfänger geeignet

ÖPNV: Tram 12 bis Merkenich, dann Bus 121 bis Oranjehofstraße

1 **Principals and principles**[1] by Daniel Handler

In San Francisco the weather never gets hot, and when it does it lasts only three days. On the first day, the hot weather is a surprise, and everyone wanders around carrying their sweaters. On the second day, everyone enjoys the heat. And on the third day, the cold weather returns and it is just as surprising, and everyone wanders around shivering[2].

One of these three-day heat waves arrived when I was in seventh grade, and on the first day everyone was grumpy[3] because we had all dressed for fog and gloom[4] and now had to drag our sweaters all over school. We all agreed that the next day we'd dress for warm weather, but just as the day ended, the principal made an announcement over the loudspeaker. "Students at Herbert Hoover Middle School are not allowed to wear shorts," she said, in the tone of voice she always used – a tone of voice that sounded friendly but was actually unbearably wicked[5].

Everyone groaned – everyone but me. "She can't do that," I said, and reached into the back of my binder. On the first day of school, we'd all received a pamphlet: "Student Rights and Responsibilities." For some reason I'd saved it, and I read one of our rights out loud: "Students have the right to free dress." I convinced everyone to wear shorts the next day in order to protest the wicked principal's unfair cancellation[6] of one of our rights.

The next day was wonderful because we were all dressed for the heat and nobody had to drag their sweaters around, but of course, I was sent to the principal's office – someone had ratted on[7] me. (To this day I suspect[8] Nancy Cutler, but I can't prove it.)
I said that free dress was one of our rights. She said that she was the principal and she was in charge[9]. I said that free dress was one of our rights. She kept pointing at me. I kept pointing at the pamphlet. The principal was one of those people who shouted at you until you cried, but I forced myself not to cry, biting my lip and blinking very, very fast, until at last she gave up and I was allowed to return to my classmates, who applauded me. In celebration, we all wore shorts the next day, too, even though we knew the cold weather would return, and it did, and we were shivering and miserable.

In eighth grade we got a new version of the pamphlet. Instead of "Students have the right to free dress," it read "Students have the responsibility to dress appropriately." I threw it away.

If you stand up for your rights, you can count on the fact that the wicked people will find sneaky ways to change the rules. But you should stand up for your rights anyway, because there aren't enough sunny days in the world, and everyone should enjoy them.

[1]principle ['prɪnsəpl] *Prinzip* [2]shiver ['ʃɪvə] *zittern* (vor Kälte) [3]grumpy *(infml)* ['grʌmpi] *mürrisch, brummig* [4]gloom [gluːm] *düstere Stimmung* [5]unbearably wicked [ʌn'beərəbli 'wɪkɪd] *unerträglich bösartig* [6]cancellation [kænsə'leɪʃn] *Aufhebung, Ungültigkeitserklärung* [7]rat on sb. *(infml)* *jn. verpfeifen, verraten* [8]suspect sb. [sə'spekt] *jn.verdächtigen* [9]be in charge *das Sagen / die Leitung haben*

- Read the tasks carefully.
- Write complete sentences.
- Make sure to write about all the aspects presented in each task.

a) **Describe** the narrator of this story. What do you learn about his or her life and personality? Give reasons for your opinion.

b) The narrator and the principal have different opinions about school clothes.
Explain the two opinions and say how they are different.

c) You have a choice here. Choose **one** of the following tasks.

1 *Students have the right to free dress.* (lines 16–17)
Comment on this statement from your point of view. Include the following aspects:
- Write about the **pros** and **cons** of rules about school clothes and uniforms.
- Give your personal opinion about free dress at school.
- Give examples from your experience at school.

or

2 *The next day I went to school wearing a new T-shirt. On the back it said "School is for idiots". That wasn't a good idea ...*
Continue in the way the story is told. Include the following aspects:
- the reactions of different people, e.g. other students, teachers and of course the principal,
- your opinion about this slogan,
- what happened in the end.

2 An email from the US

Here's part of an email from Alice, an American teenager.

Subject: What's next?

What's next?

This year I'm a Senior here at Norton High. So it's my last year at school. I'm both happy and sad about that – happy that I'm moving on to new things, sad that I'm leaving all my friends after so many years together. But life must go on. After the summer I'm going to go to a technical college in Santa Monica, California. What about you? When are you going to finish school? Are you going to study or are you going to do an apprenticeship[1]?

I want to learn to be a sound engineer. I'd love to work in the music industry some day – that'd be my dream. What kind of a job would you like to do later? Is it easy to find work in Germany? Or would you like to work abroad?

My friend's mom works at a recording studio here in LA and I've done some work experience there. It's a really cool job – you get to work with some great musicians and singers. Have you done any work experience? What was it like? ...

Write an email back to Alice and answer her questions. Write about 120–150 words.

[1]apprenticeship [ə'prentɪʃɪp] *Ausbildung, Lehre*

3 The story behind the picture

What is the story behind the picture? Imagine that this young woman is your friend. Write about the following aspects:
- Who is this young woman?
- Where is she?
- What is she doing?
- What has happened?
- How is she feeling?
- How did you help her?
- What will happen next?

Write about 150 words.

4 Creative writing

Choose one topic. Write a text of about 150–180 words. Count your words.

a) A blog entry:
Your family is planning to emigrate to South Africa. Write about how you feel about the move and leaving your home and friends.
What will you miss?
What are you looking forward to in your new home?
What will be exciting, fun, strange, difficult, different, etc.?
Write a blog entry about all this.

b) An article for an online travel magazine:
Think of a nice place that you've visited, or would like to visit. Describe it. Explain why you think it's so good. Give advice on the best time to go there, places to visit, activities, food, etc. Mention any interesting customs and traditions. Write a short article for an online travel magazine.

c) A diary entry:
A special day in my life
Think of a family celebration, a trip to a nice place, a great day with friends, an adventure, meeting someone special or any nice experience that you've had. Describe it. Say why it was so special. What were your feelings and thoughts?

Write a diary entry about this special day in your life.

d) A recommendation:
Think of a TV show, a film, a game or a book that you love. Think about these questions:
- Why do think it's so good?
- What do you like most about it?
- How often have you watched, played or read it? When?
- What do your friends or family think about it?
- Why would you recommend it? Is everything about it good?
- Do you have any criticisms?

Write a recommendation for a school magazine.

1 A great place to live

a) Describe the pictures. What can you see?

b) Talk about where you live and what it's like. Discuss the advantages and disadvantages.

c) If you could live anywhere in the world, where would that be?
Describe what it would be like. Give reasons for your answer.

2 Watch out!

a) What do you think the two people might say to each other? How are they feeling?

b) Talk about the dangers of cycling.
How can cyclists stay safe on the roads?

c) Some people say there are too many cars on our roads. What do you think? Explain.

d) Would you like to learn to drive?
Why (not)?

3 At a youth hostel

Situation: You've just checked into a youth hostel in the centre of Berlin. Pick one role card and read your role. Think about what you want to say, then speak to your partner.

Partner A

Your name is Julia/Alex. You're from Stuttgart and you're visiting Berlin for a week with your two friends. You've been in Berlin before, so you know the city quite well. You really like the zoo and also the Reichstag and you want to visit them again.
You see another traveller at the youth hostel reception, reading a travel guide in English.
You start a conversation.

> Find out some information about the other traveller.
> Suggest doing something together.

Partner B

Your name is Steven/Tanya. You're from Aberdeen in Scotland and you're visiting Berlin for the first time. You've just arrived and you don't know the city. You're here for three days. You don't speak much German and you're alone because your friend couldn't come.
You're at the reception and you're looking at your travel guide for some ideas, when someone speaks to you.

> Chat to the other person and ask him/her some questions.
> Ask for some tips for Berlin.

4 Congratulations!

Imagine that you and two friends have just won a competition. The prize – a one-week holiday together. You have five options. Discuss all of them, their advantages and disadvantages. Then decide together on one holiday.

Hiking in the Scottish Highlands

A beach holiday on the coast in Spain

A city visit – any city in Germany

A boat trip on the River Shannon, Ireland

Congratulations! You have won a week away!

A cycling tour of the Cotswold Hills in England

5 A conversation about part-time jobs

Talk about the jobs below. Ask your partner questions and react to your partner's opinions. You must keep the conversation going for at least 3 minutes.

- Would you like to do any of these jobs? Why (not)?
- What's good or bad about the jobs?
- Is there another kind of part-time job that you'd like to try? Give reasons.

6 Making plans for the weekend

Partner B: Go to p. 105. **Partner C:** Go to p. 104.

Partner A: You want to do something fun this weekend with your partners.

- First look at the cinema programme below. Choose one film that you would like to go to.
- Then talk to your partners. Tell your partners about the film. Listen to their suggestions.
- Finally agree together what you want to do.

LOST ZOMBIES

You probably think this is a horror film, but it isn't. There are a lot of zombies in it, but they aren't very scary. It's really a very funny comedy. You'll laugh a lot. The story is a bit silly, but the actors are very cool. A fun way to spend an evening.

Saturday at 6.30 pm and 9.00 pm

The heart of the sea

This is a very exciting action film. The story has been told before – a crew go out to catch a whale in terrible seas – but this film explores new worlds. The special effects are amazing, and the actors are very believable. Watch out for that whale – he will get you! Scary!

Friday at 4.00 pm, 6.00 pm and 8.30 pm

Students who are getting ready for their final exams (level A2/ A2+, **Hauptschulabschluss**) will find extra practice here. (For level B1, **Mittlerer Schulabschluss**, go to pp. 78ff.)

1 The interview

You will hear a job interview. You will hear it twice. Choose the correct picture for each question.

1 Which is Daryl's family?

A

B

C

2 Where does Daryl work?

A

B

C

3 What does Daryl like making most?

A

B

C

4 What is Daryl's strength?

A

B

C

5 Which job is Daryl applying for?

A
WANTED
Full-time waiters (37 hours)
Wednesday – Sunday
Apply: Cafola Cafe

B
Busy downtown restaurant looking for kitchen help.
Part-time only.
Apply with CV.

C
SUMMER JOB
Part-time chef wanted for small seaside cafe.
Must have experience.

▸ *Workbook Exam Preparation, pp. 58–74*

2 That's a nice car!

Three young people are looking at photos together – Stefan from Bielefeld, Taylor from California, USA, and Julie from Liverpool, England.
Listen to their conversation about driving.
Decide whether sentences 1–7 are true or false.

1 Taylor has had her car for twenty years.
2 Taylor started driving when she was 14 years old.
3 With her first license Taylor could only drive to school.
4 In the UK you can get your first licence at the age of 16.
5 Most kids in California get a provisional license at the age of 16.
6 Stefan says that he'd like a car.
7 Taylor says that her friends in California drive everywhere.

3 Teens and their parents

Listen to these teenagers. They are talking about what they fight about with their parents.
You will hear the recording twice.
Choose the correct answer A, B or C.

1 Jess says that she fights with her parents because she isn't allowed to
A stay out later than 10.30 pm.
B go out with her friends.
C stay at her friend's house.

2 Malik says that
A his parents talk too much.
B his parents always start a fight.
C he and his parents don't talk.

3 Molly says that at the moment she
A is easy to live with.
B isn't easy to live with.
C is fun to live with.

4 Ethan says that his parents
A don't care about him.
B are always checking on him.
C think he's very organized.

5 Kelly and her parents
A often fight.
B never fight.
C almost never fight.

6 Robbie had an argument with his parents because
A they won't allow him to have a party.
B he went to a party at his friend's house.
C he wants to ask the whole school to his party.

1 "I'm a European"

Complete the sentences below by choosing the best ending.

This text appeared on youthreporter, *a website for young Europeans who are studying or working in other countries.*

I'm an 18-year-old girl and I have always felt Italian and not European. Well, this was true until last October when I had the chance to go to Berlin and spend three weeks learning German. This changed my opinion.

At first I was a little unsure. For me Berlin was just the German capital, a cold city. And in the beginning I was worried about living with a host family, away from my friends.

But I was completely wrong. My journey turned into a wonderful experience.

I discovered a modern and beautiful city full of young people from all over Europe. And I lost my prejudices about German people. Here in Italy people are warm, and I expected people from the north of Europe to be cold. But I was wrong! My host family welcomed me, made me feel comfortable, showed me places where real Berlin people go, prepared my breakfast every morning, treated me like a daughter, helped me when I felt a little homesick because I was so far from my family.

I changed my opinion about the German language too. I had thought that it was an unattractive language. Now I know it can be very romantic. This was the best experience ever as I met new people and I lost the narrow-minded way of thinking of my little town in the south of Italy. I learned to be a European.

1 The writer is from ...
- A Italy.
- B Germany.
- C Berlin.

2 She went to Berlin ...
- A for a holiday.
- B to work.
- C to learn a language.

3 Before the writer went to Berlin ...
- A she was excited about it.
- B she wasn't very enthusiastic.
- C she didn't want to leave her family.

4 When she got to Germany, ...
- A she was disappointed.
- B she was surprised.
- C she was uncomfortable.

5 The writer found that people in Berlin are ...
- A friendly.
- B cold.
- C romantic.

6 Now she feels differently about ...
- A the German climate.
- B the Italian language.
- C being European.

2 **The Bracelet** by Ann Angel

1 Trevor put something into my hand. "Here," he said. Trevor didn't talk a lot. I opened my hand and saw a silver bracelet with a silver heart locket at the centre. The bracelet was beautiful.
"Happy birthday," Trevor said. "It's your birthday, right?"
"Yeah, it's my birthday."
This bracelet seemed like something you'd give a girl you loved. Trevor and I had only been on two dates so far.
"Thank you," I said.
I opened the heart locket. Inside was a piece of pink paper with the words "Worth Loving". It wasn't like Trevor's handwriting. The bracelet must have cost a lot.

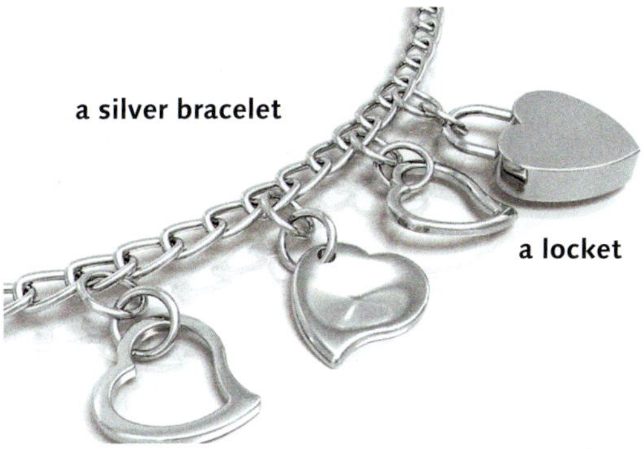

2 Trevor asked, "Which birthday is it?"
"Sixteen." Before he could ask I explained, "My family doesn't do parties. My mom usually makes a dinner for our birthdays."
I looked at the bracelet. Had Trevor searched through the lockets to find one that said "Worth Loving"? Did this mean something? I wasn't sure how I felt about him.
"This bracelet is really pretty," I said. But I couldn't accept it. I didn't like Trevor enough to call him "Worth Loving".
"I gotta go to training." He was at the back door before he turned and added, "Maybe I'll come over later. After dinner."
He was gone before I had a chance to answer.

3 My mother came in with the twins – they were arguing. She put the groceries down and turned to Will and Josh. "Boys, I told you to stop fighting in the grocery store. And in the bakery. Now I'm telling you to stop in this house!"
Josh hit Will on the shoulder. "Yeah, jackass[1]."
I put the bracelet on the table.
"What's that?" Mom asked.
"A gift[2] from Trevor."
She picked it up. "Are you and Trevor serious?"
"I didn't think so. But he's coming over later. He knows he's not invited for dinner."

4 Kat came later. She told me that she was with Trevor when he stole the bracelet.
"The note was inside," she said. "The bracelets were near the door when we walked out of the store."
I felt ill. "So the bracelet is stolen?" I stared at the bracelet. "It means nothing."
I dropped the bracelet. Kat looked at it.
"Do you want the bracelet?" I asked.
"Of course not. He gave it to you," she answered.
"I don't really like it," I said. "Go ahead. Take the bracelet. It's yours," I told her.

---

[1]jackass ['dʒækæs] *(AE, infml) Idiot* [2]gift [gɪft] *Geschenk*

a) Read the text *The Bracelet*. Then read the headings below.
Choose the correct heading (A–E) for each paragraph (1–4).
There is one more heading than you need.

Heading	Paragraph
A What does the message mean?	
B Feeling disappointed	
C The birthday party	
D A birthday present	
E The family comes home	

b) Complete the sentences about paragraphs 1 and 2 in about one to five words.

1 When the narrator opened her hand, she saw a silver ...
2 She didn't know Trevor very well because they had only been on ...
3 Inside the locket there were two words: ...
4 But Trevor didn't write these words because it wasn't like ...
5 The narrator can't invite Trevor to a party because her family ...
6 She told him that the bracelet was ...
7 Trevor couldn't stay because he had to ...
8 But he planned to ...

c) Match the sentence halves about the last two paragraphs.

1 When the family came home, ...
2 They were arguing everywhere, ...
3 When Mom saw the bracelet, ...
4 Kat told the story ...
5 When the narrator heard this, ...
6 The narrator offered Kat the bracelet, ...

A e.g. in the grocery store and the bakery.
B about stealing the bracelet.
C but she didn't want it.
D the twins were fighting.
E she asked what it was.
F she was shocked.

d) Are the statements true or false or not in the text?

1 Trevor was a chatty guy.
2 The narrator was surprised to get this present.
3 The bracelet looked expensive.
4 The narrator was in love with Trevor.
5 The narrator didn't invite Trevor to her birthday dinner.
6 The narrator never saw Trevor again.

e) Answer these questions in one to five words.

1 How do we know that Trevor didn't know a lot about the narrator?
2 How did Kat know that Trevor didn't buy the bracelet?
3 What do we learn about Trevor in this story?

1 An interesting weekend

Du möchtest zum *Climate Change Challenge Weekend* nach Irland. Du hast den Flyer ausgedruckt und möchtest einige Mitschülerinnen und Mitschüler dafür begeistern mitzukommen. Beantworte ihre Fragen. Schreibe die Antworten in Stichpunkten auf.

1 Die Veranstaltung findet an einer Uni statt? Stimmt das?
2 Was ist das Thema der Veranstaltung?
3 Wann genau findet sie statt?
4 Welche Aktivitäten werden angeboten?
5 Wo werden wir übernachten?
6 Wann ist Anmeldeschluss?
7 Was kostet die Teilnahme?

Trocaire

Working for a just world

CLIMATE CHANGE Challenge Weekend

Date: 1st – 3rd July
Location: Maynooth University, Ireland

Are you 15 – 17 years old?
Are you ready to act on climate change?

What's involved?
You will:
- take part in workshops.
- listen to guest speakers.
- watch documentary films.

Accommodation:
- All meals provided
- Accommodation on the university campus

To apply:
- Cost for the weekend: £25 / EUR 30
- Closing date: 18th June

Your planet needs YOU! Will you act?

2 Let's go in-line skating

Amira is new in Cologne. She can't speak much German, but her English is good. She's interested in this in-line skating track. Answer Amira's questions in English.

Where can you skate?
Is this track for in-line-skaters only?
How many kilometres can you skate there?
Where do you begin?
How can you get there?
Do you have to be good at skating?

Skating am Fühlinger See

Wo: Fühlinger See, Köln-Seeberg
Länge: Länge: 8,5km (einmal um die Regattastrecke und wieder zurück)
Belag: feiner Asphalt
Hinweis: Die Strecke wird auch von Spaziergängern und Sportlern genutzt.
Start: Parkplatz P1 (Oranjehofstraße)
Schwierigkeit: für Anfänger geeignet
ÖPNV: Tram 12 bis Merkenich, dann Bus 121 bis Oranjehofstraße

1 An email from the US

Alice is your teenage friend in the US. Here's an email from her.
Read her email and write back to her. Answer all her questions. Think of a good beginning and ending for your email. Write 60–100 words in complete sentences.

Subject: What's next?

Hi

It was great to get your last email – thanks. This year is my last year at school. I'm happy that I'm moving on to new things, but sad that I'm leaving all my friends.
When are you going to leave school and how do you feel about that?

After the summer I'm going to go to a technical college in Santa Monica, California.
I want to learn to be a sound engineer. **What's next for you? Are you looking for a job or an apprenticeship? Or are you going to go to a different school?**

My friend's mom works at a recording studio in LA and I've done some work experience there. It's a cool job – you work with some great musicians and singers. **Have you done any work experience? What was it like?**

I'd love to work in the music industry some day – that's my dream. **What kind of job would you like to do later?**
Write back soon. Bye for now.

Alice

2 Write about the picture

Write a text about the picture (about 60–80 words).
Write about the following aspects:
- Who is this teenager?
- Where is she?
- What is she doing?
- What has happened?
- How is she feeling now?
- What will happen next?

1 Congratulations!

Imagine that you and your partner have just won a competition. The prize is a holiday – you can spend a week in one of the three places below.

a) Talk to your partner and tell him/her which holiday you would like best and why.

b) Decide together on one holiday.

Congratulations! You have won a week away!

The Scottish Highlands

Active holiday:
hiking • visit Highland Games • mountain biking • look for the Loch Ness monster • stay in a hostel • meet lots of people your age

A beach holiday on the coast in Spain

Relaxing holiday:
weather • activities on beach • beach volleyball • swimming pool • stay on campsite in tent

A city visit – any city in Germany

Sightseeing holiday:
visit tourist places • museums • famous places

Lots to do in the evening:
cinema • concerts • stay in city hostel

2 A conversation about part-time jobs

You and your partner are thinking about applying for a part-time job.

a) Talk to your partner about your ideas for a job.

b) Say what you think of your partner's ideas.

c) Decide which job you each want to apply for. (You can choose different jobs.)

what you're good at

inside / outside

with people / children / animals

working hours

working in a shop or restaurant, car wash, ...

babysitting, ...

walking dogs, garden work, ...

Unit 1

3 SPEAKING Holiday plans ▸ Unit 1, p. 25

Partner B:

a) You're planning your summer holidays. You've found this idea for a working holiday. Read the information. Answer your partner's questions.

Camping by the sea

We are looking for active young people to work on our campsite this summer.

Dates: July 1st to August 31st

Duties: cleaning, helping with Kids Club, some office work.

You need to be able to speak English and another language (French or German).

You should have good communication skills. Experience not necessary.

Pay: 7 euros per hour

Minimum of 30 hours per week.

Accommodation: You will share a mobile home with three other campsite workers.

Apply today: skyblue@work.fr

b) Then ask your partner about his / her idea. Ask questions like:

- What kind of holiday?
- Where?
- What kind of places?
- Ideas for a route?
- How long?
- Cost/Pay?
- Stay where?

c) Agree with your partner which of the two holidays you should go on and why.

4 MEDIATION COURSE (1) I need to learn German ► Unit 1, p. 26

PARTNER B:

a) You haven't been in Germany for very long and you've been sent to the Sophie-Scholl-Schule to take a language course. You've been given a flyer with information about the course, but it's in German. Ask your partner the following questions:

1. I can already shop and get around in German. How is this language course going to help me?
2. They told me this is more than a language course. What do they mean?
3. So what kind of people do this course? Could I bring my mum here too?
4. I want to start school as soon as possible. How long does the course take?
5. How do I know how well I've done in the course?

b) Swap roles. Read the further information. Then answer your partner's questions.

FIT FOR EXAMS

- Think about who you are mediating for, what they need to know, and why.
- Choose the information that you need – don't translate everything.
- Don't translate word for word.

► Skills file 12, pp. 178–179

Willkommenskurs für Jugendliche: Deutschlernen und vieles mehr

Wie geht es nach dem Willkommenskurs weiter?
Wenn du mit dem Kurs fertig bist, kannst du an einer normalen Schulklasse teilnehmen. Das bedeutet nicht, dass du automatisch zur Sophie-Scholl-Schule gehen wirst. Es ist möglich, aber aus organisatorischen Gründen ist es eher wahrscheinlich, dass du einen Platz in einer anderen Schule in deinem Wohngebiet bekommen wirst.

Wann findet der Kurs statt?
Der nächste Kurs fängt am Montag, den 14. September an. Der Unterricht findet nach der regulären Schulzeit statt, montags bis freitags von 13.30 bis 16.30 Uhr.

Was muss man mitbringen?
Alle Materialien sind vorhanden. Du brauchst nur Motivation und Konzentration mitzubringen.

Was kostet es?
Du oder deine Eltern bezahlen nur 1,20 Euro pro Unterrichtsstunde – die restlichen Kosten übernimmt das Bundesamt für Migration und Flüchtlinge. Die Abschlussprüfung am Ende des Kurses ist kostenlos.

Wo findet der Kurs statt?
Der Kurs findet in der Sophie-Scholl-Schule statt: Eingang B, 4. Stock, Raum B412. Vom Schuleingang läuft man links über den Spielplatz zum hinteren Ende des Gebäudes. Dort befindet sich Eingang B.

Unit 2 | Stop! Check! Go!

6 SPEAKING Typically German ► *Unit 2, p. 55*

Partner B: Listen to your partner. Which typically German things is he or she describing? Then describe these things to your partner without using the German word.

Vollkornbrot

Fahrradweg

Der grüne Pfeil

Unit 3 | Stop! Check! Go!

6 Is it better to recycle or buy new? ► *Unit 3, p. 77*

Partner B:

You think it's better to buy new things.
Here are some of your arguments:

- cost (repairs take time; if they don't last long, you have to buy new things in the end)
- repairing can be unsafe and risky
- shopping can be fun / easier /quicker
- old things are uncool
- supporting businesses and (perhaps) the economy

Exam file

6 Making plans for the weekend ► *Exam file B1 SPEAKING, p. 93*

Partner C: You want to do something fun this weekend with your partners.

- First look at the concert programme below. Choose one concert that you would like to go to.
- Then talk to your partners. Tell your partners about the concert. Listen to their suggestions.
- Finally agree together what you want to do and when.

Concert by new rock band *Little Blue Bikes*

They're only 18 and some of them are still at school, but they're going places. They write their own songs and do some covers. You won't be able to stand still. A lively evening is guaranteed!

Saturday at 8 pm

Singer-songwriter Jessie Smith is back

Jessie wowed us last year with her fantastic voice and original songs. Now she's back again with new material. Her music is very special. The lyrics are often very funny, especially when she raps. Not to be missed!

Friday at 9 pm

Exam file

6 Making plans for the weekend ▸ *Exam file B1, p. 93*

Partner B: You want to do something fun this weekend with your partners.

- First look at the sports centre programme. Choose one activity that you would like to do.
- Then talk to your partners. Tell your partners about the activity. Listen to their suggestions.
- Finally agree together what you want to do.

Fenway Sports Centre

Dodgeball: Come and play with us! You can just come along and join in. No experience needed. Beginners welcome. Mixed teams. Suitable for all ages. We guarantee you'll have a fun evening.

Saturday evening 7–9.00 pm

Tag rugby: Like rugby but with tags – so no bruises! Good fun for all ages – guys and girls. Beginners welcome – just turn up and join in. It's easy to learn. Great way to meet people and keep fit.

Friday evening 6–8.00 pm

English for jobs

3 NOW YOU Two role-plays – pick one ▸ *English for jobs, p. 152*

a) Partner B: You're a Danish programmer at *Unico Design* in Copenhagen, which is doing work for the software company *Intersoft* in Berlin. You have a quick question for Nina Pfeifer at *Inter_soft* and you need her answer today. So you call her on the phone. You don't speak German.

b) Partner B: You're an online sales trainee at the Munich shoe company *Funshu*. You're travelling to the UK office in Manchester next week for a training seminar. While you're there, you'd like to meet with the sales manager and learn about their sales department. You call him directly. You only have time after 3 pm on Wednesday or Thursday.

Unit 1

More challenge 1 Nelson Mandela
▸ Unit 1, p. 11

Nelson Mandela was an important figure in South Africa's recent history. Prepare and give a presentation about his early life as a political activist, his time in prison and his life after prison.

More help 1a South Africa – then and now
▸ Unit 1, p. 12

These words and phrases can help you:

Describing
In the foreground/background ...
On the left/right ...
... there is/are ...
... you can see ...
... a girl/boy is ...

Speculating
The boy / girl looks like he / she ...
I think he/she probably has / doesn't have ...
I guess that she / he ...

- dream • feel • live • stand • study • wait • want • work • ...
- bored • disadvantaged • hard-working • hopeful • optimistic • poor • unemployed • ...
- career • dream • education • home • job • suburb • township • ...

More practice 1 A short talk
▸ Unit 1, p. 13

Choose **a)** or **b)**.

a) Prepare notes for **a short talk about apartheid**. Use the texts on pp. 10, 11 and 12. Do some research on the internet too. Think about these questions:
- What was apartheid?
- When and where did it happen?
- What was life like for non-whites under apartheid?
- Why was it wrong?
- How and when did it end?
- Who fought against it?
- Are things better in South Africa today? How?
- What still needs to change there?

Then give your talk to the class. Ask for questions.

b) Prepare notes for **a short talk about life in South Africa's townships today**. If you'd like, focus on just one township. Use the texts on pp. 10, 11 and 12. Do some research on the internet too. Think about these questions:
- What is the quality of life like?
- How many people live there?
- How diverse are the people and the living conditions?
- What do some of the residents have to say about living in a township?
- What can you find there that you wouldn't expect?
- What other problems are found there that aren't mentioned in the texts on pp. 10–12?
- If you could go there, what would you like to experience?

Then give your talk to the class. Ask for questions.

More challenge 2 An afternoon braai

▸ *Unit 1, p. 17*

Read the information about verbs of perception (= Wahrnehmung). Then complete the exercise below.

FOCUS

You usually use **verbs of perception** (see, hear, smell, taste, feel, look, listen to, watch, sound, notice) in the **simple present** when you talk about
- general perception: I hear a train. / She smells smoke. / Do you see him over there?
- appearance: It smells horrible. / That sounds like a good idea. / It seems colder today.

You use these verbs with the **present progressive** when you focus on a special object:
He's watching television. / I'm listening to music. / They're smelling the flowers.

▸ *Language file 2, p. 182*

Jonas is at his first braai – a typical South African barbecue. He's talking with Vince, his host. Complete the sentences using the *simple present* or the *present progressive*.

Vince	Welcome to our braai, Jonas! We're lucky – it ... (1 look) like nice weather today.
Jonas	It's nice to be here! Something ... (2 smell) amazing. What is that?
Vince	Those are sausages with my special braai sauce. Try one. They ... (3 taste) great.
Jonas	Mmm. It's very good. Ah, I ... (4 see) your girlfriend over there with the steaks.
Vince	Yes, she ... (5 watch) the steaks closely because my dog Vulu likes to steal them.
Jonas	Oh, yes. I ... (6 notice) that he ... (7 look) at them with those big eyes.
Vince	The steaks are from Transvaal. It's very good meat. ... (8 feel) like trying one?
Jonas	Yes, please! Hm. It ... (9 seem) different from beef. Why are you laughing?
Vince	I ... (10 look) at your puzzled face. Surprise! It's not beef – it's ostrich!

More help 4 Describing a cartoon

▸ *Unit 1, p. 17*

Write about the cartoon. Below are some useful phrases.

▸ *Skills file 11.2, p. 176*

1) Describe what you see in the cartoon – first the picture, then the words. What is happening?	In the cartoon we can see ... The elephant is sitting on ... It's holding ... It looks ...
2) What do you think the cartoon is about?	The cartoon is about the people who go to Africa to shoot ...
3) Explain what you think the artist wants to say.	In my opinion the artist wants to say that these people are ... / (wild) animals are ... / ...
4) Draw conclusions about the cartoon.	I think the cartoon is / isn't (very) funny. It is (very / quite / ...) effective because ... It makes me feel angry / cross / sad / ...

Unit 1

More challenge 3 More on relative clauses ▸ Unit 1, p. 18

a) Complete the sentences below with a ***relative pronoun*** (*who*, *which*, *that*, *whose*).
Sometimes more than one solution is possible. ▸ Language file 28, p. 197

1 Mandarin Chinese is the language ... has the largest number of native speakers.
2 But English is the language ... has the largest number of speakers worldwide.
3 This is because there are so many people ... use English as a second language.
4 Many people speak more than two languages fluently, ... is pretty amazing, in my opinion.
5 Someone ... speaks two languages is bilingual.
6 My friend, ... mum is French, speaks both English and French really well.
7 English is the language ... her family usually speaks together at home.
8 She speaks French to her mum's parents, ... don't speak English.

FOCUS

1 Sometimes the information in a relative clause is vital to the sentence.
Example: Monique is the girl whose mum is French.

The relative clause tells us which girl is meant. This is called a ***defining relative clause***.

2 A relative clause can also add extra information, which could be left out.
Example: My friend Monique, whose mum is French, speaks English at home.

Here the information about Monique's mum is extra. The sentence would make sense without it.
(> My friend Monique speaks English at home.)

So the underlined clause is a ***non-defining relative clause***.
Note that commas are used here, but not in **1**. ▸ Language file 28, p. 197

b) Three of the relative clauses in a) are non-defining. Which ones are they?

c) Add information to these sentences. Use non-defining relative clauses.

1 My Irish friend David can't speak German. His father is Austrian.
My Irish friend David, whose ...
2 He often visits his Austrian grandmother. She lives in Graz.
He often visits ..., who ...
3 His granny speaks English well. That's great.
His granny ..., which ...
4 But he can't speak to his young cousins. They can't speak English.
But he can't ..., who ...

//● 2 The story so far ▸ Unit 1, p. 21

Write seven sentences to summarize what has happened so far in the story.

More practice 2 **Questions on the text** ▸ Unit 1, p. 21

1 What is the weather like in London on this Friday?
2 Buyi seems to be in some kind of trouble. What tells us this?
3 Why do you think the story is called *Returned*?
4 What kind of a relationship does Buyi have with his neighbours? Explain.
5 Buyi isn't a model son. Give some examples.
6 Buyi's mum isn't happy about her decision to send Buyi to South Africa. How do we know this?
7 What kind of a relationship does Buyi have with his father? Why?
8 How does Buyi feel when he leaves his mum at the airport?

More practice 3 **A first meeting** ▸ Unit 1, p. 23

After Buyi arrives with the others at the nature reserve, Lwazi takes him to meet his dad. Write the next part of the story.

More practice 4 **Stylistic devices (1)** ▸ Unit 1, p. 23

Good writers use different techniques to make their texts interesting. Here are three examples of techniques that you can find in *Returned* (on pp. 19 – 23).

a) **Repetition:** Sometimes a writer repeats a phrase or a structure to stress a point and make it stronger. For example in lines 1–4 of *Returned*:
There was trouble in the air. ... For days I could feel it – in the crowded trains in the London Underground, in the school classrooms, in the streets.

1 Look at the lines above. What words are repeated? How many times? What point is the writer stressing?
2 Look at lines 17–22. What noun is repeated? How many times? What point is the writer stressing (again)?
3 Now look at lines 54–57 and find the words that are repeated. What is the writer stressing?

! You can talk about these questions in German, if you like.

b) **Similes:** Sometimes a writer compares two different things by using 'like' or 'as'. This can create a strong image. For example in line 17 of *Returned*:
I felt like a stranger.
This is called a simile.

1 What point is the writer stressing?
2 Look at lines 81–82 and find another simile. What image is the writer creating?

c) **Metaphors:** Sometimes a writer compares two very different things, without using 'like' or 'as'. For example in lines 48–49 of *Returned*:
The cheese had turned a dull yellow in a sea of olives, pineapple and some kind of meat.

1 What kind of image does this create for you? Is it negative or positive?
2 Look at line 86 and find another metaphor. Do you think this is a negative or positive image?

▸ Skills file 8, pp. 164–165

Unit 1

More challenge 4 Would you recommend this story? Why (not)? ▸ Unit 1, p. 23

Write a review of the story. Write about the main characters, the setting, the topic and the plot. Say what you like and what you don't like and give reasons. ▸ Skills file 10.9, p. 174

More practice 5 An interview with Amar ▸ Unit 1, p. 27

In the film Amar doesn't tell us about his life. Instead we see what it's like.
Imagine you have the chance to interview Amar. Write a list of questions you would ask him.

More challenge 5 SPEAKING The film-maker's aims ▸ Unit 1, p. 27

Read the interview with the film-maker Andrew Hinton.
Prepare a short talk in German (one minute):
- Explain why he decided to make the film about Amar.
- Describe what the filming was like.
- Explain why he chose not to use music, dialogue or voice-over in the film.

Interview with film-maker Andrew Hinton *by Tahiat Mahboob*

How did you meet Amar, and what made you choose him as your film's subject?
I met Amar while visiting a school in Jamshedpur. I asked if there were kids who usually worked and went to classes. When I met Amar and he quietly explained what his day consists of, six and a half days a week, 350 days a year, it really made me stop and think about how I use the time in my own life.

Your film is more than nine minutes long and contains no dialogue. Why did you decide to tell the story in this way?
Amar doesn't say much. He has a quiet determination which I think comes through in his actions so I wanted his day to speak for itself, rather than trying to explain it with voice-over or dialogue. I tried music but it just didn't seem to work. I liked the simplicity of the natural sounds.

What were the challenges in getting such intimate access to Amar's daily life? How did Amar and his family feel about being filmed?
I visited Amar's home with the school headmaster, who explained that I wanted to film him for a day, and his mother and grandmother were a little puzzled but quite happy.

You show a day in the life of Amar. Was it filmed in a day or did you have to spend some time for all of the pieces to fall into place?
It is very much filmed in one day. I'm a big fan of *vérité* film-making and so it felt important to be as honest in the process as possible. No special effects, retakes or stunts in this film.

More practice 6 Amar – a comment ▸ Unit 1, p. 27

Write a comment on the film.
- Describe the effect it had on you.
- What impressed you most about Amar's life? Explain.
- Why do you think the film won so many awards around the world? ▸ Skills file 10.2, p. 170

More practice 7 LANGUAGE Word order ▸ Unit 1, p. 31

Put the phrases in brackets in the right place.
Sometimes there is more than one possible solution.

Nelson Mandela was born in Mvezo (on 18 July 1918). He went to university (in the early 40s). He joined the ANC to fight the terrible apartheid system (during that time). He became the leader of the ANC (soon). Mandela was put in prison (for 27 years • in 1962). He became a symbol of the anti-apartheid movement (during his time in prison • quickly). Nelson Mandela was famous (by the end of the 1980s • all over the world). Although he felt desperate (during that time • often), he gave up hope (never). He left prison thanks to international pressure (in 1990). F.W. de Klerk, the last white president, worked with Mandela to end apartheid. They both got the Nobel Peace Prize (in 1993 • for their achievements). All races were allowed to vote (one year later • for the first time). Nelson Mandela became the first black president (in the same year). He gave up his presidency (finally • at the age of 81 • in 1999). Mandela died in Johannesburg (on 5 December 2013).

! Look at Language files 15–16 on p. 188 to find out more about word order.

More challenge 6 More false friends ▸ Unit 1, p. 31

a) Copy the table and add the missing words. Use a dictionary if necessary.

b) Make sentences for your partner. For examples, see 2a) on p. 31.

German	English
aktuell	
Art	
brav	
Chor	
Gymnasium	
Gift	
Platz nehmen	
sensibel	

English	German
actual	
art	
brave	
chorus	
gymnasium	
gift	
take place	
sensible	

Unit 2

More help 1a Digital citizens ▸ Unit 2, p. 35

These words and phrases can help you to tell the story:

bored • point to sth. • playground • rubbish • idea • send • campaign • post • social media • like • mayor • meet • plan • workers • clean up • help • football • slogan

More practice 1 Talking about the film ▸ Unit 2, p. 35

Work in small groups. Decide on three of these statements that you agree are true. Support your choices with examples from the story.

- This film is simple, but effective.
- It's strange that there's no talking in this film.
- We are all digital citizens now.
- The message of the film is: Young people can make a difference.
- Social media campaigns can be very good.

Then tell the class what you agreed on.

More challenge 1 UNICEF ▸ Unit 2, p. 35

This film was made by UNICEF.

a) Do some research. Find out what UNICEF is and what the organization does.

b) Tell the class what you've found out.

//● 2a Working with the text ▸ Unit 2, p. 37

Look again at paragraphs 1–5. Think of a heading for each paragraph.

Compare your ideas.

More practice 2 Online campaigns – not all positive ▸ Unit 2, p. 37

The comments below the article point to two critical or negative aspects of online campaigns.

a) Take turns describing the two aspects in your own words.

b) Discuss to what degree you or people you know have experienced the two aspects.

More help 4a WRITING Now you ▸ Unit 2, p. 37

Write an article about the student's campaign (see task 3) for the local newspaper.

Listen again and answer these questions:

- Who started the campaign?
- What was the campaign about?
- What did the students do?
- How effective was it?
- What were some positive effects of the campaign?

The answers to 3b can also help you to write your article.

More challenge 2 A successful campaign

▸ Unit 2, p.37

Prepare a short presentation about online campaigns. Choose one of the following topics.

a) Find out about an online campaign that worked well. Describe how it worked.

b) Think of an issue at your school or in your area. Talk about the kind of campaign you think is necessary for this issue and how it could work.

More practice 3 Stylistic devices (2)

▸ Unit 2, p.38

Gary Turk's poem *It's your future* uses two important stylistic devices: *repetition* and *rhyme*.

a) Look at the explanation for repetition in More practice 4 on page 109. Then look again at the extract from Gary Turk's poem.

- Identify the lines that have repetition.
- Which word or words is/are repeated?
- How many times?
- What point is the writer stressing?

b) Poems sometimes have words that sound similar – they rhyme. It's another form of repetition.
Rhyming words form patterns that give a poem rhythm and a musical feeling.

1 Look again at lines 1–4 from *It's your future*. Which of these rhyme patterns can you identify?
A abab **B** aabb **C** abba

2 Now look at lines 5–8 and 9–12 and identify the rhyme pattern.
A ccdd eeff **B** bbcc ddee **C** ccdd ccdd

3 Read these two poems and identify the rhyme pattern.

Do something
by Franziska Gross and Rory More O'Ferrall

We can't change anything
If we're passive and blind.
Come on, the clock is ticking,
Let's leave our problems behind.

History can't be deleted.
We need to learn from the past,
So our mistakes won't be repeated.
We have to do something fast!

Why not
by Franziska Gross

Why not do something for you and me
Say what we think
Be the missing link
Let's face our own reality

Why not do something for the community
Give a helping hand
Let's take a stand
And face our responsibility

▸ Skills file 8, pp. 164–165

Unit 2

More help **3 YOUR TASK Young people and politics** ▸ *Unit 2, p. 39*

STEP 4: Present your results to the class. Give a short talk – about two minutes.
Tell the class about some of these things.
- How many students did you talk to?
- How many questions did you ask?
- What did you ask about?
- Are most students that you talked to interested or not interested in politics?
- What interesting / surprising / shocking results did you find?
- Can you give any advice to politicians?

Think of interesting ways to present the results of your survey (e.g. visuals like photos, tables, charts, etc.).

Here are some useful words and phrases for your presentation.
- We asked ... (*15, 20, etc.*) young people and ...
- Of the ... young people that we asked, ...
- One of our more interesting / surprising / shocking results was that ...
- (From our results) we concluded that ...
- Most / about half of / very few / ... young people think / believe / are interested in /...
- Our advice to politicians is ...

More help **Step 5: Write a report about your survey** ▸ *Unit 2, p. 39*

Read the full report about the Irish survey.
You can use this text as a model or just pick out some useful words and phrases.

Report – a survey of Irish students

Introduction: What do young people think about politics and politicians?
We asked nearly 250 young people between the ages of 15 and 19. The results are surprising – a lot of young people are interested in politics. But they don't trust politicians.

The results: The survey found that 86% of the people we talked to do not trust politicians, while 61% would close the door if a politician came to their house. 73% believe that politicians don't really care about young people.
But most young people (67%) think that politics is important for their lives. And here's a surprising fact – most young people are interested in the news. 60% get their news on mobile phones. 48% watch the news on TV and only 16% read it in newspapers.

How interested in politics are you?

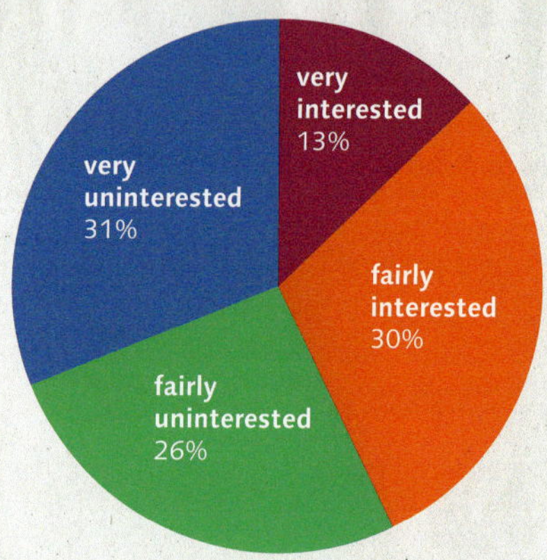

The conclusion: What does this mean?
Politicians should be more interested in young people. They should talk to young people more. They should talk to young people more and listen to what they have to say.

More practice 4 The Big Sleep Out

▸ Unit 2, p. 41

Complete the interview with the correct forms of the ***simple past***.

Reporter Yesterday fifteen Year 11 students from Green Lane School ... (1 take part) in a Big Sleep Out. I ... (2 speak) to their spokesperson Katy about the experience.
So Katy, what ... (3 happen) in the Big Sleep Out?

Katy Basically on Friday night fifteen of us ... (4 sleep) outside the school.

Reporter ... (5 you, sleep) well?

Katy We ... (6 try) to sleep, but we ... (7 not sleep) very well.

Reporter ... (8 it, rain)? ... (9 you, get) wet?

Katy At the beginning of the night the weather ... (10 be) good. We ... (11 build) little houses out of cardboard boxes. It ... (12 be) cold and we ... (13 not be) very comfortable. But it ... (14 be) OK. It ... (15 rain) a lot later though.

Reporter ... (16 the boxes, keep) you dry?

Katy No, they ... (17 not do)! We ... (18 get) very wet!

Reporter Why ... (19 you, organize) the Big Sleep Out?

Katy Well, we ... (20 have) a talk from a homeless charity and they ... (21 tell) us that they really ... (22 need) money. So we ... (23 think) this would be a good way to raise money for them.

Reporter ... (24 you, raise) much money?

Katy Yes, we ... (25 do). But we also ... (26 find out) what it's like to sleep outside in November. It ... (27 make) us think about the conditions that homeless people live in.

More practice 5 A day to remember

▸ Unit 2, p. 41

Complete the text with the correct forms of the ***simple past***, the ***past progressive***, or the ***past perfect***.

It ... (1 rain) when the soccer team left school at 7 o'clock on Saturday. But soon the sun started to shine and it ... (2 not stop) all day.
We were feeling excited by the time we ... (3 arrive) at the stadium at 11 o'clock. After we ... (4 look) around the changing rooms, we went out onto the pitch. Wow! The stadium ... (5 be) huge.
We were out there on our own because the other team ... (6 not arrive) yet. We ... (7 get) a bit worried because at 11.45 they still hadn't turned up. We ... (8 walk) back to the changing rooms when the other team came out at last. Wow, they ... (9 be) giants! We ... (10 feel) a bit scared of them, but then Mrs Brown came in and gave us a talk. After she ... (11 talk) to us for 15 minutes we felt great again.
We were ready for the match!
At half-time things ... (12 not go) well. The other team ... (13 score) two goals, and we weren't feeling confident at all. So Mrs Brown ... (14 give) us another one of her talks. Basically, she told us that if we ... (15 believe) in ourselves, we could win. Well, she was right. By the end of the second half we ... (16 score) three goals. We had won the championship! It truly was a day to remember!

Unit 2

More challenge 3 REVISION The present perfect progressive ▸ Unit 2, p.41

FOCUS

You can use the ***present perfect progressive*** when an action started in the past is still going on. It is often used with verbs like *live*, *work*, *study*.

Example: Some of the young refugees **have been living** in Australia for over a year.

▸ *Language file 6, p. 184*

Answer these questions about things you have been doing recently.

1. How long have you been learning English?
2. How long have you been going to the same school?
3. How long have you been living in the same place?
4. Do you or a friend play a sport? How long have you been playing that sport?
5. Do you or a friend play an instrument? How long have you been playing that instrument?
6. What are you doing right now? How long have you been doing it?

More practice 6 A newspaper report ▸ Unit 2, p. 45

Imagine that you're a journalist. Write a report (100–120 words) about the accident for your newspaper. Find a good title for the report – and use some headings too. ▸ *Skills file 10.8, p. 174*

More challenge 4 Mark's version ▸ Unit 2, p.45

A police officer is questioning Mark about what happened. Write their dialogue.

More practice 7 Part 4: Vanessa's granny ▸ Unit 2, p. 46

Listen to part 4 of the conversation. When you hear the bell, mediate for Vanessa.

More practice 8 NOW YOU Talking to a tourist ▸ Unit 2, p. 46

Pick at least two of these or other topics and write a short text in English to explain each one to a foreign tourist.

- Feiertage, die Menschen in Deutschland feiern (z.B. den Tag der deutschen Einheit)
- typische Hobbys in Deutschland
- beliebte Fernsehserien in Deutschland
- Einschulung und erster Schultag in Deutschland
- mein deutsches Lieblingsessen

2a LISTENING Fashion Revolution ▸ Unit 2, p. 47

A news report: First read the questions. Then listen to the news report, take notes and answer the questions.

1. How many people were killed in the Rana Plaza disaster?
2. What does *Fashion Revolution* want?
3. What should shoppers think more about?

More practice 9 **Your shopping habits** ▸ Unit 2, p. 47

a) Talk about questions 1–5 with a partner.

1 Do you buy new clothes because …
   A you really need them? B you like buying new things? C you want to look good?
2 When you go shopping for clothes, what's important?
   A low prices B good quality C fashion D who makes the clothes
3 When you're buying clothes, do you look at the label? Why (not)?
4 If you look at the label, what information do you expect to find?
   A size B washing instructions C materials D where it's made

b) Look at the labels of some of the clothes that you wear.

1 Do they tell you where the clothes are made?
2 Make a list of the countries that your clothes are made in.
3 What are the most common countries?

Compare your answers with your partner.

c) How much more do you know now about the clothes that you buy?
Are you interested in finding out more? Why (not)? Discuss in class.

More challenge 5 **What about your clothes** ▸ Unit 2, p.47

a) Look at the labels of the clothes you're wearing and pick one clothes company. Go to their website. Try to find information like:

- Does the company sell fair-trade products?
- Does the company guarantee that the clothes aren't made by children? How do they prove it?
- Does the company support the idea of a minimum wage?
- Does the company have an environment policy?

b) What can you conclude about this company and its clothes? Would you buy from them again? Make notes.

c) Present the results of your research to the class or share them with a partner.

MK **More challenge 6** WRITING **Two reviews** ▸ Unit 2, p.49

a) Write a review of the film *Walk or fly*.
OR
b) Write a review of another film that you have seen recently.

!
- Write about things like the **location**, the **characters**, the **acting**, the **costumes**, the **soundtrack**, etc.
- Does the film have a message? If yes, what is it?
- Did you enjoy it? Why (not)?
- Would you recommend it? ▸ Skills file 10.9, p. 174

Unit 2 Stop! Check! Go!

More challenge 7 Fun in Detmold ▸ Unit 2, p. 55

Freja is a friend from Sweden. Help your family to have a conversation with Freja.

Vater Nächstes Wochenende können wir einige Dinge zusammen machen und Freja etwas von unserer schönen Gegend zeigen. Frag Freja, ob sie besondere Ideen hat, was sie sehen und tun mag.

1 You (to Freja) My parents would like to take you to see some of the interesting things in our area next weekend. Is there anything you would like to see?

Freja I read something about a monument called *Hermanns-denkmal*. I'd like to see that.

2 You (to your parents) ...

Vater Sag Freja, dass wir ihr gern das Hermannsdenkmal in Detmold zeigen würden. Das ist berühmt. Viele Touristen aus aller Welt kommen, um es sich anzusehen.

3 You (to Freja) ...

Mutter In Detmold gibt es am Wochenende einen tollen Flohmarkt. Frag mal, ob Freja Lust hat, den zu besuchen.

4 You (to Freja) ...

Freja Yes, that's a great idea. I love markets.

5 You (to your parents) ...

Vater Und wenn Freja möchte, werden wir dort auch etwas typisch Deutsches essen, nämlich eine Currywurst mit Pommes. Dort gibt es die beste weit und breit.

6 You (to Freja) ...

Mutter Oder man kann einen lippischen Pickert probieren. Das ist eine westfälische Spezialität, ein bisschen wie Pfannkuchen aus Mehl, geriebenen Kartoffeln, Milch, Eiern, Hefe und mit Rosinen. Lecker, aber sehr sättigend. Frag Freja, ob sie das probieren mag.

7 You (to Freja) ...

Freja Both meals sound great. I'd like to try both. Then I can tell my friends in Sweden about some typical German food and also a speciality from Westphalia. And when I'm back in Sweden I can try making the Pickert for my family.

8 You (to your parents) ...

Unit 3

More practice 1 Working with words (1) ▸ Unit 3, p. 56

a) Write definitions for these words from pp. 56–57, using relative clauses. ▸ Language file 28, p. 197

... is a gadget / an invention / a vehicle / ... that / who ...

1 A driverless truck ...
2 Contact lenses ...
3 Piezoelectric power ...
4 A pillow ...
5 An exoskeleton ...
6 A scientist ...

b) Now use a dictionary (online, if you like) and explain these words from pages 56–57.
- blink, heart rate, outfit, generate, increase, hail

More practice 2 **Working with words (2)** ▸ Unit 3, p. 59

Explain these words from the story in complete sentences.

1 *wearable devices* (line 16)
2 *wireless headphones* (line 18)
3 *people-watching* (line 36)
4 *fitness tracker* (line 38)
5 *groaned* (line 43)
6 *head-mounted display* (line 48)

More help **1f** **A student's talk on sustainable living** ▸ Unit 3, p. 61

You can choose one of these pictures for your talk.

Travelling ...

by train or by plane?

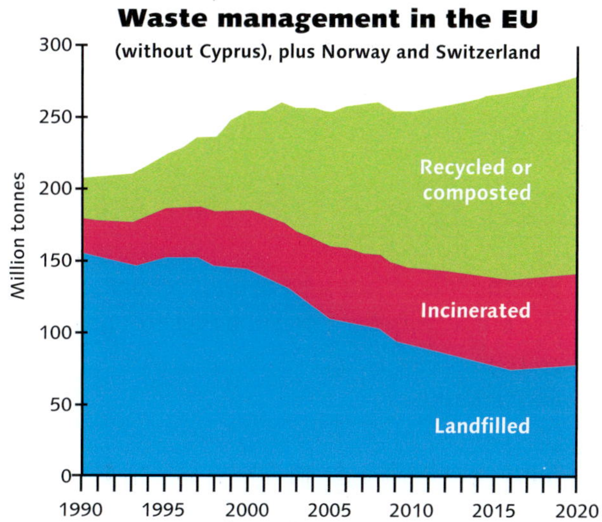

Source: *European Environment Agency (2011)*

More practice 3 **Stylistic devices (3)** ▸ Unit 3, p. 61

> These techniques are also called ***stylistic devices***.

a) Contrast: In *Sorry*, the writer uses the technique of contrast. This means he puts two opposites together.

1 Look at these lines from *Sorry*. Can you find the two opposites?
I'm guessing you probably know what is the Amazon desert, right?
Well believe it or not, it was once called the Amazon rainforest.
What effect does this contrast have? Does this technique make you feel bored or interested?

2 Now look at these lines from *Sorry*. Can you find the two opposites here?
But most of all I want to say sorry about our mindset,
Cause we had the nerve to call this destruction – progress.
What's the effect of using this contrast? How does it make you feel?

3 In these lines the contrast is very clear. What are the opposites?
And I'm sorry we didn't find another planet in time to move to.
I am s...
You know what, cut the beat, I'm not sorry.
This future, I do not accept it ...

What is Prince Ea saying here? Does he surprise you? How? ▸ Skills file 8, pp. 164–165

b) **Other techniques (stylistic devices):** Look at the lines below from *Sorry* (in 1 to 4). What writing techniques can you discover in them?

1 *Sorry, sorry we left you our mess of a planet.*
Sorry that we were too caught up in our doings to do something.
Sorry we listened to people who made excuses to do nothing.

2 *We just didn't realize how special the earth was,*
Like a marriage going wrong,
We didn't know what we had until it was gone.

3 *I'm sorry we used nature as a credit card ...*

4 *We are the root, we are the foundation, this generation.*

! You don't have to understand all the words to discover the techniques. But you can use a dictionary.

! You can find a list of good writing techniques (***stylistic devices***) in ▸ *Skills file 8, pp. 164–165.*

More help **3 YOUR TASK** **Take action** ▸ *Unit 3, p. 61*

a) Here are some ideas.
- Ban the sale of fast food in your school.
- Use public transport, travel by bike, or go on foot.
- Save energy.
- Offer advice on a green lifestyle.
- Separate rubbish.
- Reduce waste.
- Be digitally responsible.
- Become politically aware.

b) Here are some planning tips.
- Set concrete and realistic aims (e.g. make and give out 200 flyers; organize on online petition and gather 1000 signatures; set up an information stall and run it for two weeks; invite speakers to speak at your school; ...).
- Write down the necessary steps to reach your aims.
- Make a list of tasks and decide who will do what.
- Make a time plan (a time table can be helpful for this) and agree on how long your project should take.
- Choose one group member to document the project in a diary or blog. He or she could make notes on day-to-day progress including milestones along the way; record the reactions of people to your project; take notes at meetings; document things your group learns; record fun or funny moments; ...
- Meet regularly to check your progress.
- Support each other along the way with advice and help.

c) Here are some tips for your presentation.
- Choose one or two people or present your results as a group.
- Begin by describing your project and its aims.
- Present highlights from your diary/blog.
- Use visuals like photos, posters, charts, etc.
- Describe how successful you were and what it means to you.

More practice 4 Decisions, offers, promises

▸ Unit 3, p. 63

Read the dialogue. Decide if the sentences in **orange** are a) quick decisions, b) offers or c) promises.

Dan: *(on the phone)* (1) I'll talk to my mum and then I'll call you back. Okay? Bye.
Hi Mum. (2) I'll help you with those bags, if you'd like.

Mum: Oh, hi. That's sweet of you, Dan. Yes, please.

Mum: There are some new socks for you and your brother in that bag. Which ones do you prefer – the blue stripes or the red stripes?

Dan: (3) Erm, I'll take the red stripes. They remind me of Mars, my favourite planet.
And speaking of Mars, Mum, could I go see *The Martian* with Meg and Louis tonight? (4) I'll finish my homework first.

Mum: Hm, I don't know, Dan, it's a school night. (5) I'll think about it later, okay? Right now I need to water the garden.

Dan: But the film starts in an hour!

Mum: Oh, so soon? (6) Well then, I'll have to make up my mind now.

Dan: Oh, please let me go, Mum. (7) I'll come straight home when the film is over.
(8) And I'll water the garden for you, okay? Then you can relax ... and think about it.

Mum: Well, that's not a bad idea – my feet are tired. *The Martian*, did you say? ...

More practice 5 3 What do you think?

▸ Unit 3, p. 63

Complete the dialogue with suitable forms of the ***simple present*** or the ***will*-future**.

DrSpock: I ... (1 not think) humans ... (2 ever, get) to Mars. What about you?

Spacecadet: Well, I actually ... (3 believe) that it ... (4 happen) one day. Maybe it ... (5 not happen) by 2030, but I ... (6 be) sure that the scientists ... (7 be) successful in the future.

DrSpock: Let's say they make it. How long ... (8 it, take) to get there?

Spacecadet: It's likely that the trip ... (9 take) eight months. It ... (10 be) a long way!

DrSpock: What ... (11 you think) life ... (12 be) like on Mars?

Spacecadet: It ... (13 be) really difficult. The space pioneers ... (14 not be able to) go outside without special suits. They ... (15 have to) wear them all the time as it's so cold. And there's the deadly radiation. If they ... (16 stay) outside without a suit, they ... (17 die).

DrSpock: Where ... they ... (18 live) then?

Spacecadet: They ... (19 have to) live under the ground at first. But I ... (20 expect) that later they ... (21 create) new environments. I think it ... (22 be) brilliant.

DrSpock: Humans have made a big mess here on earth. I'm sure they ... (23 make) the same mistakes if they ... (24 go) somewhere else.

Spacecadet: Maybe you ... (25 be) right, but it's possible that we ... (26 do) better next time!

Unit 3

More practice 6 An evening with friends

▸ Unit 3, p. 63

Complete the sentences using the *will*-future or the *going to*-future.

! Remember: You usually use the *will*-future for predictions and the *going to*-future for plans. You can also use the *will*-future when you make a quick decision or an offer.

1 You meet your friends in town. They tell you about their plans for the evening. They say: "We ... (get) something to eat and then we ... (see) that new film at the cinema."
2 You don't think the film is very good. You say: "I don't think that I ... (like) that film."
3 One of your friends has read excellent reviews. He says: "The reviews say that people who like science fiction ... (love) it. You like science fiction, so I think you ... (enjoy) it."
4 Another friend tries to persuade you too. She says: "Please come. I'm sure we ... (have) a good time."
5 You decide to go to the cinema. You say: "OK, I ... (come) with you."
6 In the cafe one friend says: "I'm not very hungry, so I ... (order) something small. What about you two?"
7 You look at the menu and decide quickly what you want. You say: "I ... (have) a hamburger and fries."
8 Your other friend isn't sure what to have. She says: "Do you think the curry ... (be) vegetarian?
9 In the end you talk for too long and there's no time to eat anything. You say: "If we don't leave now, we ... (miss) the film!"

More challenge 1 More ways of talking about the future

▸ Unit 3, p.63

Read the text.

A grey day on Mars

Lucy woke up early. She looked out of the window of her pod. "Another grey morning on Mars," she thought. The screen on her desk said: "Monday 1st February - 6.15 am."
"I'm not getting up yet," she thought. "Breakfast isn't until 7 today."
She thought back over her time on the Red Planet. She had set off on her journey from earth over a year ago.
"In three weeks' time I'll be celebrating my birthday on Mars for the first time. We'll have been here for 6 months," she thought.
The alarm went off. "I'll get up now," she thought. "Breakfast starts in 10 minutes, and I'm not going to be late. We're having pancakes today, my favourite."
Over breakfast the team discussed their plans for the day.
"I'm going outside today," Lucy announced. "I'm going to check the solar panels. Is anybody else coming?"
"I'll come with you," said Avril. "But while you're looking at the solar panels, I'll be checking the roof of the pod."
Lucy thought, "If there's a problem with the roof, it'll be serious." But she just nodded and smiled. "I'll see you in half an hour by the main door then. Will you have finished your breakfast by then?"
"Sure," said Avril. "I've already finished. I'll see you later."
"Great. See you later."

a) True or false? Find evidence in the text for your answers.

1 Lucy has to wait over an hour for breakfast.
2 Lucy's birthday is in March.
3 Lucy has been on Mars for less than 6 months.
4 Lucy is looking forward to breakfast.
5 She knows what's on the breakfast menu.
6 Lucy has already planned her work for the day.
7 Lucy and Avril are going to work together.
8 Lucy is worried about the roof.

b) The writer uses many different verb forms to talk about the future.
Look at the examples from the text in the box below.
Then find at least one more example of each form in the text above.

FOCUS

When talking about the timetable for the day, the writer uses the ***simple present***:
Example: Breakfast starts in 10 minutes.

When talking about something that's a fixed plan, the writer uses the ***present progressive***:
Example: We're having pancakes today.

When talking about something that will come to an end in the future, the writer uses the ***future perfect***:
Example: We'll have been here for 6 months in three weeks' time.

The writer also uses the ***progressive*** form of the ***will*-future** – also called the ***future progressive***.
Example: I'll be celebrating my birthday on Mars for the first time. ► *Language files 11–14, pp. 186–187*

//● 6 Improve your English: typical mistakes ► *Unit 3, p.64*

Find the seven mistakes and improve this student's text.

Space – the new tourist destination?

I hope that space is the new tourist destination. I'd love to be a space tourist! I don't expect that I'll have the chance to go. But if I will be lucky, I'll go. I don't really believe it will happen because it simply so expensive is and I'm not sure that it will ever be cheap enough for normal people like me. But as soon as prices come down, I will on the first spacecraft. I'd really love to go into space for several reasons. First, I'd love to look down on the Earth from up there. Secondly, I'd love to explore new planets. A space pioneer's life must be so excited!

So I hope that space will be a tourist destination in the future. But unfortunately it's unlikely that I'll ever be a space tourist. A shame!

Unit 3

More practice 7 Natasha's story or Zoe's story
▸ Unit 3, p. 67

Pick a) or b).

a) Tell the story in paragraph 4 (lines 47 – 82) from Zoe's point of view. Use the first-person narrator. Write about 60 – 80 words.

b) Tell the story in paragraph 4 (lines 47 – 82) from Natasha's point of view. Use the first-person narrator. Write about 60 – 80 words.

Then compare your text with someone who has written the other text.

More challenge 2 Your view of the future
▸ Unit 3, p.67

Pick a) or b) and write a short argumentative text.

▸ Skills file 10.1, pp. 168 – 169

a) Does this story give us a pessimistic or an optimistic view of the future – or both? Give your opinion. What's your view of the future? Give reasons for your arguments.

b) *Rowing a boat is like life – you can't see what's ahead*. Do you agree or disagree with this statement? Give reasons for your answer.

More help 2a SPEAKING A gadget that I must have
▸ Unit 3, p. 68

Here are some ideas for gadgets:

- a homework robot
- mobile phone implants (in your body)
- a flying car
- a silent car
- a smart mirror for bedroom or bathroom
- an animal-human translator
- smart clothes
- a waterless washing machine
- an electric scooter

You can also do research on an idea of your own:

- Does it already exist?
- Are scientists working on it?
- Is it realistic?
- Might it come soon?
- What are the advantages?
- Are there any disadvantages?
- Are there any dangers?

More help 3b WRITING How to complain effectively
▸ Unit 3, p. 69

Match the four topics to the paragraphs in the writer's email.

- what she wants to happen next
- what exactly the problems are with the device
- what she has done so far
- what the complaint is about

More practice 8 MEDIATION An email from the drone company ▸ Unit 3, p. 70

Read the email from the drone company. Find the information that Andrea needs and make notes for a phone call with her (in German).

Senden An alle Anhang Adressen Schriften Farben

Chatwin Drones **- PUT THE FUN IN FLYING**

Dear Sir/Madam,

Thank you for getting in touch with Chatwin Drones. The Fly-Hi 100 drone is one of our most popular products. Here is some more information about it.
With a fully charged battery, the Fly-Hi 100 will fly for a maximum of nine minutes. It has a maximum speed of 1.5 metres per second. It is suitable for indoor and outdoor flying and it can fly to a height of 100 metres and a distance of 500 metres from the remote control. They are the legal limits, so we recommend that you don't exceed these limits. The drone weighs 412 g, including the battery. The battery is included when you buy the product. The current price is £159. We offer free delivery in the UK. If you are ordering from abroad, we recommend that you look up the normal postal rates. But please note, we do not deliver to the US.

Thank you for your interest in our products. Please don't hesitate to get in touch if you need more information.

Eric Brown, Chatwin Drones Sales

More challenge 3 Rules for drones in Germany ▸ Unit 3, p. 70

Do some research on the internet. Find out about the rules for drones where you live.

- Do you need a licence for a drone?
- How old do you have to be to buy a drone?
- How high can a drone fly?
- How far can it fly?
- Can it fly near airports?
- Can it fly in public places?
- Can you take photos or make films with a drone?

Unit 3

More practice 9 The characters ▸ Unit 3, p. 71

a) Pick one of the main characters in the film – Sarah, Danny or Dr Thun. Copy this table. Then watch the film again and make notes about your character.

character	
appearance	
personality	
interests	

Discuss your notes with other students who have picked the same character.

b) What do we learn about the relationship between Sarah and her mother? Does the relationship change? Write a short comment. Swap texts with other students and read their ideas.

c) Does your opinion of any of the characters change during the film? Answer this question with examples and give some reasons.

More challenge 4 A film still ▸ Unit 3, p.71

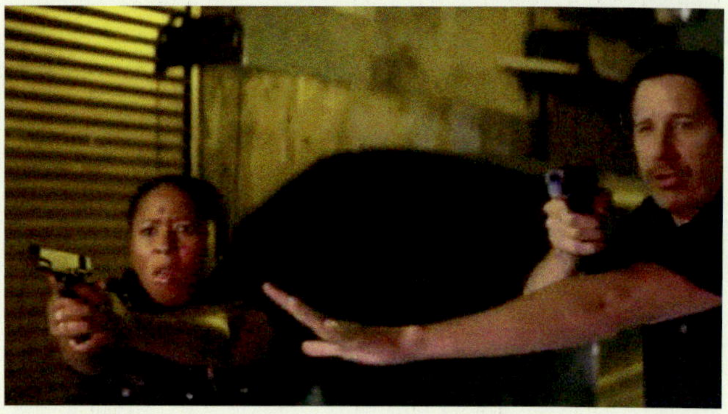

Describe the still in detail.
- Where does this scene take place?
- Describe the scene.
- How do the people look?
- What are their relationships?

Examine the still.
- What is the camera shot (a long shot / a medium shot / a close-up)?
- What body language do we see? (Are the people friendly / aggressive / ...?)
- What is the effect of the still on the viewer? (How does it make him or her feel?)

Find a caption for the still and explain why you chose the caption.

More help 6 WRITING You and superheroes ▸ Unit 3, p. 71

These questions can give you some ideas.
- What usually happens in superhero films?
- How do superhero films usually end?
- What superheroes do you know?
- What are superheroes usually like?
- If you were a superhero, what would your superhero powers be?
- Do you like superhero films?

Unit 3 | Stop! Check! Go!

More challenge 5 Use your dictionary ▸ Unit 3, p.76

a) Find suitable English words for the underlined words in these sentences.

ÜBERLEGEN

1 Beim Schwimmen ist sie mir überlegen.

2 Ich muss überlegen, ob ich nach Klasse 10 eine Ausbildung mache oder weiter zur Schule gehe.

BERECHNUNG

3 Ich hoffe, meine Berechnung des Preises ist richtig.

4 Er macht vieles aus purer Berechnung.

b) Try to guess the meaning of the underlined words, then check in a dictionary.

The world population has increased greatly and this has brought many problems including the destruction (1) of complete ecosystems (2) and global warming.

A reduction (3) in greenhouse gases (4) and the use of renewable (5) types of energy – such as solar (6), wave and wind power – are now seen as essential (7).

Text file

More practice 1 The separation of powers in Germany ▸ Text file 3, p. 136

Research the German equivalents[1] of the US branches and offices shown in the graphic on p. 136. Draw a diagram or find the missing information to complete the graphic below.

Talk about the separation of powers in the German system of government.

Legislative

Bundestag
elected for ___ (by all ___ who have the right to vote)

___
appointed by governments of the federal states

Exekutive

Schloss Bellevue, Berlin

___ *(Federal President)*
elected for ___ (by Bundesversammlung)

Kanzleramt, Berlin

___ *(Federal Chancellor)*
elected for ___ (by ___), appointed by ___

Bundesminister *(Cabinet)*
appointed by ___

Judikative

BVerfG, Karlsruhe

Bundesverfassungsgericht
16 ___, elected for 12 years (by Bundestag + Bundesrat), appointed by ___

Bundesgerichte
(Other federal courts)

[1] equivalent [ɪˈkwɪvələnt] *Entsprechung, Gegenstück*

Wordbank 1: Discourse markers

▸ More challenge 1, p. 29

Discourse markers are words and phrases that organize language in discussions and written arguments, e.g. they show the structure of an argument or the speaker's attitude. They usually stand at the beginning of a sentence.

Opening a discussion
- What do you think about ...?
- Let's discuss ...
- How about ...?
- I'd like to suggest ...

Giving your opinion
- In my opinion / view, ...
- If you ask me, ...
- I'd like to point out that ...
- Regarding ..., I think / suppose ...
- Apparently, ...

Agreeing
- I (definitely) agree (because) ...
- I think so too.
- (I think) you're right.
- It's true that ...
- That's a very good point.
- Yes, indeed.
- Certainly, ...

Disagreeing
- (I'm afraid) I don't agree.
- I'm not so sure about ...
- Yes / True, but don't forget ...
- (Sorry,) I think you're wrong. / I don't think you're right.
- However, ...
- Although ..., ...
- In spite of this, ...
- On the contrary, ...
- Even so, ...
- ..., but nevertheless ...

Giving reasons / supporting your point
- To start / begin with, ...
- Firstly / Secondly, ...
- A good example for / against ... is ...
- Think of ..., for instance.
- What's more, ...
- On the one hand ..., but on the other hand ...
- Therefore, ...
- Since ..., ...
- No doubt ...
- As a consequence, ...

Asking for clarification
- Sorry, I didn't get that.
- Could you please give an example of ...?
- Are you saying that ...?
- Does that mean ...?
- In other words, ...?

Buying time
- Well, let me see ...
- I'm not an expert, of course, but I think / I guess / I'd say that ...
- Well, that's an interesting point.
- I see what you mean.

Changing the subject
- Oh, by the way, ...
- Another aspect of ... is ...
- Right, now let's discuss ... / go on to ...

Summing up and stating the result(s)
- To sum up our discussion, we think ... / agree that ... / can't agree on ...
- Both / All of us agree that ...
- Everybody supports ... / is for / against ...
- (We voted and) a majority is for / against ...
- In any case, ...
- On the whole, ... / As a result, ...
- In short, ...
- It has become clear that ...

Wordbank 2: Pollution

▸ Unit 3, p. 61

POLLUTION

- **land**
  - rubbish

  - pesticides

  - expanding cities

  - cutting down trees
- **water**
  - chemicals

  - sewage

  - industrial waste
- **animals**
  - extinction
  - overpopulation
  - no natural balance
- **climate**
  - global warming
  - flood
  - more tornadoes
  - more deserts

- **waste of natural resources**
  - wasting energy
  - wasting water

  - using too many mineral resources

- **air**
  - exhaust fumes
    - from cars

    - from industry

---

expand [ɪk'spænd] *sich ausbreiten*   sewage ['suːɪdʒ] *Abwasser*   industrial waste [ɪn'dʌstriəl weɪst] *Industrieabfall*
natural resources ['nætʃrəl rɪ'sɔːsɪz] *natürliche Rohstoffe*   mineral resources ['mɪnərəl rɪ'sɔːsɪz] *Bodenschätze*
exhaust fumes [ɪg'zɔːst fjumz] *Abgase*

TF 1 PROJECT Around the world

1 Canada at a glance

a) Read this information from a travel guide about Canada. What did you already know?

b) If you were planning a trip to Canada, what else would you like to know? Together, note down at least five questions.

Here are some facts to get you interested in Canada. But don't stop here. Go find out more about this great country on the internet. Who knows – maybe you'll go there some day!

The beaver is a symbol of Canada

The country

It's big! Damn big! In fact, it's the world's second largest country (after Russia). It's full of different landscapes – high mountains, huge glaciers[1], vast prairies[2], forests that go on forever, wild coasts ... Canada has it all! And Canada's climate is diverse too – from freezing winter temperatures (it can go to below 60 degrees Celsius in some places) to nice warm summer weather (top temperatures are around 25 degrees). About 90% of the population of Canada is squashed into the bottom part of the country, along the border[3] with the USA (where most of the cities are). And the rest of the country is almost empty – except for the wild animals, of course!

Niagara Falls, Ontario

[1] glacier ['glæsiə] *Gletscher* [2] vast prairie [vɑːst 'preəri] *riesiges Grasland* [3] border ['bɔːdə] *Grenze*

The history

Canada's first inhabitants[4] probably came over a land bridge from Asia about 15,000 years ago and slowly moved south. Then, about 1000 years ago, the ancestors[5] of the modern Inuit people started to move down from Alaska. Around the same time the Vikings came, but they didn't stay. 500 years later, in 1497, the explorer[6] John Cabot arrived. He found cod here – a fish that Europeans liked to eat. Soon after that European fishermen started to arrive. In the 1530s the first French settlers came to Canada. They hunted beavers – for their fur[7] – and this became a huge business. So more and more Europeans came. In 1670 the English settled in the Hudson Bay area. There were many wars between the English and the French – until 1763, when France handed Canada over to Britain. In the 1850s gold was discovered in the west and lots of settlers moved there. Another important date is 1885, when the Canadian Pacific Railway was finished and many more people could travel west. In 1931 Canada became independent of Britain. However, even today the British Queen or King remains[8] the head of state[9].

Inuit family on a motorcycle at Inukjuaq

The newly married royal couple, Prince William and Catherine, on their visit to Canada in 2011

The people

For hundreds of years immigrants have been coming to Canada from all over the world – from Africa, Asia and Europe. Today Canada still has one of the highest rates of immigration in the world. As a result, Canada is a very multicultural country – and it's very accepting of[10] different cultures. Nearly every major Canadian city has a Chinatown, a Greektown, a Little Italy and a Little Punjab. Aboriginal Canadians (First Nations, Métis and Inuit) today make up about 4.3% of the population. Altogether there are about 200 different ethnic groups[11] in Canada and over 100 languages are spoken. The official languages are English and French. About 60% of the population speaks English as a first language and about 20% speaks French. One very important thing to remember is that Canadians are not Americans. If you ask Canadians what the differences are, you'll get lots of different answers: "Canadians are friendlier ... We're more polite and say 'sorry' a lot ... We're more tolerant ... We travel abroad more ... We like hockey more than football ... We don't carry guns ..." One thing is sure – Canadians get tired of being asked if they're American!

2 A talk about Canada

a) Listen to this talk. Does the talk answer any of your questions from 1b)?

b) Note down any other interesting facts that you learned about Canada from the talk.

c) Do some research to find the answers to any unanswered questions you have.

---

[4] inhabitant [ɪnˈhæbɪtənt] *Einwohner/in* [5] ancestor [ˈænsestə] *Vorfahr/in* [6] explorer [ɪkˈsplɔːrə] *Forschungsreisende/r* [7] fur [fɜː] *Fell, Pelz* [8] remain [rɪˈmeɪn] *(ver)bleiben* [9] head of state *Staatsoberhaupt* [10] be accepting of sb. *jm. annehmen, akzeptieren* [11] ethnic group [ˈeθnɪk] *Volksgruppe*

3 Your project

Pick a country where English is spoken (e.g. one of the countries in the pictures on pp. 132–133) and find some information about it. You can work alone, with a partner or in small groups. Think about the best way to present your information to the class.

Project steps

Step 1: Set your goals.
Decide what kind of information you want to find on the country you picked.
For example, are you interested in:
- information for tourists,
- the history of the country,
- why English is spoken there,
- the lives of young people,
- ...?

Note down your questions.

Step 2: Get organized.
If you're working with a partner or partners, decide who will do what and how much time you have.
Decide how you want to present the information:
- on a poster,
- as a brochure,
- as a slide show with a voice-over,
- or even as a video.

Step 3: Do your research.
Use key words to do some internet research. Take notes about what you find out. Make sure that your information is correct – double-check.

Step 4: Give your presentation.
All students should present their project to the class. Practise your presentation so that your performance is as smooth[12] as possible. ▸ *Skills file 4, p. 159*

You could ask some of these questions:
- What continent is this country in?
- What other countries is it near?
- What's the capital?
- What other big / famous cities are there?
- What's the landscape like?
- What can you find out about the history?
- What ethnic groups live there?
- Why is English spoken there?
- What can you find out about the people who live there?
- What about the wildlife, wild animals, etc.?
- What sights are there?
- What's this place famous for?
- What activities / sports can you do there?
- What famous singers and musicians come from there?
- ...

Colourful shop houses, Singapore

[12] smooth [smu:ð] *glatt, reibungslos, problemlos*

The Gateway of India in Mumbai, India

Queenstown, New Zealand

Ocho Rios, Jamaica

Lagos, Nigeria

4 Feedback

Give some helpful feedback on the projects.

Be positive. Say the things that you liked.
Use phrases like this:

- The first / second / last part was really good.
- I liked the part where you ...
- It was very interesting to learn that ...
- Your visuals were good, especially ...

Give advice. Say what could be better.
Use phrases like this:

- Try not to talk so fast / slowly / quietly / ...
- Perhaps your visuals could be a bit clearer / ...
- Don't forget to smile / look at the audience / ...
- You read from your notes a little too much.

TF 2 Wildlife tourism and conservation in South Africa

1 The wildlife industry

a) Look at the headings and pictures on pp. 134 and 135. What do you know about wildlife tourism?

b) Are your impressions of wildlife tourism positive or negative or both? Share your ideas. Think about opposite impressions and where they might come from. Then read the text.

Each year millions of tourists visit South African game parks to see wild animals in their natural habitats. The country is home to a wide diversity of animals including the "Big Five" – African elephants, rhinos, lions, leopards and Cape buffalo. Over twenty national parks and an even larger number of private game reserves offer safaris and other kinds of wildlife experiences. This industry is important both for the South African economy and for wildlife conservation. Shamwari Game Reserve is one example of a successful game park. In the 250 square kilometre private reserve visitors see and learn about the park's wild animals on informative guided safaris. During their visit they enjoy luxury accommodation. Shamwari is also active in animal conservation. Here are some of its initiatives:

- The *Wildlife Rehabilitation Centre* rescues sick or hurt animals, nurses them to health and returns them to the wild.
- The *Born Free Big Cat Rescue Centre* gives lions and leopards from circuses and zoos around the world a healthy, lifelong home.
- The *Rhino Awareness Centre* brings attention to the situation of rhinos, whose numbers worldwide have been radically reduced by poaching.
- The Education Programme works with local schools and colleges to teach young people about wildlife and conservation.

c) Who profits from wildlife tourism as described here? How?

d) Describe the ways in which Shamwari contributes to wildlife tourism.

e) Research another game reserve in South Africa. Find out how it contributes to conservation. Compare it with the information about Shamwari. Report your findings.

Key terms

awareness [əˈweənəs] *Bewusstsein*
canned hunting [kænd ˈhʌntɪŋ] *Gatterjagd (Erlegen von Tieren in einem Gehege)*
captive breeding [kæptɪv ˈbriːdɪŋ] *Zucht in Gefangenschaft*
cub [kʌb] *Junges (junges Tier)*
enclosed [ɪnˈkləʊzd] *umzäunt*
habitat [ˈhæbɪtæt] *Lebensraum*
poaching [ˈpəʊtʃɪŋ] *Wilderei*

2 The lion trade

Some of the activities in South Africa's wildlife industry are controversial. A few of them centre around the African lion, whose numbers on the African continent have gone from about 200,000 a century ago to about 30,000 today.

Captive breeding

There are about 160 lion breeding centres in South Africa. These "lion ranches" have bred more than 6000 captive lions. Critics argue that captive breeding, as it is called, doesn't help conservation because the lions can't survive in the wild. Lion cubs are taken from their mothers at birth. They lose their natural instincts through contact with humans and from living in enclosed areas. So why does the breeding continue? The lion cubs attract tourists who want to hold and stroke them, while the older lions have other uses ...

Canned hunting

Hunting big game animals in controlled numbers is a legal "sport" in South Africa. It's a huge industry that brings in more than $744 million a year. Hunters (most of them from the US) pay game park operators as much as $20,000 to "hunt" a male lion. However, the parks are not open game reserves, but enclosed areas, and the lions are captive-bred. They're easy targets with no chance to escape. Lion breeders profit from this "canned hunting" industry – and from another industry ...

Lion bones

In Vietnam and China people believe that lion bones, like rhino horns, are good for your health when they are ground up and mixed with other ingredients to make medicines. For this reason, traders pay high prices for the bones. The result is a huge international market that threatens wild lion populations. The connection with wildlife tourism is indirect. The lion bones market offers lion breeders and game parks that support canned hunting another way to profit from captive lions.

a) According to the text, how is a captive-bred lion different from a wild lion?

b) Describe two ways in which lion breeders profit from wildlife tourism.

c) **Think:** What, if anything, is wrong with the three activities described here? Make notes.
Pair: Compare your ideas.
Share: Present your arguments in class. Which are the strongest?

d) "Wildlife tourism in South Africa – an industry that we should support?" Write a comment (180 words or more) on the question.

TF 3 USA: a balance of powers

"No country can be called free which is governed by an absolute power."
Thomas Paine (1737–1809), US founding[1] father

1 Power and the federal[2] government

a) Look at the quote above. What was Thomas Paine concerned about? What makes a country free?
Share your ideas. Then read the text.

When the US Constitution was written and signed in 1787, the authors or "founding fathers" wanted a system of government that didn't give any one person or group absolute power. So the Constitution divided[3] the federal government into three separate[4] branches: the legislative, the executive and the judicial branch.

Key terms
absolute ['æbsəluːt] *uneingeschränkt*
branch [brɑːntʃ] *Abteilung*
Constitution [kɒnstɪ'tjuːʃn] *Verfassung*
enforce [ɪn'fɔːs] *vollstrecken*
executive [ɪg'zekjətɪv] *ausführend*
justice ['dʒʌstɪs] / **judge** [dʒʌdʒ] *Richter/in*
judicial [dʒu'dɪʃl] *gerichtlich*
legislative ['ledʒɪslətɪv] *gesetzgebend*
representative [reprɪ'zentətɪv] *Abgeordnete/r*

A separation of powers

Legislative branch
makes the laws

The Capitol

Congress
consists of:

- **Senate**
  100 senators, two from each state; elected for six years (one third elected every two years)
- **House of Representatives**
  435 representatives, number from each state based on[5] population; elected for two years

Executive branch
enforces the laws

The White House

President
elected for four years

Vice[6] President
elected for four years

Cabinet
Secretaries[7]: heads of most important government departments[8]; appointed by the president

Judicial branch
interprets the laws

The Supreme Court

Supreme Court
nine justices; appointed by the president for life

Other federal courts

b) According to the text, why was a separation of powers important to the authors of the US Constitution?

c) Describe the three branches of government as shown in the graphic. The phrases in the box can help you.

More practice 1 p.127

Activate your English
The ... is made up of / represented by ...
The job / role of the ... is to ...
The ... is / are elected for ... years.
The ... is / are appointed by ...

[1]found [faʊnd] *gründen* (founding father = *Gründungsvater*) [2]federal ['fedərəl] *Bundes-* [3]divide [dɪ'vaɪd] *(auf)teilen* [4]separate ['seprət] *getrennt, separat* [5]based on ['beɪst ɒn] *auf der Grundlage von* [6]vice [vaɪs] *Vize-* [7]secretary *(AE)* ['sekrətri] *Minister/in* [8]department [dɪ'pɑːtmənt] *Ministerium, Amt*

2 Checks and balances

As part of the separation of powers, the founding fathers built a system of "checks and balances" into the Constitution that allows each branch of government to "check" the other branches. This system of control "balances" the power of the three branches. For example, Congress can make new laws, but the president must sign them before they can become official.

Key terms
act [ækt] *Gesetz*
appoint [ə'pɔɪnt] *ernennen*
declare [dɪ'kleə] *erklären*
check [tʃek] *zügeln, einschränken*
override [əʊvə'raɪd] *aufheben*
propose [prə'pəʊz] *vorschlagen*
veto ['vi:təʊ] *Einspruch erheben, Veto einlegen*

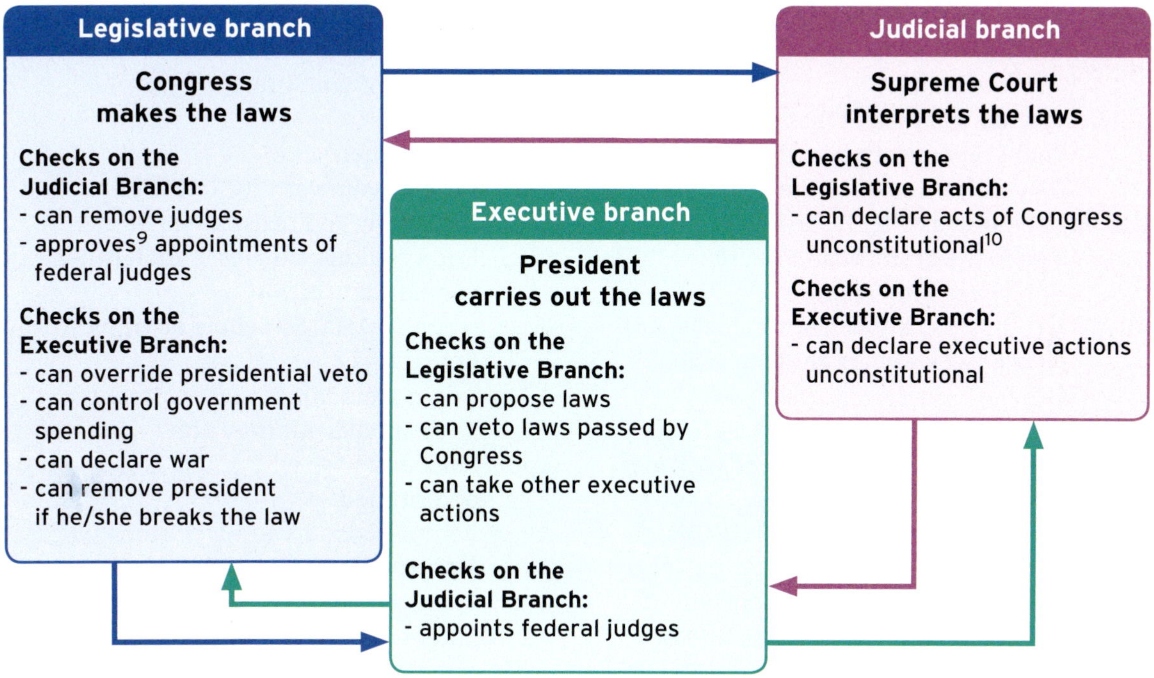

a) Complete these sentences to describe the checks and balances between the branches of government.

1 Congress can make a law, but *the president can veto the laws.*
2 The president can veto a law, but Congress ...
3 The president can take an executive action, but the Supreme Court ...
4 The Supreme Court interprets the laws, but the president ...
5 The president can appoint federal judges, but ...
6 Congress and the president can agree on a law, but ...

b) How do the role and the powers of the US president compare with those of the German chancellor and president? Do research and put your findings in a table. Present them in class.

US president	*German chancellor*	*German president*
Head[11] of government + Head of state	*Head of government*	*Head of state*
- runs the government *- represents the country*	*- runs the government*	*- mainly representative[12] functions*

[9]approve [ə'pru:v] *gutheißen, genehmigen* [10]unconstitutional [ʌnkɒnstɪ'tju:ʃənl] *verfassungswidrig* [11]head (of government/state) [hed] *Leiter/in, Vorsitzende/r (Regierungschef / Staatsoberhaupt)* [12]representative [reprɪ'zentətɪv] *repräsentativ*

TF 4 The Question (adapted from a one-act play by Brent Hartinger)

1 Before reading

Before reading this play, think about this question: What are the main differences between a play and a story? ▸ *Skills file 8, p. 164*

A teenage boy's bedroom, with a bed, desk and a few old toys (ones with high teen appeal), lots of sports equipment, colognes and hair gel, along with a tie or two sticking out of a drawer. Two boys, Eric and Allen, enter. Both are eighteen. Allen is the trendier, better dressed of the two. Eric looks like an athlete. The boys have a natural, easy rapport with each other. They're right in the middle of an energetic conversation.

Allen *(impatiently)* So? Did you ask the question?

Eric What question?

Allen What do you mean what question? What other question is there? "Do you want to go to the prom[1]?"

Eric No, I didn't ask her if she wanted to go to the prom! I can't ask her! I don't even know her!

Allen Of course you know her. You just spent the last twelve years going to school with her.

Eric Yeah, and in all that time, I've probably spoken to her a grand total of six times. In five of those times, she didn't say anything back. Allen, I can't do this! What if she turns me down[2]?

Allen *(smiling)* I already told you, she won't turn you down! That's the beauty of this. I know for a fact she thinks you're cute, and that she wants to go to the prom with you. She just doesn't have the nerve to ask you.

Eric How do you know?

Allen I already told you! She told Jessica.

Eric Okay, okay. I'll ask her tomorrow.

Allen Call her tonight. Call her now. *(He turns for the door.)* I'll dial[3].

Eric *(stopping him)* Allen! What difference does it make when I ask her?

Allen Because if you don't do it tonight, you won't ever do it.

Eric And so what if I don't ever do it? I don't see what the big deal is.

Allen The big deal is that this is your senior prom! If you don't go to your senior prom, you'll regret[4] it. Maybe not now, maybe not tomorrow, but soon, and for the rest of your life.

Eric So I regret it.

Allen Just call her.

Eric Why do you want me to ask her so bad? Oh, I get it. You're ashamed of[5] me.

Allen Eric, I couldn't care less[6] what other people think of you.

Eric *(pouncing)* Ha! So people do think I'm strange!

Allen Eric, no one thinks you're strange. They should, but they don't.

Eric I just don't see why you're so determined[7] –

Allen Because I don't wanna be alone with Jessica all night long, okay?

Eric Then you ask Brittany to the prom.

Allen I don't wanna be alone with Brittany, either.

Eric Then who –?

Allen You, you idiot! I want to go to the prom with you. *(There is a pause.)*

Allen Wait. That didn't come out right. I mean I want you and Brittany to come to the prom with Jessica and me.

Eric *(turning away)* Oh.

Allen I want someone to talk to during dinner.

Eric Okay, okay. I'll call her.

Allen Now? *(He turns for the door.)*

Eric *(irritated)* Yes, now! You're obviously not going to stop bugging me[8] until I do.

Allen Wait!

Eric Now what?

Allen Let's practise first.

---

[1] prom [prɒm] *Schulball* [1] turn sb. down *jm. absagen, einen Korb geben* [3] dial [ˈdaɪəl] *(Telefonnummer) wählen*
[4] regret [rɪˈɡret] *bereuen* [5] be ashamed of [əˈʃeɪmd] *sich schämen für* [6] I couldn't care less. *(infml) Es ist mir völlig egal.*
[7] determined [dɪˈtɜːmɪnd] *fest entschlossen* [8] bug sb. *(infml)* [bʌɡ] *jn. nerven*

Eric Oh no!

Allen Come on. Just do it. Okay, I'll pretend to be Brittany. You pretend to be you. You've just called me. *(He clears his throat; in a female voice.)* Hello? *(Eric stares at him with a smile.)*

Eric Is this really necessary?

Allen With anyone else, probably not. *("Brittany's" voice again)* Hello? Is anyone there?

Eric *(bored)* Hi, Brittany. I wanted to know if you wanted to go to the prom with me.

Allen *("Brittany's" voice)* Who is this? ... *(normal voice)* Come on! I'm just trying to get you to relax a little.

Eric *(very tense)* I'm relaxed, okay? I'm perfectly relaxed.

Allen I don't get it. Didn't you go to the prom before you met me? Last year? Or the year before?

Eric No *(quietly)*. I've never been to a dance, okay?

Allen What? Never?

Eric Never! Do I have to wear it on a sign around my neck? *(quietly)* I'm ... not sure I even know how to dance.

Allen *(smiling again)* Really?

Eric Allen!

Allen *(reassuringly[9])* Okay, okay. There's nothing to it. You just sort of ... *(he begins to sway[10])* Move to the music. That's the great thing about dancing – it's impossible to do it wrong. Do you have, like, a radio or something? Turn on some music.

Eric Yeah, sure. *(Eric turns the radio to some up-tempo song.)*

Allen Okay, just sort of ... go with the flow. *(Allen begins to dance. He's clearly practised for hours in front of a mirror, but he's actually pretty good.)*

Allen Now you try. *(Eric looks to see what Allen is doing, tries to mimic his moves.)*

Allen No, don't look at me. Just do whatever feels right. *(Eric tries again. He is embarrassingly awkward[11].)*

Allen You're too stiff. Try to loosen up[12].

Eric I thought you said it was impossible to do it wrong!

Allen I was wrong, okay? I'd never seen you dance. *(watching Eric)* That's better. *(They continue to dance. Eric is awkward.)*

Allen That's it! That's it. That's all you do. *(The song comes to an end. A slow song starts. There is an awkward pause.)*

Eric What if Brittany wants to ... slow dance?

Allen What?

Eric Slow dance. What if Brittany wants to slow dance?

Allen *(hesitantly[13])* Well ... it's sort of just the same thing, only you do it a lot slower, and you do it while holding onto someone else. *(They stare at each other for a second; the slow music continues to play.)*

Allen Oh, what the hell! *(Allen steps forward and takes Eric in his arms. They stay a foot apart.)*

Allen Okay, pretend I'm you and you be Brittany. I put my hands on your waist[14]. You put your hands on my shoulders.

Eric Like this?

Allen Close enough. Now we just sort of ... sway back and forth. I'll lead and you – Brittany – follow. *(They dance away.)*

Allen You know, there's not another guy on this planet that I'd do this with. *(They continue to dance. Eric is getting into it now – far better than before.)*

Allen Say, you're not bad. You're actually a lot better than Jessica.

Eric Come on.

Allen It's true! She dances like Frankenstein walks.

Eric Anyway ... *(An awkward silence. Then Allen speaks – less enthusiastically than before.)*

Allen Well ... I suppose we should call her now.

Eric *(quietly, head down)* Yeah, okay.

---

[9] reassuring [riːə'ʃʊərɪŋ] *beruhigend* [10] sway (back and forth) [sweɪ] *(sich hin und her) wiegen* [11] awkward ['ɔːkwəd] *unbeholfen* [12] loosen up [luːsn 'ʌp] *locker(er) werden, sich entspannen* [13] hesitant ['hezɪtənt] *zögerlich, zögernd* [14] waist [weɪst] *Taille*

(Allen starts for the door. Eric speaks, stopping him.)

Eric Well actually, there is one more thing.

Allen Yeah? *(There is another pause. Allen looks at Eric in confusion[15].)*

Eric Nothing. Never mind[16].

Allen No. Tell me.

Eric *(dismissively)* No, really. It's stupid.

Allen Come on.

Eric Well ... it's just that I ...

Allen Yeah?

Eric *(embarrassed, awkwardly)* Well, what if she wants me to ... kiss her good night?

Allen Huh?

Eric It's just that I've never actually kissed anybody before.

Allen *(quietly)* Oh.

Eric *(turning away)*
You probably think I'm an idiot asking all these stupid questions.

Allen No! No! There are no stupid questions. These aren't stupid questions. Not at all.

Eric So, um ... how do you do it?

Allen Well, there's nothing to it, really. You just sort of stand together, really close.

Eric Stand together close, okay.
(Eric and Allen step close together.)

Allen Don't pucker[17]. That's what everyone thinks at first, but it's not true.

Eric *(nodding)* Don't pucker. Okay, got it.
(They keep facing each other.)

Allen Then you just ... press your lips together.

Eric Press lips.

Allen And hold them there.

Eric Hold them there. How will I know when to stop?

Allen You just sort of ... know.

Eric Allen?

Allen Yeah?

Eric Do you ever think ...
(Suddenly, someone pounds on the door to Eric's bedroom. Both Eric and Allen start in alarm[18], then move to opposite sides of the room. The knock comes again. Eric turns to face the door.)

Eric What is it?
(A woman enters, Mrs. Sloan, Eric's mother. By interrupting, she has completely sucked the oxygen out of the room; even the light seems brighter now, and harsher.)

Mrs. Sloan Eric, your father needs to see you in the garage.

Eric Mom, I've kind of got company right now. Can you tell him I've got company?

Mrs. Sloan Oh, hello, Allen. I didn't know you were here.

Allen Hello, Mrs. Sloan.
(She notices the fact that they are on opposite sides of the room.)

Mrs. Sloan What are you boys doing?

Eric *(simultaneously with Allen)*
Reading comic books.

Allen *(simultaneously with Eric)* Playing a game!

Eric We're just hanging out! Tell dad I'll come down after Allen leaves.
(Mrs. Sloan lingers[19], staring at them suspiciously.)

Eric Anything else?

Mrs. Sloan No. No, I guess not. But we're having dinner in an hour.
Oh, and make your bed.

Eric *(quietly)* So I guess I should call Brittany now, huh?

Allen *(quietly)* Yeah, I guess you should.

Eric Okay, then. *(He starts for the door.)*

Allen Hey, maybe after the prom, we can drive up to the lake.

Eric With the girls?

Allen With 'em. Or without. Either way.
(They exit.) (BLACKOUT)
(END OF PLAY)

[15] in confusion [kən'fjuːʒn] *verwirrt* [16] Never mind. [maɪnd] *Egal.* [17] pucker ['pʌkə] *(die Lippen) kräuseln*
[18] start in alarm *vor Schreck zusammenzucken* [19] linger ['lɪŋgə] *verweilen, noch dableiben*

2 Setting

Read the play and make notes about these questions.

1 When do you think the play happens (in the present / the past)? Can you find any details that tell you this?
2 Where does the play take place? Describe how you think the stage would look.

> The **setting** of a story or play is where and when it happens.
> In a play you get information about the setting in the stage directions.

3 Plot

Pick the right ending to describe the plot. Find evidence for your answers in the text.

> The **plot** is what happens in a story or play and why it happens. Sometimes one action causes another.

1 In this play Allen wants Eric to ...
- A invite Jessica to the prom.
- B invite Brittany to the prom.
- C go to the prom alone.

2 But Eric has a problem because ...
- A he isn't interested in Brittany.
- B he hates proms.
- C he has no time.

3 We learn that Eric ...
- A doesn't know how to dance.
- B is a good dancer.
- C loves slow dancing.

4 We find out that ...
- A Eric wants to kiss Brittany.
- B Allen wants to kiss Jessica.
- C Eric is worried about kissing.

5 In the end we get the feeling that the boys ...
- A don't like each other.
- B are very good friends.
- C could be more than just friends.

4 Characterization

a) What do we learn about the two main characters? Make a table and write notes about:
AGE, APPEARANCE, PERSONALITY, FEELINGS, SENSE OF HUMOUR, WORRIES.

> We learn about the **characters** of a play or story by looking at what they say and do, how they look, what they wear, and how they feel.
> In a play the stage directions – and the performance – are important too.

b) Write a characterization of one of the boys. Give examples and use quotes from the play.

► *Wordbank 3, p. 147*

5 Atmosphere

Finish these statements about the atmosphere with examples from the play.

1 The atmosphere is light-hearted[20] when ... says ...
2 The atmosphere is a little tense when ...
3 The atmosphere changes when ...
4 In the end, the atmosphere is ...

> The **atmosphere** of a play or story is the feeling that the writer creates. It can be light-hearted or serious, positive or negative, tense or relaxed, etc. And of course the atmosphere can change.

6 Tell the story

Turn the play into a story – in not more than 180 words.
Use a first-person narrator (one of the boys) or a third-person narrator. ► *Skills file 8.2, p. 164*

[20] light-hearted *heiter, unbekümmert*

TF 5 Searching for a two-way street (a poem by Malorie Blackman)

1 While reading

Read this poem and answer the questions a) – f) on pp. 142–145.

SEARCHING FOR A TWO-WAY STREET

Before I was born,
Grown-ups[1] were passports
And driving licences
And bank accounts
And utility bills[2].

Communication was
Mobile phones
And cyber chats
And sign language
And face to face.

But people were
"Hello"
And hugs
And "Pleased to meet you"
And "How are you?"

Songs were
"Talk to me",
"See my side",
"Be with me",
"Love me."

And all those things
Were proof[3]
Of a person's identity.

All those things
Said
"I'm here,
I'm now,
I'm ready,
Willing[4]
And able
To communicate."

But that was
Before I was born.

Before I was born,
There weren't cameras
And scanners
And microchip readers
On every roof
On every street corner.

Before I was born,
School wasn't just a screen
And a virtual teacher.
Friends across the world
Had real faces,
Not faces chosen
In games or
From a menu.
We were more
Than just serial numbers[5]
And chips with everything.

Before I was born,
There was such a thing as
Secrecy[6]
Mystery
Privacy[7].
Before I was born.

Not any more.

a) What was life like before the speaker was born? Does the speaker think things were better then, or worse? Why? Give quotes from the poem.

---

[1] grown-up *Erwachsene/r* [2] utility bill [juːˈtɪləti bɪl] *Betriebskostenabrechnung (Gas, Strom, Wasser)* [3] proof [pruːf] *Beweis(e), Nachweis(e)* [4] willing [ˈwɪlɪŋ] *bereit, gewillt* [5] serial number [ˈsɪəriəl nʌmbə] *Seriennummer* [6] secrecy [ˈsiːkrəsi] *Geheimhaltung, Verschwiegenheit* [7] privacy [ˈprɪvəsi] *Privatsphäre*

When I was born,
A microchip was implanted[8]
At the base of my skull[9].
No microchip?
No state benefits[10],
No health care,
No travel,
No food aid[11],
No water deliveries,
No shelter[12],
No existence[13].
No microchip equals[14]
No anything.
Nothing.
No thing.
Not a thing.
So my Mum and Dad
Agreed,
When I was born,
To my microchip
Implant.
"We want our son
To survive in this world.
So yes to the chip."
Mum and Dad didn't like it,
They didn't want it,
But they had no choice.
And the government now knows
Where I am at all times.
Where any of us
Each of us
Are
At all times.
And we let them
Do that to us.

The government said,
"Law-abiding[15] citizens
Have nothing to fear[16]."

The government said,
"Those with nothing to hide
Have nothing to fear.
"The curtailment[17]
Of a personal freedom
Or two
Is a small price to pay
If we wish to have
Nothing to fear,"
The government said.

Those were the reasons
We gave up our mystery.

Better not to question.
Better not to know.
Better to accept.

And our information is fed
Back to computers.
State-of-the-art recording devices
That sit in silence
And capture[18] all movements
All meetings
All positions.

And Mum told me,
"Thirty years ago
This would've been
Inconceivable[19]."

And Dad said,
"Twenty years ago
This would've been
Unthinkable."

"Information shouldn't be
A one-way street," said Mum.
"Who watches the Watchmen[20]?"
Said Dad.

b) Since the speaker was born, life has changed. Describe how. Give some examples from the poem.
How does the speaker feel about these changes?

---

[8] implant [ɪm'plɑːnt] *implantieren, einpflanzen* [9] skull [skʌl] *Schädel* [10] state benefit ['steɪt benɪfɪt] *Sozialhilfe*
[11] food aid ['fuːd eɪd] *Nahrungsmittel(bei)hilfe* [12] shelter ['ʃeltə] *Unterkunft, Obdach* [13] existence [ɪg'zɪstəns] *Dasein*
[14] equal sth. ['iːkwəl] *einer Sache entsprechen* [15] law-abiding ['lɔː əbaɪdɪŋ] *gesetzestreu, die Gesetze befolgend*
[16] fear *(be)fürchten* [17] curtailment [kɜː'teɪlmənt] *Einschränkung (von Rechten)* [18] capture ['kæptʃə] *erfassen (Daten)*
[19] inconceivable [ɪnkən'siːvəbl] *unvorstellbar* [20] watchman, *pl* watchmen ['wɒtʃmən] *Wächter/in*

But they whisper the words
Behind closed doors.
It doesn't pay[21]
To stand and say
How you feel.
Not yesterday.
Not today.
Not tomorrow.
"Those days are over,"
Mum and Dad sigh.

There's a rumour[22]
Going round.
True or not?
Who can say?
But I think … true.
And this rumour?
The microchips in our heads
At the base of our brains
Relay[23] our thinking;
Maybe even control
Our thinking.

Just a rumour
But it's smoke …
So where's the fire?
Inside
Or outside
Our heads?

There's a rumour
Going round
That
Full thoughts[24]
Whole sentences
Can be tracked
Traced[25]
Monitored.
So I try
To think
In short
Sharp
Bursts[26].

My best friend
Denny told me
Staccato thoughts
Come across[27]
Like static
White noise[28].

No rhyme
No reason.
No sense
Nonsense[29].
True or not?
Who can say?

But now I think
In bursts
Like bullets[30]
Fired from a gun.
Proper[31] sentences
Could make me
… disappear.

Thoughts ought to be[32] private,
Information ought to be shared.
Communication should be
A two-way street.
An optional road to travel.
But a road we all
Can take
Nonetheless[33].

c) What do you think about the world the speaker lives in? Would you like to live in a world like that? Why (not)?

d) Do you think that the world in the poem is like our world?
- If yes, give some examples.
- If no, say why not.

[21] it doesn't pay *es zahlt sich nicht aus, es lohnt sich nicht* [22] rumour ['ruːmə] *Gerücht* [23] relay ['riːleɪ] *weitergeben, übermitteln* [24] thought *Gedanke* [25] trace sth. [treɪs] *etwas zurückverfolgen* [26] burst [bəːst] *Explosion, Salve* [27] come across *herüberkommen, ankommen* [28] static white noise ['stætɪk] *weißes Rauschen, atmosphärische Störung* [29] nonsense ['nɒnsns] *Unsinn, dummes Zeug* [30] bullet ['bʊlɪt] *Kugel (aus Schusswaffe)* [31] proper ['prɒpə] *richtig, vollständig* [32] ought to be … [ɔːt] *sollte/n … sein* [33] nonetheless [nʌnðə'les] *trotzdem, nichtsdestoweniger*

"Those days
Are over,"
Mum and Dad murmur[34].
But I'm not prepared
To believe that.
There has to be a way,
Some way,
To make my life
My own again.
Some way.

So I've started looking
For a means[35],
Some manner
To make my life
A two-way street.

And I will find it,
Because I'm not alone
In thinking
In bursts
Like bullets
Fired from a gun.
I'm not alone.
Because you are here
And I hope
You think the same.
Feel the same.
Our two-way street
We shall[36] find
We shall explore
We shall travel
Together.

e) In lines 199 – 229 of the poem, do you think that the speaker feels a little hopeful or only negative? Give reasons for your opinion.

ARTICLE 19

WE ALL HAVE THE RIGHT TO MAKE UP OUR OWN MINDS[37], TO THINK WHAT WE LIKE, TO SAY WHAT WE THINK AND TO SHARE OUR IDEAS WITH OTHER PEOPLE, WHEREVER THEY LIVE, THROUGH BOOKS, RADIO, TELEVISION AND IN OTHER WAYS.

f) Article 19 is from the Universal Declaration[38] of Human Rights. Do you think that the speaker agrees with it? Do you think this article is important? Why (not)?

2 Understanding the theme of the poem

Read the poem again. Then read these statements. Are they true or false? Quote the lines which give you the answers.

1 People weren't so friendly in the past. (Look at p. 142)
2 In the past, life was more personal. (p. 142)
3 In the modern world of the poem, you need a chip in your head to live. (p. 143)
4 In this new world, people are freer. (p. 143)
5 In this modern world, you can say what you think. (p. 144)
6 People say that the microchip controls what people think. (p. 144)
7 The computers can understand single words, but not full sentences. (p. 144)
8 The speaker asks us, the readers, to fight the microchip. (p. 145)
9 At the end of the poem, ARTICLE 19 says that we have the right to think for ourselves. (p. 145)

34 murmur ['mɜːmə] *murmeln* 35 means *(pl) Mittel, Möglichkeit* 36 we shall *wir werden (Futur)* 37 make up one's mind *sich entscheiden* 38 declaration [deklə'reɪʃn] *Erklärung* (Universal Declaration of Human Rights = *Allgemeine Erklärung der Menschenrechte*)

3 More about the poem

a) Setting: When do you think this poem is set?
b) Point of view: What do we find out about the speaker?
c) Title: What do you think the title means? Look at lines 128–129 and 193–194 for help.
d) Rhyme: What can you say about rhyme in the poem?
e) Verses: What can you say about verses in the poem? ► *Skills file 8.4–5, pp. 164–165*

4 Stylistic devices ► *Skills file 8.5, p. 165*

a) Imagery:

1 What image does the poet want to create in lines 13–17?

But people were
"Hello"
And hugs
And "Pleased to meet you"
And "How are you?"

2 The poet uses some metaphors. Find examples in lines 1–22. Can you find other examples in the poem?

3 What is the effect of the images in the poem?

b) Repetition:

1 Look at lines 1–58 on page 142 of the poem. Look for the phrase "Before I was born" How often can you find it? What point does the poet want to stress?

2 Now look at lines 60–75. What words are repeated? What point does the poet want to stress?

3 Can you find other examples of repetition in the poem? What is the writer stressing?

c) Irony: Look at lines 110–112.

Better not to question.
Better not to know.
Better to accept.

Do you think that the poet really thinks this? If not, what does she really think?

> **Imagery** is when you use language to create a picture, an **image**, in the mind of the reader. The most common stylistic devices for creating images are similes and metaphors.
>
> **A simile** is when a poet compares two things that are not really like each other using the words 'as' or 'like', e.g. in lines 184–187: "I think in bursts like bullets fired from a gun."
>
> **A metaphor** compares two things without using the words 'as' or 'like', e.g. in lines 4–7: "Grown-ups were passports and driving licences and bank accounts". These words create a picture of normal life today.

> A writer sometimes **repeats** a word or phrase to show that it's very important – to stress a point.
>
> E.g. "Before I was born" in lines 1–58.

> **Irony** is when you say the opposite of what you really think.
>
> E.g. "It's lovely weather" (when it's wet and cold outside).

5 Your response to the poem

How does the poem make you feel? Write a personal response and explain your feelings.

Wordbank 3: Talking about texts

▸ *Unit 1, pp. 23, 112* ▸ *Unit 2, pp. 45, 113* ▸ *More challenge 2, p. 51* ▸ *Unit 3, pp. 67, 120* ▸ *More challenge 3, p. 73*
▸ *Text file 4, p. 141* ▸ *Text file 5, p. 146* ▸ *Text file 6, pp. 148–149* ▸ *Skills file 8, pp. 164–165*

Title, author, publication
- I'm going to talk about … *(title)* by … *(author)*
- It was written in … *(year)* / (first) published in … *(year / for articles, interviews etc. in … title of newspaper or magazine)*

Text type and genre
- … is a non-fictional / fictional (literary) text.

Non-fictional texts:
- The text deals with … / is about …
- … is a news story / a magazine article / a biography / an interview / a review / a speech / an advertisement / …
- It shows the author's opinion about … / attitude towards …, which is …
- The text doesn't give a personal opinion, but rather global / detailed information about …
- … *(title)* tries to convince us of … / to do …

Fictional (literary) texts:
- … *(title)* is a …:
  · narrative text (novel / short story …)
  · dramatic text (play / comedy / tragedy)
  · poetic text (poem / ballad / song …)

Setting, topic and plot
- The story / novel / play is set in 1980s Britain / …
- Its central topic is freedom / life in … / …
- It's about a young couple that's … Later they … and in the end …
- The poem describes … / reflects on …

Structure
- The article has a clear argumentative structure: introduction, arguments for and against …, conclusion.
- The novel is made up of two parts / ten chapters (covering ten years) / …
- The short story is told from the end to the beginning / starts abruptly / has a surprise ending / is open-ended / …
- The play consists of one act with only one scene / three acts / …
- The poem is made of … (regular) verses / stanzas with … lines (each).

Narrator / speaker
- The story is told by a first-person narrator, … *(name)*, who is a character in the story / by a third-person narrator, … *(name)*, who is / isn't a character in the story.
- The narrator switches from one character's point of view to another's.
- The speaker of the poem describes … / feels … / shows us the world of …

Characters and characterization
- There is one main character in this short story, … *(name)*. He / She is described as …
- The other characters are not very developed / are stereotypes / …
- We get to know a lot of characters and their relationships in this novel. First there's … His / Her best friend / competitor / worst enemy / is …, who …
- In this play, there are only two characters, … and … We learn a lot about them from the way they speak, e.g. … often says / asks / claims / defends … He's described as … in the stage directions: he often behaves like … / is secretly in love with … / …

Language and style
- The author uses the following **stylistic devices** to emphasize … / to make us feel …
- The writer repeatedly **contrasts** … and …
- **Repetitions** and **parallelisms** like … intensify the speaker's point.
- The writer uses **irony** to …
- The **style** of the article / story / poem / song may seem simple (short sentences, many repetitions, …), but there are strong **images** like …
- To speak of … as … is a very impressive **metaphor**.
- The artist compares … to … and also explains this **simile** later: …
- The special sound of this poem is achieved by its regular / irregular **rhythm** and **rhyme**. There are regular rhymes at the end of each line, e.g. … / There are no regular rhymes in this poem, but we often find **similar sounds** and intensifying repetitions like …

Mood and atmosphere
- The writer makes us feel angry about … / support …
- The overall effect of the language and imagery in this poem / story / chapter is a joyful / gloomy / threatening / … atmosphere.

Personal comments
- I think … is a well-written article / a thrilling novel / a beautiful / fine poem / …
- I especially liked …
- However, the part on … was quite boring / not convincing / not well written / …
- My favourite character is … because …

TF 6 Currents[1] (adapted from a short story by Hannah Voskuil)

1 First impressions

a) Read the first two lines of this short story. Before you read on, think about what you would like to know about this story and write your questions down. For example:
- Who? - Where? - Why? - What? - When?

b) Compare your questions. Then read on. Does the story answer all your questions?

> You should **read a short story slowly**. Read it more than once.
> While you read, **make notes** about the plot and the characters to help you to understand the story better.

Gary stood on the porch and looked at the ocean. His mother had switched off the light, but he didn't protest against the dark.

Before that, his mother, Josey, put her two shivering[2], twelve-year-old granddaughters to bed. "I want you both to go swimming first thing tomorrow. We can't have two seals[3] like you afraid of the water."

Before that, one of the girls held the hand of a wordless Filipino boy. They were watching the paramedics lift the boy's dead brother into an ambulance. At this time, the other girl got sick[4] over a toilet in the cabin[5].

Before that, the girl who would feel sick watched as the drowned boy's hand slid off[6] the stretcher, Nobody put the hand back on the stretcher, and it bounced[7] and dragged and bounced.

Before that, Gary saw the brown hair sink and resurface[8] as the body bobbed[9]. At first he thought it was seaweed[10].

Before that, thirty-five people struggled out of the water at the Coast Guard's command[11]. A lifeguard shouted over jet ski motors about the increasing strength of the riptide[12].

Before that, the thirty-five people, including Gary and the two girls, formed a human chain and searched the waters for the body of a Filipino boy. The boy had gone under twenty minutes earlier and never came back up.

Before that, a lifeguard sprinted up the beach, shouting for volunteers. The two girls, resting lightly on their sandy bodyboards, stood up to help.

Before that, a Filipino boy pulled on the lifeguard's ankle[13] and gestured desperately[14] at the waves. "My brother," he said.

Before that, it was a simple summer day.

2 The narrator

a) Who tells this story – a first-person narrator or a third-person narrator?

b) Does the narrator know more about one character in the story? If yes, who? And what do we learn?

> Remember: A **first-person narrator** is someone in the story. A **third-person narrator** is outside the story and often knows more about one or more of the characters. ▸ *Skills file 8.2, p. 164*

[1] current ['kʌrənt] *Strömung* [2] shiver ['ʃɪvə] *zittern* [3] seal [siːl] *Robbe, Seehund* [4] get sick *sich übergeben (müssen)* [5] cabin ['kæbɪn] *Hütte* [6] slide off, slid, slid [slaɪd, slɪd] *heruntergleiten* [7] bounce [baʊns] *holpern* [8] resurface [riː'sɜːfɪs] *wieder auftauchen* [9] bob [bɒb] *sich auf und ab bewegen* [10] seaweed ['siːwiːd] *Seetang* [11] at sb.'s command *auf jds. Befehl* [12] riptide [rɪp 'taɪd] *gefährliche Strömung* [13] ankle ['æŋkl] *Fußgelenk, Knöchel* [14] desperate ['despərət] *verzweifelt*

3 The plot

a) What exactly happens? Tell this story in simple sentences. Begin like this:

It's a summer day.
A Filipino boy speaks to ...
The lifeguard runs ...
Two girls ...
...

> The **plot of a short story** can be very complex because the writer doesn't have a lot of words to tell you everything. So you need to **read between the lines**.
>
> The plot doesn't just tell you the story, it also tells you **why** things happen.
>
> The writer can create **tension**[15] in different ways, for example by telling the story in a special order. ► *Skills file 8.2, p. 164*

b) Now link some of the sentences in a) with some of the words below – to create a summary of the plot:
next / after that / because / but / although / however / while / when / ...

c) Compare your summary with the original story. What are the main differences?

► *Skills file 10.4, p. 171*

4 More about the story

a) Setting: Where do you think the story is set? Why do you think that?

b) Characters: Make a character network for the story and show the relationships. You can start like this:

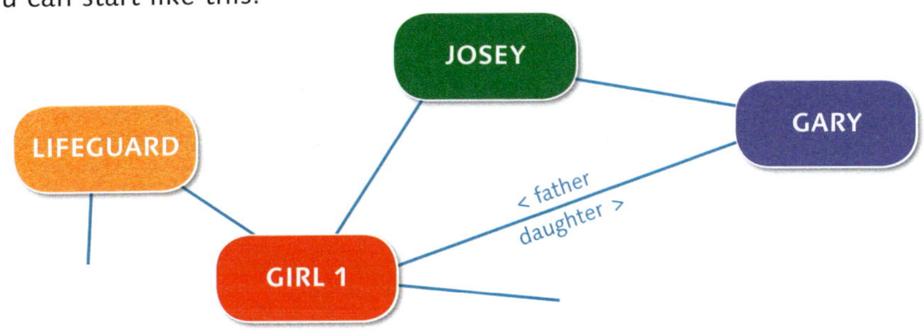

c) Imagery: What are the strongest images in the story for you?

d) Atmosphere: How does the story make you feel? What images does the writer use to create this feeling?

e) Style: How is this story different to other short stories that you have read? Is it effective?

5 Point of view

Write the story from the point of view of Gary or the lifeguard or one of the girls – in about 60 words.

---

[15] create tension ['tenʃn] *Spannung erzeugen*

Esma Nitin, 21, and Max Keller, 19, are both trainees at the company SolarGo, a German producer of solar energy systems, in Leipzig. Esma works in the marketing department and Max works in the logistics centre.

In the company

1 Small talk with visitors

Two Spanish trainees have arrived from the SolarGo office in Madrid. Esma is welcoming them.

a) Listen and correct these false statements.

1 Esma and Marta have never spoken before.
2 Marta and Luis took a taxi from the train station.
3 Luis met Max during his last visit to Leipzig.
4 Esma has to go because she has a lunch date.

b) Listen again and complete these phrases.

1 Nice to ...
2 Please ... me Esma.
3 Did you ... trip?
4 Let me ... around.
5 This is a lovely ...
6 ... is our logistics centre.
7 Please ... way.
8 Please ... seat.
9 Is this your ... to Leipzig?
10 It's great ... here.
11 I must ...
12 It was very ... you.

c) Copy the table and put the phrases in the right columns. Some fit in more than one column[1].

Greeting	Guiding a visitor	Small talk	Saying goodbye
...	...	...	...

2 NOW YOU Guided dialogue

Partner A:
You work for a German company.
- Begrüße B. Stell dich vor.
- Frage, wie die Reise war.
- Reagiere auf die Entschuldigung. Frage B nach der Unterkunft.
- Biete B an, ihm / ihr das Büro zu zeigen.
- Erkläre, dass das Gebäude ganz neu ist.
- Biete B etwas zu trinken an.

Partner B:
You arrive as a visitor.
- Reagiere, begrüße A und stelle dich vor.
- Beschreibe deine Reise. Entschuldige dich dafür, dass du spät kommst. Erkläre warum.
- Reagiere auf die Frage.
- Sage etwas Nettes über das Gebäude.
- Akzeptiere es. / Lehne es ab. Bedanke dich.

[1] column ['kɒləm] *Spalte*

3 Tell me about your job

a) Marta is interviewing Max to learn about what he does. Copy her job description form. Then listen to her interview with Max and fill in the form.

Compare your answers.

Job description

1. **Name:** MAX KELLER
2. **Job title:** ______
3. **Department:** ______
4. **Tasks:** ______
5. **Duration of traineeship[1]:** ______
6. **Further trainee tasks:** ______
7. **Full-time/Part-time:** ______
8. **Work hours:** ______

b) Luis wants to interview Esma, but he's not sure what to ask. Help him formulate a question for each of the points in the job description form above.
Listen to Max's interview again if you need to.

c) Write down Luis's interview with Esma. Use the information about her that appeared months before in the company newsletter.

d) Practise the interview.
Then swap roles.

Who's new at SolarGo?

Name:
Esma Nitin

Department:
Marketing, main office in Leipzig

Job title:
Marketing assistant trainee

My job:
mostly helping write brochures, organize events and give presentations; also assisting the marketing director

My traineeship:
18 months; includes a six-month course and a final project

My work hours:
usually 9 am to 5.30 pm, Monday-Friday

---

[1] traineeship [treɪˈniʃɪp] *Ausbildung(sverhältnis)*

Preparing for the trade fair[1]

1 Leaving a message

a) Esma is taking a phone call. Which phrase (A or B) are you more likely to hear?

	A		B
1	How can I help you?	OR	Why are you calling?
2	I want to talk to ...	OR	Could I speak to ..., please?
3	I'm sorry, but she's not at her desk right now.	OR	She's not here.
4	What do you want me to tell her?	OR	Would you like to leave a message?
5	Could you ask her to call me back ...?	OR	Tell her to call me.
6	Right. What was your name?	OR	Of course. Could you spell your last name for me, please?

b) Listen to the phone conversation and check your answers.

c) Listen again and write down how the caller and Esma begin and end their conversation. Compare notes. Then practise the conversation using different names and numbers.

2 Making appointments

a) Listen to Esma's three short phone conversations. In which conversation (A–C) do you hear the English phrases for these German ones?

1 Könnten Sie mir bitte sagen, worum es geht?
2 Ich möchte einen Telefontermin mit ihm vereinbaren.
3 Wann würde es Ihnen passen?
4 Aber nachmittags hat sie wieder Zeit.
5 Es tut mir Leid, da habe ich einen anderen Termin.
6 Das ginge gut bei mir.

b) Listen again. Write down the phrases from a) in English. Compare.

c) Ask your teacher for a printout of the three phone conversations. Practise speaking the different roles.

3 NOW YOU Two role-plays – pick one

a) **Partner B:** Go to p. 105.
Partner A: You're an office assistant at the Berlin software company *Inter_Soft*. Your boss, Nina Pfeifer, is in a meeting all afternoon. She has asked you to take a message if anyone calls for her. The phone rings. You begin the conversation – in German, of course.

b) **Partner B:** Go to p. 105.
Partner A: You're the British sales manager in the UK office of the German shoe company *Funshu*. You get a phone call from someone who wants to meet with you next week. You're free in the mornings and on Thursday afternoon.

[1] trade fair ['treɪd feə] *(Handels-)Messe, Fachmesse*

4 Ordering a product

Max is ordering equipment for the company's information stand at the trade fair.

a) Read his email to an Italian company. Find the German equivalents[1] for the underlined words.

Senden An alle Anhang Adressen Schriften Farben

An: office@aviva.it

Betreff: Product order

Dear Ms Canetti

Thank you for your reply and for your product catalogue.
With reference to our enquiry yesterday, we would like to place an order for the following items:

Catalogue No.	Description	Amount	Price/Item	Total
BN3402	Brochure shelves LUNGA	3	€78.00	€234.00

Payment will be by IBAN bank transfer to your account. Please confirm by email that you have received this order. Could you please also let us know when the delivery will be sent?

We look forward to receiving the goods soon.

Best regards
Max Keller

b) A SolarGo trainee is emailing Luc Didier at the French company *Spectra*. Rewrite her email in a formal style.
Use the email in a) as a model.

Hi Luc,

I wrote and asked about displays yesterday.

I want to order two of those big ones called "Astra". The ones that cost 270 euros.
The number in your catalogue is DF3420.
I'll pay you by IBAN.

Tell me if you get this order. And when are you going to send the displays?

Hopefully soon.

Bye, Anja (Weber)

! Writing a formal business email:
- Begin with *Dear Mr / Mrs / Ms* and the person's last name, or *Dear* and the person's full name, or *Dear Sir/Madam*.
- Close with *Regards / Best regards / Best wishes* and your full name.
- Use polite forms like *could*, *would*, *may*, etc. for questions and requests.
- Use formal words like *receive* instead of *get* and *enquiry* instead of *question*.
- Generally use *we* instead of *I*.

▸ *Skills file 10.3, p. 170*

[1] equivalent [ɪ'kwɪvələnt] *Entsprechung*

At the trade fair

1 Presenting a product

At the *Energy Expo* Esma is going to present one of the company's latest products. Her audience is mostly people who want to buy solar systems for their homes, so she decides to reduce her list of talking points today.

a) Agree on four points to drop from her list because they are less relevant.

SolarGo's EasySun system

1 Improved design
2 Easy to install
3 Invention of the solar cell (Solarzelle)
4 Fits every kind of roof
5 Produces more power than other systems
6 Saving money on electricity
7 More money-saving tips
8 Statistics on climate change
9 Helps protect the climate
10 SolarGo's 40-year success story

Price of a solar panel per watt (in $)

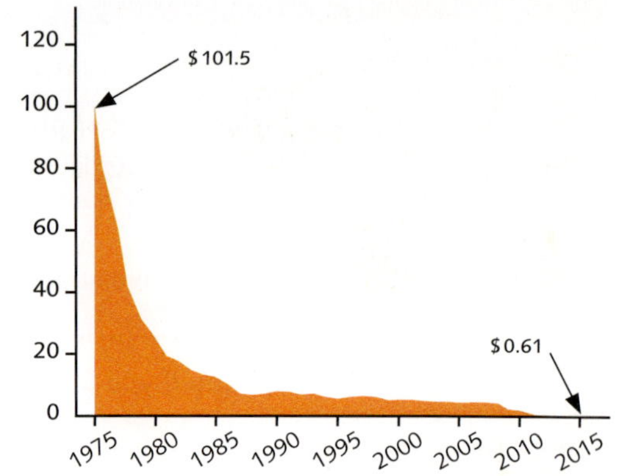

Source: *Earth Policy Institute/Bloomberg*

Now listen to the beginning of Esma's presentation. Did she drop the same points as you?

b) Esma uses two charts in her presentation. Look at charts A and B. Describe what each shows.
E.g.: The line diagram[1] shows the price of ... between ... The bar chart[2] shows how ...
Then briefly explain the changes or developments[3] that you see in the charts. ► *Skills file 11.3, p. 177*
E.g.: Between 19.. and 20.. the price went from ... to ...
Beginning in 20.., solar panel installations ...

Global solar panel installations

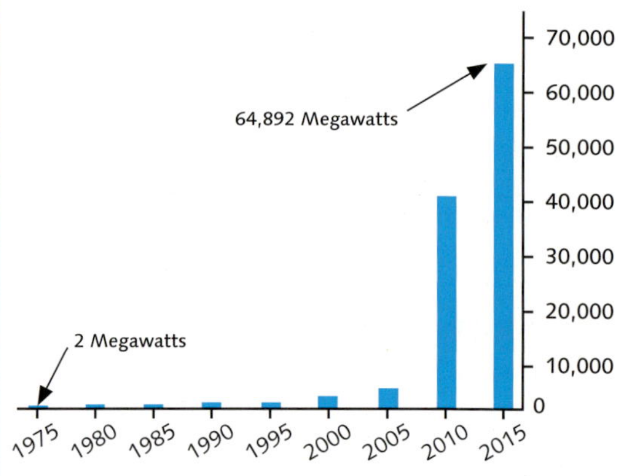

Source: *Earth Policy Institute/Bloomberg*

c) Listen to Esma's presentation and compare your answers to the information she gives.

2 NOW YOU A presentation at a trade fair

Prepare a short presentation. You could talk about a product like a tablet or a mobile phone, or a service, a holiday destination, etc. Use suitable pictures, diagrams or charts if you can. Give feedback on your classmates' presentations. ► *Skills file 11.3, p. 177*

[1] line diagram *Liniendiagramm* [2] bar chart [bɑː] *Balkendiagramm* [3] development [dɪˈveləpmənt] *Entwicklung*

3 Explaining a brochure

Max is handing out brochures and answering visitors' questions at the SolarGo stand. A Czech visitor wants to know about logistics if she orders the SolarGo system. Max has only brochures in German left today.

a) Read the information.

Vorteile des SolarGo EasySun Systems

- **Schnell und effizient:** Lieferfristen: im Inland etwa 3 Tage / im europäischen Ausland etwa 7 Tage / weltweit 14–21 Tage
- **Komplettsystem:** Das *EasySun*-System enthält alle Komponenten, die Sie zur Errichtung und zum Betrieb Ihrer Solaranlage brauchen.

- **Dokumentation und perfekte Vorplanung:** Unsere leicht verständliche Übersicht listet alle Bauteile auf. Die Bauanleitung zeigt in klaren Schritten die Montage Ihrer Dachanlage. Das spart Zeit bei der Vorbereitung und bei der Installation.
- **Hilfe:** Unsere Service-Hotline garantiert schnelle Hilfe bei Bedarf.

- **Clevere Verpackung:** Mit unserer umweltfreundlichen und äußerst stabilen Verpackung kommt Ihre Lieferung sicher bei Ihnen an. Wir holen die leere Verpackung auf Wunsch wieder ab.
- **Maximale Absicherung:** Der Bausatz kommt mit einer kostenlosen Versicherung für zwei Jahre, die ab Installation gültig ist.

b) Answer the visitor's questions. ► *Skills file 12, pp. 178–179*

1 How long will the delivery take?
2 Do I have to order any parts separately?
3 How do I know if I've received all the parts?
4 What do I do if I have questions or problems?
5 It looks complicated. I bet it takes a long time to install.
6 I'm a bit worried that the panels won't arrive safely.
7 What happens if something breaks or doesn't work?

Useful words
Bausatz assembly kit
Verpackung packaging
Versicherung insurance

SKILLS FILE

Inhalt

STUDY AND LANGUAGE SKILLS

SF 1 Dealing with unknown words ▸ *Unit 1, p. 18* ▸ *Unit 3, p. 64*

Du kannst englische Texte verstehen, auch ohne alle Wörter zu kennen. Nicht immer ist Nachschlagen nötig.

- Schau genau auf Titel und (Zwischen-) Überschriften sowie den Zusammenhang (Kontext), in dem das unbekannte Wort steht.
- Achte auf Abbildungen und Bildunterschriften.
- Leider gibt es aber einige Wörter, die im Englischen und Deutschen ähnlich klingen oder aussehen, aber jeweils eine ganz andere Bedeutung haben. In der Übersicht rechts findest du einige Beispiele dieser so genannten ***false friends***.
- Viele Wörter sind im Deutschen und in anderen Sprachen dem Englischen ähnlich, z.B. *democracy, humour, loyal, religion, souvenir*.
- Unbekannte Wörter enthalten oft bekannte Teile:
  - in **Zusammensetzungen** (Komposita, *compounds*), z.B.:
    one-way street – (Einbahnstraße)
    baby car seat – (Kindersitz)
  - in **Ableitungen** mit Vor- und Nachsilben (*prefixes and suffixes*), z.B. *antisocial, disappear, multilingual, oversleep, reappear; washable, national, useful, childish, attractive, careless, percentage, performance, foundation, opener, racism, movement, happiness, leadership, pressure*
- Kennst du das Wort evtl. schon in einer anderen Wortart? So kann z.B. *dress* Nomen oder Verb sein. Was bedeutet *Students have the right to free dress?*

Some false friends

ENGLISH	GERMAN	GERMAN	ENGLISH
actual	tatsächlich	aktuell	**current**
brave	tapfer	brav	**well-behaved**
brief	kurz	Brief	**letter**
build	bauen	bilden	**make, form**
caution	Vorsicht	Kaution	**deposit**
chips	Pommes frites	Kartoffelchips	**crisps**
critic	Kritiker/in	Kritik	**criticism**
concern	Angelegenheit, Anliegen	Konzern	**corporate group**
eventually	schließlich	eventuell	**perhaps, possible**
failure	Versagen	Fehler	**mistake**
fast	schnell	fast	**almost**
guilty	schuldig	gültig	**valid**
handy	praktisch, handlich	Handy	**(mobile) phone**
kind	freundlich	Kind	**child**
map	Karte	Mappe	**folder**
mist	Nebel	Mist (Unsinn)	**rubbish**
note	Notiz	Note, Zensur	**mark**
personal	persönlich	Personal	**staff**
rent	Miete	Rente	**pension**
rock	Fels	Rock	**skirt**
sea	Meer, die See	der See	**lake**
sensible	vernünftig	sensibel	**sensitive**
serious	ernst	seriös	**respectable**
spend	ausgeben	spenden	**donate**
sympathetic	mitfühlend	sympathisch	**nice, friendly**
when	wann	wen	**who**
where	wo	wer	**who**
while	während	weil	**because**

SF 2 Using a dictionary ▸ Unit 3, p. 76

Wenn du ein Wort nicht erschließen kannst, helfen das *Dictionary* (*English-German* S. 234–270) oder ein Wörterbuch für das Englische (entweder in Buchform oder im Internet).

1 Wörterbucheinträge sind immer alphabetisch

- *U* kommt vor *V*
- *value* kommt vor *vegetables*
- *vamping* kommt vor *vampire*

2 Zusammengesetzte Ausdrücke und *idioms*

Der Haupteintrag (z.B. *ear*) steht farbig oder fett am Anfang. Daneben oder darunter findest du oft zusammengesetzte Wörter oder Redewendungen und Idiome, z.B. ***(be) all ears***.

3 Wortarten und Wortbedeutungen

- Oft ist das gleiche Wort ein Nomen (Substantiv), ein Adjektiv oder ein Verb, mit je unterschiedlichen Bedeutungen. Überlege zuerst, zu welcher **Wortart** das gesuchte Wort gehört und suche den passenden Eintrag. Diesen liest du dann genauer.
- Die Ziffern 1, 2 usw. bei einem Eintrag zeigen, dass ein Wort mehrere **Bedeutungen** hat. Lies immer alle Einträge bei der passenden Wortart und entscheide dann, welche Bedeutung in deinem Satz passt. Zusätzlich findest du Verweise auf den Gebrauch im *American* oder *British English* (*AE* bzw. *BE*).

  Welche Bedeutungen hat *fall* hier?

  The number of unemployed people has fallen since last fall.
  Is September a summer or a fall month?
  I fell asleep very fast yesterday because I was so tired.

- Besonders wenn du ein Wort in einem deutsch-englischen Wörterbuch suchst, achte genau darauf, welche Bedeutung in deinem englischen Satz passt.

4 Weitere Informationen im Wörterbuch

- Die Lautschrift zeigt dir, wie ein Wort ausgesprochen wird.
- Unregelmäßige Verbformen, Pluralformen, Steigerungsformen usw. stehen in Klammern hinter dem Haupteintrag.

5 Online-Wörterbücher

- Wenn du ein Online-Wörterbuch verwenden möchtest, erkundige dich vorher bei deiner Lehrperson, welche zu empfehlen sind.
- Achte auf dieselben Dinge wie bei gedruckten Wörterbüchern.
- Vorteil online: Du kannst dir meist die Aussprache per Audiodatei anhören.

---

usually [ˈjuːʒuəli] meistens, normalerweise I

V

vacation [vəˈkeɪʃn], [veɪˈkeɪʃn] *(AE)* Ferien, Urlaub IV
vacuum cleaner [ˈvækjuəm kliːnə] Staubsauger V 3 (52)
vague [veɪɡ] vage, unbestimmt VI 3 (67)
vain [veɪn] eitel V 4 (79)
valley [ˈvæli] Tal IV
value [ˈvæljuː] Wert I **It's good value.** Es ist sein Geld wert. I
vamping [ˈvæmpɪŋ] *spät in der Nacht noch aktiv sein* V 4 (88)

---

ear [ɪə] *Substantiv*
1 Ohr 2 Gehör 3 Ähre
IDM **(be) all ears** ganz Ohr sein
(be) up to one's ears in sth. bis zum Hals in etwas stecken
go in one ear and out the other *(umgs)* zum einen Ohr rein- und zum anderen rausgehen

---

fall [fɔːl] *Verb, Substantiv*
***Verb* (fell, fallen)**
1 fallen, stürzen **The book fell off the table.** Das Buch fiel vom Tisch.
2 *(Zahlen)* fallen, sinken, zurückgehen **Their profits have fallen by 30%.** Ihr Gewinn ist um 30% zurückgegangen.
3 in einen Zustand geraten **fall asleep** einschlafen, **fall ill** krank werden, **fall in love (with)** sich verlieben (in)

Substantiv **1** Fall, Sturz
2 falls (Plural, bes. in Namen) (Wasser) fall **the Niagara Falls** die Niagarafälle
3 *(AE)* Herbst
4 *(Zahlen)* Rückgang

---

child [tʃaɪld] (***children*** [ˈtʃɪldrən])

SF 3 Exam skills: How to do better in tests and exams

► *Unit 1, p. 18* ► *Typical exam instructions, pp. 276–277* ► *Exam file, pp. 78–101*

1 Learning from your mistakes

- Erkenne deine Fehler, damit du sie künftig vermeiden kannst.
- Wenn du eine Klassenarbeit oder einen Test korrigiert zurück bekommst, sieh dir die Vermerke deines Lehrers / deiner Lehrerin genau an. Sie zeigen dir, welche Arten von Fehlern du gemacht hast, z.B. SP – *spelling mistake*,

  WO – *word order*, G – *grammar mistake*,

  W – *(wrong) word(s)*, FF – *false friend*
- Lege dir eine **Fehlersammlung oder -kartei** an bzw. führe sie aus den vorangehenden Schuljahren fort. Möglich ist das in Papierform (Karteikärtchen / A5-Heft) oder in Dateiform. Diese Sammlung vervollständigst du nach jedem Test um deine korrigierten Fehler.
- Praktisch ist die Sammlung nach folgenden **Arten von Fehlern**:
  - Flüchtigkeitsfehler (häufig: SP): z.B. das Auslassen oder Vertauschen von Buchstaben / Wörtern / Satzzeichen
  - Vokabelfehler (häufig: W, SP, FF): Du verwechselst z.B. Wörter und Wendungen oder kannst sie nicht korrekt schreiben bzw. aussprechen; du benutzt falsche Präpositionen (z.B. ~~*in*~~ -> *on the internet*) oder *false* friends (z.B. ~~*actually*~~ -> *at the moment / currently*)
  - Grammatikfehler (häufig: G, W, WO, SP): Beispielsweise verwendest du falsche Verbformen (z.B. *she* ~~*do*~~ -> *does*; an article *sa~~yed~~* -> *saying*), benutzt die falsche Wortart (z.B. Adverb statt Adjektiv in *real~~ly~~ danger* -> *real*) oder du hast Probleme mit der Wortstellung in Sätzen.

Elephants in danger

Yetsreday read i an	ǁ SP WO (G)
article in the internet	| W
sayed that elephants are	| G
in really danger.	| W (G)
According to the	| G
scientists it gives only	| W
352 271 elephants	| Komma!
actually in …	ǁ FF WO (G)

Was hilft?

- ✓ Konzentriere dich bei der Arbeit.
- ✓ Überprüfe alles gründlich vor der Abgabe (plane dafür genug Zeit ein).
- ✓ Lerne neue Wendungen statt nur Einzelwörter (z.B. *there is/are, on the internet, according to sb.*).
- ✓ Höre, lies, sprich und schreibe neues Vokabular regelmäßig und gründlich.
- ✓ Vermeide *false friends* ► *SF 1*.
- ✓ Lerne neue Grammatik sorgfältig; schlage stets im *Language file* (S. 181 – 205) oder in einer Englischgrammatik nach.
- ✓ Merke dir typische Wendungen als Muster.
- ✓ Wiederhole regelmäßig.
- ✓ Frage nach, wenn du etwas nicht verstehst.

2 Exam preparation

- Beginne zeitig mit der Prüfungsvorbereitung. Plane, welchen Stoff du in welchen Schritten und innerhalb welcher Zeit wiederholst. Hake Erledigtes ab.
- Lerne deine typischen Fehler zu vermeiden – mit Hilfe deiner Fehlerkartei.
- Informiere dich über typische Aufgaben. Stelle sicher, dass du sie richtig verstehst (► *Typical exam instructions, pp. 276–277*) und übe, z.B. mit dem *Exam file, pp. 78–101* und dem Workbook.

3 In the exam

- Schlafe dich vorher gut aus; sei pünktlich.
- Bleibe ruhig, optimistisch und konzentriert.
- Lies die Arbeitsanweisungen sehr genau – mehrmals! Oft hilft es, Wichtiges zu unterstreichen.
- Wenn du auswählen sollst, welche Aufgabe du bearbeitest, lies dir zuerst alle Angebote gründlich durch.
- Hake erledigte Aufgaben ab.
- Plane am Ende 5–10 Minuten ein, um alles noch einmal durchzulesen und zu korrigieren.

SF 4 Doing project work ▸ *Text file 1, pp. 130–133*

Ein Projekt ist meistens eine komplexe Aufgabe, die mehrere Stunden Arbeitszeit benötigt und in einer Gruppe bearbeitet wird. Ein mögliches Thema kann z.B. sein, dass ihr ein englischsprachiges Land vorstellen möchtet, das Produkt dazu z.B. eine mündliche Präsentation oder ein Poster.

1 Set your goals

Wählt euer Thema und entscheidet euch für ein Produkt. Schreibt auf, was euch an dem Thema interessiert und was ihr noch herausfinden möchtet.

! Das gewählte Produkt könnte sein: ein Poster, ein Vortrag, eine computergestützte Präsentation, eine Broschüre, eine Klassenzeitung, ...

2 Get organized

Macht euch einen Plan. Wer macht was bis wann? Verteilt die Aufgaben und legt einen Zeitplan fest, der regelmäßige Treffen beinhaltet. Denkt auch an eine inhaltliche Gliederung.

! Haltet die Ergebnisse in einem Protokoll fest, um bei späteren Missverständnissen nachschauen zu können.

3 Do your research

Benutzt unterschiedliche Medien für eure Recherche: Lexika, Fachbücher, Zeitschriften, Zeitungen, Karten und Atlanten. Ebenso sind schriftliche Anfragen und Interviews möglich. Bezieht auch das Internet in eure Recherchen mit ein. ▸ *SF 3*
Skimmt das Material, um euch einen Überblick zu verschaffen. Macht euch Notizen in eigenen Worten und notiert die Quellen.

! Versucht Materialien zu finden, die das Thema von unterschiedlichen Gesichtspunkten aus beleuchten – beschränkt euch nicht auf eine Perspektive.

4 Organize your materials

Sobald ihr genug Material zusammenhabt, macht eine grobe Skizze, wie das fertige Produkt aussehen soll. Sortiert das Material und schreibt eure Texte.

! Gibt es spezielle Vorgaben von eurer Lehrerin / eurem Lehrer, die ihr berücksichtigen müsst?

5 Check your materials

Überprüft eure Texte und eure Abbildungen. Korrigiert eure Texte untereinander in der Gruppe. Ist alles logisch und übersichtlich aufgebaut? Dann ordnet eure Informationen und visuellen Hilfen sorgfältig an.

6 Give your presentation

Eine gute Präsentation gelingt euch, wenn ihr folgende Tipps beachtet:

- Übt eure Präsentation, wenn ihr etwas mündlich darstellt, und benutzt Karteikarten mit stichwortartigen Notizen.
- Sagt, worum es geht und fasst am Ende das Wesentliche kurz zusammen.
- Schaut die Zuhörenden an, lächelt und sprecht langsam und deutlich.
- Verweist auf die Abbildungen (Fotos, Illustrationen, Diagramme, ...). ▸ *SF 9.1; SF 11*

7 Give feedback

Als Gruppe könnt ihr nach einzelnen Abschnitten der Arbeit am Projekt sowie abschließend besprechen, was gut lief und was beim nächsten Mal verbessert werden sollte.
Beginnt stets mit dem Positiven.
Verbindet dabei höfliche (!) Kritik immer mit guten Verbesserungsvorschlägen.

! **Include in your feeback on presentations**:
- what was great
- what the speaker could do better
- what you didn't like
- what you found interesting
- what was missing

SF 5 Doing research ▸ Unit 1, pp. 10, 33; Text file 1, p. 131; Text file 2, p. 134

1 Nutze unterschiedliche Quellen für deine Recherche

Bei der Informationssuche für ein Referat, eine Präsentation o.Ä. benutze mehrere unterschiedliche Quellen und Medien. Beachte auch die Hinweise zum Skimming und Scanning ▸ *SF 7.1, 7.2*.
Gleiche die gefundenen Informationen miteinander ab.

für alle Wissensgebiete	• Lexika (gedruckt und online, ggf. englischsprachig) • Schulbücher und Begleitmaterialien
für aktuelle Informationen	• Zeitungen, Zeitschriften (gedruckt und online, ggf. englischsprachig)
für geographische und politische Informationen	• Karten und Atlanten (gedruckt und online)

2 Tipps zur Internetrecherche

So wird deine Internetrecherche leichter und bringt bessere Ergebnisse:

Wie suche ich, um weniger und bessere Ergebnisse (*hits*) zu bekommen?

- Überlege dir gute Stichwörter für dein Thema. Bereitest du z.B. eine Präsentation über *Nigeria* vor, wären der Landesname und *history, government, geography* ein Anfang. Weitere Ideen: *culture, ethnic groups, …*
- Gib die Stichwörter in eine Suchmaschine ein und setze die Einstellungen auf englischsprachige Websites.

Welche Websites sind zuverlässig?

- Offizielle und zuverlässige Websites im englischsprachigen Internet haben *domain names*, die auf *.gov* oder *.edu* enden.
- Weniger vertrauenswürdig sind Websites von Firmen (*.com*), persönliche Blogs, Fanseiten oder Websites von Interessengruppen. Auch hier kannst du Interessantes finden, solltest aber kritisch bei der Verwendung von Inhalten sein.

Wie verschaffe ich mir einen Überblick?

- Du kannst mit dem Skimming eines Artikels in einem online-Lexikon beginnen, z.B. der englischsprachigen Wikipedia (https://en.wikipedia.org).
- Häufig finden sich im Artikel bzw. am Ende weitere Links zum Thema.
- So findest du auch genauere Stichwörter für deine weitere Recherche.

Wie finde ich Websites wieder?

- Leg dir besonders interessante Websites in die Favoriten deines Webbrowsers. Strukturiere sie in eigenen Ordnern, die du innerhalb der Favoriten anlegen kannst.

Was kommt nach dem Suchen?

- Setz dir ein Zeitlimit für deine Recherche. Danach ordne dein Material. Prüfe, was evtl. fehlt und suche dann gezielt nur danach.

Was tun mit den gefundenen Informationen?

- Mach dir Notizen in weitgehend <u>eigenen</u> Worten ▸ *SF 7.6*. *Copy and paste*, also bloßes Zusammenkopieren, ist nicht sinnvoll.
- Zu jeder Notiz vermerke die Quelle (die Webadresse sowie das Zugriffsdatum).

Was tun mit unbekannten Wörtern und Wendungen?

- Unbekannter Wortschatz begegnet dir immer wieder in fremdsprachigen Texten. Für den ersten Überblick musst du nicht jedes Wort genau verstehen – erschließe die Bedeutung ▸ *SF 1*.
- Wichtige Wörter schlage im (Online-)Wörterbuch nach, v.a. wenn du sie selbst in deiner Präsentation verwenden willst. Vergiss die Aussprache nicht! Hör dir das neue Wort online an und übe es.

LISTENING AND READING SKILLS

SF 6 Listening

▸ Unit 1, p. 24 ▸ Unit 2, p. 47
▸ Unit 3, p. 68

1 Vor dem Hören: bereite dich vor

- Lies sorgfältig die Aufgabenstellung. Die Aufgaben sagen oft, worum es in dem Text geht oder enthalten Schlüsselwörter.
- Stell dir die Situation oder die Geschichte vor: Worum wird es im Text gehen? Wer wird sprechen? Versuche vorauszuschauen.
- Überlege, was du selbst zum Thema schon weißt und welche englischen Begriffe vorkommen könnten.
- Wenn du dem Hörtext Abbildungen zuordnen sollst, schau sie dir vor dem Hören genau an.
- Konzentriere dich, denn du kannst den Text meist nur bis zu zweimal hören.

! Versuche zu erkennen, **was für eine Art Text** du hören wirst:
Nachrichten, Werbung, ein Gespräch, ein Interview, eine öffentliche Ansage oder eine *story*?

2 Beim Hören

- Beantworte schon beim ersten Hören möglichst viele Aufgaben (mach dir kurze Notizen, verwende Symbole und Abkürzungen).
- Die Informationen könnten in einer anderen Reihenfolge auftauchen.
- Im Hörtext können andere Wörter benutzt werden als in der Aufgabe, doch die Bedeutung ist ähnlich.
- Gib nicht auf, wenn du etwas nicht verstehst. Bleib ruhig und hör weiter zu. Vielleicht verstehst du beim zweiten Hören mehr.
- Achte auf Signalwörter, die dir das Verstehen erleichtern, z.B.:
  - Reihenfolge (*before, after, then, next, later, first, …*)
  - Gegensätze (*however, but, …*)
  - Gründe, Folgen (*because, so, …*)
  - Vergleiche (*larger/older than …, more, most, as … as*)
- Beachte auch, wie etwas gesagt wird: zum Beispiel verärgert oder besorgt, überrascht, freudig? Das kann ein Hinweis auf die Lösung sein.

! Höraufgaben können unterschiedliche **Arten des Zuhörens** von dir verlangen:
- **detailliertes Hören** Hier musst du genau zuhören, um wichtige Einzelheiten zu erfassen (z.B. bei einer Ansage am Bahnhof die Abfahrtszeit des Zuges).
- **globales Hören** Hier sollst du verstehen, worum es generell geht, z.B. den Hauptgedanken eines Textes erfassen. Du musst dafür nicht jedes einzelne Wort verstehen.
- **schlussfolgerndes Hören** Hier werden deine Vorüberlegungen und Vermutungen wichtig. Achte auf die Zusammenhänge. Wird etwas evtl. nur angedeutet, aber nicht vollständig ausgesprochen? Wie klingt die Stimme der Sprecher?

3 Nach dem Hören

- Vervollständige deine Notizen sofort.
- Konzentriere dich beim nächsten Hören auf eventuelle Lücken.
- Manchmal hilft auch Kombinieren (es ist in jedem Fall besser als gar nichts zu schreiben).

! **Tausche** dich mit Mitschülern und -schülerinnen **aus**. Haben sie gute **Tipps und Tricks**, z.B. für kurze Notizen und Symbole?
Ihr könnt, wenn das erlaubt ist, auch eure Notizen und Lösungen vergleichen.

SF 7 Reading course

1 Skimming ► *More challenge 1, p. 28*

Wofür? Mit dieser Technik verschaffst du dir einen **Überblick**, z.B. über eine Website oder eine Zeitungsseite.

Wie? Du musst nicht jede Einzelheit verstehen, also auch **nicht jedes Wort** lesen und verstehen. Achte vor allem auf Überschriften, Abbildungen und Bildunterschriften, hervorgehobene Wörter und den ersten Satz.

Beispiel: Du möchtest herausfinden, ob der Text „Siskeo's transformation blog" auf S. 14 für eine Präsentation über Rugby geeignet ist.

Nein, denn zwar kommt das Wort rugby vor, aber das Hauptthema des Textes ist es nicht.

2 Scanning ► *Unit 1, p. 23* ► *Unit 2, p. 45*

Wofür? Mit dieser Technik kannst du einen Text schnell nach **bestimmten Informationen** durchsuchen.

Wie? Du suchst nur bestimmte Informationen, die du über geeignete **Schlüsselwörter** findest.
Lies nur dort genauer, wo sie stehen.

Beispiel: Du möchtest herausfinden, welches die beste Reisezeit für Südafrika ist.
Überlege dir sinnvolle Schlüsselwörter und scanne dann den oder die geeignete(n) Text(e) auf S. 10–11. (Tipp: Dafür musst du zuerst skimmen, siehe ► *SF 7.1*.)

3 Finding the main point of a text ► *Unit 2, p. 48*

Wofür? Um herauszufinden, was die **Hauptaussage** eines Textes ist und wie sie sich aus seinen Hauptgedanken formt.

Wie? Für deinen **Überblick**, worum es in dem Text generell geht, benutzt du das Skimming (siehe ► *SF 7.1*).

Die **Hauptaussage** eines Textes findest du oft in seinem **ersten Absatz**, und dort oft im **ersten** oder **letzten Satz**.

Jeder **Absatz** eines Textes beinhaltet einen **Hauptgedanken**, der zur Hauptaussage beiträgt. Du findest den Hauptgedanken meist im **ersten** oder **letzten Satz** des Absatzes.

Beispiel: Du möchtest die Hauptaussage des Textes auf S. 36 formulieren. (Tipp: Beachte hier auch den Abschluss-Satz von Absatz 5.)

4 Reading for details ► *Unit 1, p. 16*

Wofür? Manchmal musst du in einem Text **jedes Detail** im Zusammenhang genau verstehen, z.B. bei Gedichten, Rezepten, Gebrauchsanweisungen und Aufgabenstellungen. In längeren Informationstexten oder Tabellen und Diagrammen ist es oft nur ein bestimmter Bereich, den du detailliert liest, weil du eine Information suchst. Welcher Bereich das ist, findest du mithilfe des Scanning heraus (siehe ► *SF 7.2*).

Wie? Lies **jedes Wort** und **jede Zahl** sehr **genau**. Achte auch auf Maßeinheiten. Benutze ein Wörterbuch für unbekannte Wörter.

Beispiel: Wie viele Ziffern musst du hier eingeben, damit der Safe schließt?
Wann sollst du den Safe offen hinterlassen?

OPERATING INSTRUCTIONS
You can operate this safe with your own 4-digit personal code.

TO LOCK: Close the door and enter your own 4-digit code.
Press # (LOCK). The safe will lock automatically and the word CLOSED will be displayed.

TO OPEN: Enter the 4-digit code that was used to lock the safe. It will unlock automatically and the word OPEN will be displayed.

IMPORTANT: Always leave the safe open at checkout.

5 Reading between the lines ► Unit 1, p. 14 ► Unit 2, p. 48

Wofür? Wenn du Fragen zu einem Text beantworten sollst, ist es möglich, dass du die Antworten nicht eins zu eins im Text findest. Hier hilft es dir, **Schlussfolgerungen** aus dem Gelesenen zu ziehen. Wichtig ist diese Technik z.B. bei Kommentaren, Tagebuch- oder Blogeinträgen, Werbung und literarischen Texten.

Wie? Einfaches Schlussfolgern bedeutet, dass du Informationen aus **unterschiedlichen Textstellen** zusammenführst.

Beispiel: Sieh dir den Text auf S. 48 an und beantworte Frage 1 rechts.

Manchmal werden im Text **andere Wörter** benutzt als in der Aufgabe, doch die Bedeutung ist ähnlich oder gleich.

Beispiel: Beantworte anhand desselben Textes nun Frage 2 rechts.

Es gibt auch Fragen, auf die du im Text gar keine direkte Antwort findest. Und doch ist sie im Text enthalten, man könnte sagen, sie steht **„zwischen den Zeilen"**. Du musst sie schlussfolgern, also z.B. dein eigenes Wissen, aber auch begründete Vermutungen beim Lesen einbringen und kritische Fragen an den Text stellen.

Beispiel: Lies den Werbetext „An adventure around every corner" und beantworte die Fragen 3–5 rechts.

(1) How do you know what I.A. Wenger thinks of the common stereotype of an engineer? *(lines 17–20; 28–30)*

(2) What prejudice against a young female software engineer did the negative comments show? *(lines 13–15; 23–25. Das Wort prejudice kommt im Text nicht vor. Erinnere dich an seine Bedeutung oder schlage es nach.)*

(3) What image of the reader is created in the text?
(4) Why should somebody be filming the reader doing a bungee jump?
(5) Name three topics that aren't mentioned at all. Why do you think they aren't?

An adventure around every corner!

Everybody knows that South Africa is full of game parks where you can go on safari and see amazing wild animals. Thanks to the work of these parks you can still see rhinos and elephants in the wild in spite of poachers who hunt and kill them. But there's more. South Africa has a great diversity of unique activities for adventure lovers. If you're looking for something different, you'll find it here.

Shark diving
See 5–20 sharks on a 30-minute dive. The boat trip includes shark watching and informative talks on sharks and conservation. The whole trip takes about two and a half hours. If you don't see any sharks, you'll get your money back.

Bungee jumping
This bungee jump drops an awesome 216 metres into the picture-perfect Bloukrans River Valley below. Make sure someone is filming as you step off the edge of the highest bungee jumping platform in the world.

6 Marking up and note-taking ► Unit 1, pp. 21, 33 ► Unit 2, p. 37

Wofür?
Du hast einen längeren Text mit vielen Fakten vor dir und sollst ihn später zusammenfassen oder inhaltliche Fragen beantworten. Wähle die für diese Aufgabe wichtigen Informationen aus und markiere sie.

Wie?
Du kannst die Stellen mit wichtigen Informationen z.B.:
- mit Textmarker hervorheben
- umkreisen
- unterstreichen

All das geht nur in elektronischen Texten oder auf Fotokopien bzw. Ausdrucken, aber nicht in geliehenen Büchern.

Wenn du dir zu den markierten Stellen **Notizen** machst (*note-taking*), kannst du diese später weiterverarbeiten, z.B. für eine Präsentation ► *SF 9.1*, einen Bericht oder eine Zusammenfassung ► *SF 9.3*.

! Schreibe nur Schlüsselwörter auf, nutze Ziffern (statt Zahlwörter: **7** statt **sieben**) und Symbole (**?**, **!**, **✓**, **≠**, **+**, **=**, **~**). Zum Beispiel:

screenagers:
- born into digital world (= world of screens)
- ~ 8 hrs daily screen time (multitasking)
- strong attraction + peer pressure
- ...

SF 8 Reading literature

► Unit 1, pp. 19–23 ► Unit 2, pp. 43–45 ► Unit 3, pp. 65–67
► Text files 4–6, pp. 138–149 ► Wordbank 3, p. 147

1 Differences between non-fictional and fictional (literary) texts

- **Sachtexte *(non-fictional texts)*** sind z.B. Texte in Zeitungen oder Online-Magazinen, Anzeigen, Kommentare, Reden, Gebrauchsanweisungen oder auch Sachbücher. Der Autor / Die Autorin schreibt über Themen der realen Welt mit dem Ziel, Lesende zu informieren oder auch zu überzeugen.
- **Literarische Texte *(fictional / literary texts)*** sind z.B. Romane, Kurzgeschichten oder Theaterstücke. Sie handeln von einer erdachten, nicht-realen Welt. Der Autor / Die Autorin entwickelt Figuren und stellt dar, was diese tun und fühlen sowie häufig auch, warum und mit welchen Folgen.

> Some **non-fictional text types**:
> (auto)biography, advert, article, comment, interview, news story, recipe, report, review, speech, travel guide

2 Narrative texts

- **Erzähltexte** sind z.B. Romane *(novels)* oder Kurzgeschichten *(short stories)* bestehen aus einem fortlaufenden Text, der manchmal in Abschnitte oder Kapitel unterteilt ist. Ein Erzähler (narrator) entwickelt um die Figuren *(characters)* einer Geschichte herum eine Handlung *(plot)*, die zu einer bestimmten Zeit und an einem bestimmten Schauplatz *(setting)* stattfindet.
- Die Charakterisierung *(characterization)* der Figuren kann direkt erfolgen (z.B. durch Adjective wie *shy*, *angry*). Oft erfolgt auch eine indirekte Charakterisierung darüber, was die Figuren sagen, denken oder fühlen.
- Durch bestimmte sprachlich-stilistische Mittel *(stylistic devices ► SF 8.5)* schafft der Erzähler eine bestimmte Atmosphäre *(mood / atmosphere)*, z.B. ruhig und friedlich oder spannungsvoll-bedrohlich.
- Die Ereignisse werden aus einer bestimmten Erzählperspektive *(point of* view) dargestellt. Dabei nimmt der Ich-Erzähler *(first-person narrator)* die Ich-Perspektive ein und ist Teil der Geschichte. Dagegen steht der Er-Erzähler *(third-person narrator)* eher außerhalb des Geschehens, kann aber auch sehr nahe bei einer Figur sein.

> **First-person narrator**: e.g. in ***Returned***, p. 19, lines 18 – 22:
> "How could this be? I had lived in London all my life. I lived here with my mum in a ..."
>
> **Third-person narrator**: e.g. in ***Face***, p. 43, lines 9 – 13:
> "The Gang of Three decided to cut through a housing estate. It used to be a nice place to live, but it wasn't any more. ..."
>
> E.g. in ***Floodland***, p. 65, lines 11 – 15:
> "Zoe was a loner. Most of the people left on Norwich hung around together ..., but she preferred to be on her own. It was safer that way ..."

3 Plays (Dramatic texts)

- **Dramen** werden von Darstellenden (Schauspielern / Sprechern) im Theater, in Filmen, Serien oder im Radio aufgeführt. Sie bestehen aus Dialogen *(dialogues)* und Monologen *(monologues)* in direkter Rede.
- Bühnenanweisungen *(stage directions)* geben meist Hinweise für die Darstellenden. Beim Lesen helfen sie dir dabei, die Aussagen der Figuren zusammen mit ihren dargestellten Handlungen zu verstehen oder auch dabei, dir den Schauplatz besser vorzustellen.

4 Poetry

- Gedichte *(poems)* werden in gebundener Sprache dargeboten, d.h. häufig in Versen *(verses / lines)* und Strophen *(stanzas)*, die auch ein wichtiges Gliederungselement sind.
- Anders als in der Alltagssprache findest du in Gedichten vielfältige stilistische Mittel wie Reim *(rhyme)*, Rhythmus *(rhythm)* und Wiederholung *(repetition)*. Die Sprechweise ist oft bildhaft, z.B. mit Hilfe von Vergleichen *(similes)* und Metaphern *(metaphors)*. ► *SF 8.5*

5 Stylistic devices (stilistische Mittel in literarischen Texten)

Begriff	Erläuterung	Beispiel
contrast *Kontrast*	Formulierung aus zwei gegensätzlichen, einander widersprechenden oder sich gegenseitig ausschließenden Begriffen	*call this destruction – progress* (from *Sorry*, p. 120) *an open secret; a controlled chaos* *in order to lead, you must walk behind*
imagery *Bildsprache*	Durch bildhafte Sprache sollen beim Lesenden Bilder erzeugt werden, um seine Sinne für das vertiefte Verstehen eines Textes anzuregen. Hierzu werden u.a. Vergleiche (*similes*) und Metaphern (*metaphors*) verwendet.	*So I've started looking* *For a means,* *Some manner* *To make my life* *A two-way street.* (from *Searching for a two-way-street*, p. 145, lines 209–213)
irony *Ironie*	Bedeutet, dass das Gegenteil von dem gesagt wird, was tatsächlich gemeint ist.	*Oh great! Now you have broken my new phone!*
metaphor *Metapher*	Metaphern sind eine Form des bildhaften Sprechens, bei der die Wörter in übertragener Bedeutung verwendet werden.	- *we must globally warm our hearts* - *change the climate of our souls* (from *Sorry*, p. 120)
parallelism *Parallelismus*	Eine bestimmte Struktur (Satzglieder oder Wörter) wird in mehreren aufeinander folgenden Satzteilen oder Sätzen beibehalten (paralleler Satzbau).	*Sorry, sorry we left you our mess of a planet.* *Sorry that we were too caught up in our doings to do something.* *Sorry we listened to people who made excuses to do nothing.* (from *Sorry*, p. 120)
repetition *Wiederholung*	Bezeichnet das mehrmalige Benennen des gleichen Wortes oder einer Wörterfolge in einem Text. Sie soll die Aussage verstärken oder bestimmte Sachverhalte betonen.	*Not yesterday. Not today. Not tomorrow.* (from *Searching for a two-way-street*, p. 144, lines 137–139)
rhyme *Reim*	Bezeichnet den Gleichklang zweier oder mehrerer Wörter vom letzten betonten Vokal an.	*You don't have to be a whisper, your voices are real,* *You can be the generation that creates a better deal* (from *It's your future*, p. 38, lines 9–10)
rhythm *Rhythmus*	Ist die Wiederholung bestimmter Gruppierungen von betonten und unbetonten Silben in einem Gedicht.	*It's the young that pay tuition, it's the young that fight the wars, It's the young who need jobs, …* (from *It's your future*, p. 38, lines 1–2)
simile *Vergleich*	Dient dem Vergleich von zwei Dingen, um die Aussage noch anschaulicher und deutlicher zu machen; ist meist an Wörtern wie *like* oder *as* erkennbar.	*But now I think* *In bursts* *Like bullets* *Fired from a gun.* (from *Searching for a two-way-street*, p. 144, lines 185–187)

SPEAKING AND WRITING SKILLS

SF 9 Speaking course

1 Giving a presentation

▸ *Unit 1, p. 25* ▸ *Unit 2, p. 113* ▸ *Unit 3, p. 68*
▸ *Text files 1, p. 132; 7, p. 154*

Beachte diese Schritte, damit deine Präsentation erfolgreich wird.

a) PLANNING YOUR PRESENTATION

- **Recherchiere** dein Thema ▸ *SF 5* und fertige dir Notizen an (am besten gleich in Englisch ▸ *SF 7.6*).
- **Strukturiere** die Informationen, z.B. in einer Mindmap oder einer Gliederung (*outline*). Prüfe, ob alle Informationen zum Thema passen.
- Wähle die **Form deiner Präsentation** aus: z.B. Vortrag, Folienpräsentation am Computer, Poster.
- Überlege, wie du dein Thema **anschaulich** und **interessant** gestaltest (Beispiele, und Visualisierungen, z.B. Abbildungen, Karten, Diagramme, evtl. Filmausschnitte). Überlege dir einen guten Einstieg.
- Bereite deine **Notizen** für die Präsentation (nur Stichwörter). Notiere kurze Erklärungen zu schwierigeren Begriffen, die deine Zuhörer/innen evtl. nicht verstehen.
- Bereite deine **Materialien** sorgfältig vor (Grafiken, Diagramme, Fotos usw.): Achte auf Lesbarkeit und Übersichtlichkeit.
- **Übe** deine Präsentation zu Hause und / oder mit Freunden. Achte auf die Zeit. Nummeriere deine Notizzettel bzw. Karteikärtchen. Überprüfe die technischen Hilfsmittel, die du verwenden willst (Laptop, Beamer usw.).

b) GIVING YOUR PRESENTATION

- **Schau** die Zuhörenden **an**. Warte, bis es ruhig ist. **Erkläre**, worüber du sprechen wirst und wie deine Präsentation aufgebaut ist.
- **Sprich langsam**, deutlich und möglichst **frei** (d.h. lies nicht nur ab).
- **Schau** die Zuhörenden **an**, **lächle**. Zeige, dass du deinen Vortrag gern hältst.
- Sprich in **kurzen**, **verständlichen Sätzen**. Vermeide zu viele unbekannte oder schwierige Wörter. Erkläre sie bei Bedarf.
- **Verweise** auf deine **Abbildungen** oder Fotos. Erkläre sie bei Bedarf.
- **Beende** deine Präsentation mit einer kurzen **Zusammenfassung** der wichtigsten Punkte, evtl. auch mit einer abschließenden Schlussfolgerung.
- **Bedanke** dich fürs Zuhören und frage, ob jemand **Fragen** hat oder sich äußern möchte.

2 Successful conversations

Unterhaltungen mit Menschen aus anderen Ländern gelingen gut, wenn du diese Hinweise beachtest. Sei höflich und aufgeschlossen! Verwende häufig *please*, *thank you* und *sorry*.

a) STARTING OFF

- **Eröffne** das Gespräch mit einer freundlichen Anrede oder Frage, möglichst mit etwas **Verbindendem**, z.B. über den Ort, die Situation usw. Mit jemandem, den du zum ersten Mal triffst, sprichst du etwas förmlicher als mit jemandem, den du schon kennst.
- Wenn es angebracht ist, stell dich vor.

USEFUL PHRASES
Excuse me, please.
Do you know ...? / Can I sit here?
Hello, how are you?
My name is ... Nice to meet you.

Hi there, are you from Sydney?
Hi, how is it going?
Hi, have you been here before?

b) KEEP THE CONVERSATION GOING

- Zeige dein **Interesse**, indem du Fragen stellst, z.B. auch Nachfragen.
- Antworte nicht nur mit wenigen Worten, das kann unfreundlich wirken.
- Erzähle auch etwas **von dir**, möglichst auf eine **positive** Art (vermeide es, zu jammern oder zu nörgeln).
- Wenn du etwas nicht verstehst, frage höflich nach.
- Wenn du etwas nicht sagen kannst, umschreibe das Wort.

USEFUL PHRASES
Fine, thanks. / Yeah, sure.
Yes, I am. / No, not really.

What about you? Do you like ...?/ I'm new here in ... / I really like these ...
What do you think ...?

Could you say that again, please?
I don't know the English word. It's something that ... / like ...

c) A GOOD ENDING

- **Beende** das Gespräch so freundlich, wie du es begonnen hast.
- **Bedanke** dich, wenn du um Hilfe gebeten oder z.B. Tipps bekommen hast.
- **Verabschiede** dich höflich.

! Mache dir vor dem Gespräch möglichst klar, mit wem du sprichst. So wirst du z.B. mit Gleichaltrigen informeller umgehen als mit Älteren.

Denke auch an eventuelle kulturelle Unterschiede, z.B. beim Begrüßen und Verabschieden.

3 Doing well in job interviews

a) PREPARE YOURSELF

- **Bereite dich sorgfältig** auf das Vorstellungsgespräch **vor**. Übe deine **Gesprächsanteile**, z.B. vor einem Spiegel oder mit Freunden. Achte besonders auf eine freundliche, aber angemessen formelle **Körpersprache**.
- Wo liegen deine **Stärken** und **Schwächen**? Was sind deine besonderen **Interessen**?
- **Warum** bewirbst du dich um diese Tätigkeit?
- Welche **Arbeitserfahrungen** hast du?
- **Informiere dich vorab** über das Unternehmen bzw. den Betrieb und bereite auch einige **Fragen** an die Interviewer vor.

USEFUL PHRASES
Good morning, Ms / Mr ...
My name is ... and I'm really interested in this job because I like working with ...

I think this is a job I could do well because I already have some experience with ...
I'm quite good at ... / I'm not very good at ...

I'd like to know if I'll be working in a team or on my own.
Do I have to work at the weekends?

b) IN THE INTERVIEW

- Plane **genügend Zeit** für die Anfahrt und das Finden des genauen Interviewortes ein. Schalte dein **Smartphone stumm**, bevor du dort ankommst.
- **Begrüße** dein Gegenüber freundlich, stell dich vor.
- Bleib **ruhig**, sei **freundlich** und **positiv**.
- Hör gut zu, sprich **deutlich** und nicht zu schnell. Sieh dein Gegenüber beim Gespräch an.
- Kontrolliere immer mal wieder deine **Köperhaltung**.
- Bleibe **ehrlich**, übertreibe nicht.
- Am Ende des Gesprächs **bedanke** dich und **verabschiede** dich freundlich.

4 Taking part in discussions

► Unit 1, pp. 15, 27 ► Unit 2, pp. 47, 49 ► Unit 3, pp. 57, 61, 71
► Wordbank 1, p. 128

In einer (Klassen-)Diskussion tauschst du dich über Ideen und Meinungen aus. Dabei sollst du auf die Äußerungen deiner Gesprächspartner/innen eingehen und gleichzeitig deinen eigenen Standpunkt darstellen und begründen.

a) PREPARING A DISCUSSION

- Eine **inhaltliche Vorbereitung** auf das Thema der Diskussion ist sinnvoll, damit du nützliche **Wörter** und **Wendungen** parat hast. Notiere sie dir.
- Mache dich mit **unterschiedlichen Standpunkten** zum Thema vertraut und denke darüber nach, was deine Position ist.
- Notiere dir **Argumente**, die deinen bzw. andere Standpunkte unterstützen. (Beispielsweise in einem Rollenspiel kann deine Aufgabe sein, einen anderen Standpunkt als den eigenen zu vertreten.)
- Bereite deine **erste Äußerung**, mit der du in die Diskussion eintrittst, besonders gut vor.

STATING YOUR OPINION
In my opinion, / view, ...
Well, I'd say ...
(Personally,) I think / feel / believe ...
If you ask me, ...
First of all, ...
To start with, I'd like to point out that ...

b) HAVING THE DISCUSSION

- Wenn du die Diskussion **eröffnest**, beginne mit deinem vorbereiteten **Einstieg**.
- Häufiger wirst du dich auf deine **Vorredner/innen** beziehen. Du kannst ihrem Standpunkt **zustimmen** oder **nicht zustimmen** und dann deine vorbereitete Äußerung und passende **Argumente** vorbringen.
- In jedem Fall **höre** den Argumenten der anderen **genau zu** und beziehe dich in deiner Äußerung darauf.
- Bleibe stets **höflich** und lass andere ausreden.
- Manchmal wirst du **nachfragen** müssen, wenn dir etwas unklar oder unverständlich ist.

AGREEING
I quite agree. (+)
You're quite right. (+)
I think so too. (+)
You've got a (good) point there. (+)
That's true / right. / That's just it. (++)
I agree completely. (++)
I couldn't agree with you more. (+++)

DISAGREEING
I'm afraid I don't (quite) agree (there). (-)
I'm not so sure, really. (-)
Well, that's one way of looking at it, but ... (-)
It's not as simple as that (I'm afraid). (-)
I don't believe that at all. (--)
I don't agree with you at all. (--)
(Sorry,) I definitely disagree. (--)
(Sorry,) I think you're wrong. (--)

ASKING FOR CLARIFICATION
Sorry, I didn't get that. / Are you saying that ... ?
Does your last statement mean that ... ?
Could you please give an example of ... ?

SF 10 Writing course

1 The steps of text writing

a) PLANNING YOUR TEXT

- Über welches Thema willst / sollst du genau schreiben?
- Was für einen Text sollst du schreiben: z.B. eine E-Mail, das Ende einer Geschichte oder einen Sachtext (Beschreibung – *Describe ...*; Erläuterung – *Explain ...*; Erörterung – *Discuss ...*; Zusammenfassung – *Summarize ...*)?
- Sammle Ideen und / oder Argumente – z.B. in einem Mindmap oder in einer Liste.
- Recherchiere die für dein Thema notwendigen Informationen ► SF 5.
- Strukturiere dein Material: Schreibe deine geplante Gliederung (*outline*) auf.

Du brauchst

- eine Einleitung (*beginning / introduction*): Hier steht, worum es im Text insgesamt geht.
- einen Hauptteil (*middle / main body*): Dieser Teil ist in mehrere Absätze (*paragraphs*) gegliedert, die Details (Fakten, Beispiele usw.) und Argumente enthalten.
- einen Schluss (*ending / summary / conclusion*): Hier gibst du dem Text ein passendes, einprägsames Ende.

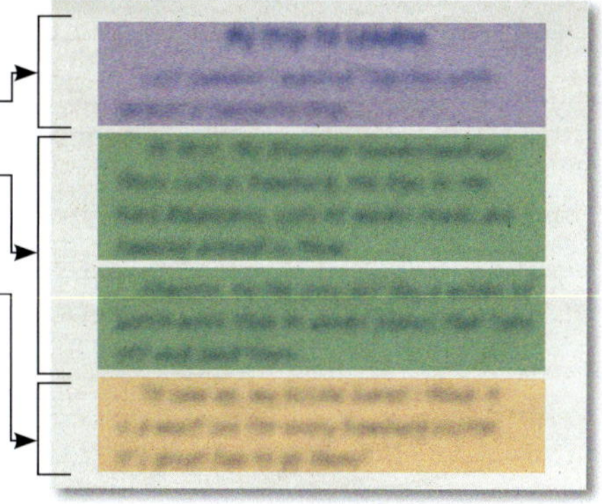

b) WRITING YOUR TEXT ▸ *Unit 3, p. 64*

- Nun schreibe den **ersten Textentwurf**. Halte dich an deine Gliederung.
- Beginne für jeden neuen Gedanken einen **neuen Absatz**.
- Jeder Absatz sollte mit einem **Einleitungssatz** (*topic sentence*) beginnen. Er drückt aus, worum es in diesem Absatz gehen wird.
- **Verbinde** deine Sätze mit passenden *linking* und *time phrases*.
- Verwende passende, **ausdrucksstarke** Wörter und Wendungen, z.B.:
  - **Adjektive** (zum näheren Beschreiben von Personen, Dingen, Orten usw.): *a peaceful voice*
  - **Adverbien** zum näheren Beschreiben von Handlungen, Vorgängen und Zuständen:
    It was raining heavily.
    oder zum Verstärken von Adjektiven: *an extremely sad story*; *He was deeply disappointed.*

USEFUL LINKING PHRASES

Konjunktionen (***conjunctions***):
but, ***and***, ***because***, ***so***, ***on the one hand – on the other hand*** (einerseits – andererseits), ***although***, ***however***
Demonstrativpronomen (***demonstrative pronouns***): *This is exactly .... That's the point.*
Relativsätze (***relative clauses***):
The platypus is an animal that I've never seen in real life.

USEFUL TIME PHRASES

Adverbiale Bestimmungen der Zeit (*time markers*): ***at first***, ***next***, ***finally*** (Reihenfolge)
for half an hour (Dauer), ***immediately***, ***faster than ...*** (Geschwindigkeit)
during our holiday, ***as he arrived***, ***while ...*** (zeitgleiches Geschehen)
two years ago, ***last spring*** (Zeitpunkt)

c) CHECKING AND REWRITING YOUR TEXT

- Wenn dein erster Textentwurf geschrieben ist, hast du viel geschafft, bist aber noch nicht fertig. Jetzt solltest du deinen Text **jemand anderem** zu lesen geben und um **Feedback** bitten.
- **Lies** selbst deinen Text **mehrmals** durch, je mit einem anderen Schwerpunkt:
  - Stimmt der **logische Aufbau**, die Struktur (Einleitung – Hauptteil – Schluss)? Sind die Absätze in sich logisch?
  - Sind die Sätze gut verbunden, liest sich der Text **flüssig** (*linking and time phrases*)?
  - Hast du deine **typischen Fehler vermieden**? (Gleiche mit deiner Fehlersammlung ab ▸ *SF 3.1*.)
  - Mithilfe der Übungen **Improve your English: typical mistakes** (S. 18, 42, 64) kannst du herausfinden, welche Fehler du häufig machst und gezielt üben, typische und häufige Fehler zu vermeiden.
  - Wenn du am Computer schreibst und ein **Rechtschreibprogramm** benutzt, wähle die richtige Sprache aus (z. B. *British/American English*). Überprüfe jeden Korrekturvorschlag in einem Wörterbuch. Achte auf den Kontext ▸ *SF 2*.
  - Schau dir ein eventuelles **Feedback** genau an und überlege, was du davon übernehmen willst.
- Schreibe nun deinen Text in der **endgültigen Version**. Lass dir etwas Zeit, dann lies auch diese Version noch einmal kritisch durch und verbessere, wo das noch nötig ist.

! **Typische Fehlerquellen**

- Groß- und Kleinschreibung
- Wörter die ähnlich klingen, aber unterschiedlich geschrieben werden: *your / you're; than – then; quiet – quite*
- unregelmäßige Pluralformen: *woman – women, child – children*
- Wörter mit „stummen" Buchstaben: *know, talk, listen*
- *word order* in Aussagen, Fragen
  ▸ *Language files 15, 16, pp. 188–189*
- unregelmäßige Verben und unregelmäßige Schreibungen: *try → tries, tried*
- Präpositionen: *on the internet, in the photo, go by bus, be good at ...*
- Typische Wendungen, z. B.: „Was gibt's zum Abendbrot?" – *What's for dinner?* „Alles Gute!" – *All the best!*

2 Writing a comment ▸ Unit 1, p. 23 ▸ Unit 2, pp. 45, 48 ▸ Unit 3, pp. 64, 71

Auch beim Verfassen eines Kommentars bzw. einer Stellungnahme beachte die *Steps of text writing.* ▸ SF 10.1
In einem *comment* vermittelst du deine persönliche Meinung, begründest und argumentierst.

a) PLANNING YOUR COMMENT

- Lies die Aufgabe und den evtl. dazugehörigen Text genau. Notiere dir z.B. Stichwörter, fertige ein Mindmap an.
- Wenn du für oder gegen etwas Stellung nehmen sollst, sortiere deine Ideen schon in Pro und Contra-Argumente.

smartphones in class?	
PRO	CONTRA
- looking up words easily	- noisy - unconcentrated

Denke bei der Gliederung (*outline*) an:

- ***beginning / introduction*** (Einleitung): Hier teilst du deinen Lesern mit, worauf du dich beziehst und was deine Meinung ist.
- ***middle / main body*** (Mittelteil): Hier begründest du deine Meinung mit (Pro-)Argumenten und Beispielen. Berücksichtige auch Gegenargumente (Contra).
- ***end / conclusion*** (Schluss): Hier ziehst du deine Schlussfolgerung aus den Argumenten des Mittelteils. Greife deine Meinung vom Anfang wieder auf.

USEFUL PHRASES FOR COMMENTS

- In my opinion, / experience, …
- I (definitely / really) think / don't think (that) …
- I agree / don't agree / disagree with …

- First of all, / first(ly), second(ly), …
- On the one hand – on the other hand / Additionally, …

- To sum up, …
- I'd like to finish by saying / underlining …

b) WRITING YOUR COMMENT

- Einige *useful phrases for comments* findest du rechts sowie in der ▸ *Wordbank 1, p. 128*.

c) CHECK AND CORRECT YOUR COMMENT

- Auch bei *comments* plane mindestens einen Textentwurf und eine gründliche Überarbeitung ein.

3 Writing a formal letter / an email of complaint ▸ Unit 3, p. 69

Für Beschwerdeschreiben (*letters / emails of complaint*) gelten die Regeln für formelle Briefe / E-Mails:

- klare Gliederung
- keine Kurzformen (*I'm -> I am* usw.)
- gründlicher Fehlercheck
- höflicher, aber bestimmter Stil

! Briefkopf mit Adressen und Datum →

[your address]

[the company's address]

[the date]

! Anlass der Beschwerde und Details: Beschreibe das Produkt und die Probleme bzw. Fehlfunktionen genau. →

Dear Sir / Madam

I recently bought … from your online shop. When I tried to use this product, I discovered that … does not work / does not last as long as promised / is faulty / is damaged / … Please find a copy of the receipt / credit card bill / … attached.

! Deine Vorschläge und höflichen Forderungen: möglichst mit Fristsetzung. →

Since the return form and label were missing, I ask you to send them to me within seven days. I would like a full refund within 30 days of the date of this letter.

! Ein höflicher Abschlusssatz und die Abschiedsformel mit deinem vollen Namen. →

I look forward to your reply and hope this matter can be sorted out quickly.

Yours faithfully

[your first name and surname]

4 Summarizing texts ► *Unit 1, p. 10* ► *Unit 2 p. 49* ► *More challenge 2, p. 50*

Wenn du einen Text (mündlich oder schriftlich) zusammenfasst, gibst du die wichtigsten Informationen oder Ereignisse in kurzer Form wieder.

a) PLANNING YOUR SUMMARY

- Lies den Text: Für den ersten Überblick beginne mit dem Skimming und lies danach genauer, aber noch ohne etwas zu markieren oder dir Notizen zu machen.
- Bestimme die **Textsorte**, denn einen erzählenden Text fasst du etwas anders zusammen als einen Sachtext.
- Beim Finden der **wichtigen Informationen** helfen dir die **fünf *wh*-Fragen**. Markiere die wichtigsten Informationen im Text (auf einer Kopie) und fertige dann kurze Notizen an. Mit diesen schreibst du dann deine Zusammenfassung.

ERZÄHLENDE TEXTE (Geschichten, Romane, Romanauszüge usw.):	**SACHTEXTE** (Zeitungs- oder Magazinartikel usw.):
Thema, Ort, Zeit, grobe Handlungszüge	Thema, Fakten, Argumente (und ggf. wichtige Ereignisse)
↓	↓
WHO	**WHAT**
is the text about?	
WHAT happens	**WHAT** are the **main points** or **arguments**
in the text?	
WHERE / WHEN / WHY does it happen?	**WHERE / WHEN / WHY** is it important?

b) WRITING YOUR SUMMARY

- ***beginning / introduction***: Hier nennst du das Thema, Titel und Autor/in des Originaltexts. Bei Zeitungsartikeln solltest du hier auch die Quelle nennen.
- Im **Hauptteil** fasst du die wichtigsten Fakten (eines Sachtexts) bzw. Handlungsschritte (eines erzählenden Textes) zusammen.
  - Fasse dich **kurz** (Der Umfang einer Zusammenfassung ist maximal **20%** des Originaltexts).
  - Fasse jeden Abschnitt in einem kurzen Satz zusammen.
  - Verwende deine eigenen Worte, schreibe den Text nicht ab.
  - Verwende keine direkte Rede.
  - Verzichte auf Einzelheiten und Beispiele.
  - Schreibe im ***simple present***, auch wenn der Originaltext eine oder mehrere andere Zeitformen verwendet.
  - Verbinde die Sätze und Textteile, so dass sich deine Zusammenfassung gut und flüssig liest. ► *p. 169*

USEFUL PHRASES
- The text / story is about ...
- ... is a story about ...
- The article shows ... / deals with ...

c) CHECK AND CORRECT YOUR SUMMARY

- Auch bei *summaries* plane mindestens einen Textentwurf und eine gründliche Überarbeitung ein.
  - Enthält deine Zusammenfassung das Thema und die wesentlichen Fakten bzw. Handlungsschritte?
  - Hast du unwichtige Einzelheiten weggelassen?
  - Korrigiere Rechtschreib- und Grammatikfehler. ► *p. 169*
  - Ist dein Text logisch aufgebaut und gut zu verstehen?

Falls möglich, überprüft eure Zusammenfassungen im *partner check*.

5 Writing a cover letter (Bewerbungsschreiben)

Beginne mit *Dear Sir/Madam* oder *Dear Mrs/Mr/Ms ...*

Sage, wie du auf die Stelle aufmerksam geworden bist, und dass du dich bewerben möchtest.

Nenne deine Arbeitserfahrungen und sage, warum du dich für die Stelle eignest.

Verwende keine Kurzformen: *I'm => I am; it's => it is*

Diesen Satz kannst du immer verwenden.

Schreibe am Ende *Yours faithfully* und deinen Namen.

Dear Sir/Madam

I read your online advertisement for an assistant in your hostel and I would like to apply for this job.

I am a student and last year I had a Saturday job in a small hotel for five months. I helped with making beds and with the cleaning, and assisted at the reception desk, so I think that I would be very suitable for the job.

I am 16 years old and I speak English, German and Turkish. I am reliable and I enjoy working with people. My teachers say that I am a good team worker, and I have no problems working under pressure.

I attach my CV and I look forward to hearing from you.

Yours faithfully
Samed Celik

6 Writing a CV (*curriculum vitae*, Lebenslauf)

Schreibe ganz oben deinen Namen, deine Adresse, Telefonnummer und Emailadresse.

Sage, wieso du dich für die Stelle interessierst und eignest.

Nenne deine Stärken.

Sage, welche Schulen du besucht hast.

Nenne Praktika, Ferienjobs oder andere Berufserfahrungen.

Zähle deine wichtigsten Hobbys und Interessen auf – vor allem Teamsportarten oder ehrenamtliche Tätigkeiten.

Gib Referenzen an. Wer kann Positives über dich berichten?

Samed Celik

Address: Grahnstr. 83a, 30165 Hannover
Mobile: 0151 555 5010 Email: Samed.Celik@phone.de

Personal statement
I am a confident student with good communication and telephone skills. I have some work experience, and I would like to learn new skills.

Key skills
- Strong team member
- Good computer skills
- Friendly and polite
- Turkish, German, good English

Education
2012 to now: Berg Gesamtschule, Hannover
2008 to 2012: Grundschule Sonnenstr., Hannover

Work experience
Hotel Adler: Cleaning, making beds, helping at the reception desk (part-time job)

Interests
I am interested in computers and programming.
I love playing basketball and I am in the school's basketball team.

References
Sibylle Renz (English teacher)
Berg Gesamtschule

Christian Adler (manager)
Hotel Adler

7 A written discussion ▸ Unit 1, p. 30 ▸ Unit 3 p. 59

Oft sollst du zu strittigen Fragen schriftlich Stellung nehmen und deine Sichtweise überzeugend darlegen. Zeige dabei, dass du dich gründlich mit dem Thema beschäftigt und die Pro-/ Contra-Argumente abgewogen hast.

a) PREPARING YOUR TEXT

- **Sammle** zuerst alle **Argumente** (z.B. in einem kurzen Brainstorming). Evtl. musst du vorher weiter recherchieren ▸ SF 5.
- Ordne deine Argumente gleich beim Sammeln in zwei Listen: ***pro*** und ***contra***.
- Schau dir die Argumentlisten an und bereite so die Gliederung *(outline)* deines Texts vor:
  - Was sind die **besten drei Argumente *contra*** und die **besten drei *pro***? Diese verwendest du, jeweils beginnend mit dem stärksten Argument.
  - **Nummeriere** die Argumente entsprechend dem Schema rechts.
- Notiere deine **Gliederung *(outline)*** gemäß dem Schema rechts.
  - Beginne mit den Argumenten, die **gegen *(contra)*** deine Sichtweise sprechen und stell **danach** die Argumente vor, die deine Meinung **unterstützen *(pro)***. (Auf diese Weise lassen sich die Contra-Argumente wirkungsvoller entkräften. Prinzipiell kannst du aber auch mit den Pro-Argumenten beginnen.)
  - Notiere jeweils **Beispiele** zu den Argumenten.
  - Überlege und notiere, in welche Richtung deine **Schlussfolgerung *(conclusion)*** gehen soll.

OUTLINE FOR A WRITTEN DISCUSSION

Topic: Can students do enough to save the planet?

1) Introduction: …
2) Arguments contra / against
   2.1) First argument: …
   2.2) Second argument: …
   2.3) Third argument: …
3) Arguments pro / for / supporting
   2.1) First argument: …
   2.2) Second argument: …
   2.3) Third argument: …
4) Conclusion: …

b) WRITING YOUR TEXT

- Nun formuliere mithilfe deiner *outline* die *written discussion* **ausführlich**.
- In der **Einleitung *(introduction)*** stellst du das Thema vor und beschreibst, worum es geht. Geh dabei von einem allgemein bekannten Problem oder einer persönlichen Erfahrung aus.
- Im **Hauptteil *(main body)*** präsentiere die Argumente *contra* und *pro*.
  - Nenne jeweils das Argument.
  - Erläutere es näher und begründe deine Meinung.
  - Unterstütze deine Meinung durch Fakten und Beispiele (aus deiner Recherche bzw. aus eigener Erfahrung).
  - Formuliere logisch und flüssig, verbinde deine Argumente. ▸ p. 169
- Am Textende steht deine persönliche **Schlussfolgerung *(conclusion)***. Achtung: Hier keine neuen Argumente und auch keine Argument-Wiederholungen aus dem Hauptteil!

USEFUL PHRASES

… for your introduction:
A lot of people think …
You often hear people say that …,
… so the questions is: should … or not?

… for the main body of your text:
Firstly, …; Secondly, …;
Another argument for / against … is …
For example, …
People think that because …
However, a lot of people feel …
On the one hand, …
On the other hand, we should not forget …
So …; That is why …; Finally, …

… for your conclusion:
To sum up, I think / I would say …
After looking at all the arguments, I think / I come to the conclusion that …

c) CHECK AND CORRECT YOUR TEXT

- Auch bei *written discussions* plane mindestens einen Textentwurf und eine gründliche Überarbeitung ein. ▸ p. 169

8 Writing a report ▸ Unit 2, pp. 39, 114, 116

Auch beim Verfassen eines Berichts beachte *The steps of text writing*. ▸ SF 10.1
In einem *report* gibst du deinen Lesern kurze und sachliche Informationen.

a) PLANNING YOUR REPORT

Collect ideas
Notiere dir Stichwörter zu den fünf *wh*-Fragen und *how* in einer Mindmap oder Tabelle. Beispiel:

Footballers support refugees

Gelsenkirchen-Schalke, Germany – Yesterday Schalke's former professional Gerald Asamoah and Schalke's fans stood up for human rights and refugees.
Ghana born Asamoah started a campaign for refugees earlier this month. His campaign is called *#Stand up for human rights!* and was supported by thousands of fans who stood up holding posters with *#stehtauf* in their hands.
Asamoah started the campaign because he wanted to show that everybody could help. He said, "Everybody must show courage and they must hold up a sign that says, "Stand up." The campaign is supported in many social networks by well-known footballers, e.g. Schalke's Benedikt Höwedes or Hamburg's Rene Adler.

Plan the structure of your report
Auch ein Bericht besteht aus *beginning*, *middle* und *end*.
Beginne mit den **wichtigsten Informationen**, um deinen Lesern eine schnelle Orientierung zu ermöglichen. **Weitere Informationen** kannst du ans Ende setzen. Informiere deine Leser kurz und knapp.

b) WRITING YOUR REPORT

Schreibe deinen Bericht auf und bilde Sinnabschnitte. Beachte: Wenn du über Vergangenes berichtest, musst du das *simple past* verwenden.

c) CHECK AND CORRECT YOUR REPORT

Plane auch bei einem *report* mindestens einen Textentwurf und eine gründliche Überarbeitung ein.

9 Writing a book or film review ▸ Unit 1, p. 111 ▸ Unit 2, p. 123

1 Worum geht es?

Nicht nur Fachleute wie Journalisten oder Kritiker schreiben Kritiken zu Filmen oder Büchern, sondern auch viele Nicht-Profis geben zunehmend ihre Meinung zu Büchern und Filmen, die sie gelesen oder gesehen haben, in Internetportalen wieder. Auch Mitschüler sind daran interessiert, wie dir ein Film oder ein Buch gefallen hat.

2 Wie schreibe ich eine Kritik?

Überlege dir vorab, ob du den Film / das Buch weiterempfehlen oder davon abraten möchtest. Dann baue deine Kritik wie folgt auf.

- **Einleitung** (*background information*)
  Nenne den Titel und das Genre (z. B. Komödie oder Thriller; Roman oder Sachbuch). Sag etwas über die wichtigsten Schauspieler bzw. Figuren und auch etwas zum Regisseur bzw. Autor. Du kannst wichtige zusätzliche Informationen zum Film oder Buch ergänzen (z.B. gewonnene Preise etc.)

USEFUL PHRASES
for writing a book or film review
... is a film / book by ...
It's a comedy / thriller / adventure film / documentary ...
The main actors / characters are ...

- **Hauptteil** (*specific information*)
  Gib eine kurze Zusammenfassung: Ort und Zeit der Handlung, Hauptpersonen und die wichtigsten Inhalte. Benutze dafür das ***simple present***. Schreibe über den Aufbau, den Handlungsverlauf (*plot*), den Schauplatz (*setting*), die Figuren (*characters*) und die Stimmung (*mood*).
  ► *Skills file 7.7, p. 164*

- **Bewertung und Empfehlung**
  (*your opinion and recommendation*)
  Schreib, wie dir der Film oder das Buch gefallen hat und sag, woran das lag. Fandest du Handlung spannend und interessant oder langweilig? Warum? Was war ansprechend und ungewöhnlich?

  Falls du einen Film kritisierst: Wie waren die Schauspieler, wie gefiel dir die Filmmusik? Kannst du Buch oder Film empfehlen oder nicht? Wem könnte der Film bzw. das Buch gefallen?

3 Check and correct your review

Plane auch bei einem *review* mindestens einen Textentwurf und eine gründliche Überarbeitung ein.

USEFUL PHRASES

The film / book is about ...
It's the story of ...
The action takes place in ...
The story begins when ...
Later ... In the end ...

I really enjoyed ...

I think it's one of the best films of the last few years because ...

Personally I think the story is exciting / weak/ boring ...

The actors are just super / convincing ...

The special effects are amazing and the music is wonderful.

If you like action/romantic feelings/ to laugh, *(film title)* is the movie for you.

I can recommend / wouldn't read this book / watch this film because I'm (not) interested in ...

I think that this film / book will be popular with girls / boys / anybody who likes ...

SF 11 Talking about visuals

1 Describing photos, pictures, filmstills ► *Unit 3, pp. 61, 126*

- Beginne **allgemein**: Welchen Ort, welche Gegenstände und welche Menschen siehst du? Was tun sie?
  In the photo we can see a little girl and a young man. They're sitting inside a big room, but not together.
- Beachte eine **Reihenfolge**: **Wen** oder **was** siehst du **wo** im Foto? Du kannst im Vorder- oder Hintergrund (*in the foreground / background*) beginnen. Benutze passende Ortsangaben (z.B. *in the middle of / at the top / ...*) und Präpositionen (z.B. *at / behind / between / in the background / in front of / near / next to / on ...*).
- Beschreibe **Personen** und **Handlungen**: z.B. ihr Aussehen, was sie gerade tun (dies im ***present progressive***):
  The girl is building something with dominoes. She looks happy.
- Formuliere **Vermutungen** über die **Personen** und ihre **Beziehung(en)** zueinander. Was fühlen oder denken sie (vermutlich) gerade?
  Was könnte als nächstes passieren?
  The man might be working. He looks busy. I think he is the girl's father. The girl is probably having fun and she's happy that her father is at home. Maybe they're going to have a video-call with grandma.

! Beachte die "***non-progressive***" ***verbs***
► *Language file 2, p. 182*.

2 Talking about cartoons ▸ Unit 1, pp. 17, 107

- Cartoons (Karikaturen) sind humorvolle Zeichnungen mit oder ohne Text, die häufig ein aktuelles Thema kommentieren. Diese Schritte helfen dir beim Beschreiben und Verstehen eines Cartoons:

supremacy [suː'preməsi] – *Vorherrschaft*

- ***(I) Describe what you see***

  Beschreibe die **Personen** / **Tiere** / **Dinge**: ihr **Aussehen** und ihre **Handlungen**. Beginne wieder allgemein und beschreibe in einer Reihenfolge mit Hilfe von Ortsangaben und Präpositionen.
  We see a protest situation, not with people, but with two penguins as angry protesters. Both birds are black and white. They seem to be alone in a polar landscape.
  The penguin on the left is holding a protest sign saying "White supremacy" and the one on the right is confronting him with a sign carrying the slogan "Black power!".

- ***(II) Name the topic / problem***

  Worum geht es deiner Meinung nach in diesem Cartoon?
  I think this cartoon is about racial problems and prejudices.

- ***(III) Explain the message***

  Was will der Cartoonist zum Ausdruck bringen / kritisieren / unterstützen? Was ist positiv, was negativ dargestellt?
  I think the cartoon criticizes racial prejudices. It is making fun of a serious human problem by employing animal protagonists.

- ***(IV) Evaluate the cartoon / Give your opinion***

  „Funktioniert" die Karikatur aus deiner Sicht, d.h. sind die eingesetzten Mittel (Figurenwahl, eventueller Text …) effektiv? Hier kannst du auch Hintergrundwissen zum Thema des Cartoons einsetzen.
  Both penguins are shown as equally black and white and equally narrow-minded. The one on the left sees itself as only "white" and the one on the right as only "black". I think they have a lot in common and should stick together instead of fighting each other.
  The two slogans are historical, which makes this cartoon more serious. …

USEFUL PHRASES
for talking about cartoons:

(I) At the top / bottom / in the middle / … of the cartoon there is …
The caption reads "…"

(II) This cartoon is about / shows / provides proof (for / against) … / deals with …

(III) The cartoon may be meant to …
It's layout / use of colour … / caption … shows / criticizes / makes fun of …

(IV) The cartoon addresses / doesn't address the problem / topic of … very effectively …
Using … is very amusing / funny / …
I especially like its irony seen against the complicated / tragic / … background of …

3 Talking about charts and diagrams ▸ Unit 1, p. 16 ▸ Unit 2, p. 39

- Diagramme stellen statistische Vergleiche zwischen mindestens zwei Dingen dar. Dabei helfen sie komplexe Informationen zu veranschaulichen und leichter zu verstehen.

- Unterschiedliche **Formen von Diagrammen**:
  - Bar charts (Säulendiagramme) beschreiben in der Regel die Anzahl oder Größe von zwei oder mehr Dingen.
  - Pie charts (Kreis- / Tortendiagramme) geben einen Überblick über die prozentuale Verteilung.
  - Line graphs (Kurvendiagramme) stellen den Zusammenhang zwischen zwei oder mehr Variablen (Parameter) dar.
  - Charts (Tabellen) ermöglichen den Vergleich unterschiedlicher Daten anhand von Zahlen.

- So **beschreibst** du **Diagramme**:

  Um Diagramme zu beschreiben, ist es hilfreich, folgende Struktur zu nutzen.
  A: Einleitung
  What is the graph / chart about?
  The bar / pie chart / line graph is about … / deals with …
  The (horizontal) x-axis / (vertical) y-axis shows …
  The slices of the pie chart compare …
  Du solltest auch sagen, wo du das Diagramm gefunden hast.
  It is taken from …
  B: Beschreibung der dargestellten Informationen
  What does the graph / chart compare? What information does it give?
  … has the largest / smallest … is twice / three times … as big as …
  There are more than / almost twice as many … as there are …
  A majority / minority / … per cent of …
  Less than half / More than one third …
  The number … grows by … / sinks by … / does not change.
  C: Schlussfolgerung
  What is the general conclusion?
  I was really surprised / shocked by …
  So / To sum up / All in all we can say …

- **Beachte** außerdem:

  Benutze das ***simple present***, wenn das Diagramm sich auf Fakten in der Gegenwart bezieht oder bei allgemeingültigen Aussagen:
  More than 55 per cent of German students under 10 have a smartphone.
  Benutze das ***simple past*** bei Fakten, die in der Vergangenheit liegen:
  73 per cent of the 10–12-year-olds had their own TV in 2012.
  Benutze das **present perfect**, wenn du dich auf einen Zeitraum beziehst, der von der Vergangenheit bis heute reicht:
  The number of young people using social media has nearly doubled since 2011.

What do 10 to 18-years-olds use their mobile for?

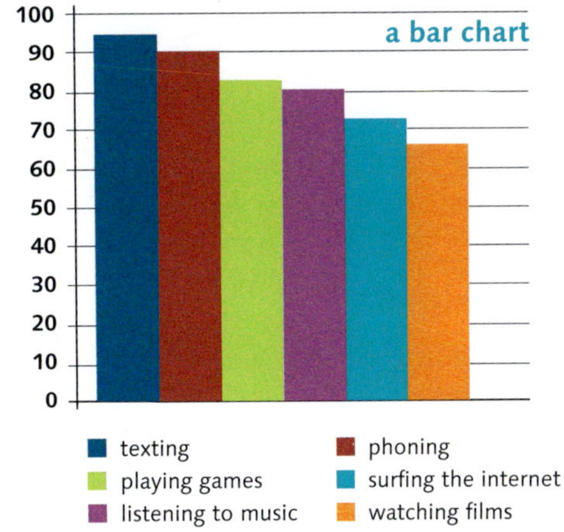

source: Bitkom

Use of social networks (10–18 yrs)

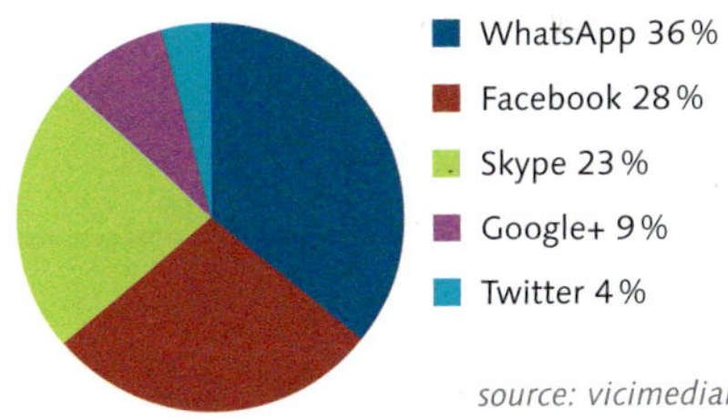

source: vicimediainc

a pie chart

Hours spent on media per day

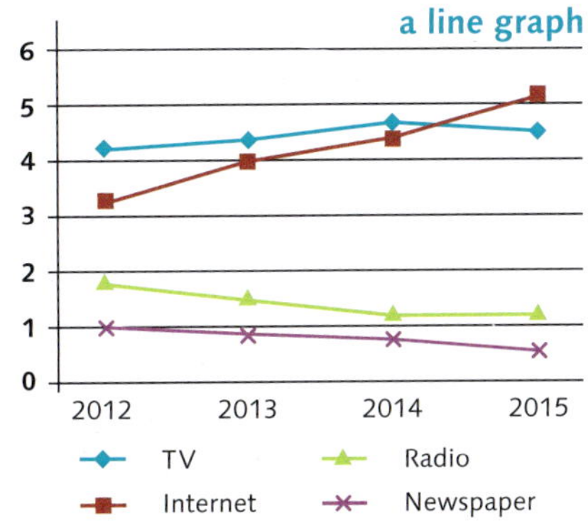

source: Bitkom

SF 12 MEDIATION COURSE ▸ Unit 1, pp. 26, 103 ▸ Unit 2, p. 46 ▸ Unit 3, p. 70

Mediation (auch: Sprachmittlung) bedeutet, zwischen Sprecher/innen unterschiedlicher Sprachen zu vermitteln und Informationen in der jeweiligen Sprache wiederzugeben.

1 Worum geht es?

- Du gibst englische Informationen mündlich **auf Deutsch** wieder, wie im Beispiel rechts.
- Oder du vermittelst deutsche Informationen **auf Englisch**, z.B. wenn bei dir an der Schule ein Austauschschüler zu Gast ist. Das kann mündlich geschehen (im Gespräch mit Anderen) oder auch schriftlich, wenn du dem Gastschüler z.B. eine Nachricht schreibst.
- Die unterschiedlichen Möglichkeiten von *mediation* (Deutsch ↔ Englisch, mündlich / schriftlich) fasst dieses Schema zusammen:

Freund: Können wir hier parken? Was sollen wir machen?

Du: Ja. Wir sollen einen Parkschein lösen und ihn sichtbar ins Auto legen.

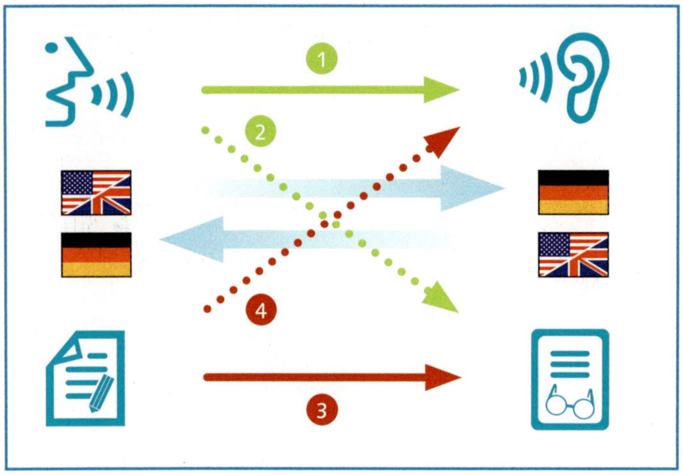

Beispiele:

1. Einem englischsprachigen Reisenden in Deutschland sagst du, was eben in der Bahnhofsdurchsage Wichtiges zu hören war.
2. Bei einem Telefonat mit einem englischen Jobanbieter machst du Notizen, die du einem Freund mailst.
3. Du mailst einer künftigen Gastschülerin die wichtigsten Inhalte eurer Schulordnung auf Englisch.
4. Du erklärst eine schriftliche Information mündlich in der anderen Sprache, vgl. das Beispiel im Foto oben.

2 Worauf musst du achten?

- *Mediation* ist keine Übersetzung. Gib also nur das **Wesentliche** sinngemäß wieder, lasse unwichtige Informationen weg.
- Verwende kurze und einfache Sätze.
- Wenn du **schriftliche Informationen** sprachmitteln sollst:
  - **Scanne** den Text gezielt nach den notwendigen Informationen. ▸ SF 7.2
  - Ist der Text länger und du brauchst viele Informationen daraus, **markiere** die wichtigsten Textstellen und mach dir ggf. **Notizen** in deinen eigenen Worten. ▸ SF 7.6
- Wenn du **mündliche Informationen** sprachmitteln sollst:
  - **Höre zielgerichtet** auf die notwendigen Informationen. ▸ SF 6
- Bei längeren Hörtexten und umfangreichen Informationen mach dir **kurze Notizen** während des Hörens. Überlege anschließend, wie du sie am besten in der anderen Sprache wiedergeben kannst.

! Wenn du schriftlich sprachmittelst, achte darauf, dass dein Text in der anderen Sprache nicht länger als ca. 40% des Originaltexts ist.

3 Paraphrasieren (Umschreiben unbekannter Wörter)

Manchmal fällt es schwer, Inhalte auf Englisch wiederzugeben, z.B. wenn dein Wortschatz nicht ausreicht oder dir manche Wörter im Stress nicht gleich einfallen. Dann nutze das Umschreiben *(paraphrasing)*. Die folgenden **Strategien** helfen dir.

- Umschreibe mit Wörtern, die eine ähnliche oder die **gleiche Bedeutung** haben (Synonyme) oder mit Vergleichen:
  It's the same as … / It's (very) similar to … / It works like …
- Umschreibe mit **gegensätzlichen** Wörtern (Antonymen):
  It's the opposite of …
  Seine Eltern leben getrennt. – *His parents don't live together.*
  Der See ist künstlich angelegt. – *The lake is not a natural one.*
- Umschreibe mit dem **Oberbegriff** statt der einzelnen Unterbegriffe (das hilft dir auch, dich kurz zu fassen):
  Wir müssen noch ein paar Tulpen und Osterglocken kaufen.
  – *We need (to buy) some flowers.*
  Oh nein, Fahrradventil und Schlauch sind kaputt!
  – *She's angry because she can't ride her bike.*
- Umschreibe mit **Unterbegriffen**, wenn du den Oberbegriff nicht kennst:
  Haben wir ausreichend Geschirr für die Party heute Abend?
  – *Are there enough plates and glasses, etc. for the party?*
- Umschreibe mit einer näheren Erläuterung, z.B. in **Relativsätzen**. ▸ *Language file 28, p. 197*
  It's somebody / a person who is known for …
  It's something that you use for …
  It's a place that … / where …
- Oft hilft das Prinzip ***Keep it simple***. Fällt dir eine einfache Erklärung des gesuchten Begriffs ein? Diese kannst du dann leicht auf Englisch formulieren, z.B.
  Selbstbedienung – *no waiter / waitress*
  Vollsperrung der A20 bis 24 Uhr
  – *The A20 motorway will be (completely) closed till midnight.*
  Schienenersatzverkehr
  – *There is no train, so we have to take the bus instead.*

4 Kulturelle und regionale Unterschiede

- Manche ‚typisch deutschen' Alltagsdinge oder Traditionen wird dein Gegenüber eventuell nicht kennen. Hierfür gibt es im Englischen meist gar keinen direkten Begriff. Du musst dann erklären, was du meinst. Typische Beispiele:
- **Rosenmontag** – *It's the most important day of carnival for people in the Rhine area. It's a holiday. People celebrate and wear costumes, and there are parades in the streets.*
- **Schultüte** – *It's a kind of special bag kids are given on their first day at school. There are sweets in it and little things you need at school, like pens and exercise books.*
- Natürlich wird es für dich auch Unbekanntes geben, wovon dein Gegenüber ganz selbstverständlich spricht. Dann frage höflich nach und bitte um eine Erklärung:
- *I'm sorry, I'm afraid I don't know this tradition / rule / habit / meal …*
  Could you please explain it?
  I've never done / eaten … this before. Could you help me, please?

SF 13 VIEWING SKILLS

▸ Unit 1, p. 27 ▸ Unit 2, pp. 34–35, 49 ▸ Unit 3, pp. 61, 71

1 Vor dem Sehen: bereite dich vor

- Welche Art von Film wirst du sehen: a documentary, a movie, a commercial, a soap, the news, …? Was weißt du bereits über die Art des Films?
- Lies sorgfältig die Aufgabenstellung. Worum könnte es gehen?
- Worauf musst du besonders achten? Was kann dir beim Verstehen helfen?
- Betrachte die Filmszenen im Buch vor dem Anschauen.

2 Beim Sehen

Nutze ein Viewing log, um über die meisten Aspekte des Films sprechen zu können, wie Schauplatz (*setting*), Figuren (*characters*), Handlungsverlauf (*plot*) und Stimmung (*mood*).

Who?	What?	When?	Where?	camera work	comments
…	…	…	…	…	…

Versuche beim ersten Sehen die wesentlichen Inhalte des Films zu erfassen. Beim zweiten Sehen kannst du dann auf Einzelheiten achten und deine Notizen ergänzen.

Kameraeinstellungen helfen dir, Inhalte und Gefühle besser zu verstehen.

- close-up
  Ein *close-up* ist eine Nahaufnahme eines Gesichts oder einer Gegenstandes. So kannst du z.B. am Gesichtsausdruck die Gefühle einer Person erkennen.
  What does Amar look like in this close-up?

close-up

- long shot
  Ein *long shot* (auch: *wide shot*), die Totale, gibt dir einen Eindruck der gesamten Szene und des Schauplatzes.
  How many people are there? What impression do you get?

long shot

Achte auf die Erzählstruktur des Filmes, z. B. monologue. Ein Monolog gibt dir die Möglichkeit, die Motive einer einzelnen Person besser zu verstehen.

Ein *flashback* (Rückblende) verändert die chronologische Reihenfolge. Dadurch kannst du Ereignisse besser verstehen oder erkennen, wieso jemand dieses oder jenes gemacht hat. Filmtechniken werden eingesetzt, um z. B. Spannung, Lachen, Angst oder Freude auszulösen.
Weitere wichtige Aspekte beim Anschauen, auf die du achten kannst, um dein Verständnis zu schulen, wie Filme funktionieren: Farbe, Kameraführung, Kontraste, Licht, Perspektive, Schnitt und Ton, insbesondere die Filmmusik.

3 Nach dem Sehen

Vervollständige deine Notizen.
Dabei helfen dir die Redewendungen rechts.

USEFUL PHRASES

The film is about …. / It tells the story of …

The close-ups of …. make it easier to understand …

The wide shot of the classroom shows …

The monologues helped me to understand …

The flashbacks showed …

There is no music in the film / The music is dramatic / sad / … because…

I (don't) like the film because …

LANGUAGE FILE

Inhalt

TALKING ABOUT THE PRESENT

LF 1 The simple present (Die einfache Form der Gegenwart) ▸ *Unit 1, p. 17*

Mit dem ***simple present*** drückst du aus, was **wiederholt** oder **nie** geschieht. Es steht häufig mit: *always, sometimes, often, never* oder Zeitangaben wie *every day, in the morning, at the weekend, on Monday.* Du benutzt das ***simple present*** auch, um **Gewohnheiten**, **Dauerzustände** oder **allgemein gültige Tatsachen** auszudrücken, z.B. *Mia likes football. Dublin lies on the coast. No means no.*

Bejahte und verneinte Aussagen

I/You/We/They He/She/It	like likes	sport.

I/You/We/They He/She/It	don't like doesn't like	sport.

Bei **bejahten Aussagen** fügst du bei *he/she/it* ein -*s* an das Verb.

! *he/she/it goes, watches, tries, hurries*

! Das Verb nach doesn't (hier: *like*) steht immer in der Grundform. Das gilt auch für does in Fragen.

Ja-/Nein-Fragen und Kurzantworten

Do you like Does he like	sport?	Yes, I do./No, I don't. Yes, he does./No, he doesn't.

Ja-/Nein-Fragen im ***simple present*** beginnst du mit *Do* oder *Does*.

Fragen mit Fragewort

Why do Ben's friends love football?

Wenn die Frage mit einem **Fragewort** anfängt, folgt direkt *do* bzw. *does*.

! Fragen mit **Fragewort** *Who* findest du in ▸ *LF 16*.

LF 2 The present progressive (Die Verlaufsform der Gegenwart) ▸ Unit 1, p. 17

Mit dem ***present progressive*** sagst du, dass etwas **gerade jetzt** geschieht oder dass jemand **gerade etwas tut**. Das ***present progressive*** benutzt du auch, um Bilder zu beschreiben.
Häufige Zeitangaben in Sätzen im ***present progressive*** sind: *now*, *at the moment*, *just*, *still*.
Eine Verlaufsform gibt es im Deutschen nicht. Man sagt aber z.B.: „Ich bin gerade dabei, etwas zu tun."

Bejahte Aussagen	
I'm / You're He's / She's They're	waiting.

Verneinte Aussagen	
I'm not / You aren't He / She isn't They aren't	waiting.

Das ***present progressive*** bildest du mit einer Form von ***be*** + *verb* + ***-ing***.

! Beachte beim Schreiben:
write → writing *make → making*
plan → planning *stop → stopping*

Ja-/Nein-Fragen und Kurzantworten		
Am I Are you Is he / she Are they	waiting?	Yes, I am. / No, I'm not. Yes, he / she is. / No, ... isn't. Yes, they are. / No, they aren't.

Ja-/Nein-Fragen beginnst du mit *Am / Are / Is*:
Is Mia going to football practice?
- Yes, she is. / No, she isn't. She's waiting for Li.

Fragen mit Fragewort
What's Mia doing today?

Ein **Fragewort** steht vor *am / are / is:*
Where are Mia and her friend going?

Present progressive or simple present?

Mia is playing football. (*present progressive*)
Mia spielt Fußball. (= gerade, jetzt im Moment)

Mia plays football. (*simple present*)
Mia spielt Fußball. (= regelmäßig, es ist ihr Sport)

Mia often plays football, but she isn't playing today because it's raining. ... oft ..., aber heute nicht, weil ... .

Für den Satz „Mia spielt Fußball." kannst du entweder das ***present progressive*** oder das ***simple present*** benutzen, je nachdem, was du ausdrücken möchtest:

present progressive:	***simple present:***
just, at the moment, now	*always, often, every day, on ...*

! Verben, die **Zustände** oder **Sinneswahrnehmungen** bezeichnen (z.B. *be*, *know*, *love*, *seem*, *want*, *weigh*), werden meist **nicht** in der ***progressive form*** verwendet, sondern **nur** in der ***simple form***. (Anders als Tätigkeits- und **Vorgangsverben** wie *go*, *read*, *rain*, die sowohl in der ***simple*** als **auch** in der ***progressive form*** auftreten.) ▸ Unit 1, p. 107
Merke dir folgende dieser **Verben** (sie werden auch ***"non-progressive" verbs*** genannt):
> für Sinneswahrnehmungen, Meinungen, Wissen: *hear*, *see*, *seem*, *believe*, *(dis-)agree*, *suppose*, *understand*, *know*, z.B.: *He doesn't see well without his glasses. There seems to be a problem.*
> für Regeln, Eigenschaften, Eigentum, Zugehörigkeit: *mean* („bedeuten"), *be*, *look* („aussehen"), *own*, *need*, *belong*, *include*, z.B.: *Practice means work. I need a day off. Li often looks* happy*.*
> für Gefühle/Vorlieben: *like*, *love*, *prefer*, *hate*, *mind*, *want*, *wish*, z.B.: *Mia loves football. She wants to be really good at it.*

*Je nach Bedeutung und Aussageabsicht kann auch die ***progressive form*** möglich sein: *You look* („aussehen") *sad. What's wrong? - I'm looking for* („suchen") *my phone, but I can't find it. What do you think of* („denken von/über") *our new coach? - What are you thinking about?* („Worüber denkst du gerade nach?")

TALKING ABOUT THE PAST

LF 3 The simple past (Die einfache Form der Vergangenheit) ▸ Unit 2, p. 41

Mit dem ***simple past*** sagst du, was **zu einer bestimmten Zeit** in der Vergangenheit geschah. Du verwendest es oft mit Zeitangaben wie *yesterday*, *last week*, *in July*, *two years ago*. Oft benutzt wird es für **Berichte** und beim **Erzählen von Geschichten**.

Bejahte Aussagen (regelmäßige Verben)	
I/He/We/…	laughed a lot.

Bei **regelmäßigen** Verben bildest du das ***simple past*** durch Anhängen von -***ed*** an das Verb.

Bejahte Aussagen (unregelmäßige Verben)	
I/He/We/…	bought a book.

Lerne die ***simple past***-Formen **unregelmäßiger** Verben. ▸ pp. 272–273

Verneinte Aussagen	
I/He/We/…	didn't know all the people.

Wenn du sagen willst, was **nicht** geschah, setzt du *didn't* vor das Verb in der **Grundform**.

! Das Verb *be* (*was/were*) verneinst du **ohne** ~~*did*~~. *The comics weren't new.*

Ja-/Nein-Fragen und Kurzantworten		
Did you/she /…	like it?	Yes, I did./No, I didn't. Yes, she did./No, she didn't.

Ja-/Nein-Fragen im ***simple past*** beginnst du mit *Did*.

Fragen mit *be* (*was/were*) und Kurzantworten		
Was I/he/she/it Were we/you/they	happy?	Yes, he was./No, he wasn't. Yes, we were./No, we weren't.

! *Ja-/Nein*-Fragen mit *Was/Were* bildest du **ohne** ~~*did*~~, ebenso die Kurzantworten.

Fragen mit Fragewort
What did Mia like best about the comic?

Did folgt direkt auf das **Fragewort**.

! Das Verb nach *did* (hier: *like*) steht immer in der Grundform. ▸ LF 15

LF 4 The past progressive (Die Verlaufsform der Vergangenheit)

Mit dem ***past progressive*** drückst du aus, dass eine Handlung in der Vergangenheit gerade im Gange war (zu einem Zeitpunkt oder als etwas anderes geschah).

Bejahte und verneinte Aussagen		
I/He/She/It You/We/They	was/wasn't were/weren't	sleeping at 5pm.

Das ***past progressive*** bildest du mit ***was/were*** + *verb* + -***ing***. ▸ LF 2

Ja-/Nein-Fragen und Kurzantworten	
Was/Were … taking …?	Yes, I/he was./ No, they weren´t.

Fragen mit Fragewort
What was Ben doing at 5 pm?

LF 5 The present perfect (Das *present perfect*) ▸ Unit 2, p. 41

Mia and Li are shopping. They've already been to six shops. "We haven't found a shirt for me yet, Mia." – "I know, but I'm hungry. I haven't eaten much today."

! Das ***present perfect*** wird **immer** mit *have/has* gebildet, auch wenn im Deutschen eine Form von „sein" steht.

Das ***present perfect*** drückt aus, dass etwas **irgendwann** geschehen ist. Der Zeitpunkt ist unwichtig. Es steht häufig mit: *just, already, always, ever, never, not … yet.*

Du bildest das ***present perfect*** mit ***have/has*** + dritte Form des Verbs (***past participle***).

! Beachte unregelmäßige Verben ▸ pp. 272–273.

Bejahte/verneinte Aussagen	
I/… 've/haven't He/… has/hasn't	bought …

Ja-/Nein-Fragen	
Have you/we … Has she/he …	bought …?

Fragen mit Fragewort
Why have Mia and Li gone to the new mall?

Kurzantworten
Yes, I /we … have. / No, I / we … haven't. Yes, she / … has. / No, she /… hasn't.

Present perfect with *since* and *for*

! Trotz Präsens im Deutschen benutzt du mit *since* und *for* das ***present perfect*** auf Englisch:
I've lived next door to Mia **since** my family came to the US. Mia has been my friend **for** six years. Ich bin Mias Nachbarin **seit** …

Das ***present perfect*** mit *since* oder *for* drückt aus, **seit wann / wie lange** etwas andauert.

Since nennt einen Anfangs**zeitpunkt**: *since 6 am, since 2018, since I was a baby, …*

For umfasst einen **Zeitraum**: *for two months/ for years/for hours /for a long time.*

Present perfect or simple past?

! Das ***present perfect*** steht häufig in Sätzen mit Zeitangaben wie *just, already, often, always, never, ever, not … yet, before, since / for.*

- um zu sagen, dass etwas **irgendwann** geschehen ist, oft mit **Auswirkungen auf die Gegenwart.**
  Ben has **just** come back from LA.
- in Fragen mit *ever …?*
  Have you **ever** been to LA before, Ben?
- in Sätzen mit *since* und *for*
  His uncle has lived in LA **for** three years now.

! Das ***simple past*** muss stehen in Sätzen mit Zeitangaben wie *yesterday, last week, in July, two years ago, in 2016.*

- um zu sagen, dass etwas **zu einer bestimmten Zeit** geschehen ist, oft mit genauer Zeitangabe.
  In 2016 Ben's uncle started a cafe in LA.
- in Berichten und Erzählungen
  Ben wanted to help him. His uncle agreed.
- in Fragen mit ***When** …?*
  When did you leave for LA, Ben?

LF 6 *The present perfect progressive ▸ Unit 2, p. 116

(Die Verlaufsform des *present perfect*)

Mit dem ***present perfect progressive*** sagst du, dass etwas **in der Vergangenheit** begonnen hat und **bis jetzt andauert** bzw. **gerade vorbei** ist. Es steht häufig mit Zeitangaben wie *since …* oder *for …*

Bejahte und verneinte Aussagen

I/...'ve/haven't He/...'s/hasn't	been waiting long.

Du bildest das ***present perfect progressive*** mit ***have/has been*** + *verb* + ***-ing***.

***Ja-/Nein*-Fragen und Kurzantworten**

Have you/... Has he/...	been waiting long?	Yes, ... have/has. No, ... haven't/hasn't.

Fragen mit Fragewort

How long have you been waiting?
Wie lange wartest du schon?

LF 7 The past perfect (Das *past perfect*)

When Li arrived at the party, Ben had already gone home. *(Erst ging Ben, dann kam Li.)*

Ben thought that Li had forgotten about the party.

! Das ***past perfect*** wird **immer** mit ***had*** gebildet, auch wenn im Deutschen „war" steht.

Mit dem ***past perfect*** (Plusquamperfekt oder **Vor**vergangenheit) drückst du aus, dass etwas noch **vor** etwas anderem in der Vergangenheit stattgefunden hatte.

Du bildest das ***past perfect*** mit ***had*** **+** 3. Form des Verbs (***past participle***).

► *pp. 272–273*

Bejahte und verneinte Aussagen

I/... He/...	had/hadn't	forgotten ...

***Ja-/Nein*-Fragen und Kurzantworten**

Had I .../he ...	forgotten ...?	Yes, ... had. No, ... hadn't.

Simple past or past perfect?

Before Li left home, it had started to rain heavily.

Mit dem ***past perfect*** sagt du, was zeitlich vorangegangen war. Oft stehen dabei Zeitangaben wie *after, when, before, already*.

So Li took an umbrella with her, but she forgot her phone.

! Keine Vorvergangenheit (sondern ***simple past***), wenn etwas zur gleichen Zeit geschah.

NEW LF 8 *The past perfect progressive (Die Verlaufsform des *past perfect*)

► *Unit 2, p. 52*

Ben had been sleeping for ten hours when his phone rang.
(er hatte über einen langen Zeitraum geschlafen)

Mit dem ***past perfect progressive*** sagst du, dass etwas noch **vor** einem weiteren Ereignis **in der Vergangenheit** über **einen gewissen Zeitraum angedauert** hat.

Du bildest das ***past perfect progressive*** mit ***had been*** + *verb* + ***-ing***.

Bejahte und verneinte Aussagen

I/... He/...	had / hadn't been	... *ing*.

***Ja-/Nein*-Fragen und Kurzantworten**

Had I/.../he/...	been ...*ing*?	Yes, ... had. No, ... hadn't.

Fragen mit Fragewort

What had ... been you doing (when/before ...)?

TALKING ABOUT THE FUTURE

LF 9 The *going to*-future (Das Futur mit *going to*) ▸ Unit 3, p. 63

Mia's going to have a football match next Saturday.
Mia wird nächsten Samstag … haben.

Her brother Ben isn't going to come to the match.
Ihr Bruder hat nicht vor, es zu sehen.

What are we going to do on Sunday?
Was wollen wir am Sonntag machen?

Is the weather going to be fine?
Wird das Wetter gut?

! Stark umgangssprachlich hörst/liest du häufig gonna, z.B. *They're gonna watch the match.*

Wenn du ausdrücken möchtest, was jemand in der Zukunft **plant** oder **vorhat** sowie für **Vorhersagen** benutzt du das Futur mit ***going to***.

Es wird mit einer Form von *be* (*am/are/is*) gebildet, oft mit den Kurzformen:
'm/'re/'s + going to + verb

Verneinung:
Ben isn't going to be at Mia's match.
But she's not going to be angry with him.

Fragen und Kurzantworten:
Is it going to rain?
- (Look at the sky!) Yes, it is./No, it isn't.

LF 10 The *will*-future (Das Futur mit *will*) ▸ Unit 3, p. 63

Bejahte und verneinte Aussagen

I/You/He/She/It We/You/They	will like the concert. won't like all the songs.

Ja-/Nein-Fragen und Kurzantworten

Will	I/you/ he /…	like all the songs?	Yes, … will. No, … won't.

Fragen mit Fragewort

Who will win the match tomorrow?
When will we get home?

! Englisch *I will* heißt im Deutschen „ich werde" und nicht „ich will".

Mit dem ***will-future*** kannst du über die Zukunft sprechen, z.B. über **Vermutungen** und **Vorhersagen** oder **spontane Entschlüsse**.
Es steht häufig mit Zeitangaben wie *tomorrow, (sometime) next week/year …*

Eine **Vermutung** beginnt oft mit *Maybe / I'm sure: I think I'll enjoy the concert. – I'm sure you will.*

Bei **Vorhersagen** geht es oft um Dinge, die man nicht direkt beeinflussen kann: *It'll be winter soon.*

Ein **spontaner Entschluss** ist oft ein Versprechen oder Angebot.
It's so hot! I'll buy you an ice cream.

Das ***will*-future** wird mit ***will* + verb** gebildet.

Die Kurzform von ***will*** heißt ***'ll***. Die Kurzform der **Verneinung *will not*** heißt ***won't***.

! Verwechsle nicht ***won't*** mit ***wouldn't***, der Verneinung von ***would*** (*würden*). ▸ LF 26

NEW LF 11 *The simple present with future meaning (Einfache Gegenwart mit Zukunftsbedeutung) ▸ Unit 3, p. 123

A note at the door said 'Breakfast is at 7 tomorrow'.
… „Frühstück ist …".

Ben told his friends, 'My plane for LA leaves at 9.30 am.'
…: „Mein Flug(zeug) … geht um halb zehn."

'My holiday job starts on Monday', said Li.
„Montag beginnt mein Ferienjob", …

Zukünftiges Geschehen drückst du mit dem ***simple present*** aus, wenn es durch einen **Fahrplan**, ein **Programm**, den **Kalender** o.ä. genau bestimmt ist.

Das ***simple present*** wird in solchen Fällen auch als ***'timetable future'*** bezeichnet und betrifft oft Verben wie *arrive, close, end, leave, open, start, stop, take place.*

NEW LF 12 *The present progressive with future meaning (Verlaufsform der Gegenwart mit Zukunftsbedeutung)

▸ Unit 3, p. 123

When discussing plans for the day Lucy said, 'I'm going outside today.' (fest geplant)

Ben told a friend, 'We're all meeting again next Monday.' (fest verabredet)

Li is coming back from her uncle's tomorrow morning. (fest geplant)

Wenn etwas für die Zukunft **fest geplant** oder **verabredet** ist, verwendest du das ***present progressive***.

Das **Zukünftige** muss durch den **Zusammenhang** oder **Signalwörter** erkennbar sein, z.B. *next week*, *tomorrow* oder an zukünftigen Daten, z.B. *in 2031 / on Monday*, …

NEW LF 13 *The future progressive (Die Verlaufsform des *will-future*)

▸ Unit 3, p. 123

Avril told Lucy, 'While you're looking at the panels, I'll be checking the roof.'
(Avril plant, währenddessen etwas anderes zu tun.)

Ben won't be practising all afternoon.
(… nicht den gesamten Nachmittag lang …)

Mit dem ***future progressive***, der Verlaufsform des ***will-future***, sagst du, dass etwas **in der Zukunft wie vermutet / geplant / gewohnt ablaufen** wird. Es steht häufig mit *next Monday/summer/…* , *tomorrow* oder zukünftigen Daten nach *in… / on …*

Du bildest das ***future progressive*** mit:
will /'ll + ***be*** + verb + ***-ing***.

Bejahte und verneinte Aussagen

I/… He/…	will / won't be	waiting for you.

***Ja-/Nein*-Fragen und Kurzantworten**

Will … be missing me?	Yes, … will. / No, … won't.

Fragen mit Fragewort

What will Li be doing while …?

NEW LF 14 *The future perfect (Die vollendete Form des *will-future*)

▸ Unit 3, p. 123

Lucy asked Avril, 'Will you have finished breakfast by 7.30?' (… „Wirst du um … haben?")

Ben will have repaired his bike when Li arrives.
(Er wird es geschafft haben, wenn sie kommt.)

Mia won't have written her graduation speech by next Friday. (Sie wird es bis … nicht geschafft haben.)

Mit dem ***future perfect*** drückst du aus, dass etwas zu einem **bestimmten Zeitpunkt in der Zukunft abgeschlossen** sein wird.

Das ***future perfect*** steht oft mit ***by*** *tomorrow / next year/…* oder einer Zeitbestimmung wie ***When*** *we get there, …*

Du bildest das ***future perfect*** mit:
will / 'll + ***have*** + ***past participle*** (dritte Form)

▸ pp. 272–273

Bejahte und verneinte Aussagen

I/… He/…	will / won't have	done that by …

***Ja-/Nein*-Fragen und Kurzantworten**

Will	…	have done your homework by 8 pm?	Yes, … will. No, … won't.

Fragen mit Fragewort

What will you have achieved by your 20th birthday?

LF 15 Word order in statements
(Die Wortstellung in Aussagen)

Die Regel zur Wortstellung im englischen Satz ist **subject – verb – object**, kurz **S-V-(O)**.
Subjekt – Prädikat – (Objekt) (Ein Objekt gibt es nicht immer.)

! Anders als im Deutschen wird von **S-V-O nicht** abgewichen, z.B. bei Angaben des Orts, der Art und Weise *(In englischen Sätzen stellst du nicht um.)* bzw. Zeitangaben *(Gestern wusste ich das noch.)*

subject	verb	object	adverbial *(Adverbialbestimmung)*	
Mia	plays	football.		
She	can't play	an instrument.		
Ben and Mia	have bought	tickets.		
Ben and Mia	are interested in	music.		
They	didn't go		to concerts	last year.

Mia usually plays football. Ben sometimes phones Li.

Die **Adverbien der Häufigkeit** *usually, always, often, sometimes, never* stehen **zwischen Subjekt** und **Verb**.

Mia and Ben have already bought tickets.
They're just planning how to get to the concert.
Have you ever been to a concert?

Die **Adverbien der Zeit**, wie *already, ever, just, never* stehen **vor** dem ***present participle*** (*-ing*-Form) bzw. dem ***past participle*** (dritte Form) **des Verbs**.

Luckily Ben and Mia still got cheap tickets.
Ben und Mia bekamen glücklicherweise noch …

Die **Adverbien**, die sich auf den **gesamten Satz** beziehen, wie *perhaps/maybe, suddenly, finally, of course, at first* stehen meist am **Satzanfang**.

After the date with Li, Ben walked home happily.

Adverbien, die sich auf ein Verb bzw. eine Tätigkeit beziehen, stehen in der Regel **am Satzende**.

Ben had first met Li **at Mia's club two months ago**.

! Gibt es in einem Satz eine **Orts- und** eine **Zeitangabe**, gilt die **Regel „Ort vor Zeit"**.

LF 16 Word order in questions (Die Wortstellung in Fragen)

Du erkennst einen Fragesatz daran, dass hier **vor** dem **Subjekt** eine gebeugte Form von *do*, *be*, *have* bzw. *will*, *can*, *may* steht.

Fragen mit *do/does* und *did*

Viele Fragen bildest du mit einer Form von *do*, einem Hilfsverb (*auxiliary*). Es „hilft" sozusagen dabei, dass die Wortstellung des zugrundeliegenden Aussagesatzes einfach erhalten bleiben kann. Vergleiche:

Aussagesatz (S-V-O)
Mia and Li play football.

→

Fragesatz (Hilfsverb-S-V-O)
Do Mia and Li play football? (*Ja-/Nein*-Frage)
When do Mia and Li play football? (Frage mit Fragewort)

Weitere Fragesätze:

question word	auxiliary *do(es)/did*	subject	(main) verb	
	Does	Ben	work	on Fridays?
	Did	he and Li	go	to the cinema?
What	does	Ben	watch	on TV?
Where	did	you	buy	that DVD?

Du beginnst die Frage mit (Fragewort +) *do/does/did*, dann folgen Subjekt und Hauptverb *(main verb)*.

! Keine **Umstellungen** von **Verb** und **Subjekt** wie im Deutschen:
Arbeitet Ben? → *Does Ben work?*

Fragen mit Formen von *be* und *have*

Wenn der Fragesatz eine Form von ***be*** oder ***have*** enthält, steht diese **vor** dem **Subjekt**.

question word	verb (forms of *be / have*)	subject	
	Is	Mia	Ben's sister?
	Are	Mia and Li	good friends?
	Have	you	been to school?
Where	were	you	last weekend?
What	are	Mia and Li	planning for Friday?

Ein **Fragesatz** mit *be* oder *have* wird gebildet, indem du die entsprechende Form, z.B. *is, was, were; have, has* **vor** das **Subjekt** stellst.

Fragewörter – *who, what, when, where, why, how, how long* – stehen am **Satzanfang**.

Subject and object questions (Fragen nach dem Subjekt oder dem Objekt)

***Ben** likes Li.*

Who **likes** Li? – **Ben**.
Wer mag Li?

Who **does Ben** like? – Li.
Wen mag Ben?

***The noise** disturbed Li.*
What **disturbed** Li? – **The noise.**
Was störte Li? – Der Lärm.

***Li** shut the window.*
What **did Li** shut? – The window.
Was schloss Li? – Das Fenster.

Mit den Fragewörtern *who/what/which* kannst du nach dem Subjekt oder nach dem Objekt fragen.

! Beachte bei der Fragebildung die **S-V-(O)-Regel**.

Wenn das **Fragewort** nach dem **Subjekt** *(wer?/was?)* fragt, **folgt direkt das Vollverb – nie ~~do~~/~~does~~/~~did~~ als Hilfsverb**.

Wenn das **Fragewort** nach dem **Objekt** fragt *(wen?/wem?/was?)*, **folgt *do/does/did***.

! Das Hauptverb steht in der Grundform (Infinitiv).

LF 17 Questions with the passive and with modals

(Fragen im Passiv und mit Modalverben)

Fragen im Passiv

question word	form of *be*	subject	*past participle*	
	Is	Ben	called	*Benny* by his fans?
	Was	he	invited	to a party?
When	were	you	born,	Ben?
Why	isn't	your team	supported	by sponsors?

Da du das Passiv mit ***be + past participle*** bildest, beginnst du *Ja-/Nein*-Fragen mit der Form von ***be***, die hier Hilfsverb ist.

Bei Fragen mit **Fragewort** steht die Form von ***be* zwischen** Fragewort und Subjekt.

Fragen mit Modalverben

question word	*modal verb*	subject	(main) verb	
	Can	Ben	meet	Li on Friday?
	May	she	go	to a party then?
	Should	Li	ask	her parents?
When	will	Ben and Li	meet?	
What else	must	Ben	prepare	for the party?

Ja-/Nein-Fragen mit ***modals*** beginnen mit dem **Modalverb**.

Bei Fragen mit **Fragewort** steht das ***modal* zwischen** Fragewort und Subjekt.

LF 18 NEW *Questions with prepositions (Fragen mit Fragewörtern und Präpositionen)

Ben waved goodbye to his team. Then he walked with Li to her house.

Ben and Li spent the afternoon with Li's family. They laughed at her mum's funny stories.

Now they are looking forward to next weekend. They're waiting for a visitor from Germany.

Who did Ben wave goodbye **to**?
 Wem winkte Ben zum Abschied **zu**?

Who did he walk **with**?
 Mit wem ging er spazieren?

Who did Ben and Li spend the afternoon **with**?
 Mit wem verbrachten … den Nachmittag?

What did they laugh **at**?
 Worüber haben sie gelacht/lachten sie?

What are they looking **forward to**?
 Worauf freuen sie sich?

Who / What are they waiting **for**?
 Auf wen / Worauf warten sie?

Präpositionen, z.B. *after, at, for, from, in, of, on, to* stehen **vor Nomen** oder **Pronomen**.

Es gibt auch viele typische **Wendungen** (Verb + Präposition), z.B. *look at, wait for, be afraid of, wave to, …* .

Wenn du **Fragen mit Präpositionen** bildest, stehen die **Fragewörter** *Who/What* **am Anfang**, die **Präpositionen** stehen häufig **am Ende der Frage**.

! Im Deutschen stehen die Präpositionen meist vor dem Fragewort, z.B.
*Mit **wem** spielst du gern?* → **Who** do you like to play **with**?

Häufig gibt es im Deutschen besondere Fragewörter, z.B.
Womit *spielst du gern?* → **What** do you like to play **with**?

LF 19 The comparison of adjectives (Die Steigerung der Adjektive)

The comparison with *-er / -est* and *more / most*

Wenn du Personen oder Dinge vergleichst, benutzt du Steigerungsformen.
Mit der 1. Steigerungsform + ***than*** („als") vergleichst du zwei **unterschiedliche** Personen oder Dinge.

Ben thinks English is hard, but maths is harder than English. But today French seems to be the hardest of all.

Bei **kurzen** (einsilbigen) Adjektiven und bei Adjektiven mit der Endung -***y*** hängst du für die Steigerung *-er* und *-est* an das Adjektiv:

cheap	*cheaper*	*(the) cheapest*

Li prefers a big bowl of ice cream – the biggest she can get.
But she doesn't have enough money for the most expensive one.

Bei **längeren** (zwei- oder dreisilbigen) Adjektiven stellst du ***more*** und ***most*** *vor* das Adjektiv:

expensive	*more expensive*	*(the) most expensive*

Chocolate looks good, it's better than vanilla.
It's the best – and it's cheap too.

! Merke dir die **unregelmäßig** gesteigerten Adjektive, z.B.:

good	*better*	*(the) best*
much/many	*more*	*(the) most*

The comparison with *as … as*

Li doesn't think that ice cream is unhealthy.
It's as healthy as all the other things on the menu.

Mit dem Vergleich (***not***) ***as*** … ***as*** … kannst du ausdrücken, dass zwei Personen oder Dinge gleich (oder nicht gleich) sind.

LF 20 Adverbs of manner (Adverbien der Art und Weise)

Adjektive beschreiben **Nomen** näher. *Li was a happy girl after the basketball match.*

Adverbien der Art und Weise beschreiben **Verben** näher. *Li walked home happily.*

Adverbien der Art und Weise stehen nach dem Verb, oft am Satzende:

Li's morning was going terribly.
*(**Wie** lief der Morgen für Li? – Schrecklich.)*

She couldn't find her ticket and looked for it very carefully, but still couldn't find it.
She left the house angrily.

Then she ran to school fast.
She worked very hard in maths that day.
In the evening her team played well.

So Li walked home happily. She felt good in the end.

Du bildest ein Adverb der Art und Weise meist durch Anhängen von *-ly* an das Adjektiv.

! Merke dir **unregelmäßige** Adverbformen:

Adjektiv	**Adverb**
*Li is a **fast** runner.*	*Li ran **fast**.*
*She had a **hard** day at school.*	*She worked **hard** in class.*
*But she was **good** at sport.*	*She played **well**.*

! Nach Verben der Sinneswahrnehmung *feel, look, sound, taste, smell* folgt **kein** Adverb, sondern ein Adjektiv.

LF 21 Adverbs of frequency (Adverbien der Häufigkeit)

Diese drücken aus, wie häufig jemand etwas tut oder wie häufig etwas geschieht: *always, usually, often, sometimes, never*. (Zur Wortstellung in Sätzen ▸ *LF 15–16*)

Hi Li,
How's life back home? I sometimes wish you were here. LA is always so exciting! I've never seen a place like this before.
I don't often check my emails as there's a lot of work to do in my uncle's cafe.
...

Adverbien der Häufigkeit stehen:

- nach ***be***:
  *LA **is** always exciting for tourists.*
- vor einem Vollverb:
  *I sometimes **wish** you were here.*
- bei zusammengesetzten Verbformen nach dem Hilfsverb (*don't, have, ...*):
  *I **don't** often **check** my emails.*

LF 22 The comparison of adverbs (Die Steigerung der Adverbien)

Du kannst auch Adverbien steigern. Du bildest die zwei Steigerungsformen wie bei Adjektiven. ▸ *LF 19*

Ben spoke more slowly to help the new exchange student understand.
Of all the students, Ben was the most friendly to Moritz.
Everyone was fast, but Li was the fastest.

Adverbien, die auf *-**ly*** enden, steigerst du mit ***more*/*most***, z.B.

slowly — *more slowly* — *(the) most slowly*

Einsilbige Adverbien werden mit *-er*/*-est* gesteigert:

fast — *faster* — *(the) fastest*

The race went well, much better than Li had expected.

! Beachte:

well — *better* — *(the) best*

LF 23 Indirect speech (Indirekte Rede)

Direct speech (Direkte Rede)

Mia says, "I like my new friend Kai."

Mia sagt: „Ich mag meinen neuen Freund Kai."

Indirect speech (Indirekte Rede)

Mia says _ (that) she likes her new friend Kai.

Mia sagt, dass sie ihren neuen Freund Kai mag.

! Im Englischen steht vor der indirekten Rede **kein** Komma, und *that* („dass") wird oft weggelassen.

Mit der **direkten Rede** gibst du ***wörtlich*** wieder, was jemand sagt, schreibt oder denkt (bzw. gesagt/geschrieben/gedacht hat).

Mit der **indirekten Rede berichtest** du, was jemand sagt/schreibt/denkt. Einleitende Verben sind z.B.: *say, tell, add, answer, think, explain*.

! Achte bei der **indirekten Rede** darauf, dass sich Personen, Pronomen, Verbformen sowie Orts- und Zeitangaben ändern:
"I like my new friend." → ... she likes her new friend.
"We are going to meet here again tonight." → (retold two days later) They were going to meet there again that night.

Indirect speech: backshift in statements (Indirekte Rede: *backshift* in Aussagen)

Mia said_ (that) she liked Kai.

Mia sagte, dass sie Kai mag/gut finden würde.

She told Kai her name was Mia and she hadn't been to that club before.

Sie sagte (zu) Kai, ihr Name sei/wäre Mia und sie wäre noch nie in diesem Club gewesen.

Mia: "I'm 16. I live in Braxton."

→ Kai to Dan: "Mia told me she's (*was*) 16. And she lives (*lived*) in Braxton."

Steht das einleitende Verb im ***simple past***, z.B. *said, told, added, answered, thought, explained*, verschiebt sich auch die Zeitform des Verbs der ursprünglichen Aussage meist ins ***simple past*** oder ins ***past perfect*** (letzteres häufiger in der Schriftsprache).
Dieses (Rück-)Verschieben in die Vergangenheit heißt auf Englisch ***backshift*** *(of tenses)*.
In der **Umgangssprache** wendet man den ***backshift*** (*of tenses*) bei immer noch gültigen (oder allgemeinen) Tatsachen **nicht immer** an.

Indirect speech: questions (Indirekte Rede: Fragen)

Dan asked Mia, "Where do you live?"

→ Dan asked Mia_where she lived.

Dan fragte Mia, wo sie wohnt/wohne/wohnte.

He also asked, "How did you get here?"

→ He also wanted to know how she had got there.

Er wollte auch wissen, wie sie hergekommen war.

Mia asked, "How often are you at this club?"

→ Mia asked how often he was at that club.

... wie oft er ... sei/wäre/sein würde.

Bei der Wiedergabe von **Fragen in indirekter Rede** musst du die **gleichen Regeln** wie bei Aussagen beachten:
- Personen, Pronomen, Verbformen sowie Orts- und Zeitangaben können sich ändern.
- Steht das **einleitende Verb** im ***simple past***, (rück)verschiebt sich auch hier die Zeitform des Verbs (***backshift***).

! Wie im Deutschen steht **am Ende** einer indirekten Frage **kein Fragezeichen**, sondern ein **Punkt**.

Fragewörter werden übernommen, jedoch entspricht die Wortstellung im Nebensatz jetzt Aussagesätzen, vgl. ... *where ~~do/does/did~~ she lived.* -> ***subject*** – ***verb***: **S-V-(O)** ► *LF 15*

Dan asked Mia, "Do you like our music?"

→ Dan asked Mia_ **if** she liked their music.
Dan fragte Mia, **ob** sie die Musik seiner Band mochte.

Bei ***Ja-/Nein*-Fragen** wird (wie im Deutschen „ob") im Englischen ***if*** (oder *whether)* eingefügt. Auch hier gilt die **Wortstellung** von **Aussagesätzen**: **S-V-(O)**. ▸ *LF 15*

Indirect speech: commands, requests, advice
(Aufforderungen, Bitten, Ratschläge in indirekter Rede)

Ben told Dan, "Go and get us something to drink."
→ Ben told Dan **to** go and get them something to drink.
Ben forderte Dan auf, ihnen etwas zu trinken zu holen.

Aufforderungen, Befehle und **Ratschläge** werden in **indirekter Rede** meist eingeleitet mit: *tell/told sb.* ***to*** *(do sth.)*

And he added, "Don't hurry!"
→ And he told him **not to** hurry.
Und er fügte hinzu, dass er sich nicht zu beeilen brauche/bräuchte.

Bei **Verboten** und **Verneinungen** wird vor dem Infinitiv mit *to* das ***not*** eingeschoben:
tell/told sb. ***not to*** *(do sth.)*
bzw. *ask/asked sb.* ***not to*** *(do sth.)*

Ben told Mia, "You shouldn't listen to Dan."
→ Ben told Mia not to listen to Dan.
Ben empfahl Mia, Dan nicht zuzuhören.

Ben said to Mia, "Please, don't trust that boy."
→ Ben asked Mia not to trust that boy.
Ben bat Mia, dem Jungen nicht zu trauen.

Bitten werden in **indirekter Rede** meist eingeleitet mit: *ask/asked sb.* ***to*** *(do sth.)*.

Dan asked her, "Can you give me your address, please?"
→ Dan asked her to give him her address.
Dan bat sie, ihm ihre Adresse zu geben.

Indirect speech: More on backshift (Indirekte Rede: Weiteres zum *backshift*)

Den ***backshift of tenses*** – das Rückverschieben in eine andere Zeitstufe in der Vergangenheit – kennst du von der Veränderung ***simple present*** zu **simple past**, wenn der **Einleitungssatz im *simple past*** steht, z.B.
Mia: "I like Dan." → *Later Mia told her best friend (that) she liked Dan.*

Mia: "Dan is a nice guy."
→ Mia told her friend Dan was a nice guy.

Mia: "We met at a music club."
→ Mia told her they had met at a music club.

Mia: "And I've never been there before."
→ Mia added she had never been there before.

She thought, "Next Saturday I'll meet him again."
→ She thought she would meet him again the following Saturday.

"And maybe I can learn more about their songs."
→ (And) Maybe she could learn more about their songs.

!
simple present *(is)* wird ***simple past*** *(was)*

simple past *(met)* wird ***past perfect*** *(had met)*

present perfect *(have been)* wird ebenfalls ***past perfect*** *(had been)*

> ***will (future)*** *(will meet)* wird ***would*** *(would meet)*

> ***can*** *(can learn)* wird ***could*** *(could learn)*

LF 24 Modal verbs and their substitutes

(Modalverben und ihre Ersatzformen)

Modal verbs (modale Hilfsverben) sind z.B. *can, must, should* und ihre Verneinungen. Du benutzt sie, um auszudrücken, was jemand **kann**, **darf**, **muss**, **soll** oder **nicht kann** usw.

Coach said, "You may leave earlier tonight."
Great! Ben could go to the party and meet Li.
Der Trainer sagte: „Du darfst ...". Ben war ..., weil er ... konnte.

Modal verbs haben nur eine Form, z.B. *can*, *must* oder *may* für alle Personen, d.h. kein *-s* bei *he/she/it*.

He added that Ben shouldn't forget the match next week. "Well, should I stay then?", Ben thought.
... dass Ben ... nicht vergessen sollte. „Hhm, soll ich ...?"

Die **Verneinung** und die **Frage** werden **ohne** ~~do/does/did~~ gebildet.

"Can/May I borrow your black dress for the party, please?" Li asked her mum.
- "Yes, you can/may./No, you can't/may not."
„Darf ich ... - „Ja, du darfst./Nein, du darfst nicht."

Modal verbs stehen nur in Kurzantworten allein.

Li to Mia: "I'm sorry, I must go now. I have got to pick up mum's black dress from the dry-cleaner's. I'm allowed to wear it to the party!"
"I wasn't able to do it yesterday. I had to prepare the maths test today."

Modal verbs haben nur eine ***simple present***-Form. Weitere Zeitformen bildest du **mit anderen Verben** mit ähnlicher Bedeutung:

müssen:	*must*	→ ***have (got) to****
dürfen:	*can/may*	→ ***be allowed to***
können:	*can*	→ ***be able to***

Verneinte Aussagen

You mustn't play in the street.
! Du darfst nicht ...
You don't have/haven't got to play in a team.
You needn't play in a team.
Du musst/brauchst nicht ...

Verneinte Aussagen

You can't You aren't allowed to Du darfst nicht ...	play in the street. play in a team.

Verneinte Aussagen

The team can't The team isn't able to The team is unable to	win the game today.

***Ja-/Nein*-Fragen**

Can/May/Should/Must	I/he practise now?

Mit diesen Verben kannst du **alle Zeitformen** bilden, auch das *simple present*:

müssen
simple present: *must*; *have/has (got) to** (muss)
simple past: *had to* (musste)
future: *will have to* (wird ... müssen)
(**have got to*: umgangssprachlicher; wird inhaltlich wie *have to* verwendet)

dürfen
simple present: *can/may*
oder *am/are/is allowed to* (darf)
simple past: *was/were allowed to* (durfte)
future: *will be allowed to* (wird ... dürfen)

können (fähig sein)
simple present: *can*; *am/are/is able to* (kann)
simple past: *could*; *was/were able to* (konnte)
future: *will be able to* (wird ... können)

Ja-/*Nein*-Fragen (Forts.)		
Do/Did I/you/they Does/Did he/she Have you/Has she	have to got to	practise hard?

Am/Are/Is ... Was/Were ... Will ... be	allowed to ...? able to ...?

Kurzantworten	
Yes, you ... can / may / should / must. Yes, you ... do / did. Yes, you ... are. Yes, you ... was. Yes, you ... will.	No, you can't / may not / shouldn't / don't have to. No, you don't / didn't. No, you aren't. No, you wasn't. No, you won't.

LF 25 *If* ... (Conditional sentences type 1) (Bedingungssätze Typ 1)

Mit ***if***-Sätzen (Bedingungssätzen Typ 1) sagst du, was unter bestimmten Bedingungen geschieht oder geschehen wird: „**Was ist, wenn ...**"

Nebensatz

If Mia's team plays well next time,

Hauptsatz

they'll win the summer contest.

Wenn Mias Team nächstes Mal gut spielt, werden sie den Sommer-Wettbewerb gewinnen.

Bedingungssätze bestehen aus zwei Teilsätzen:

Die **Bedingung** wird im ***if***-Satz (Nebensatz) genannt. Das Verb steht im ***simple present***:

*If they **play** ...,*

Their team will only finish in second place _ if they don't fight hard.

Ihr Team wird nur Zweiter sein, wenn sie nicht kämpfen.

Die **Folge für die Zukunft** steht im **Hauptsatz**. Hier steht meist das ***will-future***:

*... they **will** ...*

▸ LF 10

= If they don't fight hard, their team will only finish in second place.

Wenn sie nicht kämpfen, wird ihr Team nur Zweiter sein.

Der ***if***-Teil kann am Anfang oder am Ende stehen.

! Anders als im Deutschen setzt man **kein Komma**, wenn der ***if***-Teil am **Ende** steht.

"I'll ask the coach for her advice when I see her."

... wenn ich sie sehe.

(Es steht fest, dass Mia die Trainerin trifft. Dann fragt sie.)

! Nicht verwechseln:

- ***when*** bedeutet „sobald wie", „dann, wenn"
- ***if*** bedeutet „wenn", „falls"

"I'll ask the coach for her advice if I see her."

... falls ich sie sehe. *(Es ist unsicher, ob sie sich treffen.)*

If you need advice, you **can/should** ask the coach.

Wenn ihr Rat braucht, könnt ihr /solltet ihr die Trainerin fragen.

Im **Hauptsatz** können auch stehen:

- *can, must, should* + Infinitiv

▸ LF 24

Please **phone** me if you want to talk to me.

Bitte ruft mich an, wenn ihr ... wollt.

- oder eine Aufforderung bzw. Bitte (ein **Imperativ**).

LF 26 *If* … (Conditional sentences type 2) (Bedingungssätze Typ 2)

Mit Bedingungssätzen Typ 2 sagst du, was unter unwahrscheinlichen oder unsicheren Bedingungen geschehen würde: **„Was wäre, wenn …"**

Nebensatz
If Ben had enough money,
Hauptsatz
he'd travel everywhere.
Wenn Ben genug Geld hätte, würde er …

Hauptsatz
But Li wouldn't travel
Nebensatz
even if she won a trip around the world.
Aber Li würde nicht reisen, selbst/sogar wenn sie … gewinnen würde.

If you were on a world trip, you **could** forget about school.
Wenn du auf … wärst, könntest du … vergessen.

Da die **Bedingung** im ***if***-Satz unwahrscheinlich ist (hier: genug Geld), ist unsicher, ob die **Folge** im **Hauptsatz** (hier: das Reisen überall hin) Wirklichkeit wird.
Im Deutschen verwendet man hier oft ***würde/wäre/hätte***.

Auch ***if***-Sätze Typ 2 bestehen wie ***if***-Sätze Typ 1 aus zwei Teilsätzen: ▸ *LF 25*

Die (unwahrscheinliche) **Bedingung** steht im ***if***-Satz. Das Verb steht im ***simple past***, z.B. *had, won*.

Die (unsichere) **Folge** steht im **Hauptsatz**. Dort benutzt du *would* (Kurzform *'d*) bzw. für die Verneinung *wouldn't* + Infinitiv.

! Auch bei Typ 2 kein Komma vor dem ***if***-Teil.
Im **Hauptsatz** kann auch *could* + Infinitiv stehen.

Forms of *would*

Bejahte und verneinte Aussagen

I/You/He/… We/…	'd/would/wouldn't	travel …

Ben would travel everywhere if he could, but Li wouldn't come with him.

***Ja-/Nein*-Fragen mit Kurzantworten**

Would I/he/we/…	travel …	Yes, … would. No, … wouldn't.

Would you go on a trip around the world if you had the chance? – Yes, you would.

Fragen mit Fragewort

Where/How/… would I/you/he/… …?

Where would you travel first – to the US or to South Africa?

LF 27 *If* … (Conditional sentences type 3) (Bedingungssätze Typ 3)

Mit Bedingungssätzen Typ 3 **stellst du dir vor**, was **in der Vergangenheit** unter bestimmten Bedingungen hätte geschehen können: **„Was wäre gewesen, wenn …"**

Nebensatz
If it had been warmer yesterday,
Hauptsatz
Li would have gone to the beach.
Wenn es gestern wärmer gewesen wäre, wäre Li zum Strand gegangen. *(Es war aber nicht wärmer, und Li war nicht am Strand.)*

Da die **Bedingung** im ***if***-Satz **nicht erfüllt** ist, können über die **Folge** im **Hauptsatz** nur Vermutungen angestellt werden.

Im Deutschen verwendet man oft ***wäre*** *gewesen/gegangen/…* oder ***hätte*** *gehabt/gegeben* oder auch ***würde*** gewesen sein/gehabt haben.

Hauptsatz
Li would have phoned Mia
Nebensatz
if she had had her new number.

Li hätte Mia (ja) angerufen, wenn sie deren neue Telefonnummer gehabt hätte. *(Aber sie kannte sie nicht oder hatte sie verlegt.)*

Die (nicht erfüllte) **Bedingung** steht im ***if*-Satz**. Das Verb steht im ***past perfect*** z.B. *had been, had had, had helped.*

Die (vermutete) **Folge** steht im **Hauptsatz**. Dort benutzt du ***would/wouldn't*** + ***have past participle*** (3. Form).

! Auch hier steht kein Komma vor dem ***if***-Teil.

If Li had asked Mia's brother Ben, he could have helped her. ... hätte er ihr helfen können.

Im **Hauptsatz** kann auch ***could*** + ***have past participle*** stehen.

If she'd asked Ben, he'd have given her Mia's number. ... gefragt hätte, hätte er ihr ... gegeben.

! Die **Kurzform** von ***would*** und von ***had*** ist ***'d***:
he'd (= he would) have given.
she'd (= she had) asked.

LF 28 Relative clauses (Relativsätze)

Someone who/that uses social media often has several profile pictures.

Li prefers pictures that/which are creative.

Mit Relativsätzen sagst du genauer, **wen** oder **was** du meinst. Sie werden eingeleitet mit den Relativpronomen

- ***who*** oder ***that*** für **Personen** und
- ***which*** oder ***that*** für **Dinge**.

! Relativsätze, die Personen oder Dinge näher bestimmen, stehen **ohne Komma** (anders als im Deutschen: Jemand, der ... / Bilder, die ...).

*Defining and non-defining relative clauses (Bestimmende und nicht bestimmende Relativsätze)

▸ *Unit 1, p. 108*

Im Englischen unterscheidet man **bestimmende** und **nicht bestimmende** Relativsätze.

Ben chose the photo _ that Li took.
(Ohne den Relativsatz *that Li took* wüsste man nicht, welches Foto gemeint ist.)

Bestimmende Relativsätze (***defining relative clauses***) sind **notwendig** dafür, dass man den Satz versteht und weiß, wer/was genau gemeint ist.

! ***Defining relative clauses*** stehen **ohne Komma**.

This photo**,** which was taken by Li**,** shows Ben on his bike. (Auch ohne den Relativsatz ist klar, was das Foto zeigt, also welches Foto genau gemeint ist.)

Li used a drone for the photo, which was really exciting. (Zusätzliche Bewertung, die sich auf den gesamten vorangehenden Satz bezieht.)

Mia**, who** is Ben's sister**,** doesn't like drones. Li**, whose** best friend Mia is**,** owns a drone**, which** she isn't allowed to use in Mia's garden.

Nicht bestimmende Relativsätze (***non-defining relative clauses***) geben **Zusatz**informationen, die man nicht unbedingt braucht, um zu wissen, von welcher Person/Sache die Rede ist. Man findet sie häufiger in geschriebenem Englisch.

! ***Non-defining relative clauses*** werden **mit Komma** abgetrennt.

! Es können nur die Relativprononomen ***who***, ***which*** und ***whose*** („dessen/deren") verwendet werden, nicht aber ~~***that***~~.

! In ***non-defining relative clauses*** darf das Relativpronomen nie weggelassen werden.

▸ *LF 29*

LF 29 Contact clauses (Relativsätze ohne Relativpronomen)

Objekt **Subjekt** des Relativsatzes

That's the girl ~~*who*~~ **I** chatted with yesterday.

Das ist das Mädchen, mit **dem** ich …

Objekt **Subjekt** des Relativsatzes

These are the pictures ~~*that*~~ **our friends** shared the most.

Das sind die Bilder, **die** unsere Freunde am häufigsten teilten.

Subjekt des Relativsatzes

That's the girl **who** chatted with me yesterday.

Das ist das Mädchen, **das** gestern … hat.

Subjekt des Relativsatzes

These are the pictures **that** were shared the most.

Das sind die Bilder, **die** am häufigsten … wurden.

Relativsätze **ohne** *who/that* heißen ***contact clauses***.
Wenn **nach** dem Relativpronomen (*who/that*) ein Pronomen oder Nomen folgt und vor dem Verb steht, darfst du *who/that* **weglassen**. (Denn hier ist das Relativpronomen **Objekt** des Relativsatzes und zum Verständnis nicht unbedingt notwendig.)

! Wenn das Relativpronomen (*who/that*) **direkt vor dem Verb** im Relativsatz steht, darfst du es **nicht** weglassen (weil es hier das **Subjekt** des Relativsatzes ist).

LF 30 *Participle clauses instead of subordinate clauses (Partizipialsätze anstelle von Nebensätzen)

(1) Walking down the street, Ben noticed a broken shop window.
(1a) **While** he was walking down the street, Ben noticed a broken shop window.
(1b) ***Während*** *er … entlang ging, bemerkte Ben …*

(2) Seeing two men near a van, he decided to watch them.
(2a) He saw two men near a van **and** decided to …
(2b) *Er sah zwei Männer nahe bei …* ***und*** *beschloss, …*

(3) Ben shouted loudly, expecting some sort of crime.
(3a) Ben shouted loudly **because** he expected … crime.
(3b) *Ben rief laut,* ***weil*** *er … Verbrechen erwartete.*

(4) Having noticed Ben, the men laughed, "It's OK. We're here to put in a new window."
(4a) **When** they had noticed Ben, the men laughed, "…
(4b) ***Als*** *sie Ben bemerkt hatten, lachten die Männer: „…*

(5) The men working at the window talked to Ben.
(5a) The men **who** were working … talked to Ben.
(5b) *Die Männer,* ***die*** *gerade …, sprachen mit Ben.*

Zur Verkürzung langer Sätze kann man **Partizipialsätze** verwenden. Sie enthalten Formen des Partizips:
- ***present participle***: ***verb*** + ***-ing***
- ***past participle***: ***verb*** + ***-ed*** (regelmäßige Verben; **!** <u>**un**</u>regelmäßige Verben ▸ *pp. 273–274*)

Im Englischen können Partizipialsätze anstelle eines (längeren) Nebensatzes stehen, vergleiche 1 und 1a. Im Deutschen braucht man aber immer den vollständigen Nebensatz (1b).

Partizipialsätze können u.a. **ersetzen**:
- **Nebensätze der <u>Zeit</u>** (oft bei Gleichzeitigkeit), die mit ***while***, ***when*** beginnen (1 ersetzt 1a).
- zwei **Hauptsätze**, die mit ***and*** verbunden wären (2 ersetzt 2a).
- **<u>begründende</u> Nebensätze**, die mit ***because***, ***as*** beginnen (3 ersetzt 3a).
- **Nebensätze**, die eine **<u>Folge</u>** ausdrücken (4 ersetzt 4a).
- **<u>Relativsätze</u>**, die beschreiben, was gerade vor sich geht (***present progressive***) oder ging (***past progressive***) (5 ersetzt 5a).

LF 31 Reflexive pronouns (Reflexivpronomen)

I ask myself how we can enjoy ourselves this evening.
Ich frage mich, wie wir uns heute Abend amüsieren können.

I think your little sister is old enough to look after herself.
Ich finde, deine …, auf sich selbst aufzupassen.

Reflexivpronomen (***myself***, ***yourself***, ***ourselves***, …) beziehen sich auf das Subjekt:
(*I* – ***myself***, *you* – ***yourself***, *people* – ***themselves***):

Subjekt		Reflexivpronomen
I	*asked*	***myself*** …
We	*can enjoy*	***ourselves***.
Your sister	*can look after*	***herself***.

Reflexive pronouns

(I)	myself	(ich)	mir/mich
(you)	yourself	(du)	dir/dich
(he)	himself	(er)	sich
(she)	herself	(sie)	sich
(it)	itself	(er/sie/es)	sich

(we)	ourselves	(wir) uns
(you)	yourselves	(ihr) euch
(they)	themselves	(sie) sich

! Den Plural bildest du mit ***-selves***.

! Es gibt Verben, die im Deutschen reflexiv sind, im Englischen jedoch nicht. Das „sich, mich, mir, dir" usw. wird nicht übersetzt, z.B.:

		Beispiele:	
(to) feel	sich fühlen	*He doesn't feel well.*	Er fühlt sich nicht gut.
(to) hide	sich verstecken	*Let's hide!*	Verstecken wir uns!
(to) imagine	sich etwas vorstellen	*I can imagine that.*	Das kann ich mir vorstellen.
(to) look forward to sth.	sich auf etwas freuen	*I'm looking forward to it.*	Ich freue mich darauf.
(to) meet	sich treffen	*Let's meet at six!*	Treffen wir uns um sechs!
(to) remember	sich an etwas erinnern	*I don't remember.*	Ich erinnere mich nicht.
(to) wonder	sich fragen	*I wonder if …*	Ich frage mich, ob …
(to) worry	sich Sorgen machen	*Don't worry.*	Mach dir keine Sorgen.

LF 32 The *-ing*-form (the gerund) (Die *-ing*-Form bzw. das Gerundium)

Du kannst von vielen Verben eine ***-ing*-Form** bilden, etwa für die Verlaufsform (*present progressive*), z.B. *Li is driving to school in her own car today.* ▸ *LF 2*

Driving a car is cool.
(Das) **Autofahren** ist cool./Ein Auto **zu fahren**, ist *cool*.

I love driving a car.
Ich liebe das **Autofahren**./Ich liebe es, **Auto zu fahren**.

Als ***gerund*** bezeichnet man die *-ing*-Form, wenn sie als **Nomen** verwendet wird, hier z.B. als **Subjekt** oder **Objekt**:

Sport is cool. ◂▸ ***Driving*** *is cool.* **(Subjekt des Satzes)**

I love sport. ◂▸ *I love* ***driving***. **(Objekt des Satzes)**

Im Deutschen wird das ***gerund*** oft durch einen Infinitiv mit „zu" wiedergegeben.

I enjoy **helping** people. So I keep **working** with kids. I'd miss **teaching** them music.

Die ***-ing*-Form** (***gerund***) folgt oft auf bestimmte **Verben** als **Objekt**, z.B. *(dis-)like, enjoy, hate, keep, miss, start, finish, …*

I prefer **learning** languages. (or: *I prefer **to** learn languages.*)
I'll start **learning** German next term.
(or: *I'll start **to** learn German …*)

! Nach *like/love/hate/prefer/start/begin* kann auch ***to*** **+ Infinitiv** *folgen:*
love/like to play *hate to learn* *begin/start to sing*

! Nach einigen Verben – z. B. *enjoy, finish, imagine, mind, miss, practise, suggest* – muss die ***-ing*-Form** (***gerund***) verwendet werden, nie ***to*** **+ Infinitiv**.

I'm good at **playing** basketball. Our team is looking forward to **playing** against Boston City. We've always dreamed of **winning** against them.

Die ***-ing*-Form** (***gerund***) folgt nach **Präpositionen:** *at, about, after, for, in, of, to.*

! Es gibt einige **Wendungen**, denen das ***gerund*** **folgen muss**, z.B.:
- *dream of/about …ing*
- *(be) good/bad at …ing*
- *(be) interested in …ing*
- *get used to …ing*
- *look forward to …ing*

*-*ing*-form (gerund) or *to*-infinitive? (Gerundium oder *to*-Infinitiv?)

Ben: I enjoy **chatting** with people.

Das ***gerund*** **(*-ing*-Form)** folgt meist nach bestimmten Verben als **Objekt**, z.B. *(dis-)like, enjoy, hate, start, …*

I want **to tell** them everything.

Nach **bestimmten Verben** darfst du **nur** den ***to*-Infinitiv** verwenden, z.B. *want to, would like to, need to, hope to …*

Li prefers **meeting** people. She prefers **to meet** them in real life.

Nach bestimmten Verben kannst du das ***gerund*** oder den ***to*-Infinitiv** verwenden. Die **Bedeutung** ändert sich **nicht**, z.B. bei *like, love, hate prefer, start, begin*.

"Stop **chatting** all day long."
Hör auf, … zu chatten.

! **Unterschiedliche Bedeutungen** hat die Verwendung von ***gerund*** oder ***to*-Infinitiv** nach diesen Verben:

stop + *gerund* ◂ mit etwas aufhören (… es zu tun)
stop + *to …* ◂ aufhören/anhalten, um etwas anders zu tun
forget + *gerund* ◂ vergessen, was man (früher mal) getan hat
forget + *to …* ◂ vergessen, was später (noch) zu tun ist
remember + *gerund* ◂ sich erinnern, was man mal getan hat
remember + *to …* ◂ daran denken, etwas (noch) zu tun

At the door Ben stopped **to check** his emails. … blieb Ben stehen, **um** seine …

I'll never forget **skiing** for the first time.
Ich werde nie vergessen, wie ich …

Oh, I won't forget **to send** you the photos.
… werde nicht vergessen, dir die Fotos …

Mum remembers **buying** her first mobile.
… erinnert sich, dass/wie sie … hat.

Will dad remember **to give** me his headphones? … daran denken, dass er …?

LF 33 The passive (Das Passiv)

Advertising companies make all sorts of ads.
Werbefirmen machen alle Arten von Werbung.

Special ads are made to target teens only.
... Werbung wird gemacht, nur um auf Teens abzuzielen.

"I'm often asked how much money is spent on ads."
Ich werde oft gefragt, ... ausgegeben wird.

Of course, ads aren't made for teens only.
Natürlich wird Werbung nicht nur ... produziert.

Yesterday a new tablet was presented on TV.
Gestern wurde ein neues Tablet ...präsentiert.

Years ago ads for cigarettes were shown everywhere.
Vor Jahren wurde noch Werbung ... überall gezeigt.

Slogans are often repeated in ads.
Man wiederholt oft Slogans in der Werbung.

The song in this ad was first sung **by** the *Beatles*.
Das Lied ... wurde zuerst von ... gesungen.

New tablet presented yesterday

Mit einem **Aktivsatz** sagst du, wer oder was etwas tut. Das Subjekt des Aktivsatzes führt die Handlung aus.

Ein **Passivsatz** drückt aus, mit wem oder was (= womit) **etwas geschieht**, oft ohne zu sagen, wer der/die „Verursachende" ist. (Subjekt ist im Passivsatz der, die bzw. das, womit etwas geschieht.)

Du bildest das Passiv mit einer **Form von *be*** und dem ***past participle*** (der **3. Form des Verbs**). ▸ *pp. 272–273*

simple present: *am/are/is* + ***past participle*:**
I'm ***asked*** *...*
how much money is ***spent*** *on ...*

simple past: *was/were* + ***past participle*:**
The street was ***used*** *in ...*
The houses that were ***shown*** *...*

! In vielen Passivsätzen wird ***be*** im Deutschen mit ***werden*** ausgedrückt (*werde, wird, wurdest, wurde, ...*).

! Im Deutschen gibt man englische Passivsätze häufig durch einen Aktivsatz mit „man" wieder:

! Zum Nennen des „Verursachers" verwendet man die Präposition ***by*** (*von/durch*).

In Überschriften und Schlagzeilen entfallen zudem meist die Artikel, die Form von *be* sowie Satzzeichen:
~~A~~ new tablet ~~was~~ presented yesterday~~.~~

*Other forms of the passive

▸ *More challenge 3, pp. 73–74*

Das ***passive*** im ***simple present*** und ***simple past*** kennst du bereits. Passivsätze können auch in anderen Zeitformen, mit Modalverben oder im Infinitiv stehen. Das Passiv bildest du immer mit einer Form von ***be*** + ***past participle***.

present perfect	*All games have been sold.*
past perfect	*I took part in the game because I had been invited.*
going to-future	*The new game is going to be launched in a week.*
will-future* and *modal verbs	*The game will be sold all over the world. It* ***can*** *be downloaded from next week on. It* ***shouldn't*** *be played by kids.*
future perfect	*Millions of new games will have been invented by 2030.*
present progressive	*All sorts of games are being played today.*
past progressive	*The shop was closed. It was being prepared for a games event.*
passive infinitive	*This game is not to be played by children under twelve years.*

*The passive of verbs with two objects (Das Passiv von Verben mit zwei Objekten)

(active) Someone sent **her** a photo.

personal object — thing object

subject

(passive) **She** was sent a photo.
(**Ihr** wurde … geschickt.)

We were paid a lot of money for our new game.
(**Uns** wurde … bezahlt. / Wir bekamen … / Man zahlte uns …)

He will be given a prize for inventing this game.
(**Ihm** wird ein Preis für … gegeben werden. / Er wird einen Preis für … bekommen / Man wird ihm einen Preis für … geben.)

Students are supposed to work hard.
(Von Studenten wird hartes Arbeiten erwartet. / Von Studenten wird erwartet, dass sie hart arbeiten. / … erwartet, hart zu arbeiten.)

What are we supposed to do?
(Was erwartet man von uns? / Was sollen wir tun?)

Manche Verben können **zwei Objekte** haben, z.B. *give / lend / offer / pay / promise / send / show / tell **somebody something***.
(**jemandem etwas** geben / leihen / anbieten / bezahlen / versprechen / schicken / zeigen / erzählen)

Englische Passivsätze mit diesen Verben beginnen meist mit der Person (die vom indirekten Objekt des Aktivsatzes zum Subjekt des Passivsatzes wird).

Deshalb heißt diese Form auch ***personal passive*** („persönliches Passiv"). Im Deutschen gibt es keine direkte Entsprechung dafür. Hier bleibt die Person Objekt des Passivsatzes (und steht im Dativ): **Ihr** wurde … geschickt. (Wem …?)

Man kann aber auch andere deutsche Formulierungen benutzen, z.B.: Man schickte ihr … / Sie erhielt …

Ähnlich wie das ***personal passive*** funktioniert auch die englische Wendung ***be supposed to*** (*do something*), mit der man Erwartungen oder Verpflichtungen ausdrückt.

*The passive with prepositional verbs (Das Passiv von Verben mit Präpositionen)

(active) Everybody is talking **about** them.

verb form + **preposition** — object

(passive) **They** are being talked **about**.

subject — verb form + **preposition**
(Über sie wird geredet.)

Auch von vielen Verben, die fest mit einer Präposition verbunden sind (***prepositional verbs***), kann man das Passiv bilden, z.B.: *listen to / look at / look after / shout at / talk about / think of*.
Wie im Aktivsatz folgt auch im Passiv die Präposition direkt nach dem Verb.

LF 34 Question tags (Frageanhängsel)

Question tags werden im Englischen **in Gesprächen** oft verwendet. Diese Frageanhängsel an Aussagesätze benutzt man, um **Zustimmung** beim Gesprächspartner zu erreichen.
Sie werden aber auch verwendet als „echte" **Nachfrage**, wenn man unsicher ist.

Im Deutschen kennen wir „…, nicht wahr?" oder „…, nicht?" bzw. auch „ne?/ gell?/woll?/ja?/oder? /…?".

Look, **it's** a nice day today, **isn't** it? … nicht wahr?

You and I **can** go swimming, **can't** we? … oder?

And Ben **will** come too, **won't** he? … ja?

Im Englischen muss das Frageanhängsel aber jeweils unter **Rückbezug** auf das **(Modal-) Verb** und **die Person** des Aussagesatzes neu gebildet werden.

Wenn der **Aussagesatz bejaht** ist, wird das **Frageanhängsel verneint**.
Das Personalpronomen steht wie in einer Frage hinten.

The weather **wasn't** fine last week, **was** it?
But we **can't** expect too much, **can** we?

Wenn der **Aussagesatz verneint** ist, wird das **Frageanhängsel bejaht**.

The bus to the beach **leaves** at 4 pm, **doesn't** it?
You **didn't repair** your bike, **did** you?
And you **don't want** to walk there, **do** you?

Vollverben werden im Frageanhängsel durch *do/does* im ***simple present*** bzw. *did* im ***simple past*** ersetzt.

I'm your best friend, **aren't** I?

Das **verneinende *question tag*** für *I'm …* lautet ***aren't** I …?*.

LF 35 The definite and the indefinite article

(Der bestimmte und der unbestimmte Artikel)

Der bestimmte Artikel **the** entfällt, wenn ein Nomen ganz allgemein gebraucht wird.

Life here is sometimes hard.

Solche allgemein gebrauchten Nomen sind oft
- **abstrakte Begriffe** wie *life*, *history*, *nature*, *traffic*
- **Stoffbezeichnungen** wie *food*, *oil*, *water*, *air*
- **Nomen im Plural** wie *schools*, *students*, *people*

Wenn diese Nomen aber **näher bestimmt** sind, stehen sie **mit dem bestimmten Artikel *the***.

The film described the life of a singer.
The digital habits of the teens that you know …

! Der bestimmte Artikel steht im Englischen meist bei **Musikinstrumenten**:

play the piano, the guitar, the drums, …

Du benutzt den **unbestimmten Artikel a /an** im Englischen meist genauso wie im Deutschen.

Besonders zu beachten ist der unbestimmte Artikel aber
- **vor Berufsbezeichnungen** wie a teacher, …
  I'm **a student**. Ich bin Schüler/Schülerin.
- **in Wendungen** wie …
  *be in **a** hurry* es eilig haben
  *have/take **a** bath/shower* baden/duschen
  *have / take **a** look* mal sehen/schauen
- **im Sinne von „pro"** wie bei *a month, a kilo*, …
  *Our car does 70 miles **an hour**.* … pro Stunde.
- **vor vielen Krankheiten** wie *a cold, a headache*, …
  *I've got **a temperature**.* Ich habe Fieber.

Anders als im Deutschen gibt es **Zeitangaben** sowie viele **Ortsangaben** und viele **Wendungen**, in denen **im Englischen kein bestimmter Artikel** steht. Diese musst du wie Vokabeln lernen.

Zeitangaben und Mahlzeiten:	*in May, on Monday, at night, at breakfast, after lunch*	im Mai, am Montag, in der Nacht, zum Frühstück, nach dem Essen
Straßen- und Eigennamen:	*along Main Street, on 14th Street*	entlang der …, in der …
Einrichtungen (allgemein):	*be at school, go to hospital*	in der Schule …, ins Krankenhaus …
Wendungen wie:	*on TV, at work, by bike/car/plane …*	im Fernsehen, bei der Arbeit, mit dem …

LF 36 Countable and uncountable nouns

(Zählbare und nicht zählbare Nomen)

countable nouns
a point — two points
a butterfly — these butterflies

uncountable nouns
advice • butter • damage • equipment • fruit • health • homework • information • meat • money • music • news • plastic • shopping • traffic • work

! Nicht zählbare Nomen haben **keinen Plural** und stehen **nie** mit ***a/an*** oder Zahlwörtern wie ***one/two/three/...*** .

Die meisten Nomen sind **zählbar**, du benutzt sie auch im **Plural**.

Von **nicht zählbaren** Nomen gibt es **keine Pluralform**, z.B. bei Dingen, die meist als **Masse** gesehen werden, wie *water*, *sugar*, *milk*, *wood*, *rice*, *bacon*, *furniture*, ... oder **abstrakten** Begriffen, wie *damage*, *love*, *peace*, ...

Mit Angaben wie *a piece of*, *a kilo of* kannst du die Menge oder Anzahl eines nicht zählbaren Nomens bestimmen, z.B.
two pieces of cake, *ten kilos of meat*, *three litres / bottles of milk*

Für „viel" verwendest du bei nicht zählbaren Nomen neben *a lot of* auch ***much***, z.B. *much homework*, *much fun*, *much money*
Bei zählbaren Nomen heißt es ***many***.

! Anders als im Deutschen sind einige Nomen **nicht zählbar**, d.h. sie haben **keinen Plural**, z.B. *damage*, *homework*, *information*.
I need some information about ... Ich brauche Informationen über ...
That's good news! Das ist eine gute Nachricht! / sind gute Nachrichten!

Grammatical terms (Grammatische Fachbegriffe)

active	['aktɪv]	Aktiv	*Li **went** to the party.*
adjective	['ædʒɪktɪv]	Adjektiv	*good, red, new, boring, ...*
adverb	['advɜːb]	Adverb	*today, there, outside, very, ...*
adverb of frequency	['friːkwənsi]	Häufigkeitsadverb	*always, often, never, ...*
adverb of manner	[ædvɜːb əv 'mænə]	Adverb der Art und Weise	*slowly, happily, well, ...*
article	['ɑːtɪkl]	Artikel	*the, a, an*
auxiliary	[ɔːg'zɪliəri]	Hilfsverb (zur Bildung von Fragesätzen, Zeitformen usw.)	***Did** Ben go to the party?*
backshift of tenses	['bakʃɪft]	Rückverschiebung der Zeitformen	*"I'**m** tired." She said she **was** tired.*
comparative	[kəm'pærətɪv]	Komparativ (1. Steigerungsform)	*older; more expensive*
comparison	[kəm'pærɪsn]	Steigerung	*old – older – oldest*
conditional sentence	[kən'dɪʃənl 'sentəns]	Bedingungssatz	*If we win, we'll go to London.*
contact clause	['kɒntækt klɔːz]	Relativsatz ohne Relativpronomen	*She's the girl **I love**.*
defining relative clause	[dɪ'faɪnɪŋ]	bestimmender Relativsatz	*I like teachers **who laugh a lot**.*
direct speech	[ˌdaɪrekt 'spiːtʃ]	direkte Rede	*"I love my dog."*
future	['fjuːtʃə]	Zukunft, Futur	
gerund	['dʒerənd]	Gerundium, *-ing*-Form	*I like **dancing**.*
***going to*-future**	['gəʊɪŋ tʊ fjuːtʃə]	Futur mit *going to*	***I'm going to stay** at home tonight.*
***if*-clause**	['if klɔːz]	*if*-Satz, Nebensatz mit *if*	***If we meet**, we'll talk.*
imperative	[ɪm'perətɪv]	Imperativ (Befehlsform)	***Open** your books. **Don't** talk.*
indirect speech	[ˌɪndərekt 'spiːtʃ]	indirekte Rede	*She said (that) **she loved her dog**.*
infinitive	[ɪn'fɪnətɪv]	Grundform des Verbs, Infinitiv	*go, open, see, read, ...*
***-ing*-form**		Gerundium, *-ing*-Form	*I like **dancing**.*
irregular verb	[ɪ'regjələ 'vɜːb]	unregelmäßiges Verb	*go – went – gone*
main clause	[ˌmeɪn 'klɔːz]	Hauptsatz	*If we meet, **we'll talk**.*
main verb	[meɪn vɜːb]	Hauptverb	*Did Ben **go** to the party?*

modal verb	[ˌməʊdl ˈvɜːb]	Modalverb, modales Hilfsverb	*can, must, should, may, …*
negative statement	[ˈnegətɪv]	verneinter Aussagesatz	*I don't like oranges.*
noun	[naʊn]	Nomen, Substantiv	*Ben, girl, man, time, name, …*
object	[ˈɒbdʒɪkt]	Objekt	*Ben has* ***an idea****.*
object question		Objektfrage, Frage nach dem Objekt	***Who did*** *Mrs Miller invite to tea?*
participle clause	[ˌpɑːtɪsɪpl ˈklɔːz]	Partizipialsatz	*Li shook her head,* ***laughing out loud****.* ***Warned by her dad****, she escaped.*
passive	[ˈpæsɪv]	Passiv	*Lots of films* ***are made*** *in LA.*
past participle	[pɑːst ˈpɑːtɪsɪpl]	Partizip Perfekt, 3. Form des Verbs	*happened, eaten, gone, …*
past perfect	[ˌpɑːst ˈpɜːfɪkt]	*past perfect* (Vorvergangenheit, Plusquamperfekt)	*I* ***had*** *already* ***gone*** *to bed when they arrived.*
past progressive	[pɑːst prəˈgresɪv]	Verlaufsform der Vergangenheit	*He* ***was playing*** *a drum.*
personal pronoun	[pɜːsənl ˈprəʊnaʊn]	Personalpronomen	*I, you, he, she, it, we, they, …*
plural	[ˈplʊərəl]	Plural, Mehrzahl	*sweets, carrots, sheep, …*
positive statement	[ˈpɒzətɪv]	bejahter Aussagesatz	*I like oranges.*
possessive determiner	[pəˌzesɪv dɪˈtɜːmɪnə]	Possessivbegleiter	*my, your, his, her, its, our, their*
possessive pronoun	[pəˌzesɪv ˈprəʊnaʊn]	Possessivpronomen	*mine, yours, his, hers, ours, theirs*
preposition	[prepəˈzɪʃn]	Präposition	*after, at, in, next to, under, with, …*
present participle	[preznt ˈpɑːtɪsɪpl]	Partizip Präsens	*checking, phoning, trying, planning, going, …*
present perfect	[preznt ˈpɜːfɪkt]	*present perfect*	*He* ***has drunk*** *your water.*
present perfect progressive		Verlaufsform des *present perfect*	*We****'ve been playing*** *for hours.*
present progressive	[preznt prəˈgresɪv]	Verlaufsform der Gegenwart	*They****'re having*** *lunch.*
pronoun	[ˈprəʊnaʊn]	Pronomen, Fürwort	
question	[ˈkwestʃən]	Frage(satz)	*What did you do yesterday?*
question tag	[ˈkwestʃn tag]	Frageanhängsel	*isn't he?, are you?, can't we?, …*
question word	[ˈkwestʃən wɜːd]	Fragewort	*what?, when?, where?, how?, …*
reflexive pronoun	[rɪˌfleksɪv ˈprəʊnaʊn]	Reflexivpronomen	*myself, yourself, himself, …*
regular verb	[ˈregjələ ˈvɜːb]	regelmäßiges Verb	*help – helped – helped*
relative clause	[ˈrelətɪv klɔːz]	Relativsatz	*This is the dog* ***that bit me****.*
relative pronoun	[ˌrelətɪv ˈprəʊnaʊn]	Relativpronomen	*who, that, which, whose*
short answer	[ʃɔːt ˈɑːnsə]	Kurzantwort	*Yes, I am./No, I don't./…*
simple past	[sɪmpl ˈpɑːst]	einfache Form der Vergangenheit	*I* ***loved*** *the holidays.*
simple present	[sɪmpl ˈpreznt]	einfache Form der Gegenwart	*I always* ***go*** *to school by bike.*
singular	[ˈsɪŋgjələ]	Singular, Einzahl	
statement	[ˈsteɪtmənt]	Aussage(satz)	
subject	[ˈsʌbdʒɪkt]	Subjekt	***My dad*** *is working.*
subject question		Subjektfrage	***Who invited*** *Ben?*
subordinate clause (*also*: sub-clause)	[səˈbɔːdɪnət klɔːz] [ˈsʌbklɔːz]	Nebensatz	*I like cycling* ***because I like the sport****.*
substitute	[ˈsʌbstɪtjuːt]	Ersatzverb (anstelle v. Modalverb)	*be able to, be allowed to, have to*
superlative	[suˈpɜːlətɪv]	Superlativ	*cheapest, most expensive, …*
tense	[tens]	Zeitform des Verbs	
time word / time phrase	[ˈtaɪm wɜːd] [ˈtaɪm freɪz]	Zeitangabe	*yesterday, this morning, after school, before lunch*
verb	[vɜːb]	1. Verb 2. Prädikat	*go, help, look, see, …* ***Can*** *we* ***do*** *it alone? He****'s gone****.*
***will*-future**	[ˈwɪl fjuːtʃə]	Futur mit *will*	*I think our trip* ***will be*** *fun.*
***yes / no*-question**	[ˈjes ˈnəʊ kwestʃən]	Entscheidungsfrage	*Are you 15? Do you like films?*
word order		Wortstellung (im Satz)	

Das **Vocabulary** (S. 206–233) enthält alle neuen Wörter und Wendungen des Buches, die du lernen musst.
Sie stehen in der Reihenfolge, in der sie im Buch zum ersten Mal vorkommen.

Wenn du **nachschlagen** möchtest, was ein englisches Wort bedeutet oder wie man es ausspricht, dann solltest du das **Dictionary English – German** auf den Seiten 234–270 verwenden.

p.	=	page (Seite)
pp.	=	pages (Seiten)
sb.	=	somebody (jemand)
sth.	=	something (etwas)
pl	=	*plural* (Mehrzahl)
fml	=	formal (formell)
infml	=	*informal* (umgangssprachlich)
AE	=	*American English*
BE	=	*British English*

English connects

p. 9	**entertainment** [entə'teɪnmənt]	Unterhaltung	
	politics ['pɒlətɪks]	Politik	noun: **politics** – adjective: **political** [pə'lɪtɪkl] ! **politics** ist Singular, trotz des **-s** am Ende: **Politics is** very interesting for some people, and **it is** very boring for others.
	engineering [endʒɪ'nɪərɪŋ]	Ingenieurwesen, Maschinenbau, Technik	

Unit 1: A diverse nation

p. 10	**multicultural** [mʌlti'kʌltʃərəl]	multikulturell	There are people from many different cultures in the USA. It is a ~ society. **cultural** ['kʌltʃərəl] = kulturell
	rainbow ['reɪnbəʊ]	Regenbogen	a **rainbow** 
	diversity [daɪ'vɜːsəti]	Vielfalt	noun: **diversity** – adjective: **diverse**
	Dutch [dʌtʃ]	holländisch, niederländisch; Niederländisch	noun/country: **Holland** *or* **the Netherlands** – adjective/language: **Dutch** **the Dutch** = die Holländer, die Niederländer
	colonize ['kɒlənaɪz]	kolonisieren	noun: **colony** – verb: **colonize**
	diamond ['daɪəmənd]	Diamant	! Betonung auf der 1. Silbe: **di**amond ['daɪəmənd]
	religion [rɪ'lɪdʒən]	Religion	
	multilingual [mʌlti'lɪŋgwəl]	mehrsprachig	David speaks English and Spanish at home and German at school. He is ~.
	vegetation [vedʒə'teɪʃn]	Vegetation	There isn't **much vegetation**. = There aren't **many plants**.
	wildlife ['waɪldlaɪf]	Tiere *(in freier Wildbahn)*, Tierwelt	You can find all kinds of ~ in Africa's national parks. The ~ of Africa is very different from the ~ in Europe.
p. 11	**apartheid** [ə'pɑːtaɪt]	Apartheid *(früheres System der Trennung zwischen Weißen und Schwarzen in Südafrika)*	
	anti- ['ænti]	anti-, gegen-	
	worldwide ['wɜːldwaɪd]	weltweit	= all over the world

free sb. [fri:]	jn. befreien	verb: **free** (befreien) – adjective: **free** (frei; kostenlos)
democratic [demə'krætɪk]	demokratisch	
democracy [dɪ'mɒkrəsi]	Demokratie	adjective: **democratic** – noun: **democracy** **!** Betonung auf der 2. Silbe: de**mo**cracy [dɪ'mɒkrəsi]
election [ɪ'lekʃn]	Wahl *(Abstimmung)*	
elect sb. **(to be)** sth. [ɪ'lekt]	jn. zu etwas wählen	verb: **elect** – noun: **election** **!** *English*: They **elected** him president. *German*: Sie **wählten** ihn **zum** Präsidenten.
in (the) case of [keɪs]	im Falle von	**In (the) ~ of** fire, don't panic. Let's take an umbrella, **(just) in ~** it rains. ((nur) für den Fall, dass ...)
people ['pi:pl]	Volk	**!** **people** = **1.** Menschen – A lot of **people** are afraid of dogs. **2.** Volk – the Zulu **people** (das Volk der Zulu) the native **peoples** of Africa (die Urvölker Afrikas)
tribal ['traɪbl]	Stammes-	noun: **tribe** – adjective: **tribal**
economic [i:kə'nɒmɪk]	wirtschaftlich, Wirtschafts-	A few very rich people and more and more poor people – the country should change its ~ policy.
embrace [ɪm'breɪs]	annehmen, mit offenen Armen begrüßen; (sich) umarmen	Are you ready to ~ new ideas? They said goodbye and **~d**.

Theme 1

p. 12	**(back) then** [ðen]	damals	My grandma was born in 1952. Life was a lot slower **(back) ~**, she says. **!** **then** = **1.** dann, danach; **2.** damals
	race [reɪs]	Rasse	Racism is discrimination against people because of their ~.
	suburb ['sʌbɜ:b]	Vorstadt, Vorort	It's so noisy here in the town centre that we have decided to move to a ~.
	perform [pə'fɔ:m]	aufführen; durchführen; auftreten *(Künstler/in)*	**Perform** the play/scene/dialogue for your class. The Beatles first **~ed** in the USA in 1964.

performer – performance – performing arts *(pl)*

• **performer**	Künstler/in	We walked along the Thames and watched the street **performers** on the Embankment.
• **performance**	Aufführung, Vorstellung; Auftritt	The Beatles' first **performance** in the USA was a huge success.
• **performing arts *(pl)***	darstellende Kunst	Music, dance and drama are **performing arts**.

document ['dɒkjument]	dokumentieren	**!** **document** = **1.** dokumentieren ['dɒkjument]; **2.** Dokument ['dɒkjumənt]
inequality [ɪnɪ'kwɒləti]	Ungleichheit	nouns: **equality** ◄► **inequality** adjectives: **equal** ◄► **unequal**

	responsibility [rɪspɒnsə'bɪləti]	Verantwortung	**take responsibility for** = Verantwortung übernehmen für ! **responsibility** = **1.** Verantwortung; **2.** Aufgabe, Zuständigkeit
p. 13	**feature** ['fiːtʃə]	Merkmal, Eigenschaft	
	protester [prə'testə]	Demonstrant/in	
	protest ['prəʊtest]	Protest(demonstration)	! verb: **protest** [prə'test] – noun: **protest** ['prəʊtest] Beachte auch die unterschiedliche Betonung.

Theme 2

p. 14	**transform** [træns'fɔːm]	umwandeln, verändern, umgestalten	= change sth. completely
	transformation [trænsfə'meɪʃn]	Umwandlung, Veränderung, Umgestaltung	verb: **transform** – noun: **transformation**
	process ['prəʊses]	Verfahren, Ablauf, Prozess	! Betonung auf der 1. Silbe: **pro**cess ['prəʊses]
	progress ['prəʊgres]	Fortschritt(e)	**make progress** = Fortschritte erzielen/ machen; vorankommen
	few	wenige	I talked to **a few** people at the party. *(einige, ein paar)* Only **few** people came to the party. *(nur wenige)*

(a) little – (a) few

(a) little steht mit **nicht zählbaren Nomen** wie **cheese, milk, money, time, traffic**.
few steht mit dem Plural von **zählbaren Nomen**.

! Beachte die Unterschiede zwischen **little** und **a little** und **few** und **a few**.

We had very **little money** *(= not much money)* when we were young.	**wenig/nicht viel** Geld
Dad gave me **a little money** *(= some money)* and sent me to the shops.	**etwas/ein bisschen** Geld
There were **few people** *(= not many people)* in the streets, so I felt a bit scared.	**wenige/nicht viele** Leute
There were **a few people** *(= some people)* at the ticket office, but I didn't have to wait long.	**einige/ein paar** Leute

	level ['levl]	Niveau, Ebene; Grad, Stufe	**at the basic level** = **an** der Basis **at the professional level** = **auf** Profi-Ebene
	access ['ækses]	Zugang, Zutritt	
	disadvantaged [dɪsəd'vɑːntɪdʒd]	benachteiligt	With a good education ~ children (= children from poor families) can be really successful in life.
p. 15	**reply** [rɪ'plaɪ]	Antwort	= answer noun: **reply** – verb: **reply** (antworten)
	athlete ['æθliːt]	(Leicht-)Athlet/in, Sportler/in	! Betonung auf der 1. Silbe: **ath**lete ['æθliːt]

	athletes **of colour**	nicht-weiße Athleten/-innen	people **of colour** = Nichtweiße, Menschen nicht-weißer Hautfarbe
	unbeatable [ʌn'bi:təbl]	unschlagbar; unübertrefflich	No team has won against us this season! We're just ~!
	male [meɪl]	männlich; männliche Person, männliches Tier	The police are looking for a 40-year-old ~. **male ◄► female**

Focus on language

p. 16	**instead of** [ɪn'sted əv]	anstatt, anstelle von	→ **instead of – instead** • I'd like pasta **instead of** chips, please. (= **anstelle von**) • I don't like chips. Can I have pasta **instead**? (= **stattdessen**)
	confuse [kən'fju:z]	verwirren; verwechseln	I was **~d** when someone called traffic lights a "robot". I always ~ right **with** left / right **and** left.
	lingua franca [lɪŋgwə 'fræŋkə]	Lingua Franca *(Verkehrssprache)*	English is a ~ **franca** in many parts of the world.
	communicate (with sb.**)** [kə'mju:nɪkeɪt]	(mit jm.) kommunizieren; sich (mit jm.) verständigen	verb: **communicate (with)** – noun: **communication**
	century ['sentʃəri]	Jahrhundert	There are one hundred years in a ~.
p. 17	**question mark** ['kwestʃən mɑ:k]	Fragezeichen	

Punctuation [pʌŋktʃu'eɪʃn] **(Zeichensetzung)**

.	**full stop** [fʊl 'stɒp]	Punkt	?	**question mark** ['kwestʃən mɑ:k]	Fragezeichen
,	**comma** ['kɒmə]	Komma	!	**exclamation mark** [ekskIə'meɪʃn mɑ:k]	Ausrufezeichen
:	**colon** ['kəʊlən]	Doppelpunkt	-	**hyphen** ['haɪfn]	Bindestrich

	humour ['hju:mə]	Humor	**!** Betonung auf der 1. Silbe: **hu**mour ['hju:mə] *English:* She has **a good sense of humour**. / She has no **sense of humour**. *German:* Sie hat **Humor.** / Sie hat **keinen (Sinn für) Humor**.
p. 18	**in fact** [ɪn 'fækt]	eigentlich, um genau zu sein	My homework wasn't hard. **In ~**, it only took me 10 minutes.
	mark [mɑ:k]	(Schul-)Note, Zensur	= grade *(AE)* **!** **mark** = **1.** kennzeichnen, markieren; **2.** (Schul-)Note, Zensur

Text

p. 19	**tunnel** ['tʌnl]	Tunnel	**!** Aussprache: **tunnel** ['tʌnl]
	cover ['kʌvə]	bedecken	Black and grey clouds **~ed** the sky. 

sudden ['sʌdn]	plötzliche(r, s)	! • His **sudden** departure surprised us all. (Seine **plötzliche** Abreise …) • We were surprised when he **suddenly** left. (…, als er **plötzlich** aufbrach)
glimpse [glɪmps]	kurzer Blick	**catch a glimpse of sth.** = einen Blick von/auf etwas erhaschen; etwas nur kurz zu sehen bekommen I was shocked when I caught a **~** of myself in the mirror.
stranger ['streɪndʒə]	Fremde/r	Don't talk to **~s**. (= to people you don't know)
council flat ['kaʊnsl flæt]	Sozialwohnung	**council** = Rat, Gemeinderat, Stadtverwaltung
somehow ['sʌmhaʊ]	irgendwie	**Somehow** I'll earn enough money for a new computer.
echo ['ekəʊ]	(wider)hallen	verb: **echo** – noun: **echo**, *pl* **echoes**
every now and again	ab und zu, von Zeit zu Zeit	= sometimes
certainly ['sɜːtnli]	sicher(lich), gewiss	I can **~** understand that you do not want to take the train at 5 am, but it is 100 euros cheaper than the train at 7 am.
… and neither did I. ['naɪðə]	… und ich auch nicht.	You didn't buy milk? Well, **~ did I**.

Inversion (Wortstellung **verb – subject**)

Nach Adverbien mit **negativer** oder **einschränkender** Bedeutung am **Anfang des Satzes** ändert sich die Wortstellung:
Die normale Wortstellung **subject – verb** wird umgedreht zu **verb – subject**.

Beim *simple present* und *simple past* musst du **do/does** oder **did** benutzen.

subject – verb	**verb – subject**
I am not happy. – **I am not** happy **either**.	**Neither am I**.
Cycling keeps the air clean and is good for your health.	**Not only does cycling keep** the air clean, but it's also good for your health.
This would not help us **in any way**.	**In no way would this help** us.
I had never heard of such a thing.	**Never had I heard** of such a thing.
We only found out about this **later**.	**Only later did we find out** about this.

straight [streɪt]	direkt, gleich	We bought a takeaway pizza and ate it **~** from the box.
carton ['kɑːtn]	(Papp-)Karton; Packung	! Betonung auf der 1. Silbe: **car**ton ['kɑːtn]
glass [glɑːs]	Glas	Would you like a **~ of** orange juice? ! **glas** = Glas; **glasses** *(pl)* = **1.** Gläser; **2.** eine Brille
p. 20 **leftover** pizza/cake/… ['leftəʊvə]	übrig gebliebene Pizza/ übrig gebliebener Kuchen/…	
turn yellow	gelb werden	= go yellow
olive ['ɒlɪv]	Olive	
pineapple ['paɪnæpl]	Ananas	

olives

pineapple

heat [hiːt]	erwärmen, erhitzen	adjective: **hot** – verb: **heat** – noun: **heat**
microwave ['maɪkrəweɪv]	Mikrowelle	**heating** a meal in the **microwave** 
mind [maɪnd]	Geist, Verstand; Gedanken	I couldn't sleep. All kinds of questions were running through my **~**.
drift [drɪft]	sich bewegen, driften, *(Gedanken)* wandern	The crowd **~ed** towards the stage when the concert started. When I read the story, my thoughts **~ed** to California and the beach.
sigh [saɪ]	seufzen	 **rings** 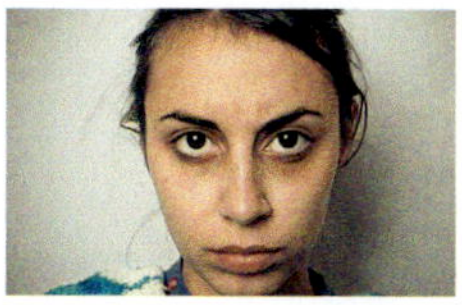 She has dark **rings** under her eyes.
ring [rɪŋ]	Ring	
pale [peɪl]	blass, bleich	
besides [bɪ'saɪdz]	außerdem	It's too late to go to the cinema. And **~**, I've already seen the film.
dishes *(pl)* ['dɪʃɪz]	Geschirr	**dirty dishes** 
dustbin ['dʌstbɪn]	Mülleimer	
struggle ['strʌgl]	kämpfen, sich abmühen	I am **struggling** to understand my French homework. I have so much trouble with the conditional! verb: **struggle** – noun: **struggle** (Kampf)
stream [striːm]	strömen	Tears were **~ing** down the little boy's face. verb: **stream** – noun: **stream** (Bach)
silent ['saɪlənt]	still, ruhig; lautlos	**fall silent** = still werden, verstummen
be about to do sth.	im Begriff sein, etwas zu tun	I **was ~ to** leave the house when my phone rang.
financial [faɪ'nænʃl]	finanziell	! Betonung auf der 2. Silbe: fi**nan**cial [faɪ'nænʃl]
difficulty ['dɪfɪkəlti]	Schwierigkeit(en)	adjective: **difficult** – noun: **difficulty**
talk sth. **over (with** sb.**)**	etwas (mit jm.) besprechen	I need to **talk** something **~** with Mr Clark, then I'll come over to your house.
terror ['terə]	(panische) Angst	
Where the hell is Africa? [hel] *(infml)*	Wo zum Teufel ist Afrika?	**hell** = Hölle
p. 21 **bits** *(pl)* [bɪts] *(infml)*	Teile, Stückchen	I have seen **bits** on television … = Ich hab (mal) ein bisschen (was) im Fernsehen gesehen … ! **bits** = Teile, Stückchen **a bit** = ein bisschen

…evision ['telɪvɪʒn]	Fernsehen	= TV
make notes [meɪk 'nəʊts]	(sich) Notizen machen *(zur Vorbereitung)*	**!** **make notes** sagt man, wenn man eigene Ideen aufschreibt als Vorbereitung auf z.B. einen Vortrag oder eine Präsentation. **take notes** verwendet man, wenn man sich beim Lesen oder Zuhören Notizen macht.
ladies and gentlemen [leɪdiːz ənd 'dʒentlmən]	meine Damen und Herren	
device [dɪ'vaɪs]	Gerät, Apparat	A clock is a ~ that tells you the time.
seat belt ['siːt belt]	Sicherheitsgurt	All car passengers must wear their **seat belts**. It's the law.
dread [dred]	fürchten	= be very afraid of
there is no doing sth.	man kann etwas nicht tun	**There's** no avoid**ing** it. = It can't be avoided.
turn back	umkehren	**There was no turning back**. = Es gab kein Zurück (mehr).
scenery ['siːnəri]	Landschaft	Scotland has some beautiful ~.
silver ['sɪlvə]	Silber; silberfarben	a **silver** necklace with a heart 
tiny ['taɪni]	winzig	= very small
p. 22 **tour operator** ['tʊər ɒpəreɪtə]	Reiseveranstalter/in	
chauffeur ['ʃəʊfə]	Chauffeur/in	**!** Aussprache: **chauffeur** ['ʃəʊfə]
pick sb. **up** [pɪk 'ʌp]	jn. abholen	He's **picking up** Mrs Carter. 
mind-blowing ['maɪnd bləʊɪŋ] *(infml)*	irre, wahnsinnig	= very exciting
gentle ['dʒentl]	behutsam, leicht, sanft(mütig)	Our dog is huge, but very friendly. He's a ~ giant!
feel at ease [iːz]	sich wohl/entspannt fühlen	My new boss introduced me to everyone. That helped me to **feel** more **at** ~.
get going	in Gang kommen; sich auf den Weg machen	Let's ~ **going** or we'll miss our train!
ahead [ə'hed]	voraus, vorausliegend	**There is still a long road ahead.** = Es liegt noch ein langer/weiter Weg vor uns.
glance [glɑːns]	(kurzer) Blick	**steal quick glances at** = verstohlene Blicke werfen auf
fly [flaɪ]	Hosenschlitz	
do sth. **up**	etwas zumachen *(Kleidung)*	"Before you start your presentation, **do up** your **fly**!" my friend whispered. **your fly is done up** = dein Hosenschlitz ist zu

as well	auch	❗ *German* **„auch"**: Beachte die Wortstellung! I speak French, German and English, and … I **also** speak Chinese. I speak Chinese **too**. I speak Chinese **as well**.
crazy about sth.	wild auf etwas, versessen auf etwas	I think football is boring, but my sister is really ~ **about** it.
security [sɪ'kjʊərəti]	Sicherheit	 **a security check at the airport**
security guard [sɪ'kjʊərəti gɑːd]	Sicherheitsbedienstete/r	
minibus ['mɪnibʌs]	Kleinbus	
care about sth. [keə]	etwas wichtig nehmen	

care (about)

Do you care?	Kümmert dich das? / Interessiert dich das?
Does anybody care about our oceans?	Interessiert sich irgendjemand für unsere Ozeane?
I didn't care about money when I was younger.	Geld war mir egal / war mir nicht wichtig, ….
You should care about your health.	Deine Gesundheit sollte dir wichtig sein.
I don't eat meat. **I really care about** animals.	… Tiere liegen mir sehr am Herzen.
They are really rich. – **Who cares?**	… – Na und? / Wen interessiert das?

space [speɪs]	Raum, Fläche	❗ **space** = **1.** Platz; **2.** Raum, Fläche
hut [hʌt]	Hütte	= a small and very simple house
p. 23 **dirt road** ['dɜːt rəʊd]	unbefestigte Straße	
distance ['dɪstəns]	Distanz, Entfernung	**in the distance** = in der Ferne
buzz [bʌz]	*(ein/das)* Summen	noun: **buzz** – verb: **buzz** (summen)
game [geɪm]	Wild *(Tiere)*	= wild animals or birds ❗ **game** = **1.** Spiel; **2.** Wild *(Tiere)*
quote [kwəʊt]	Zitat	Do you know a famous ~ from Shakespeare? – "To be or not to be …" noun: **quote** – verb: **quote** (zitieren)
response (to) [rɪ'spɒns]	Reaktion, Antwort (auf)	noun: **response** – verb: **respond** [rɪ'spɒnd] (reagieren, antworten)
impression [ɪm'preʃn]	Eindruck	When I apply for the job, I want to make a good ~. verb: **impress** – noun: **impression**

Skills training

p. 24 **facilities** *(pl)* [fə'sɪlətiz]	Einrichtungen, Anlage(n)	The ~ at the first hotel were much better than the ones here!

	stop [stɒp]	Halt, Haltepunkt	**make stops** = anhalten The train **makes three stops** on the way to London. (... hält dreimal an ...)
	schedule sth. **for** (a time) ['ʃedju:l]	etwas (für eine Uhrzeit) ansetzen	Our team **~d** the meeting **for** Monday afternoon. ! The meeting **was scheduled for** Monday. *or* The meeting **was scheduled to take place** on Monday. The train **was scheduled for** 14.18. *or* The train **was scheduled to leave at** 14.18. (Der Zug sollte planmäßig um 14.18 abfahren.)
	announcer [ə'naʊnsə]	Ansager/in, Sprecher/in	
p. 25	**politician** [pɒlə'tɪʃn]	Politiker/in	
p. 27	**require** [rɪ'kwaɪə]	erfordern, benötigen	This isn't an easy task. It **requires** a lot of thinking.
	reaction (to) [ri'ækʃn]	Reaktion (auf)	verb: **react (to)** – noun: **reaction (to)**
	stick [stɪk], **stuck, stuck** [stʌk]	(haften) bleiben	I will never forget the final scene of that film. It will always ~ in my mind. (... wird mir immer im Gedächtnis bleiben)
	technique [tek'ni:k]	Methode, Technik	! Betonung auf der 2. Silbe: **tech<u>nique</u>** [tek'ni:k]

Unit 2: Take a stand!

p. 34	**take a stand (on/against** sth.**)**	Stellung beziehen (zu/gegen etwas)	I think it's important to **take a** strong **~ on/against** cyberbullying. (= make it very clear that you are against cyberbullying) **stand** = Standpunkt, Haltung
p. 35	**create** [kri'eɪt]	(er)schaffen, kreieren	Jonathan **~d** a special smoothie for his mum.
	cancel sth. ['kænsl]	etwas abbrechen; absagen, ausfallen lassen	The outdoor concert had to be **~led** because of the rain.
	mayor [meə]	Bürgermeister/in	Our town has a new ~. Ms Jackson won the election.

Theme 1

p. 36	**activism** ['æktɪvɪzəm]	Aktivismus	**activist** ['æktɪvɪst] = Aktivist/in
	demonstration [demən'streɪʃn]	Demonstration	
	these days	heutzutage	! Betonung auf **these**: **<u>these</u> days** ['ði:z deɪz]
	airbrush ['eəbrʌʃ]	*(Foto)* retuschieren, nachbessern	That photo doesn't look like you at all. Did someone ~ it?
	petition [pə'tɪʃn]	Petition, Unterschriftensammlung	
	signature ['sɪgnətʃə]	Unterschrift	Verb: **sign** [saɪn] – Nomen: **signature** ['sɪgnətʃə]
	power ['paʊə]	Macht, Kraft, Stärke	

estimate ['estɪmeɪt]	schätzen	It is **~d** that ... (es wird geschätzt, dass ...) = **Estimates** say that ... (Schätzungen besagen, dass ...) verb: **estimate** ['estɪmeɪt] – noun: **estimate** ['estɪmət] (Schätzung)
be involved (in) [ɪn'vɒlvd]	sich an etwas beteiligen, sich bei etwas engagieren →	**get involved – be involved** • Lots of young people **get involved in** social projects. (**sich beteiligen/engagieren**) • **Are** you **involved in** this year's school play? (**beteiligt/engagiert sein**)
issue ['ɪʃuː]	(Streit-)Frage, Problem, Thema	Bullying is a big ~ at a lot of schools.
meme [miːm]	Internet-Mem, Internetphänomen	= an idea, image, video, website, etc. which people get to know via the internet
series ['sɪəriːz], *pl* **series**	Serie; (Sende-)Reihe	
relative ['relətɪv]	relativ	Our town is **relatively** big. ! **relative** = **1.** relativ; **2.** Verwandte/r
replace (with) [rɪ'pleɪs]	ersetzen (durch), austauschen (gegen)	I should get rid of my old phone and ~ it **with** a new one.
effect [ɪ'fekt]	(Aus-)Wirkung, Einfluss, Effekt	noun: **effect** – adjective: **effective** [ɪ'fektɪv]
point sth. **out** [pɔɪnt 'aʊt]	auf etwas hinweisen, aufmerksam machen	At the meeting Mr Jones **~ed out** that profits had gone down.
raise [reɪz]	(er)heben	**raise one's eyes** from sth. (von etwas aufschauen) **raise one's voice** (die Stimme erheben)
both ... and ...	sowohl ... als auch ...	I like **both my sisters**. (meine beiden Schwestern) I like **both** Anne **and** Julia. (sowohl Anne als auch Julia)
troll [trəʊl]	Troll, Kobold; *(in Online-Medien)* Provokateur/in	a **troll** 
hurtful ['hɜːtfl]	verletzend	a ~ comment = a comment that hurts/that might hurt
loads (of) [ləʊdz] *(infml)*	eine Menge	= lots (of)

Theme 2

p. 38 **tuition** [tju'ɪʃn]	Unterricht, Anleitung; Studiengebühren	Studiengebühren = **tuition** *oder* **tuition fees** *(pl)* [tju'ɪʃn fiːz]
end up	(schließlich) gelangen, landen, enden →	If you go on like this, you might ... **end up in** prison. **end up as** a gangster. **end up** sick and poor. **end up asking** others for help. ! **end up doing** sth. = am Ende/schließlich etwas tun
planet ['plænɪt]	Planet	! Betonung auf der 1. Silbe: **pla**net ['plænɪt]

	hypocrisy [hɪ'pɒkrəsi]	Heuchelei, Scheinheiligkeit	You tell your children always to be honest,
	fate [feɪt]	Schicksal	
	show up *(infml)*	erscheinen, kommen, sich zeigen	It's unfair if you reserve a table at a restaurant and then don't **~ up**.
	in my/your/... view [vjuː]	meiner/deiner/... Ansicht nach	= in my/your/... opinion
p. 39	**publish** ['pʌblɪʃ]	veröffentlichen, herausbringen	
	majority [mə'dʒɒrəti]	Mehrheit, Mehrzahl	There are 16 girls and 13 boys in my class. The girls are in the **~**.
	pie chart ['paɪ tʃɑːt]	Tortendiagramm, Kreisdiagramm	This is a funny **pie chart**! 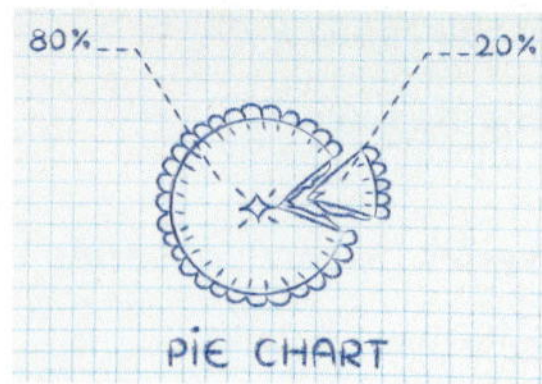

Focus on language

p. 40	**robber** ['rɒbə]	Räuber/in	a **robber** 
	demand [dɪ'mɑːnd]	fordern, verlangen	The workers **~ed** more money. verb: **demand** – noun: **demand** (Forderung)
	praise [preɪz]	loben, rühmen	His teacher **~d** him for his hard work. verb: **praise** – noun: **praise** (Lob)
	come across sth.	auf etwas stoßen, etwas (zufällig) finden	After two hours we **came ~** a beautiful village.
	refugee [refju'dʒiː]	Flüchtling	
	survival [sə'vaɪvl]	*(das)* Überleben	noun: **survival** – verb: **survive** [sə'vaɪv] (überleben)
	remarkable [rɪ'mɑːkəbl]	bemerkenswert	My grandfather died at the **~** age of 104.
	stage [steɪdʒ]	Bühne	
	news item ['njuːz aɪtəm]	Nachrichtenmeldung, Pressemeldung	**item** = Artikel, Gegenstand I took my **~s** to the cash desk.
	report sth./sb. **(to)** [rɪ'pɔːt]	etwas/jn. melden, anzeigen (bei) *(z.B. bei der Polizei)*	You should **~** this **to** the police. The car **was ~ed** stolen. (... wurde als gestohlen gemeldet.) **!** **1. report on sth.** = über etwas berichten; **2. report sth. (to the police)** = etwas (bei der Polizei) melden, anzeigen
p. 41	**be in progress** ['prəʊgres]	im Gange sein	 

	interrupt [ɪntə'rʌpt]	unterbrechen	It's rude to ~ people when they're talking.
	since then	seitdem	I was attacked last May, and **since then** I've been having horrible dreams at night. (= **Since I was attacked** last May, I've been having horrible dreams at night.)
	concrete ['kɒŋkriːt]	konkret	! Betonung auf der 1. Silbe: **<u>con</u>**crete ['kɒŋkriːt]
	foreign ['fɒrən]	ausländisch, fremd	**foreign language** = Fremdsprache
p. 42	**delicious** [dɪ'lɪʃəs]	köstlich, lecker	The pizza looked ~, but it didn't smell very nice.
	afterwards ['ɑːftəwədz]	hinterher, danach	We had fish and chips, and ~ we went for an ice cream.
	drop [drɒp]	fallen; fallen lassen	! **drop** = **1.** fallen – The book **dropped** to the floor. **2.** fallen lassen – Please don't **drop** that glass.

Text

p. 43	**cut through** sth.	etwas durchqueren; eine Abkürzung durch … nehmen	
	housing estate ['haʊzɪŋ ɪsteɪt]	Wohnsiedlung	
	high-rise building [haɪ raɪz 'bɪldɪŋ]	Hochhaus	

a **housing estate**

high-rise buildings

	needle ['niːdl]	Nadel; Kanüle	

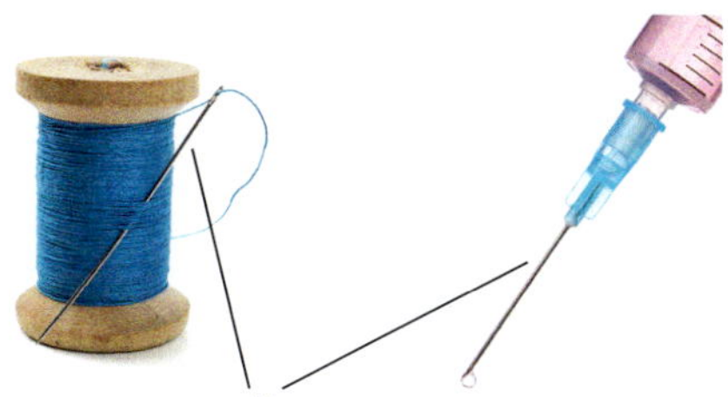

needles

	screech [skriːtʃ]	kreischen; *(Reifen, Bremsen)* quietschen	The car came to a stop with **~ing** tyres.
	come sb.'s **way**	auf jn. zu kommen	Can you hear the train **coming our ~**?

way

1. Art und Weise	I like the **way** they dance in the video.	… die Art und Weise, wie sie … tanzen
2. Weg	Excuse me, can you tell us the **way** to the station?	… den Weg zum Bahnhof …
3. Richtung	Stop! You're going **the wrong way**. We have to go **this way**.	… in die falsche Richtung. … hier entlang/in diese Richtung

	headlight ['hedlaɪt]	Scheinwerfer(licht)	

headlights

approach [ə'prəʊtʃ]	sich nähern, näher kommen	As we **~ed** our house, we saw that the front door was open. verb: **approach** – noun: **approach** (Ansatz, Herangehensweise)
the headlights were on full beam [biːm]	das Fernlicht war eingeschaltet	**beam** = (Licht-)Strahl
pull up	anhalten, an den Straßenrand fahren	A taxi **~ed up** beside the man, and he got in.
lift [lɪft]	Mitfahrgelegenheit	Anyone going to Brighton next Saturday? I'm looking for a **~**. **!** *English:* You don't have to walk. I can **give you a lift**. *German:* … Ich kann **dich mitnehmen**.
furious ['fjʊəriəs]	wütend	= very angry
mad [mæd]	wahnsinnig, verrückt	You want to go out in this weather? You must be **~**. **!** **mad – madder – maddest**
be supposed to be/do sth. [sə'pəʊzd]	etwas sein sollen/ etwas tun sollen	We**'re** not **~ to** use our mobiles at school, but some of us do. I haven't heard their new CD yet, but it**'s ~ to** be really good.
speed [spiːd], **sped, sped** [sped]	rasen, zu schnell fahren	verb: **speed** – noun: **speed** (Geschwindigkeit) The car was racing along the street **at a speed** of 100 km/h. (mit einer Geschwindigkeit von …)
speed hump ['spiːd hʌmp]	Bodenschwelle, Bremsschwelle *(zur Verkehrsberuhigung)*	a **speed hump**  **hump** = Buckel, Hindernis
mate [meɪt] *(infml)*	Freund/in, Kumpel	On Saturdays I always hang out with my **~s**.
scar [skɑː]	Narbe	noun: **scar** – verb: **scar** sb. (bei jm. Narben hinterlassen) His face was **scarred**. = Sein Gesicht war von Narben bedeckt. a **scar** 
p. 44 **cop** [kɒp] *(infml)*	Bulle *(Polizist/in)*	= a police officer
flash [flæʃ]	blinken, leuchten	The police car's blue light was **~ing**. **!** **flash one's headlights** = aufblenden, die Lichthupe betätigen  **flashing lights**  **flashlight** *(AE)*/ **torch** *(BE)*

right behind him	direkt hinter ihm	❗ **right** = **1.** richtig; **2.** (nach) rechts; **3.** genau, direkt *(adverb)*
lose the police *(infml)*	die Polizei abhängen, abschütteln	The robber escaped through the crowded streets on foot and managed to **~ the police**.
siren ['saɪrən]	Sirene	❗ Betonung und Aussprache: **siren** ['saɪrən]
junction ['dʒʌŋkʃn]	(Straßen-)Kreuzung	a **junction** 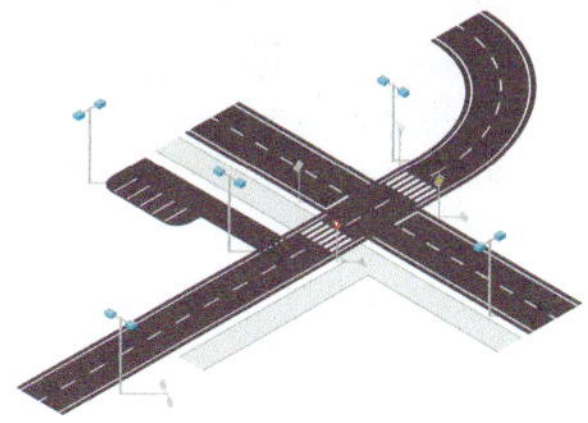
unconscious [ʌn'kɒnʃəs]	bewusstlos	
bloody ['blʌdi]	blutig, voller Blut	verb: **bleed, bled, bled** – noun: **blood** – adjective: **bloody**
explosion [ɪk'spləʊʒn]	Explosion	❗ Betonung auf der 2. Silbe: ex**plo**sion [ɪk'spləʊʒn]
paramedic [pærə'medɪk]	Rettungssanitäter/in	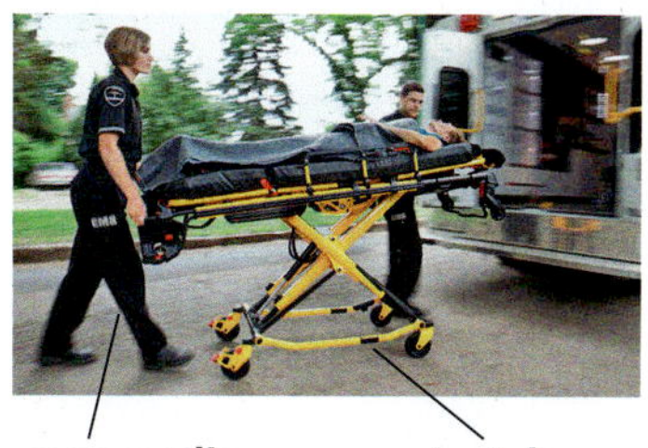
stretcher ['stretʃə]	Trage, (Trag-)Bahre	
rush sb. **to ...** [rʌʃ]	jn. auf dem schnellsten Weg nach .../zu ... bringen	The driver was badly hurt, so the paramedics **~ed** him **to** the nearest hospital.
burn [bɜːn]	Verbrennung, Brandverletzung	verb: **burn** – noun: **burn** **burns unit** *(in a hospital)* = Abteilung für Verbrennungen/Brandverletzungen
take it easy	sich schonen	❗ **Take it easy.** *(infml)* = **1.** Reg dich nicht auf. / Bleib mal locker. **2.** Schone dich.
nurse [nɜːs]	(Kranken-)Pfleger/in	three **nurses** 
bruise [bruːz]	Bluterguss, Prellung	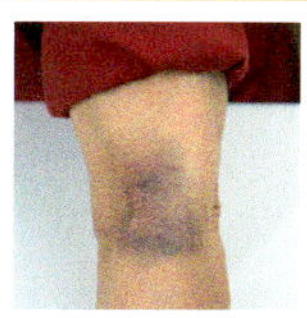 a **bruise**  **bones**
bone [bəʊn]	Knochen	
alarmed [ə'lɑːmd]	beunruhigt	The manager was ~ because profits had gone down.
over time	im Laufe der Zeit	**Over ~** I learned to love vegetarian food.

	counsellor [ˈkaʊnsələ]	Berater/in; Betreuer/in	The high school ~ will help you if you have
p. 45	**joyriding** [ˈdʒɔɪraɪdɪŋ]	Joyriding *(eine Spritztour mit einem gestohlenen Auto machen)*	

Skills training

p. 47	**revolution** [revəˈluːʃn]	Revolution	! Betonung auf der 3. Silbe: **revolution** [revəˈluːʃn]
	wage [weɪdʒ], *oft auch:* **wages** *(pl)*	Lohn, Gehalt	When dad was young, he had a ~ of £180 per week. These days, his **~s** are much higher.
	quality [ˈkwɒləti]	Qualität, Qualitäts-; Eigenschaft	I always buy high **quality** clothes. = … clothes of high **quality.** What **personal qualities** do you need for the job? (persönliche Eigenschaften)
	conditions *(pl)* [kənˈdɪʃnz]	Bedingungen, Verhältnisse	It's too cold and too noisy in this office. I can't work in these ~.
	sweatshop [ˈswetʃɒp]	Ausbeutungsbetrieb	
	factory [ˈfæktri]	Fabrik	a **factory** 
	impossible [ɪmˈpɒsəbl]	unmöglich	It's ~ to run a mile in two minutes. **possible ◄► impossible**
	inside out [ɪnsaɪd ˈaʊt]	verkehrt herum, auf links *(Kleidung)*	You're wearing your T-shirt **inside ~**.
p. 48	**recruitment** [rɪˈkruːtmənt]	Anwerbung, Einstellung *(von Personal)*	The ~ campaign for next year's teachers will start in February.
	put sth. **up**	etwas aufhängen *(Bild etc.)*	 They're **putting up** a picture.
	feature [ˈfiːtʃə]	vorkommen, mitwirken	She **was ~d** in the campaign. (Sie wurde in der Kampagne gezeigt/war Teil der Kampagne.)
	receive [rɪˈsiːv]	erhalten, empfangen	a more formal word for **get** **receive a letter ◄► send a letter**
	encourage [ɪnˈkʌrɪdʒ]	ermutigen, ermuntern	My parents **~d** me to apply for the job.
	prove [pruːv]	beweisen; nachweisen	• I'm innocent! I didn't take the money. – Can you ~ it? • **prove sb. wrong** = beweisen, dass jemand Unrecht hat
	stereotype [ˈsteriətaɪp]	Stereotyp, Klischee(vorstellung)	The film's main character doesn't seem real to me. It's just the ~ of a schoolgirl in love.

minority [maɪ'nɒrəti]	Minderheit	The boys in our class are in the **~**. (= There are more girls than boys in our class.)
gender ['dʒendə]	Geschlecht *(als soziales Merkmal)*	
just about	so ziemlich, nahezu; (so) ungefähr	She knows **just ~** everything about cars. Oh no! My train is leaving … **just ~** now!
relevant ['reləvənt]	relevant, wichtig	! Betonung auf der 1. Silbe: relevant ['reləvənt]
p. 49 **location** [ləʊ'keɪʃn]	Ort *(Standort; Einsatzort, Drehort)*	
storyline ['stɔːrilaɪn]	Handlung *(z.B. eines Films/ einer Geschichte)*	
script [skrɪpt]	Drehbuch	
rescue ['reskjuː]	retten	He fell into the river, but a dog **~d** him. verb: **rescue** – noun: **rescue** (Rettung, Rettungsdienst)
bomb [bɒm]	Bombe	noun: **bomb** – verb: **bomb** sth. (einen Bombenanschlag auf etwas verüben, etwas bombardieren)

Unit 3: Future visions

p. 56 **vision** ['vɪʒn]	Vision; Vorstellung	Is the driverless car just a **~** of the future? ! Betonung auf der 1. Silbe: vision ['vɪʒn]
exoskeleton ['eksəʊskelɪtn]	Exoskelett, Außenskelett	**skeleton** ['skelɪtn] = Skelett 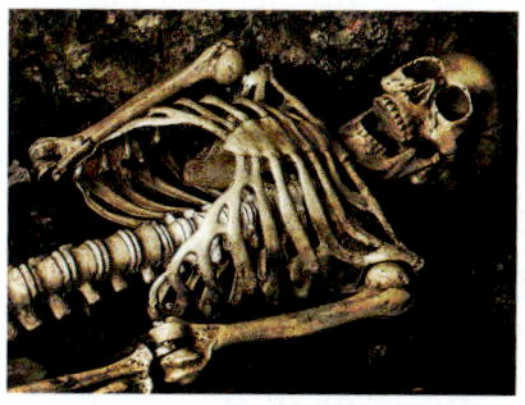
mechanical [mɪ'kænɪkl]	mechanisch	Grandma has a very old **~** clock. It's a bit slow and sometimes it stops, but it's lovely.
use [juːs]	Gebrauch, Verwendung	**make use of** sth. = Gebrauch machen von etwas, etwas nutzen Our flat is very small, so we have to find clever ways to **make ~ of** the little space we have. ! verb: **use** [juːz] – noun: **use** [juːs]
lift [lɪft]	heben, hochheben	This box is very heavy. I can't even **~** it from the ground! ! **lift** = **1.** Lift, Fahrstuhl; Mitfahrgelegenheit; **2.** heben, hochheben
object ['ɒbdʒɪkt]	Objekt, Gegenstand	This robot can lift and move heavy **~s**. ! Betonung auf der 1. Silbe: object ['ɒbdʒɪkt]
contact lens ['kɒntækt lenz]	Kontaktlinse	
blink (your eyes) [blɪŋk]	blinzeln, (mit den Augen) zwinkern	= shut and open your eyes very quickly

heart rate ['hɑːt reɪt]	Herzfrequenz, Puls	**rate** = Quote, Rate, Tempo
power ['paʊə]	Energie, Strom	! **power** = **1.** Energie, Strom; **2.** Macht, Kraft, Stärke
electric [ɪ'lektrɪk]	elektrisch, Elektro-	I play the ~ guitar in our rock band.
generate ['dʒenəreɪt]	erzeugen, generieren	We have solar panels on the roof of our house – devices which can **generate electricity** from the sunlight. adjective: **electric** – noun: **electricity**
electricity [ɪlek'trɪsəti]	Strom, Elektrizität	
p. 57 **pillow** ['pɪləʊ]	Kopfkissen	
psychology [saɪ'kɒlədʒi]	Psychologie	! Das **p-** am Anfang von **psychology** wird nicht gesprochen: [saɪ'kɒlədʒi]
wireless ['waɪələs]	drahtlos, Funk-	

-less („-los")

driverless	fahrerlos, führerlos	**helpless**	hilflos	**meatless**	fleischlos
endless	endlos	**homeless**	obdachlos	**sleepless**	schlaflos
		hopeless	hoffnungslos	**wireless**	drahtlos

allow sb. **to do** sth. [ə'laʊ]	jm. erlauben, etwas zu tun	Will your parents **allow** you **to** go to the concert? = Will you **be allowed to** go to the concert? We can't **allow** people **to** smoke in the building. = Smoking isn't **allowed** in the building.
saving ['seɪvɪŋ]	Einsparung, Ersparnis	I try to save some money every month. I want to buy a new bike with my **~s**.
pass sth. **on (to** sb.**)** [pɑːs]	etwas weitergeben (an jn.)	Take as many potatoes as you want from the dish and then please ~ it **on** to Lucie.
consumer [kən'sjuːmə]	Konsument/in, Verbraucher/in	
scientist ['saɪəntɪst]	(Natur-)Wissenschaftler/in	a **scientist** in a lab 
seed sth. [siːd]	etwas säen	"Freshly **~ed** grass! Please don't walk here."
increase (by) [ɪn'kriːs]	steigern, (sich) erhöhen; steigen, zunehmen (um)	Our profits **increased by** 10% last year. (stiegen um 10%) We were able to **increase** our profits **by** 10%. (erhöhen)
hail [heɪl]	Hagel	We ran inside when a bad ~ shower started. (= a shower with small balls of ice)
chemical ['kemɪkl]	Chemikalie; chemisch	Please describe the ~ reaction you see. (chemisch) Be careful! This is a dangerous ~. (Chemikalie)
agricultural [ægrɪ'kʌltʃərəl]	landwirtschaftlich, Agrar-	noun: **agriculture** – adjective: **agricultural**
region ['riːdʒən]	Region, Gegend	! Betonung auf der 1. Silbe: **re**gion ['riːdʒən]

p.58	**watch** [wɒtʃ]	Armbanduhr	a **watch** 
	vocabulary [və'kæbjələri]	Wortschatz, Vokabular; Vokabelverzeichnis	I understand these French words, but they're not part of my active ~. (aktiver Wortschatz) You find the new words of each unit in the ~ at the back of your English book. (Vokabelverzeichnis)
	wearable ['weərəbl]	tragbar *(Kleidung)*	How many ~ electronic products do you own?
	headphones *(pl)* ['hedfəʊnz]	*(ein)* Kopfhörer	a pair of wireless **headphones** 
	data ['deɪtə]	Daten	**!** *English:* The **data shows** that ... / The **data was** collected in ... *German:* Die **Daten zeigen**, dass ... / Die **Daten wurden** in ... gesammelt.
	exercise *(no pl)*	Bewegung, *(körperliches)* Training	**!** **1. exercise** *(no pl)* = Bewegung – My parents say I need more **exercise**. **2. exercise(s)** = Übung(en) – I couldn't do **exercises** 4 and 5. noun: **exercise** – verb: **exercise** (sich bewegen, trainieren) *auch:* **take exercise**
p.59	**display** [dɪ'spleɪ]	Bildschirm, Anzeige(gerät)	noun: **display** – verb: **display** (anzeigen, zeigen, zur Schau stellen)
	groan [grəʊn]	stöhnen	He **~ed** when he read the message.
	head-mounted display [hed maʊntɪd dɪ'spleɪ]	Datenhelm, Datenbrille, Videobrille	
	tense [tens]	sich anspannen, sich verkrampfen	verb: **tense** – adjective: **tense** (angespannt, verkrampft) I **~d** when I heard someone behind me in the darkness. (sich anspannen/ verkrampfen) Time for a holiday? You seem very stressed and ~. (angespannt)
	shatter (into) ['ʃætə]	zerbrechen (in)	If you break a car window, it will ~ into hundreds of very small pieces.
	efficient [ɪ'fɪʃnt]	effizient, rationell; *(Person)* tüchtig	A person can be ~ in their workplace. (= they work well with good time management) Service or the organization of an event can be ~. (= well-organized) A car can be fuel-~. (= it uses very little fuel)
	check on sb.	nach jm. schauen, jn. kontrollieren	Note to babysitter: Please put Lily to bed around 8 pm and then ~ **on** her again to make sure she's sleeping.
	spy on sb. ['spaɪ ɒn]	jm. nachspionieren, jn. bespitzeln	How do you know these details from my life? Are you **~ing on** me? (= watching me secretly)

Theme 2

p. 60 **keep on**	weitermachen	**keep (on) doing sth. ◄► stop doing sth.**

keep, kept, kept

1. keep	Can I **keep** your pen or do you want it back? You should **keep** milk in a cool place. Put on some gloves to **keep** your hands warm. Be careful. **Keep away** from the fire. **Keep me posted**, please.	**behalten** **aufbewahren** **(warm/...) halten** **sich fernhalten von** **auf dem Laufenden halten**
2. keep sth. up	You're doing a good job. **Keep it up!**	**Mach weiter so!**
3. keep on	If you **keep on** like this, you'll get in trouble.	**weitermachen**
keep (on) doing sth.	We **kept (on) walking** till we got to a village. I tried to talk to him, but he **kept shouting** at me.	**etwas immer weiter/immer wieder/ständig tun**

sustainable [sə'steɪnəbl]	nachhaltig, umweltverträglich; zukunftsfähig	To be ~, we have to plant as many trees as we cut down. **sustainable living** = nachhaltige Lebensweise
growth [grəʊθ]	Wachstum	verb: **grow** – noun: **growth**
the Middle Ages *(pl)* [mɪdl 'eɪdʒɪz]	das Mittelalter	**!** *English:* The **Middle Ages are** sometimes called "The Dark Ages". *German:* Das **Mittelalter wird** manchmal „das Dunkle Zeitalter" genannt.
billion ['bɪliən]	Milliarde	= one thousand million (1,000,000,000)
7000 BC [biː 'siː]	7000 v. Chr.	
1000 AD [eɪ 'diː]	1000 n. Chr.	
p. 61 **graph** [græf], *BE auch:* [grɑːf]	Diagramm, Kurve	What do these **~s** tell us? 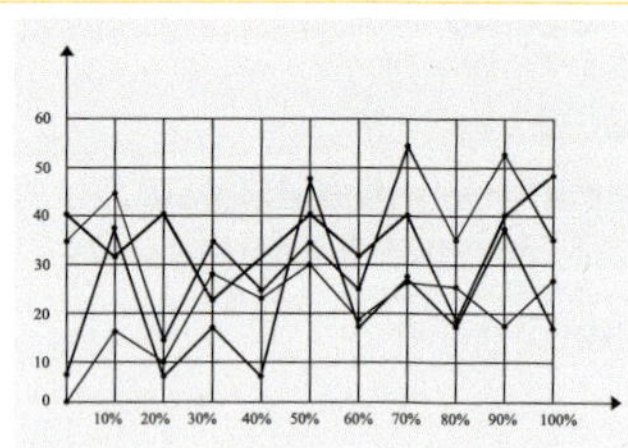
pessimistic [pesɪ'mɪstɪk]	pessimistisch	adjective: **pessimistic** – noun: **1. pessimist** ['pesɪmɪst] (Pessimist/in); **2. pessimism** ['pesɪmɪzəm] (Pessimismus)

Focus on language

p. 62 **frontier (with)** ['frʌntɪə]	Grenze (zu)	**new frontiers** = Neuland, neue Ufer
fascinate ['fæsɪneɪt]	faszinieren	I've always been **~d** by stories about other planets.
Martian ['mɑːʃn]	Marsmensch	a person or creature from the planet **Mars** [mɑːz]
go wrong [rɒŋ]	schiefgehen	Murphy's Law: Anything that can **go ~**, will **go ~**.
controversial [kɒntrə'vɜːʃl]	kontrovers, umstritten	His last book was ~ . Some loved it, but most people hated it.

prediction [prɪˈdɪkʃn]	Vorhersage, Voraussage	noun: **prediction** – verb: **predict** [prɪˈdɪkt] (voraussagen, vorhersagen)
by 8 pm/by next year/ by 2030/...	bis 20 Uhr/bis nächstes Jahr/ bis (zum Jahr) 2030/...	They should be here **~ 8 pm**. (= not later than 8 pm)
optimist [ˈɒptɪmɪst]	Optimist/in	**optimist ◄► pessimist** adjective: **optimistic** – noun: **1. optimist** [ˈɒptɪmɪst] **2. optimism** [ˈɒptɪmɪzəm] (Optimismus)
in spite of [spaɪt]	trotz	**in ~ of** the bad weather = **although** the weather was bad
pioneer [paɪəˈnɪə]	Pionier/in	
environment [ɪnˈvaɪrənmənt]	Umwelt; Umfeld, Umgebung	Cycling is good for the **environment**. *(Umwelt)* working/learning **environment** *(-Umfeld, -Umgebung)*
would-be [ˈwʊd biː]	künftige(r, s), angehende(r, s); Möchtegern-	What training do **~-be** space travellers need? I don't like those TV programmes with all the **~-be** pop stars. I think they're boring.
sign up (for) [saɪn]	sich anmelden (für)	Dad has just **~ed up** for for a cooking class.
even though	auch wenn, obwohl *(betont)*	! *English:* He's world-famous, **even though** he isn't really an artist. *German:* ... weltberühmt, **und das, obwohl** er gar kein wirklicher Künstler ist.
one-way ticket [wʌn ˈweɪ tɪkɪt]	einfache Fahrkarte	**one-way ticket ◄► return (ticket)** [rɪˈtɜːn] (Rückfahrkarte)
recommend sth. **(to** sb.**)** [rekəˈmend]	(jm.) etwas empfehlen	I can ~ the music store on 3rd Street. They have great stuff! verb: **recommend** – noun: **recommendation**
concentrate (on) [ˈkɒnsntreɪt]	sich konzentrieren (auf)	verb: **concentrate** [ˈkɒnsntreɪt] – noun: **concentration** [kɒnsnˈtreɪʃn] (Konzentration) ! *English:* I can't **concentrate on** the test. *German:* Ich kann **mich** nicht **auf** den Test **konzentrieren**.
p. 63 **choir** [ˈkwaɪə]	Chor	a **choir** 
p. 64 **destination** [destɪˈneɪʃn]	Reiseziel, Fahrtziel	You will reach your ~ in seven hours.
unfortunately [ʌnˈfɔːtʃənətli]	unglücklicherweise, leider	We were planning a barbecue, but ~ it rained. **fortunately ◄► unfortunately** (glücklicherweise ◄► unglücklicherweise)

Text

p. 65 **global warming** [gləʊbl ˈwɔːmɪŋ]	Erderwärmung	

cause sth. [kɔːz]	etwas bewirken, verursachen	The bad weather **~d** many problems. ! *English:* The bad weather **caused** many trains **to be** late. *German:* Das schlechte Wetter **bewirkte**, dass sich viele Züge **verspäteten**. / Das schlechte Wetter **verursachte die Verspätung** vieler Züge.
by accident	aus Versehen; zufällig	! **accident** = **1.** Unfall; **2.** Versehen; Zufall
mainland [ˈmeɪnlænd]	Festland	**mainland** ◄► **island**
deserted [dɪˈzɜːtɪd]	menschenleer, wie ausgestorben	**deserted** streets = streets with no people in them
derelict [ˈderəlɪkt]	heruntergekommen, verfallen	**derelict buildings** 
slow down [sləʊ ˈdaʊn]	(sich) verlangsamen, langsamer werden	Don't drive so fast! There are children in the road – please **~ down**. 
put sth. **off**	etwas verschieben, hinauszögern	Don't **~** it **off** till tomorrow. Do it now.

put

put sth. in	Please **put in** (= fill in) your name and address.	einsetzen, eingeben
put sth. off	Do it now. Don't **put** it **off** till tomorrow.	verschieben, hinauszögern
put sth. on	It's cold outside. I'd **put on** a pullover. The driver **put on** the police car's siren.	**1.** anziehen; aufsetzen **2.** einschalten
put sth. up	Can you help me to **put up** this picture?	aufhängen

row [rəʊ]	rudern	 **rowing boat** [ˈrəʊɪŋ bəʊt] = Ruderboot
loner [ˈləʊnə]	Einzelgänger/in	To me, other people are often a pain. I prefer to be on my own. I'm really a **~**.
hang around *(infml)*, **hung, hung**	herumhängen	After school we often **~ around** at the bus stop.

... whom you could trust. [huːm] *(fml)*	..., wem man trauen konnte.	→ **Whom** did you see? **Whom** can I trust? (Fragewort: Wen?/ Wem?) The expert **whom** they called in ... / People **whom** we asked / **whom** we talked to ... (Relativpronomen: den/dem/die/denen)
mob [mɒb]	Mob, Menschenmenge	A ~ of about 20 football fans was waiting on the platform.
shed [ʃed]	Schuppen *(Hütte, Lagerraum)*	a **garden shed** 
slip [slɪp]	(aus)rutschen	He **~ped** on the wet grass and fell down.
contain [kən'teɪn]	enthalten	I can't eat this chocolate. It **~s** nuts.
pant [pænt]	keuchen, hecheln	You're **~ing** like a dog. You ran too fast.
p. 66 **storm** [stɔːm]	stürmen	The soldiers **~ed** down the hill and into the village.
gravestone ['greɪvstəʊn]	Grabstein	**gravestones** 
splash [splæʃ]	spritzen, platschen	Dogs love **~ing** through the water.
crowd [kraʊd]	(Menschen-)Menge	a **huge crowd** 
shore [ʃɔː]	Ufer *(eines Sees)*	**shore** 
pause [pɔːz]	kurz innehalten, Pause machen	She **~d** a moment before she answered my question. verb: **pause** – noun: **pause** (Pause) ! Pause in der Schule: **break**
breath [breθ]	Atem	**pause for breath** = kurz Pause machen, um Luft zu holen

they would sit ... — sie saßen (früher) immer ...

German "früher" – <u>used to</u> + infinitive / <u>would</u> + infinitive

- Wenn man beschreiben will, was **früher** der Fall war, aber heute nicht mehr, dann kann man **used to ...** verwenden:

We **used to live** in Manchester.	Wir wohnten früher in Manchester.
Manchester United **used to be** my favourite team.	Früher war Manchester United meine Lieblingsmannschaft.
I **used to spend** a lot of money on sports magazines.	Ich habe früher immer viel Geld für Sportzeitschriften ausgegeben.

- Wenn es um <u>Handlungen</u> geht – also um Dinge, die man **früher immer gemacht** hat –, kann man auch **would ...** benutzen:

Grandpa **would visit** us every Sunday after church.	Opa besuchte uns jeden Sonntag nach der Kirche. / Opa pflegte uns jeden Sonntag ... zu besuchen.
We **would** often **go** for long walks in the woods.	Wir haben oft lange Spaziergänge im Wald gemacht.

bath [bɑːθ] — Bad; Badewanne — ! *English*: **have a bath** *or* **take a bath** *German:* **baden, ein Bad nehmen** *(in der Badewanne)*

backwards [ˈbækwədz] — rückwärts; nach hinten — I'm learning to drive. I find it hard to drive ~. And I often forget to look ~ in the mirror. **forward(s) ◄► backward(s)**

It's the way you do it. — So macht man das.

German "man"

you	**You** should wash **your** hands before every meal.	▶ **Man (Jede/r)** sollte sich vor jeder Mahlzeit die Hände waschen.
one	**One** should wash **one's** hands before every meal.	
	! In der <u>Umgangssprache</u> wird meist **you** für das deutsche „man" verwendet, während **one** eher förmlich klingt.	
they	**They** say it always rains in England, but that's not true.	▶ **Man** sagt (**Die Leute** sagen), dass es in England immer regnet, ...
people	**People** say it always rains in England, but that's not true.	
the passive	The boy **was taken** to hospital, but it was too late. Nothing **could be done**.	▶ **Man** brachte den Jungen ins Krankenhaus, ... **Man** konnte nichts mehr tun.

facing forwards/ backwards [ˈfeɪsɪŋ] — nach vorn/hinten schauend; mit dem Gesicht nach vorn/hinten

He just stood there **facing** the sea.

a restaurant table **facing** the sea

p.67 **narrator** [nəˈreɪtə] — Erzähler/in — **first-person narrator** = Ich-Erzähler/in

Skills training

p. 68	**robot** ['rəʊbɒt]	Roboter	
	exhibition [eksɪ'bɪʃn]	Messe; Ausstellung	This new device was presented at last year's technology **~**. (Messe) I want to see the Chagall ~ at the museum. (Ausstellung)
	gadget ['gædʒɪt]	Gerät, technischer Krimskrams	= a device, usually a small one, that does something useful
	no matter what/how/who ['mætə]	(ganz) egal, was/wie/wer	I want to do this, **no ~ how** long it takes, **what** it costs or **whom** I have to ask for help.
	alternative [ɔːl'tɜːnətɪv]	Alternative; alternativ	I hate planes, but when I go to Australia there's really no ~ to flying. Our factory is closing, but our company has offered us ~ jobs.
	and so on	und so weiter	= etc.
p. 69	**take** sth. **off**	etwas abnehmen, ausziehen *(Kleidung)*	**put** sth. **on** ◄► **take** sth. **off**
	battery ['bætri]	Batterie, Akku	**battery life** = Batterie-/Akku-Laufzeit
	poor [pɔː], [pʊə]	schlecht, schwach, minderwertig	! **poor** = **1.** arm; **2.** schlecht, schwach, minderwertig
	in addition [ə'dɪʃn]	außerdem	This mobile is very expensive. **In ~**, it's made of plastic and will break easily.
	accurate ['ækjərət]	genau, präzise	= exact
	circumstances *(pl)* ['sɜːkəmstənsɪz]	Umstände	**under the circumstances** = unter diesen Umständen
	refund ['riːfʌnd]	Rückzahlung, (Kosten-) Erstattung	noun: **refund** ['riːfʌnd] – verb: **refund** [rɪ'fʌnd] (erstatten, rückerstatten)
	attach (to) [ə'tætʃ]	anfügen; anhängen (an) *(Brief, E-Mail)*	Can you ~ the photos and mail them to me? I'm **~ing** some photos of Ashley's party.
	receipt [rɪ'siːt]	(Kauf-)Beleg, Quittung, Kassenzettel	! **false friends:** *English* **receipt** [rɪ'siːt] = *German* **Beleg, Quittung, Kassenzettel** *English* **recipe** ['resəpi] = *German* **(Koch-)Rezept**
	within [wɪ'ðɪn]	innerhalb (von), in	We have to finish our project ~ two weeks.
	complaint [kəm'pleɪnt]	Beschwerde	verb: **complain** – noun: **complaint** **make a complaint (about sth.)** = eine Beschwerde vorbringen (über etwas), etwas beanstanden
p. 70	**drone** [drəʊn]	Drohne	 a **drone**

	informal [ɪn'fɔːml]	informell, locker	When you apply for a job, your letter should be quite formal, but emails to your friends can be ~.
p. 71	**thunder** ['θʌndə]	Donner	
	shot [ʃɒt]	Aufnahme, Foto; *(Film)* Einstellung	! **shot** = **1.** Schuss; **2.** (Kamera-)Einstellung, Aufnahme *(Film)*
	long shot ['lɒŋ ʃɒt]	Totale *(Film)*	
	medium shot ['miːdiəm ʃɒt]	Halbtotale *(Film)*	**medium** = mittel(groß); mittlere(r, s)
	close-up ['kləʊs ʌp]	Nahaufnahme *(Film)*	! • adjective: **close (to)** [kləʊs] nah, dicht (bei, an) Many people don't like it if you stand too ~ **to** them. • verb: **close** [kləʊz] schließen

MORE CHALLENGE 1

p. 28	°**poach** [pəʊtʃ]	wildern, unerlaubt jagen	= hunt illegally Someone who **~es** is a **poacher**.
	°**record** ['rekɔːd]	Rekord	be at **record** level(s) = einen Höchststand/ein Rekordniveau erreicht haben
	°**consequence** ['kɒnsɪkwəns]	Konsequenz, Folge	I've been a bit lazy recently. The ~ was that I did badly in two exams. / As a ~, I did badly in two exams. **as a consequence** = als Folge, folglich ! Betonung auf der 1. Silbe: <u>con</u>sequence ['kɒnsɪkwəns]
	°**certain** ['sɜːtn]	gewisse(r, s), bestimmte(r, s)	I don't want to give any names, but ~ people in our team are a bit difficult to work with.
	°**notably** ['nəʊtəbli]	insbesondere, hauptsächlich	
	°**rhino** ['raɪnəʊ], *pl* **rhinos** *(infml)*	Nashorn	
	°**extinction** [ɪk'stɪŋkʃn]	Ausrottung, Aussterben	noun: **extinction** – adjective: **extinct** [ɪk'stɪŋkt] (ausgestorben)
	°**moon** [muːn]	Mond	the **moon** 
	°**surround** [sə'raʊnd]	umgeben	An island is **~ed** by water on all sides.
	°**track** [træk]	(zurück-, nach)verfolgen, beobachten	! **track** = **1.** Pfad, (Feld-)Weg; **2.** (zurück-, nach)verfolgen, beobachten
	°**since**	weil, da	! **since** = **1.** seit; **2.** seitdem, seither; **3.** weil, da
	°**armed** [ɑːmd]	bewaffnet	**armed soldiers** 
	°**confront** sb. [kən'frʌnt]	jn. konfrontieren, jm. entgegentreten	! Betonung auf der 2. Silbe: con<u>front</u> [kən'frʌnt]

°**leopard** ['lepəd]	Leopard	! Betonung auf der 1. Silbe: **leo**pard ['lepəd]
°**cheetah** ['tʃiːtə]	Gepard	
°**hippo** ['hɪpəʊ], *pl* **hippos**	Nilpferd	
°**medicine** ['medsn]	Medizin, Medikament(e)	
°**put** sth. *(+ Adverb)*	etwas *(auf eine bestimmte Art)* ausdrücken, formulieren	

a **leopard**
a **hippo**
a **cheetah**

put sth. politely/simply ... (etwas höflich/einfach/ ... ausdrücken)

I don't understand. Can you **put it more simply**?	... Kannst du es einfacher ausdrücken?
To put it mildly, the service at the hotel was a disaster.	Gelinde gesagt, ...
The food was ... how shall I **put it**? ... a bit disappointing.	Das Essen war ... wie soll ich sagen? ...
As my brother put it, "You can't have everything."	Wie mein Bruder es ausdrückte, ...
I often find it difficult to **put my feelings into words**.	... meine Gefühle in Worten auszudrücken.

°**unemployment** [ʌnɪm'plɔɪmənt]	Arbeitslosigkeit	**unemployment** ◄► **employment** [ɪm'plɔɪmənt] (Arbeit, Anstellung)
°**therefore** ['ðeəfɔː]	daher, deshalb	= a more formal word for "so" or "that's why"
°**at a time**	jeweils, ununterbrochen	**three weeks at a time** = drei Wochen am Stück
°**despite** [dɪ'spaɪt]	trotz	**despite** the dangers = **although** it is/was dangerous
p. 30 °**poverty** ['pɒvəti]	Armut	adjective: **poor** – noun: **poverty**
°**conservation** [kɒnsə'veɪʃn]	(Natur-)Schutz, Erhaltung, Bewahrung	I am interested in animal ~ because too many animals are dying out!

MORE CHALLENGE 2

p. 50 °**bicycle** ['baɪsɪkl]	Fahrrad	The word "bike" is short for "~".
°**shameful** ['ʃeɪmfl]	schändlich, beschämend	
°**reasonable** ['riːznəbl]	vernünftig, angemessen	**reasonably** happy = quite happy (ziemlich/ durchaus glücklich)
°**well heeled** [wel 'hiːld] *(infml)*	gut betucht, wohlhabend	A **well-heeled** area is one where lots of rich people live.
°**draw** sb.'s **attention to** sth.	js. Aufmerksamkeit auf etwas lenken	
°**instinctive** [ɪn'stɪŋktɪv]	instinktiv	! Betonung auf der 2. Silbe: in**stinc**tive [ɪn'stɪŋktɪv]
°**intervene (in)** [ɪntə'viːn]	eingreifen, einschreiten (in, bei); sich einmischen (in)	The kids are fighting again ... should we ~?
°**state** [steɪt]	Zustand	I was in a ~ of shock when I heard the news. ! **state** = **1.** Staat; **2.** Zustand
°**menacing** ['menəsɪŋ]	drohend, bedrohlich	If something or someone is ~, you're afraid of it/them.
°**curse** [kɜːs]	fluchen	He **~d** when he arrived on the platform and saw that his train had just left.

	°**be about**	da sein, anwesend sein, sich aufhalten	There **weren't** many people ~ when the attack happened.
	°**concerned (for/about)** [kən'sɜːnd]	besorgt (um)	A boy is missing from his home in Stoke-on-Trent. The police are **concerned** for his **welfare**.
	°**welfare** ['welfeə]	Wohl, Wohlergehen	
	°**motorcycle** ['məʊtəsaɪkl]	Motorrad	a **motorcycle** 
	°**conclude** [kən'kluːd]	schließen, schlussfolgern	From her accent we **~d** that she was German.
	°**If he were to …**	Wenn/Falls er …	• **If he were to win** the race, he would get a lot of money. (**Wenn/Falls er gewinnen sollte, … / Sollte er gewinnen, …**) • **If it were to snow** tomorrow, we could go skiing. (**Wenn/Falls es schneien sollte, … / Sollte es schneien, …**)
	°**retreat** [rɪ'triːt]	sich zurückziehen	I didn't want to get into a fight, so I **~ed**.
	°**inexplicable** [ɪnɪk'splɪkəbl]	unerklärlich	When something is ~, it cannot be explained.
	°**incident** ['ɪnsɪdənt]	Vorfall, Begebenheit	= something that happens
	°**pass** [pɑːs]	vorübergehen, vorbeigehen *(Zeit, Moment, Gelegenheit)*	When the first wave of shock has **~ed**, we'll be able to think clearly again. I wanted to tell her the truth, but the moment **~ed**, and then it was too late.
	°**account** [ə'kaʊnt]	Bericht, Beschreibung	Your ~ of the incident sounds very different from your friend's!
	°**that sort of thing** [sɔːt]	so etwas; dergleichen	What kind of music do you like? – Hip hop, rap, **that ~ of thing**.
	°**misgivings** *(pl)* [mɪs'gɪvɪŋz]	Bedenken	= bad feelings
p. 51	°**enrich** [ɪn'rɪtʃ]	bereichern, anreichern	= make sth. better, e.g. by adding things You can ~ this sauce by adding some cream.
p. 52	°**referendum (on sth.)** [refə'rendəm]	Volksentscheid (über etwas)	
	°**divide (into)** [dɪ'vaɪd]	spalten; teilen (in)	The teacher **~d** the class **into** groups of four. These government decisions threaten to ~ our nation. (= people disagree about the decisions)
	°**anger** ['æŋgə]	Zorn, Wut	noun: **anger** – adjective: **angry**
	°**open-minded** [əʊpən 'maɪndɪd]	aufgeschlossen, offen	
	°**tolerant** ['tɒlərənt]	tolerant	
	°**worldly** ['wɜːldli]	welterfahren, weltgewandt	= having a lot of experience in life, knowing about the ways of the world
	°**shut** sb./sth. **off from**	jn./etwas abschneiden, abkapseln von	
	°**form** [fɔːm]	(sich) formen, bilden	

	°**change one's mind**	es sich anders überlegen	Daniel had wanted to go out, but then he **~d his mind** and stayed home.
	°**builder** ['bɪldə]	Bauarbeiter/in	! **builder** = **1.** Bauunternehmer/in; **2.** Bauarbeiter/in

MORE CHALLENGE 3

p. 72	°**graduate (from)** ['grædʒueɪt]	den Abschluss machen (an) *(Schule, Hochschule)*	Sean **~d from** Oxford University last month and is now looking for a job.
	°**fellow** student ['feləʊ]	Mitschüler/in	Our ~ passengers on the plane were very patient when our baby cried.
	°**memory (of)** ['meməri]	Gedächtnis, Erinnerung (an)	My dad lived in Berlin twenty years ago. He says he has very nice **memories** of the city. **in memory of** = in Gedenken an
	°**rhetorical question** [rɪtɒrɪkl 'kwestʃən]	rhetorische Frage	
	°**repetition** [repə'tɪʃn]	Wiederholung	verb: **repeat** – noun: **repetition**
	°**provoke** [prə'vəʊk]	provozieren	
	°**successively** [sək'sesɪvli]	hintereinander, nacheinander	= one after the other Please do these tasks **~**.
	°**clarify** ['klærəfaɪ]	klären, klarstellen	= make sth. clear(er)
	°**passage** ['pæsɪdʒ]	Passage *(z.B. Text, Musikstück)*	
	°**found** [faʊnd]	gründen	The University of Cambridge is very old. It was **founded** in 1209. ! **found** = **1.** *simple past/past participle* of **find, found, found** (finden) **2.** gründen (**found, founded, founded**)
	°**patience** ['peɪʃns]	Geduld	adjective: **patient** – noun: **patience**
p. 73	°**bore** sb. [bɔː]	jn. langweilen	something **bores** you = you find it **boring** = you are **bored** by it
	°**embarrass** sb. [ɪm'bærəs]	jn. in Verlegenheit bringen	I hate it when my parents **~** me in front of my friends. It **~es** me when this happens. = I'm embarrassed by what happens.
	°**have bumps** [bʌmps]	holprig sein	
p. 74	°**senior** ['siːniə]	*Schüler/in im letzten Schuljahr*	
	°**expression** [ɪk'spreʃn]	Ausdruck	
	°**be expected to do** sth.	etwas tun sollen/müssen; es wird erwartet, dass man etwas tut	I **was expected to** make a speech. = People **expected** me **to** make a speech.
	°**have** sth. **done (by** sb.)	etwas (von jm.) machen lassen	Your hair looks nice. Did you cut it yourself or did you **~ it cut**?
	°**decorate** ['dekəreɪt]	dekorieren, schmücken	! Betonung auf der 1. Silbe: **de**corate ['dekəreɪt]
	°**ceremony** ['serəməni]	Feier, Zeremonie	! Betonung auf der 1. Silbe: **ce**remony ['serəməni]
	°**colour**	färben	noun: **colour** – verb: **colour** sth.

Das **English – German dictionary** enthält den Wortschatz der Bände 1 bis 6 von *Headlight*. Wenn du wissen möchtest, was ein englisches Wort bedeutet, wie man es ausspricht oder wie es genau geschrieben wird, dann kannst du hier nachschlagen.

Im **Dictionary** werden folgende **Abkürzungen und Symbole** verwendet:

sb. = somebody | sth. = something | jn. = jemanden | jm. = jemandem
pl = *plural* (Mehrzahl) | *BE* = British English | *AE* = American English | *(in)fml* = *(in)formal* (formell/informell)

° Mit diesem Kringel sind Wörter markiert, die nicht zum Lernwortschatz gehören.
Die **Fundstellenangaben** zeigen, wo ein Wort zum ersten Mal vorkommt.
Die Ziffern in Klammern bezeichnen Seitenzahlen:

I = *Headlight* Band 1 • II = *Headlight* Band 2 • III = *Headlight* Band 3 • IV = *Headlight* Band 4 • V = *Headlight* Band 5 • VI 1 (8) = *Headlight* Band 6, Unit 1, Seite 8

Tipps zur Arbeit mit einem Wörterbuch findest du im Skills file auf Seite 157.

A

a [ə] ein, eine I **£10 a week** 10 Pfund pro Woche II
ability [ə'bɪləti] Fähigkeit, Können V
able ['eɪbl]: **be able to do sth.** etwas tun können, in der Lage sein etwas zu tun III
aboard [ə'bɔːd] an Bord I
Aboriginal [æbə'rɪdʒənl] Aborigine- *(die Ureinwohner/innen Australiens betreffend)* V **Aboriginal Australian** australische/r Ureinwohner/in V
about [ə'baʊt]:
1. ungefähr I
2. über I
about me über mich I **be about to do sth.** im Begriff sein, etwas zu tun VI 1 (20) **good about my house** gut an meinem Haus I **What about you?** Und du? / Was ist mit dir? I °**be about** da sein, anwesend sein, sich aufhalten °**do sth. about it** etwas daran tun, etwas dagegen unternehmen
above [ə'bʌv] oben; über, oberhalb (von) V
°**abreast (of sb./sth.)** [ə'brest] auf gleicher Höhe (mit jm./etwas)
°**abroad** [ə'brɔːd] im/ins Ausland
absolute ['æbsəluːt] absolut IV
academy [ə'kædəmi] Akademie VI 1 (14)
accent ['æksent] Akzent III
accept [ək'sept] akzeptieren, annehmen V
access ['ækses] Zugang, Zutritt VI 1 (14)
accident ['æksɪdənt]:
1. Unfall II
2. Versehen; Zufall VI 3 (65)
by accident aus Versehen; zufällig VI 3 (65)
accommodation [əkɒmə'deɪʃn] Unterkunft III
according to [ə'kɔːdɪŋ] laut, zufolge V
account [ə'kaʊnt]:
1. Account, Konto V
°2. Bericht, Beschreibung
accurate ['ækjərət] genau, präzise VI 3 (69)
°**ace** [eɪs] Ass
ache [eɪk] Schmerz(en) II
achievement [ə'tʃiːvmənt] Errungenschaft, Leistung V
across [ə'krɒs] (quer) über II
act [ækt]:
1. Theater spielen, schauspielern II
2. handeln, sich verhalten; so tun, als ob V
acting school ['æktɪŋ skuːl] Schauspielschule V
action ['ækʃn] Aktion, Handlung V **take action** Maßnahmen ergreifen, etwas unternehmen V
active ['æktɪv] aktiv II **active vocabulary** aktiver Wortschatz VI 3 (58)
activism ['æktɪvɪzəm] Aktivismus VI 2 (36)
activist ['æktɪvɪst] Aktivist/in VI 2 (36)
activity [æk'tɪvəti] Aktivität, Tätigkeit II
actor ['æktə] Schauspieler/in V
°**actual** ['æktʃuəl] tatsächliche(r, s), eigentliche(r, s)
actually ['æktʃuəli] eigentlich; tatsächlich III
AD [eɪ 'diː]: **1000 AD** 1000 n. Chr. VI 3 (60)
ad [æd] *(infml)* Anzeige, Inserat, Annonce V
adapted from [ə'dæptɪd frɒm] basierend auf, (frei) nach V
adapter [ə'dæptə] Adapter III
add (to) [æd] hinzufügen (zu) III
addicted (to) [ə'dɪktɪd] süchtig (nach), abhängig (von) V
addition [ə'dɪʃn]: **in addition** außerdem VI 3 (69)
address [ə'dres]:
1. Adresse I
°2. **address sb.** jn. ansprechen, sich an jn. richten
admire [əd'maɪə] bewundern V
admission [əd'mɪʃn] Eintritt(spreis) IV
adopt [ə'dɒpt] adoptieren; *(Tier)* bei sich aufnehmen II
adult ['ædʌlt] Erwachsene/r II
advantage [əd'vɑːntɪdʒ] Vorteil IV
adventure [əd'ventʃə] Abenteuer I
advert ['ædvɜːt] Anzeige, Werbung I
advertise (sth.) ['ædvətaɪz] Werbung machen (für etwas) V
advertisement [əd'vɜːtɪsmənt] Anzeige, Inserat, Annonce V
advertiser ['ædvətaɪzə] Werber/in, Werbetreibende/r V
advertising ['ædvətaɪzɪŋ] Werbung, Reklame V
advice [əd'vaɪs] Rat(schlag), Ratschläge II **a piece of advice** ein Rat(schlag) IV
°**affect** [ə'fekt] beeinflussen, sich auswirken auf
afraid [ə'freɪd]: **be afraid (of)** Angst haben (vor) IV **I'm afraid** leider, ich fürchte III
African American [æfrɪkən ə'merɪkən] afroamerikanisch; Afroamerikaner/in IV
after ['ɑːftə]:
1. nachdem III
2. nach *(zeitlich)* I
after that danach IV
after-class activities *(pl)* [ɑːftə klɑːs æk'tɪvətiz] AGs *(freiwillige Veranstaltungen nach Unterrichtsschluss)* IV
afternoon [ɑːftə'nuːn] Nachmittag I **in the afternoon** am Nachmittag I
afterwards ['ɑːftəwədz] hinterher, danach VI 2 (42)
again [ə'gen] wieder, noch einmal I **every now and again** ab und zu, von Zeit zu Zeit VI 1 (19)
against [ə'genst] gegen II
age [eɪdʒ]:
1. Alter I
2. Zeitalter VI 3 (60)
°**agency** ['eɪdʒənsi] Agentur, Organisation
aggressive [ə'gresɪv] aggressiv IV
ago [ə'gəʊ]: **a long time ago** vor langer Zeit II
agree [ə'griː]: **agree with sb./sth.** jm. zustimmen; mit etwas einverstan-

den sein II **°agree (on) sth.** vereinbaren, sich einigen auf
agricultural [ægrɪ'kʌltʃərəl] landwirtschaftlich, Agrar- VI 3 (57)
agriculture ['ægrɪkʌltʃə] Landwirtschaft IV
ahead [ə'hed] voraus, vorausliegend VI 1 (22) **There is still a long road ahead.** Es liegt noch ein langer/weiter Weg vor uns. VI 1 (22)
°aim [eɪm] Ziel
air [eə] Luft II
airbrush ['eəbrʌʃ] *(Foto)* retuschieren, nachbessern VI 2 (36)
airport ['eəpɔːt] Flughafen III
°alarm [ə'lɑːm] Alarm; Alarmanlage
alarm clock [ə'lɑːm klɒk] Wecker I
alarmed [ə'lɑːmd] beunruhigt VI 2 (44)
alcohol ['ælkəhɒl] Alkohol III
alive [ə'laɪv] lebendig, am Leben II **come alive** lebendig werden, (wieder) aufleben II
all [ɔːl] alle(s) I **all over the country** überall im Land, im ganzen Land II **all summer** den ganzen Sommer I **in all** insgesamt III
all right [ɔːl 'raɪt] gut; in Ordnung; OK IV
allergic (to) [ə'lɜːdʒɪk] allergisch (gegen) V
alligator ['ælɪgeɪtə] Alligator IV
allow sb. to do sth. [ə'laʊ] jm. erlauben, etwas zu tun VI 3 (57)
allowed [ə'laʊd]: **be allowed to do sth.** etwas tun dürfen III
almond ['ɑːmənd] Mandel III
almost ['ɔːlməʊst] fast, nahezu, beinahe IV
alone [ə'ləʊn] allein II **leave sb. alone** jn. in Ruhe lassen V
along [ə'lɒŋ]:
1. **along the road** die Straße entlang II
2. **(come/sing/...) along** *(infml)* mit(kommen/singen/...) V
drag sb. along *(infml)* jn. mitschleifen V
alphabet ['ælfəbet] Alphabet I
already [ɔːl'redi] schon II
also ['ɔːlsəʊ] auch II
alternative [ɔːl'tɜːnətɪv] Alternative; alternativ VI 3 (68)
although [ɔːl'ðəʊ] obwohl V
altogether [ɔːltə'geðə] insgesamt IV
always ['ɔːlweɪz] immer I
am [eɪ'em]: **9 am/9 a.m.** 9 Uhr morgens/vormittags I
amazing [ə'meɪzɪŋ] erstaunlich II
ambulance ['æmbjələns] Krankenwagen II
among [ə'mʌŋ] unter, zwischen *(mehreren Personen oder Dingen)* IV
an [ən] ein, eine I
°analyse ['ænəlaɪz] analysieren, untersuchen

ancient ['eɪnʃənt] uralt, antik IV
and [ænd], [ənd] und I
°anger ['æŋgə] Zorn, Wut
angry ['æŋgri] wütend II
animal ['ænɪml] Tier I
°announce [ə'naʊns] verkünden, bekanntgeben
announcement [ə'naʊnsmənt] Durchsage, Ansage; Bekanntgabe, Ankündigung IV
announcer [ə'naʊnsə] Ansager/in, Sprecher/in VI 1 (24)
another [ə'nʌðə] ein/e andere/r/s; noch ein/e I
answer ['ɑːnsə]:
1. Antwort II
2. antworten (auf), beantworten II
answer the door aufmachen, zur/an die Tür gehen V **answer the phone** ans Telefon gehen V
anti- ['ænti] anti-, gegen- VI 1 (11)
any ['eni] jegliche/r/s, jede/r beliebige IV **Any ideas?** Irgendwelche Ideen? I **(at) any time** zu jeder Zeit, jederzeit IV **It wasn't just any car.** Es war kein beliebiges / nicht einfach irgendein Auto. V **not (...) any more** nicht mehr II **we don't have any** wir haben kein/e II
anybody ['enibɒdi] (irgend)jemand; jede/r (beliebige) IV **not ... anybody** niemand IV
anyone ['eniwʌn] (irgend)jemand; jede/r (beliebige) IV **not ... anyone** niemand IV
anything ['eniθɪŋ] *(in Fragen)* (irgend) etwas III **not (...) anything** nichts II **Would you like anything else?** Möchten Sie sonst noch etwas? I
anytime ['enitaɪm] jederzeit IV
anyway ['eniweɪ]: **Anyway, ...** Also, ... / So, ... / Gut, ... III **Where ... anyway?** Wo ... überhaupt? VI 1 (20)
anywhere ['eniweə]: **not ... anywhere** nirgendwo(hin) III
apartheid [ə'pɑːtaɪt] Apartheid *(früheres System der Trennung zwischen Weißen und Schwarzen in Südafrika)* VI 1 (11)
apartment [ə'pɑːtmənt] *(AE)* Wohnung IV
appear (to be/do) [ə'pɪə] auftauchen, erscheinen; (zu sein/tun) scheinen V
appearance [ə'pɪərəns] Erscheinung(sbild), Aussehen V
appetite ['æpɪtaɪt] Appetit III
apple ['æpl] Apfel I
°appliance [ə'plaɪəns] (Haushalts-)Gerät
application [æplɪ'keɪʃn] Bewerbung, Antrag V
application form [æplɪ'keɪʃn fɔːm] Bewerbungsformular, Antragsformular V
apply (for) [ə'plaɪ] sich bewerben (um) V

appointment [ə'pɔɪntmənt] Termin; Verabredung II
apprentice [ə'prentɪs] Lehrling, Auszubildende/r V
approach [ə'prəʊtʃ]:
1. Ansatz, Herangehensweise V
2. sich nähern, näher kommen VI 2 (43)
appropriate [ə'prəʊpriət] angemessen, passend, geeignet IV
April ['eɪprəl] April I
aquarium [ə'kweəriəm] Aquarium I
arch [ɑːtʃ] Bogen *(z.B. Torbogen)* III
archery ['ɑːtʃəri] Bogenschießen II
°architect ['ɑːkɪtekt] Architekt/in
architecture ['ɑːkɪtektʃə] Architektur V
are [ɑː] bist, sind, seid I **The posters are £ 1.** Die Poster kosten £ 1. I
area ['eəriə] Gebiet, Gegend III
arena [ə'riːnə] Arena V
argue ['ɑːgjuː] argumentieren; streiten IV
argument ['ɑːgjumənt] Argument; Streit V
°argumentative [ɑːgju'mentətɪv] argumentativ
arm [ɑːm] Arm II
°armed [ɑːmd] bewaffnet
army ['ɑːmi] Armee IV **join the army** zur Armee gehen IV
around [ə'raʊnd]:
1. in ... umher III
2. um ... herum III
3. umher(-) II
around here hier in der Nähe II
get around sich fortbewegen *(mobil sein)* IV **walk around** umhergehen II
arrange [ə'reɪndʒ] arrangieren; (an) ordnen V
arrest sb. [ə'rest] jn. festnehmen, verhaften IV
arrival [ə'raɪvl] Ankunft III
arrive [ə'raɪv] ankommen II
art [ɑːt] Kunst I
article ['ɑːtɪkl] Artikel III
artist ['ɑːtɪst] Künstler/in III
artistic [ɑː'tɪstɪk] künstlerisch; künstlerisch begabt IV
arty ['ɑːti] *(infml)* (gewollt) künstlerisch V
as [æz], [əz]:
1. als, während II
2. da, weil IV
3. **as a footballer** als Fußballer/in III
as fast as he could so schnell (wie) er konnte II **as much as ...** bis zu ...; nicht weniger als ... IV **as well** auch VI 1 (22)
ask [ɑːsk]:
1. fragen I
ask questions Fragen stellen I **ask sb. about sth.** sich bei jm. nach etwas erkundigen II
2. **ask for sth.** um etwas bitten IV

ask sb. to do sth. jn. bitten, etwas zu tun II
asleep [ə'sli:p]: **be asleep** schlafen IV **fall asleep** einschlafen IV
°**aspect** ['æspekt] Aspekt
assembly [ə'sembli] Schulversammlung I
assist (with) [ə'sɪst] assistieren, helfen (bei) V
assistant [ə'sɪstənt] Helfer/in, Assistent/in V **early years teaching assistant** Hilfskraft im Kindergarten, Sozialassistent/in V
astronaut ['æstrənɔ:t] Astronaut/in V
at [æt], [ət]: **at 1 o'clock** um 1 Uhr / um 13 Uhr I **at a restaurant** in einem Restaurant I **at home** zu Hause, daheim I **at least** wenigstens, zumindest II **at MARTINS** bei MARTINS I **at night** nachts, in der Nacht I **at school** in der Schule I **at the bottom** unten, am unteren Ende I **at the cinema** im Kino I **at the moment** im Moment, gerade I **at the same time** zur selben Zeit, gleichzeitig V **at the top** oben, am oberen Ende; an der Spitze I **at the weekend** am Wochenende I **at this school** auf/an dieser Schule I **at work** bei der Arbeit, am Arbeitsplatz I **be good at sth.** etwas gut können; gut in etwas sein III
ate [eɪt], [et] *siehe* **eat**
athlete ['æθli:t] (Leicht-)Athlet/in, Sportler/in VI 1 (15)
attach (to) [ə'tætʃ] anfügen; anhängen (an) *(Brief, E-Mail)* VI 3 (69)
attack [ə'tæk] angreifen II
attention [ə'tenʃn] Aufmerksamkeit V **pay attention (to)** achten (auf), aufpassen (auf) V °**draw sb.'s attention to sth.** js. Aufmerksamkeit auf etwas lenken
attention-getter [ə'tenʃn getə] Blickfang; etwas, was Aufmerksamkeit erregt V
attic ['ætɪk] Dachboden IV **in the attic** auf dem Dachboden IV
attitude (to/towards) ['ætɪtju:d] Einstellung, (Geistes-)Haltung (zu/gegenüber) V
attract [ə'trækt] anziehen, anlocken IV
attraction [ə'trækʃn] Attraktion; Anziehungskraft V
attractive [ə'træktɪv] attraktiv V
audience ['ɔ:diəns] Publikum; Zuschauer/innen, Zuhörer/innen V
August ['ɔ:gəst] August I
aunt [ɑ:nt] Tante I
author ['ɔ:θə] Autor/in IV
autumn ['ɔ:təm] Herbst II
available [ə'veɪləbl] erhältlich, verfügbar, *(Stelle)* frei IV **be available** zur Verfügung stehen, Zeit haben V
avatar ['ævətɑ:] Avatar *(virtuelle Figur)* V
average ['ævərɪdʒ] durchschnittlich, Durchschnitt V **on average** im Durchschnitt, durchschnittlich V
avoid [ə'vɔɪd] (ver)meiden IV
°**award** [ə'wɔ:d] Preis *(Auszeichnung)*
°**aware** [ə'weə]: **politically aware** politisch interessiert/bewusst
away [ə'weɪ] weg, fort I
awesome ['ɔ:səm] *(AE, infml)* klasse, stark, großartig IV

B

babysitting ['beɪbisɪtɪŋ] Babysitten I
back [bæk]:
1. zurück I
back and forth hin und her V
2. Rücken; Rückseite II
back of the hand Handrücken V
at the back hinten, im hinteren Teil IV **know sth. like the back of one's hand** etwas wie seine Westentasche kennen; etwas in- und auswendig kennen V
back away (from) [bæk] zurückweichen (von) V
°**back cover** [bæk 'kʌvə] Umschlagrückseite *(Buch)*
background ['bækgraʊnd] Hintergrund III
backpack ['bækpæk]:
1. Rucksack V
2. als Rucksacktourist/in unterwegs sein V
backstreet ['bækstri:t] *(kleinere)* Seitenstraße *(weitab von den Hauptstraßen)* V
backward(s) ['bækwədz] rückwärts; nach hinten VI 3 (66)
backyard [bæk'jɑ:d] *(AE)* (Hinter-)Hof; Garten hinter dem Haus IV
bacon ['beɪkən] Speck IV
bad [bæd] schlecht; schlimm I **... is bad news.** ... ist gefährlich. / ... ist (gar) nicht gut. V
badge [bædʒ]:
1. Anstecknadel, Button III
2. Abzeichen, Dienstmarke IV
badger ['bædʒə] Dachs II
badminton ['bædmɪntən] Badminton, Federball IV
bag [bæg] Tasche I
bagel ['beɪgl] Bagel *(ringförmiges Brötchen)* IV
baggage ['bægɪdʒ] Gepäck III
baggage reclaim [rɪ'kleɪm] Gepäckausgabe III
baggy ['bægi] weit (geschnitten), sackig *(Kleidung)* IV
bagpipes *(pl)* ['bægpaɪps] *(ein)* Dudelsack III
bake [beɪk] backen II
baked potato [beɪkt pə'teɪtəʊ] Ofenkartoffel *(in der Schale gebacken)* II
baker ['beɪkə] Bäcker/in IV
bakery ['beɪkəri] Bäckerei III
balcony ['bælkəni] Balkon I
ball [bɔ:l] Ball I
balloon [bə'lu:n] Ballon III
ballroom dancing [bɔ:lru:m 'dɑ:nsɪŋ] Standardtanz II
ban [bæn]:
1. verbieten IV
be banned verboten sein/werden IV
2. **ban (on)** Verbot (von) V
banana [bə'nɑ:nə] Banane III
bank [bæŋk]:
1. Bank *(Geldinstitut)* II
2. Ufer III
Baptist ['bæptɪst] Baptist/in; Baptisten- IV
bar [bɑ:] **(chocolate/energy) bar** (Schoko-/Energie-)Riegel V
barbecue ['bɑ:bɪkju:] Grillfest, Grillparty II
barbecued ['bɑ:bɪkju:d] gegrillt IV
bark (at sb.) [bɑ:k] (jn. an)bellen II
barn [bɑ:n] Scheune, Stall I
basic ['beɪsɪk] einfach, elementar V
basically ['beɪsɪkli] im Prinzip, grundsätzlich V
basketball ['bɑ:skɪtbɔ:l] Basketball I
°**bastard** ['bɑ:stəd] *(taboo)* Arschloch, Schwein
bat [bæt]:
1. Fledermaus III
2. Schläger *(Sport)* IV
bath [bɑ:θ] Bad; Badewanne VI 3 (66)
have/take a bath baden, ein Bad nehmen *(in der Badewanne)* VI 3 (66)
bathroom ['bɑ:θru:m]:
1. Bad(ezimmer) I
2. *(AE)* Toilette *(in Privathäusern)* IV
battery ['bætri] Batterie, Akku VI 3 (69)
battery life ['bætəri laɪf] Batterie-/Akku-Laufzeit VI 3 (69)
battle ['bætl]:
1. Wettstreit, Battle *(im Rap)* I
2. Schlacht; Kampf IV
°**bay** [beɪ] Bucht
BC [bi: 'si:]: **7000 BC** 7000 v. Chr. VI 3 (60)
be [bi:], **was/were, been** sein I **I want to be a baker.** Ich möchte Bäcker/in werden. IV
beach [bi:tʃ] Strand I **on the beach** am Strand I
°**beadwork** ['bi:dwɜ:k] Perlstickerei, Perlarbeit
beam [bi:m] (Licht-)Strahl VI 2 (43)
the headlights were on full beam das Fernlicht war eingeschaltet VI 2 (43)
bean [bi:n] Bohne III
bear [beə] Bär I
beat [bi:t]:
1. *(Musik)* Beat, Rhythmus I

2. **beat, beat, beaten** schlagen, besiegen III
beaten ['bi:tn] *siehe* **beat**
became [bɪ'keɪm] *siehe* **become**
because [bɪ'kɒz] weil I
because of [bɪ'kɒz əv] wegen IV
become [bɪ'kʌm], **became, become** werden II
bed [bed] Bett I
bed and breakfast (B&B) [bed ən 'brekfəst] Frühstückspension; Zimmer mit Frühstück III
bedroom ['bedru:m] Schlafzimmer I
°**bedroomed** ['bedru:md]: **a two-bedroomed flat** eine Wohnung mit zwei Schlafzimmern
bedtime ['bedtaɪm] Schlafenszeit V
bee [bi:] Biene III
°**beef** [bi:f] Rind(fleisch)
been [bi:n] *siehe* **be**
before [bɪ'fɔ:]:
1. bevor; vor *(zeitlich)* I
2. vorher; zuvor II
began [bɪ'gæn] *siehe* **begin**
begin [bɪ'gɪn], **began, begun** anfangen, beginnen II
beginning [bɪ'gɪnɪŋ] Anfang III
begun [bɪ'gʌn] *siehe* **begin**
behave [bɪ'heɪv] sich benehmen; sich verhalten IV
behind [bɪ'haɪnd] hinter I
beige [beɪʒ] beige V
believe (in) [bɪ'li:v] glauben (an) II
bell [bel] Glocke; Klingel III
belly button ['beli bʌtn] *(infml)* Bauchnabel IV
belong to sb./sth. [bɪ'lɒŋ] jm. gehören, zu etwas gehören IV
belongings *(pl)* [bɪ'lɒŋɪŋz] Sachen, Besitz IV
below [bɪ'ləʊ] unten; unter, unterhalb (von) V
belt [belt] (Gepäck-)Band III
°**bench** [bentʃ] Bank *(zu Sitzen)*
bend [bend] Kurve III
beside [bɪ'saɪd] neben III
besides [bɪ'saɪdz] außerdem VI 1 (20)
best [best] beste(r, s); am besten I **Best wishes** Viele Grüße ... *(Briefschluss)* I **like sth. best** etwas am liebsten mögen II **the best of both worlds** das Beste von beidem I
best-known [best 'nəʊn] der/die/das bekannteste; am bekanntesten V
bet [bet], **bet, bet** wetten III
better ['betə] besser I **do better** besser abschneiden II **like sth. better** etwas lieber mögen II
better-known [betə 'nəʊn] bekannter V
between [bɪ'twi:n] zwischen I °**in between** dazwischen
°**bicycle** ['baɪsɪkl] Fahrrad
big [bɪg]:
1. groß I
2. dick, schwer *(Person)* V

bike [baɪk] Fahrrad I
biking ['baɪkɪŋ] *(das)* Radfahren IV
°**bilingual** [baɪ'lɪŋgwəl] zweisprachig
billboard ['bɪlbɔ:d] *(AE)* Plakatwand, Werbeplakat V
billion ['bɪliən] Milliarde VI 3 (60)
bin [bɪn] (Müll-)Eimer II
bird [bɜ:d] Vogel I
birthday ['bɜ:θdeɪ] Geburtstag I **Happy birthday!** Herzlichen Glückwunsch zum Geburtstag! I **It's her birthday.** Sie hat Geburtstag. I
biscuit ['bɪskɪt] Keks, Plätzchen I
bit [bɪt] *siehe* **bite**
bit [bɪt]: **bits** *(pl, infml)* Teile, Stückchen VI 1 (21) **a bit** ein bisschen I
bite [baɪt]:
1. Biss, (Insekten-)Stich V
2. **bite, bit, bitten** beißen II
bitten ['bɪtn] *siehe* **bite**
black [blæk] schwarz I
blame sb. (for) [bleɪm] jm. die Schuld geben (an), jm. Vorwürfe machen (wegen) III
blanket ['blæŋkɪt] Decke *(zum Zudecken u. Ä.)* I
blazer ['bleɪzə] Blazer *(Jackett, oft Teil der Schuluniform)* I
bled [bled] *siehe* **bleed**
bleed [bli:d], **bled, bled** bluten V
blew [blu:] *siehe* **blow**
blind [blaɪnd] blind II
blink (your eyes) [blɪŋk] blinzeln, (mit den Augen) zwinkern VI 3 (56)
block [blɒk] (Häuser-)Block IV
block of flats [blɒk əv 'flæts] Mehrfamilienhaus, Wohnblock I
blog [blɒg] bloggen VI 1 (14)
blood [blʌd] Blut IV
bloody ['blʌdi] blutig, voller Blut VI 2 (44) °**bloody** *(taboo)* verdammt, Scheiß-
blouse [blaʊz] Bluse II
blow [bləʊ], **blew, blown** blasen (in); wehen *(Wind)* V
blown [bləʊn] *siehe* **blow**
blue [blu:] blau I
blurb [blɜ:b] Klappentext *(eines Buches)* V
blush [blʌʃ] erröten, rot werden III
BMX [bi: em 'eks] BMX-Rad I
board [bɔ:d]:
1. Tafel I
°2. Surfboard, Surfbrett
board [bɔ:d]:
1. einsteigen, an Bord gehen IV
2. **board sth. up** etwas mit Brettern vernageln/zunageln V
boardwalk ['bɔ:dwɔ:k] Steg, Uferpromenade *(aus Holz)* V
boat [bəʊt] Boot; Schiff II
body ['bɒdi] Körper V
body painting ['bɒdi peɪntɪŋ] Körperbemalung V

boil [bɔɪl] zum Kochen bringen, kochen *(sieden)* III
bold [bəʊld] fett (gedruckt) III
bomb [bɒm]:
1. Bombe VI 2 (49)
2. einen Bombenanschlag verüben auf, bombardieren VI 2 (49)
bone [bəʊn] Knochen VI 2 (44)
bonfire ['bɒnfaɪə] *(großes Freuden-)* Feuer II
book [bʊk]:
1. Buch I
2. buchen, reservieren III
booking ['bʊkɪŋ] Buchung, Reservierung; Bestellung III
bookshop ['bʊkʃɒp] Buchladen II
boot [bu:t]:
1. Stiefel II
2. Kofferraum *(Auto)* V
booth [bu:ð] Nische, (Sitz-)Ecke *(im Restaurant)* IV
°**bore sb.** [bɔ:] jn. langweilen
bored [bɔ:d] gelangweilt II **feel bored** Langeweile haben II
boredom ['bɔ:dəm] Langeweile IV
boring ['bɔ:rɪŋ] langweilig I
born [bɔ:n]: **be born** geboren sein/werden IV
borough ['bʌrə] *(AE)* (Stadt-)Bezirk IV
borrow ['bɒrəʊ] (aus)leihen, sich borgen I
boss [bɒs] Boss, Chef/in III
bossy ['bɒsi] herrisch, rechthaberisch I
both [bəʊθ] beide I **both ... and ...** sowohl ... als auch ... VI 2 (36) **the best of both worlds** das Beste von beidem I
bottle ['bɒtl] Flasche I
bottom ['bɒtəm]:
1. unteres Ende I **at the bottom** unten, am unteren Ende I
2. Gesäß, Po III
bought [bɔ:t] *siehe* **buy**
bowling ['bəʊlɪŋ] Bowling, Kegeln II
box [bɒks] Kasten, Kiste, Kästchen I
box [bɒks] boxen III
boxer ['bɒksə] Boxer/in III
boy [bɔɪ] Junge I
boycott ['bɔɪkɒt]:
1. Boykott IV
2. boykottieren IV
boyfriend ['bɔɪfrend] (fester) Freund I
°**braai** [braɪ] Grillfest *(südafrikanisch)*
°**bracket** ['brækɪt] Klammer
brave [breɪv] mutig III
bread [bred] Brot I
break [breɪk]:
1. Kurzurlaub, (kurze) Schulferien IV
2. Pause I **at break** in der Pause *(zwischen Schulstunden)* II
break [breɪk], **broke, broken** (zer)brechen; kaputtgehen; kaputtmachen III **break a contract** einen Vertrag ver-

letzen, brechen IV **break down** eine Panne haben, kaputtgehen *(Auto)* V
breakfast ['brekfəst] Frühstück I
have breakfast frühstücken I
breath [breθ] Atem VI 3 (66) **pause for breath** kurz Pause machen, um Luft zu holen VI 3 (66)
°**breathtaking** ['breθteɪkɪŋ] atemberaubend
bridge [brɪdʒ] Brücke II
brief [bri:f] kurz (gefasst), knapp IV
be brief sich kurzfassen IV
brilliant ['brɪliənt] genial, toll III
bring [brɪŋ], **brought, brought** bringen, mitbringen I
Britain ['brɪtn] Großbritannien II
British ['brɪtɪʃ] britisch I
°**Brittany** ['brɪtəni] die Bretagne
brochure ['brəʊʃə] Broschüre, Prospekt I
broke [brəʊk] *siehe* **break**
broken ['brəʊkən]:
1. *siehe* **break**
2. zerbrochen, kaputt III
°**Bronze Age** ['brɒnz eɪdʒ] Bronzezeit
brother ['brʌðə] Bruder I
brought [brɔ:t] *siehe* **bring**
brown [braʊn] braun I
bruise [bru:z] Bluterguss, Prellung VI 2 (44)
budget ['bʌdʒɪt]:
1. Budget, Haushalt V
2. haushalten *(sparsam sein)* V
budgie ['bʌdʒi] Wellensittich II
buffalo, *pl* **buffalo** *or* **buffaloes** ['bʌfələʊ] Büffel; Bison IV
build [bɪld], **built, built** bauen II
builder ['bɪldə]:
1. Bauunternehmer/in V
°2. Bauarbeiter/in
building ['bɪldɪŋ] Gebäude III
built [bɪlt] *siehe* **build**
bull [bʊl] Stier, Bulle I
bully ['bʊli]:
1. Mobber/in, Tyrann/in V
2. tyrannisieren, mobben V
bump [bʌmp]:
1. **bump into** zusammenstoßen mit; zufällig treffen IV
°2. **have bumps** holprig sein
burger ['bɜ:gə] Hamburger *(Frikadelle)* II
burn [bɜ:n]:
1. brennen; verbrennen IV
2. Verbrennung, Brandverletzung VI 2 (44)
burns unit Abteilung für Verbrennungen/Brandverletzungen *(im Krankenhaus)* VI 2 (44)
burst [bɜ:st], **burst, burst** brechen, bersten, platzen IV **burst with excitement** vor Aufregung ganz außer sich sein IV

bus [bʌs] Bus I **go by bus** mit dem Bus fahren I **on the bus** im Bus I
bus station ['bʌs steɪʃn] Busbahnhof I
bus stop ['bʌs stɒp] Bushaltestelle II
bush [bʊʃ] Busch III
business ['bɪznəs] Geschäft, Betrieb III **start a business** ein Geschäft aufmachen, einen Betrieb gründen/eröffnen III
business people ['bɪznəs pi:pl] Geschäftsleute III
business person ['bɪznəs pɜ:sn] Geschäftsperson III
business studies *(pl)* ['bɪznəs stʌdi:z] Wirtschaft(slehre) *(Unterrichtsfach)* III
busker ['bʌskə] Straßenmusiker/in III
busy ['bɪzi]: **be busy** beschäftigt sein; viel zu tun haben I **The kitchen is too busy.** In der Küche ist zu viel los. I
busybody ['bɪzibɒdi] Wichtigtuer/in V
but [bʌt], [bət] aber I
butter ['bʌtə] Butter II
butterfly ['bʌtəflaɪ] Schmetterling V
buy [baɪ], **bought, bought** kaufen I
buzz [bʌz]:
1. *(ein/das)* Summen VI 1 (23)
2. summen VI 1 (23)
by [baɪ]: **by 8 pm/by next year/ by 2030** bis 20 Uhr/bis nächstes Jahr/bis (zum Jahr) 2030 VI 3 (62) **by the trail** am Weg, neben dem Weg IV **come by** *(AE)* vorbeikommen, vorbeischauen *(besuchen)* IV **go by bus** mit dem Bus fahren I **side by side** Seite an Seite IV **written by …** geschrieben von … III °**by the end of the second half** bis zum Ende der zweiten Halbzeit
Bye. [baɪ] Tschüs. I
bystander ['baɪstændə] Zuschauer/in, (unbeteiligte/r) Beobachter/in V

C

cable ['keɪbl] Kabel; Seil *(aus Draht/Stahl)* IV
cafe ['kæfeɪ] Café I
cafeteria [kæfə'tɪəriə] *(AE)* Kantine; Cafeteria IV
cage [keɪdʒ] Käfig I
cake [keɪk] Kuchen, Torte I
calculator ['kælkjuleɪtə] Taschenrechner I
calendar ['kælɪndə] Kalender IV
calf, *pl* **calves** [kɑ:f], [kɑ:vz] Kalb IV
call [kɔ:l]:
1. (Telefon-)Anruf II
2. Ruf, Schrei V
3. rufen; anrufen; nennen II
be called heißen *(genannt werden)* III
calm [kɑ:m] ruhig, still; besonnen III
came [keɪm] *siehe* **come**
camel ['kæml] Kamel V
camera ['kæmərə] Fotoapparat; Kamera I

camp [kæmp]:
1. zelten, campen IV
2. (Zelt-)Lager II
make camp sein Lager/Zelt aufschlagen V
campaign [kæm'peɪn] Kampagne V
campground ['kæmpgraʊnd] *(AE)* Campingplatz V
campsite ['kæmpsaɪt] Campingplatz V
can [kæn], [kən] können I **I can't (= cannot) do my homework.** Ich kann meine Hausaufgaben nicht machen. I
can [kæn] Dose V
cancel sth. ['kænsl] etwas abbrechen; absagen, ausfallen lassen VI 2 (35)
candidate ['kændɪdət] Bewerber/in, Kandidat/in V
candle ['kændl] Kerze V
°**candlelit** ['kændllɪt] bei Kerzenschein
candy ['kændi] *(AE)* Süßigkeiten II
canoe [kə'nu:] Kanu, Paddelboot I
canteen [kæn'ti:n] Kantine, (Schul-) Mensa I
°**canyon** ['kænjən] Cañon
cap [kæp] Kappe, (Schirm-)Mütze II
capital ['kæpɪtl]:
1. Hauptstadt III
2. **capital (letter)** Großbuchstabe II
captain ['kæptɪn] Kapitän/in II
caption ['kæpʃn] Bildunterschrift III
car [kɑ:] Auto I
car park ['kɑ: pɑ:k] Parkplatz II
°**caramel** ['kærəmel] Karamell
card [kɑ:d] Karte I
°**cardboard** ['kɑ:dbɔ:d] Pappe
care [keə]:
1. Sorgfalt, Vorsicht V
with care vorsichtig, mit Bedacht V
2. Versorgung, Betreuung V
take care of sth. sich um etwas kümmern V
care [keə]: **care about sth.** etwas wichtig nehmen VI 1 (22) **Do you care?** Kümmert dich das? / Interessiert dich das? VI 1 (22) **I care about you.** Du bist mir nicht egal. / Du liegst mir am Herzen. IV **People don't care.** Es ist den Leuten egal. / Den Leuten ist alles egal. IV **Who cares?** Wen interessiert das? / Was soll's? / Na und? IV
career [kə'rɪə] Karriere; (schulischer/beruflicher) Werdegang V
careful ['keəfl] vorsichtig; sorgfältig II
drive carefully vorsichtig fahren II
carnival ['kɑ:nɪvl] Karneval III
carpenter ['kɑ:pəntə] Schreiner/in IV
carriage ['kærɪdʒ] Kutsche II
carrot ['kærət] Möhre, Karotte II
carry ['kæri] tragen; befördern, transportieren IV
cart [kɑ:t] Wagen *(Einkaufswagen, Golfwagen etc.)* IV
carton ['kɑ:tn] (Papp-)Karton; Packung VI 1 (19)

cartoon [kɑː'tuːn] Zeichentrickfilm; Comic II
case [keɪs] Fall VI 1 (11) **(just) in case ...** (nur) für den Fall, dass ... VI 1 (11) **in (the) case of** im Falle von VI 1 (11)
casino [kə'siːnəʊ] (Spiel-)Kasino IV
castle ['kɑːsl] Burg II
cat [kæt] Katze I **Has the cat got his tongue?** Hat's ihm die Sprache verschlagen? IV
catch [kætʃ], **caught, caught** (ein)fangen, erwischen III **catch sth.** sich mit etwas anstecken; sich etwas einfangen *(Krankheit)* V
category ['kætəgəri] Kategorie IV
cathedral [kə'θiːdrəl] Kathedrale, Dom III
Catholic ['kæθlɪk] Katholik/in; katholisch II
cattle *(pl)* ['kætl] Vieh, Rinder IV
caught [kɔːt] *siehe* **catch** °**be caught up in sth.** von etwas gefangen sein, sich in etwas verheddern
cause sth. [kɔːz] etwas bewirken, verursachen VI 3 (65)
cave [keɪv] Höhle II
CCTV camera [siː siː tiː 'viː] Überwachungskamera III
CD [siː 'diː] CD I
CD player [siː'diː pleɪə] CD-Player II
celebrate ['selɪbreɪt] feiern II
°**celebration** [selɪ'breɪʃn] Feier
celebrity [sə'lebrəti] Prominente/r, Promi V
cell phone ['sel fəʊn] *(AE)* Handy IV
Celsius (C) ['selsiəs] Celsius IV
cent [sent] Cent III
central ['sentrəl] zentral III
centre ['sentə] Zentrum, (Stadt-)Mitte I
century ['sentʃəri] Jahrhundert VI 1 (16)
cereals *(pl)* ['sɪəriəlz] Getreide-, Frühstücksflocken II
°**ceremony** ['serəməni] Feier, Zeremonie
°**certain** ['sɜːtn] gewisse/r/s, bestimmte/r/s
certainly ['sɜːtnli] sicher(lich), gewiss VI 1 (19)
certificate [sə'tɪfɪkət] Urkunde, Bescheinigung V
chain [tʃeɪn] Kette I
chainsaw ['tʃeɪn sɔː] Kettensäge IV
chair [tʃeə] Stuhl I
challenge ['tʃælɪndʒ] Herausforderung III
°**championship** ['tʃæmpiənʃɪp] Meisterschaft
chance [tʃɑːns] Chance, Gelegenheit II
change [tʃeɪndʒ]:
1. (ver)ändern; wechseln IV **change (clothes)** sich umziehen, sich andere Sachen anziehen II **change (trains)** umsteigen *(Zug)* III °**change one's mind** es sich anders überlegen
2. Veränderung, Wechsel III
°**3.** Wechselgeld
channel ['tʃænl] Kanal II
chant [tʃɑːnt] Sprechgesang I
character ['kærəktə] Figur, Person *(in Roman, Film usw.)* III
characterization [kærəktəraɪ'zeɪʃn] Charakterisierung V
characterize ['kærəktəraɪz] charakteristisch sein für; beschreiben, darstellen V
charge [tʃɑːdʒ] (auf)laden *(Batterie, Handy)* III
charity ['tʃærəti] wohltätige Organisation II **charity shop** *Geschäft, das gespendete Waren für wohltätige Zwecke verkauft* II
chart [tʃɑːt] Diagramm, Tabelle IV
chase [tʃeɪs]:
1. verfolgen, jagen III
°**2. give chase** die Verfolgung aufnehmen
chat [tʃæt]:
1. chat (with) plaudern, „chatten", sich unterhalten (mit) II
2. Unterhaltung; Chat II
have a chat eine Unterhaltung führen, sich unterhalten II
chauffeur ['ʃəʊfə] Chauffeur/in VI 1 (22)
cheap [tʃiːp] billig, preiswert II
check [tʃek]:
1. (Über-)Prüfung, Kontrolle IV
2. (über)prüfen, kontrollieren II
check a website auf einer Website nachschauen II **check on sb.** nach jm. schauen, jn. kontrollieren VI 3 (59)
check sb./sth. out *(infml)* sich etwas anschauen, anhören; etwas ausprobieren IV
check in [tʃek 'ɪn] einchecken III
check-in ['tʃek ɪn] Check-in, *(das)* Einchecken III
checklist ['tʃeklɪst] Checkliste V
cheek [tʃiːk] Wange IV
cheer [tʃɪə] jubeln, *(Sportler/innen)* anfeuern IV
cheerful ['tʃɪəfl] fröhlich, gut gelaunt V
cheese [tʃiːz] Käse IV
°**cheetah** ['tʃiːtə] Gepard
°**chef** [ʃef] Koch, Köchin *(als Beruf)*
chemical ['kemɪkl] Chemikalie; chemisch VI 3 (57)
chest [tʃest] Brust(korb) V
chicken ['tʃɪkɪn] Huhn; (Brat-)Hähnchen I
child, *pl* **children** [tʃaɪld], ['tʃɪldrən] Kind I
childcare ['tʃaɪldkeə] Kinderbetreuung V
chill [tʃɪl] *(infml)* relaxen, sich ausruhen II
chin [tʃɪn] Kinn V
chip [tʃɪp] Stück(chen), Splitter IV
chipmunk ['tʃɪpmʌŋk] Streifenhörnchen I
chips *(pl)* [tʃɪps] Pommes frites I
(potato) chips *(AE)* Kartoffelchips IV
chocolate ['tʃɒklət] Schokolade I
choice [tʃɔɪs] (Aus-)Wahl IV
choir ['kwaɪə] Chor VI 3 (63)
choose [tʃuːz], **chose, chosen** (aus) wählen II
chore [tʃɔː] (Haus-)Arbeit, *(lästige)* Pflicht II **do chores** (Haus-)Arbeiten erledigen II
°**chorus** ['kɔːrəs] Refrain *(Lied)*
chose [tʃəuz] *siehe* **choose**
chosen ['tʃəuzn] *siehe* **choose**
Christmas ['krɪsməs] Weihnachten II
chronological [krɒnə'lɒdʒɪkl] chronologisch V
church [tʃɜːtʃ] Kirche I
cinema ['sɪnəmə] Kino I
circle ['sɜːkl] Kreis II
circumstances *(pl)* ['sɜːkəmstənsɪz] Umstände VI 3 (69) **under the circumstances** unter diesen Umständen VI 3 (69)
circus ['sɜːkəs] runder Platz *(in einer Stadt)* III
citizen ['sɪtɪzn] Bürger/in V
city ['sɪti] (Groß-)Stadt I
city slicker ['slɪkə] *(infml)* Großstadtsnob III
civil rights *(pl)* [sɪvl 'raɪts] Bürgerrechte IV
°**clarify** ['klærəfaɪ] klären, klarstellen
class [klɑːs]:
1. Klasse I
2. Unterricht; Kurs II
class teacher ['klɑːs tiːtʃə] Klassenlehrer/in I
classmate ['klɑːsmeɪt] Mitschüler/in V
classroom ['klɑːsruːm] Klassenraum I
clean [kliːn]:
1. sauber IV
2. sauber machen, putzen I
clean sth. off etwas abwaschen, abwischen, abputzen VI 2 (40) **clean sth. up** etwas aufräumen, sauber machen VI 1 (20)
cleaner ['kliːnə] Reinigungskraft V
cleaning ['kliːnɪŋ]: **do the cleaning** sauber machen, putzen V
clean-up ['kliːn ʌp] Reinemachen, Hausputz V
clear [klɪə]:
1. klar, deutlich II
2. (auf-/ab-/weg)räumen; *(Augen z.B. von Tränen)* frei machen IV
clearing ['klɪərɪŋ] Lichtung V
clerk [klɑːk] Angestellte/r V
clever ['klevə] schlau, klug II
cleverness ['klevənəs] Klugheit V
click (on) [klɪk] klicken (auf) III
°**cliff** [klɪf] Klippe, Felsen
°**cliff walk** ['klɪf wɔːk] Klippenpfad
climate ['klaɪmət] Klima V

°**climate change** ['klaɪmət tʃeɪndʒ] Klimawandel
climb [klaɪm] klettern (auf) II
cloak [kləʊk] Umhang IV
clock [klɒk] (Wand-, Stand-, Turm-) Uhr I
close [kləʊz] schließen, zumachen I **close on sb.** jm. näher kommen, zu jm. aufholen V **close sth. down** etwas schließen, stilllegen *(Fabrik, Geschäft)* III **closed** gesperrt *(Straße)* V
close [kləʊs]:
1. dicht, eng V
2. **close (to)** nahe (bei, an) IV **step closer** näher treten, näher (heran)kommen IV
3. genau *(eingehend)* IV **look closely** genau/näher hinschauen IV
close-up ['kləʊs ʌp] Nahaufnahme *(Film)* VI 3 (71)
clothes *(pl)* [kləʊðz] Kleidung(sstücke) II
cloud [klaʊd] Wolke II
cloudy ['klaʊdi] wolkig, bewölkt II
club [klʌb] Klub I **Join the club.** Da bist du nicht der/die Einzige. II
clue [klu:] Hinweis III
coach [kəʊtʃ] Trainer/in II
coast [kəʊst] Küste II **on the coast** an der Küste II
°**coastal** ['kəʊstl] Küsten-
coat [kəʊt] Mantel; Jacke III
cocktail ['kɒkteɪl] Cocktail VI 3 (59)
cocoa ['kəʊkəʊ] Kakao II
coconut ['kəʊkənʌt] Kokosnuss III
cod, *pl* **cod** [kɒd] Kabeljau, Dorsch III
coffee ['kɒfi] Kaffee I
cold [kəʊld]:
1. kalt II
2. Erkältung II
collar ['kɒlə] Halsband II
collect [kə'lekt] sammeln II
college ['kɒlɪdʒ] höhere Schule, Fach(hoch)schule V
°**Cologne** [kə'ləʊn] Köln
colon ['kəʊlən] Doppelpunkt VI 1 (17)
colonize ['kɒlənaɪz] kolonisieren VI 1 (10)
colony ['kɒləni] Kolonie V
colour ['kʌlə]:
1. Farbe I **(athletes) of colour** nicht-weiße Athleten/-innen VI 1 (15)
°2. färben
colourful ['kʌləfl] farbenfroh, bunt VI 1 (10)
comb [kəʊm]:
1. Kamm IV
2. **comb (your hair)** (sich die Haare) kämmen IV
combat ['kɒmbæt]:
1. Kampf V
2. kämpfen (gegen) V

come [kʌm], **came, come:**
1. (mit)kommen I **come across sth.** auf etwas stoßen, etwas (zufällig) finden VI 2 (40) **come by** *(AE)* vorbeikommen, vorbeischauen *(besuchen)* IV **Come on!** Na los! / Komm(t) (schon)! I **come up** aufgehen *(Sonne)* I **the sea's coming in** die Flut kommt; das Wasser steigt I **when it comes to ...** wenn es um ... geht IV
2. werden II **come alive** lebendig werden, (wieder) aufleben II **come true** wahr werden V **a dream come true** ein wahr gewordener Traum V
comedy ['kɒmədi] Comedyshow; Komödie II
comfortable ['kʌmftəbl] bequem, gemütlich II **be/feel comfortable (with)** sich wohlfühlen (bei/mit) V **make yourself comfortable** es sich gemütlich machen III
comma ['kɒmə] Komma VI 1 (17)
command [kə'mɑ:nd] Befehl V
comment ['kɒment]:
1. Kommentar III
°2. **comment on sth.** etwas kommentieren
commercial [kə'mɜ:ʃl] kommerziell *(auf Gewinn ausgerichtet)* IV
common ['kɒmən] häufig, weit verbreitet, gewöhnlich IV
communicate (with sb.) [kə'mju:nɪkeɪt] (mit jm.) kommunizieren; sich (mit jm.) verständigen VI 1 (16)
communication [kəmju:nɪ'keɪʃn] Kommunikation, Verständigung V
community [kə'mju:nəti] Gemeinschaft, Gemeinde IV **community service** gemeinnützige Arbeit, Sozialdienst IV
community college [kə'mju:nəti kɒlɪdʒ] weiterführende Schule *(BE)* I
company ['kʌmpəni] Firma, Gesellschaft IV
compare [kəm'peə] vergleichen IV °**compare (with/to)** vergleichbar sein (mit), sich vergleichen lassen (mit)
compass ['kʌmpəs] Kompass II
compete (with) [kəm'pi:t] konkurrieren (mit); *(in Wettbewerben)* antreten (gegen) V
competition [kɒmpə'tɪʃn] Wettbewerb III
complain (about/of) [kəm'pleɪn] sich beschweren (über); jammern III
complaint [kəm'pleɪnt] Beschwerde VI 3 (69) **make a complaint (about sth.)** eine Beschwerde vorbringen (über etwas), etwas beanstanden VI 3 (69)

complete [kəm'pli:t]:
1. vollständig, komplett IV
°2. vervollständigen, fertigstellen
°**complex** ['kɒmpleks] (Gebäude-)Komplex, Anlage
complicated ['kɒmplɪkeɪtɪd] kompliziert V
°**compost** ['kɒmpɒst] kompostieren
concentrate (on) ['kɒnsntreɪt] sich konzentrieren (auf) VI 3 (62)
concentration [kɒnsn'treɪʃn] Konzentration VI 3 (62)
°**concerned (for/about)** [kən'sɜ:nd] besorgt (um)
concert ['kɒnsət] Konzert I
°**conclude** [kən'klu:d] schließen, schlussfolgern
conclusion [kən'klu:ʒn] Schluss(folgerung) IV **draw conclusions** Rückschlüsse ziehen IV
concrete ['kɒŋkri:t] konkret VI 2 (41)
conditions *(pl)* [kən'dɪʃnz] Bedingungen, Verhältnisse VI 2 (47) °**living conditions** *(pl)* Lebensbedingungen, Lebensumstände
confectionery [kɒn'fekʃənəri] Süßwaren III
confident ['kɒnfɪdənt] (selbst)sicher; zuversichtlich V
confirm [kən'fɜ:m] bestätigen III
confiscate ['kɒnfɪskeɪt] konfiszieren, beschlagnahmen III
°**confront sb.** [kən'frʌnt] jn. konfrontieren, jm. entgegentreten
confuse [kən'fju:z] verwirren; verwechseln VI 1 (16)
connect (with/to) [kə'nekt] verbinden (mit) IV
connection [kə'nekʃn] Verbindung, Anschluss III
cons *(pl)* [kɒnz]: **the pros and cons** das Pro und Kontra; das Für und Wider V
°**consequence** ['kɒnsɪkwəns] Konsequenz, Folge **as a consequence** als Folge, folglich
°**conservation** [kɒnsə'veɪʃn] (Natur-) Schutz, Erhaltung, Bewahrung
°**consist of** [kən'sɪst] bestehen aus
consumer [kən'sju:mə] Konsument/in, Verbraucher/in VI 3 (57)
contact ['kɒntækt]:
1. Kontakt III
2. **contact sb.** Kontakt aufnehmen zu, sich melden bei V
contact lens ['kɒntækt lenz] Kontaktlinse VI 3 (56)
°**contact rugby** ['kɒntækt rʌgbi] Kontaktrugby
contain [kən'teɪn] enthalten VI 3 (65)
°**container** [kən'teɪnə] Behälter, Gefäß
°**content** ['kɒntent] Inhalt
continent ['kɒntɪnənt] Kontinent; europäisches Festland IV

continue [kən'tɪnjuː] weitergehen, weitermachen, (sich) fortsetzen IV **continue to …** weitergehen, weiterfahren, weiterreisen nach … IV
contract ['kɒntrækt] Vertrag IV **break a contract** einen Vertrag verletzen, brechen IV
°**contrast** ['kɒntrɑːst] Kontrast, Gegensatz
°**contrast** [kən'trɑːst] vergleichen, (einander) gegenüberstellen
control [kən'trəʊl]:
1. kontrollieren, regulieren V
2. Kontrolle I
lose control die Kontrolle verlieren I
controversial [kɒntrə'vɜːʃl] kontrovers, umstritten VI 3 (62)
conversation [kɒnvə'seɪʃn] Gespräch, Unterhaltung V
convince [kən'vɪns] überzeugen V
convincing [kən'vɪnsɪŋ] überzeugend V
cook [kʊk]:
1. kochen, *(Essen)* zubereiten I
2. Koch, Köchin I
cooker ['kʊkə] Herd III
cookie ['kʊki] Keks, Plätzchen III
cool [kuːl]:
1. kühl II
2. cool I
play it cool *(infml)* sich cool geben IV
cool down [kuːl 'daʊn] sich abkühlen; sich beruhigen V
cop [kɒp] *(infml)* Bulle *(Polizist/in)* VI 2 (44)
copy ['kɒpi] kopieren, abschreiben V
corn [kɔːn] *(BE)* Korn, Getreide; *(AE)* Mais IV
cornbread ['kɔːnbred] Maisbrot IV
corner ['kɔːnə] Ecke I **corner of your eye** Augenwinkel IV **pets corner** Streichelzoo I
correct [kə'rekt]:
1. korrigieren, berichtigen II
2. korrekt IV
°**correction** [kə'rekʃn] Berichtigung, Korrektur
cost [kɒst], **cost, cost** kosten *(Geld)* III
costs *(pl)* [kɒsts] Kosten V **travel costs** Reisekosten V
costume ['kɒstjuːm] Kostüm, Verkleidung II
cottage ['kɒtɪdʒ] Häuschen, Hütte II
cotton ['kɒtn] Baumwolle IV
couch [kaʊtʃ] Couch VI 1 (20)
cougar ['kuːgə] *(bes. AE)* Puma IV
could [kʊd]:
1. **he could** er konnte II
2. **I could** ich könnte II
council ['kaʊnsl] Rat, Gemeinderat, Stadtverwaltung VI 1 (19)
council flat ['kaʊnsl flæt] Sozialwohnung VI 1 (19)
counsellor ['kaʊnsələ] Berater/in; Betreuer/in VI 2 (44)
count [kaʊnt] zählen III
counter ['kaʊntə] (Verkaufs-)Schalter, Ladentheke V
country ['kʌntri] Land I **in the country** auf dem Land I
country bumpkin ['bʌmpkɪn] *(infml)* Landei, Bauerntrampel III
countryside ['kʌntrisaɪd] Land(schaft); Natur III
couple ['kʌpl] Paar III **a couple (of)** ein paar; ein Paar III
°**courage** ['kʌrɪdʒ] Mut **act of courage** mutiger Schritt
course [kɔːs] Kurs(us) III
court [kɔːt] Platz, Court *(Tennis, Basketball)* IV
cousin ['kʌzn] Cousin/e I
cover ['kʌvə] bedecken VI 1 (19)
cover letter ['kʌvə letə] Anschreiben, Begleitschreiben, Motivationsschreiben V
cow [kaʊ] Kuh I
crab [kræb] Krebs *(Tier)* I
cracker ['krækə] Cracker *(Gebäck)* IV
crash (into) [kræʃ] einen Unfall haben, zusammenstoßen (mit) V
crazy ['kreɪzi] verrückt I **crazy about sth.** wild auf etwas, versessen auf etwas VI 1 (22) **go crazy** verrückt werden V
cream [kriːm]:
1. Sahne I
2. Creme II
create [kri'eɪt] (er)schaffen, kreieren VI 2 (35)
creative [kri'eɪtɪv] kreativ V
credit card ['kredɪt kɑːd] Kreditkarte V
creep [kriːp], **crept, crept** schleichen, kriechen V **creep up (on sb.)** sich heranschleichen (an jn.) V
crept [krept] *siehe* **creep**
crew [kruː] Mannschaft, Team; Clique V
°**cricket** ['krɪkɪt] Kricket *(Mannschaftssportart)*
°**cricketer** ['krɪkɪtə] Kricketspieler/in
crime [kraɪm] Kriminalität; Verbrechen IV
crime series, *pl* **crime series** ['kraɪm sɪəriːz] Krimiserie II
crisps *(pl)* [krɪsps] (Kartoffel-)Chips I
critic ['krɪtɪk] Kritiker/in V
°**critical (of)** ['krɪtɪkl] kritisch (gegenüber)
criticism ['krɪtɪsɪzəm] Kritik V **react to criticism well** mit Kritik gut umgehen, Kritik vertragen V
°**criticize** ['krɪtɪsaɪz] kritisieren
crocodile ['krɒkədaɪl] Krokodil I
cross [krɒs]:
1. Kreuz II
2. überqueren II
3. **cross (with)** böse, sauer (auf) III
crossroads, *pl* **crossroads** ['krɒsrəʊdz] (Straßen-)Kreuzung III
crowd [kraʊd] (Menschen-)Menge VI 3 (66)
crowded ['kraʊdɪd] überfüllt, vollgestopft III
crown [kraʊn] Krone IV
cruise [kruːz]:
1. Kreuzfahrt, Schiffsreise IV
2. herumfahren (in) *(ohne Ziel)* IV
°**crutches** *(pl)* ['krʌtʃɪz] Krücken
cry [kraɪ] weinen II
cucumber ['kjuːkʌmbə] (Salat-)Gurke III
cultural ['kʌltʃərəl] kulturell VI 1 (10)
culture ['kʌltʃə] Kultur III
cup [kʌp] Tasse I
cupcake ['kʌpkeɪk] Cupcake *(kleiner runder Kuchen)* III
curious about ['kjʊəriəs] neugierig auf II
curly ['kɜːli] lockig V
°**current** [kʌrənt] aktuell, gegenwärtig
curry ['kʌri] Curry(gericht), Curry- III
°**curse** [kɜːs] fluchen
curtain ['kɜːtn] Vorhang, Gardine V
cushion ['kʊʃn] Kissen I
customer ['kʌstəmə] Kunde, Kundin I
cut [kʌt]:
1. Schnitt VI 1 (19)
2. **cut, cut, cut** schneiden; *(Rasen)* mähen II
cut down trees Bäume abholzen IV
cut through sth. etwas durchqueren; eine Abkürzung durch … nehmen VI 2 (43) °**cut sth.** etwas abbrechen, aufhören mit etwas
cute [kjuːt] niedlich, süß I
CV (= curriculum vitae) [siː 'viː], [kərɪkjələm 'viːtaɪ] *(BE)* Lebenslauf V
cyberbullying [saɪbə'bʊliɪŋ] Cybermobbing V
cycle ['saɪkl] Rad fahren III
cycle tour ['saɪkl tʊə] Radtour III

D

dad [dæd] Papa, Vati I
daily ['deɪli] täglich II
damage ['dæmɪdʒ]:
1. (be)schädigen, schaden VI 2 (44)
2. **damage (to)** *(no pl)* Schaden, Schäden (an) V
dance [dɑːns]:
1. tanzen I
2. Tanz(veranstaltung) III
dancer ['dɑːnsə] Tänzer/in III
danger ['deɪndʒə] Gefahr II
dangerous ['deɪndʒərəs] gefährlich I
dare [deə]:
1. Mutprobe IV
2. **dare sb. to do sth.** jn. herausfordern, etwas zu tun IV
dark [dɑːk]:
1. dunkel II
2. **(the) dark** (die) Dunkelheit VI 2 (43)
°**darkened** ['dɑːkənd] dunkel, verdunkelt, nicht angestrahlt *(z.B. Gebäude)*
darkness ['dɑːknəs] Dunkelheit IV

dart [dɑːt] (Wurf-)Pfeil II
dartboard ['dɑːtbɔːd] Dartscheibe II
data ['deɪtə] Daten VI 3 (58)
date [deɪt]:
1. Datum I
2. Verabredung, Date *(auch die Person, mit der man ausgeht)* IV
daughter ['dɔːtə] Tochter I
day [deɪ] Tag I **day-to-day** tagtäglich V **I haven't eaten in days.** Ich habe tagelang nichts gegessen. V **in the old days** früher II **one day** eines Tages IV **the next day** am anderen/nächsten Tag III **the other day** neulich III **these days** heutzutage VI 2 (36) **three-day trip** dreitägiger Ausflug II
day out, *pl* **days out** [deɪ 'aʊt] (Tages-)Ausflug II
dead [ded] tot III
deadly ['dedli] tödlich IV
deal [diːl] Geschäft; Vereinbarung II **a big deal** eine große Sache, viel Aufhebens III **It's a deal!** Abgemacht! II
deal with sth. [diːl], **dealt, dealt:**
1. umgehen mit etwas, mit etwas fertigwerden, klarkommen V
2. sich um jn./etwas kümmern, sich mit jm./einer Sache befassen VI 2 (44)
dealt [delt] *siehe* **deal**
Dear … [dɪə] Liebe/r … I **Dear Sir/Madam** Sehr geehrte Damen und Herren V **Oh dear.** Oje! I
debate [dɪ'beɪt] debattieren, diskutieren IV
December [dɪ'sembə] Dezember I
decide (to do sth.) [dɪ'saɪd] beschließen, (sich) entscheiden (etwas zu tun) IV
decision [dɪ'sɪʒn] Entscheidung III **make a decision** eine Entscheidung fällen III
deck [dek] Deck IV **on deck** an Deck IV
°**decorate** ['dekəreɪt] dekorieren, schmücken
deep [diːp] tief III
°**define** [dɪ'faɪn] definieren
definite ['defɪnət] klar, deutlich, sicher III
definitely ['defɪnətli] auf jeden Fall; ganz bestimmt III
°**definition** [defɪ'nɪʃn] Definition
degree [dɪ'griː] Grad II
delete [dɪ'liːt] löschen V
delicious [dɪ'lɪʃəs] köstlich, lecker VI 2 (42)
°**deliver** [dɪ'lɪvə] (aus)liefern **deliver a speech** eine Rede halten
°**delivery** [dɪ'lɪvəri] Lieferung
demand [dɪ'mɑːnd]:
1. fordern, verlangen VI 2 (40)
2. Forderung VI 2 (40)
democracy [dɪ'mɒkrəsi] Demokratie VI 1 (11)
democratic [demə'krætɪk] demokratisch VI 1 (11)
°**demonstrate** ['demənstreɪt] zeigen, demonstrieren
demonstration [demən'streɪʃn] Demonstration VI 2 (36)
den [den] Versteck; Hobbyraum II
department [dɪ'pɑːtmənt] Abteilung V
department store [dɪ'pɑːtmənt stɔː] Kaufhaus IV
departure [dɪ'pɑːtʃə] Abfahrt; Abflug III
depressing [dɪ'presɪŋ] deprimierend V
deputy ['depjuti] Stellvertreter/in; stellvertretende/r IV **deputy prime minister** Vizepremierminister/in IV **deputy sheriff** Hilfssheriff IV
derelict ['derəlɪkt] heruntergekommen, verfallen VI 3 (65)
descended [dɪ'sendɪd]: **be descended from** abstammen von IV
describe [dɪ'skraɪb] beschreiben I
°**description** [dɪ'skrɪpʃn] Beschreibung
desert ['dezət] Wüste IV
deserted [dɪ'zɜːtɪd] menschenleer, wie ausgestorben VI 3 (65)
design [dɪ'zaɪn] entwerfen, gestalten, entwickeln V
desk [desk] Schreibtisch I **front desk** Rezeption, Empfang *(z.B. Hotel)* V
desk clerk ['desk klɑːk] Empfangsmitarbeiter/in V
°**desperate** ['despərət] verzweifelt
°**despite** [dɪ'spaɪt] trotz
dessert [dɪ'zɜːt] Nachspeise, Dessert II
destination [destɪ'neɪʃn] Reiseziel, Fahrtziel VI 3 (64)
destroy [dɪ'strɔɪ] zerstören, vernichten II
°**destruction** [dɪ'strʌkʃn] Zerstörung, Vernichtung
detail ['diːteɪl] Detail, Einzelheit III
detective [dɪ'tektɪv] Detektiv/in III
°**determination** [dɪtɜːmɪ'neɪʃn] Entschlossenheit
device [dɪ'vaɪs]:
1. Gerät, Apparat VI 1 (21)
°2. Mittel *(Verfahren, Methode)*
diagram ['daɪəgræm] Diagramm III
dialogue ['daɪəlɒg] Dialog I
diamond ['daɪəmənd] Diamant VI 1 (10)
diary ['daɪəri] Tagebuch; Kalender I
dictionary ['dɪkʃənri] Wörterbuch, *(alphabetisches)* Wörterverzeichnis I
dictionary entry ['dɪkʃənri entri] Wörterbucheintrag II
did [dɪd] *siehe* **do** **I didn't want to … (= did not)** ich wollte nicht … II **Which club did you join?** In welchen Klub bist du eingetreten? II
die [daɪ] sterben II
difference ['dɪfrəns] Unterschied I **make a difference** etwas bewirken, etwas ausmachen I
different ['dɪfrənt] verschieden; anders I
difficult ['dɪfɪkəlt] schwierig I
difficulty ['dɪfɪkəlti] Schwierigkeit(en) VI 1 (20)
dig [dɪg], **dug, dug** graben V
digital ['dɪdʒɪtl] digital V
diner ['daɪnə] *(AE)* (kleines, preiswertes) Restaurant IV
dining room ['daɪnɪŋ ruːm] Esszimmer III
dinner ['dɪnə] Abendessen I
dinosaur ['daɪnəsɔː] Dinosaurier III
direct [də'rekt] direkt, unmittelbar V
direction [də'rekʃn] Richtung IV **directions** *(pl)* Wegbeschreibung(en) II
director [də'rektə] Geschäftsführer/in, Chef/in V
dirt road ['dɜːt rəʊd] unbefestigte Straße VI 1 (23)
dirty ['dɜːti] schmutzig III
disability [dɪsə'bɪləti] Behinderung IV
disabled [dɪs'eɪbld] (körper)behindert I
disadvantage [dɪsəd'vɑːntɪdʒ] Nachteil IV **at a disadvantage** im Nachteil IV
disadvantaged [dɪsəd'vɑːntɪdʒd] benachteiligt VI 1 (14)
disagree [dɪsə'griː] nicht zustimmen, widersprechen III
disappear [dɪsə'pɪə] verschwinden IV
disappoint sb. [dɪsə'pɔɪnt] jn. enttäuschen IV **disappointed (with)** enttäuscht (von) II **disappointing** enttäuschend IV
disaster [dɪ'zɑːstə] Katastrophe, Unglück III
disco ['dɪskəʊ] Disco III
°**discourse marker** ['dɪskɔːs mɑːkə] Redemittel, Wendungen *(in Diskussionen und argumentativen Texten)*
discover [dɪ'skʌvə] entdecken II
discrimination (against sb.) [dɪskrɪmɪ'neɪʃn] Diskriminierung *(eines Menschen)* V
discuss [dɪ'skʌs] diskutieren III
discussion [dɪ'skʌʃn] Diskussion I
disease [dɪ'ziːz] Krankheit V
disgusting [dɪs'gʌstɪŋ] ekelhaft, widerlich IV
dish [dɪʃ] Gericht *(Mahlzeit)*; Schüssel III **dishes** *(pl)* Geschirr VI 1 (20)
dishwasher ['dɪʃwɒʃə] Geschirrspülmaschine II
dislike [dɪs'laɪk] nicht mögen IV
dislikes *(pl)* ['dɪslaɪks]: **likes and dislikes** Vorlieben und Abneigungen III
display [dɪ'spleɪ]:
1. (an)zeigen, zur Schau stellen VI 3 (59)
2. Bildschirm, Anzeige(gerät) VI 3 (59)
head-mounted display Datenhelm, Datenbrille, Videobrille VI 3 (59)
distance ['dɪstəns] Distanz, Entfernung VI 1 (23) **in the distance** in der Ferne VI 1 (23)
disturb [dɪ'stɜːb] stören III

dive [daɪv]:
1. einen Kopfsprung machen I
2. (ein)tauchen II
diver ['daɪvə] Taucher/in III
diverse [daɪ'vɜːs] unterschiedlich, vielfältig V
diversity [daɪ'vɜːsəti] Vielfalt VI 1 (10)
°**divide (into)** [dɪ'vaɪd] spalten; teilen (in)
divorce [dɪ'vɔːs] (Ehe-)Scheidung IV
get a divorce sich scheiden lassen IV
do [duː], **did, done** machen, tun I
do a paper round Zeitungen austragen II **do better** besser abschneiden II **do sport** Sport treiben I
do sth. up etwas zumachen *(Kleidung)* VI 1 (22) **dos and don'ts** *(pl)* was man tun und lassen sollte V
she doesn't like ... sie mag ... nicht I
you do have ... du hast (ja/wohl) doch ... IV
doctor ['dɒktə] Arzt, Ärztin II
document ['dɒkjumənt] Dokument VI 1 (12)
document ['dɒkjument] dokumentieren VI 1 (12)
documentary [dɒkju'mentri] Dokumentarfilm II
dog [dɒg] Hund I **dogs' home** Hundeheim II
°**doing** ['duːɪŋ] *(das)* Tun, Tat
doll [dɒl] Puppe IV **doll's house** Puppenhaus IV
dollar ($) ['dɒlə] Dollar IV
°**donate** [dəʊ'neɪt] *(Geld für gute Zwecke)* spenden
done [dʌn] *siehe* **do** **Well done.** Gut gemacht! I **your fly is done up** dein Hosenschlitz ist zu VI 1 (22)
donkey ['dɒŋki] Esel I
donut ['dəʊnʌt] *(AE)* Donut *(ringförmiges Gebäck aus Hefeteig)* VI 3 (59)
door [dɔː] Tür I **answer the door** aufmachen, zur/an die Tür gehen V
dormitory ['dɔːmətri] Schlafsaal III
°**dossier** ['dɒsieɪ] Mappe, Dossier
dot [dɒt] Punkt, Pünktchen V
dot painting ['dɒt peɪntɪŋ] Punktmalerei; Punktgemälde V
°**doubt** [daʊt] Zweifel
down [daʊn] hinunter, herunter II
down the hill den Hügel hinunter I
look down your nose at sb. herabblicken auf jn. IV
downside ['daʊnsaɪd] Nachteil III
downstairs [daʊn'steəz] (nach) unten *(die Treppe hinunter)* I
downtown [daʊn'taʊn] *(AE)* (im/ins) Stadtzentrum IV
°**draft** [drɑːft] Entwurf
drag [dræg] ziehen, schleifen IV **drag sb. along** *(infml)* jn. mitschleifen V
drama ['drɑːmə]:
1. Schauspiel, darstellende Kunst I
2. Drama IV
dramatic [drə'mætɪk] dramatisch IV

drank [dræŋk] *siehe* **drink**
draw [drɔː], **drew, drawn** zeichnen; ziehen IV °**draw sb.'s attention to sth.** js. Aufmerksamkeit auf etwas lenken
drawing ['drɔːɪŋ] Zeichnung IV
drawn [drɔːn] *siehe* **draw**
dread [dred] fürchten VI 1 (21)
dream [driːm]:
1. Traum I
a dream come true ein wahr gewordener Traum V
2. dream (of/about sth.) träumen (von etwas) IV
dress [dres]:
1. sich kleiden, sich anziehen IV
get dressed up sich schick anziehen III
2. Kleid II
3. Kleidung IV
formal dress formelle Kleidung, Gesellschaftskleidung IV **formal evening dress** Abendkleid, festliche Abendgarderobe IV
drew [druː] *siehe* **draw**
drift [drɪft] sich bewegen, driften, *(Gedanken)* wandern VI 1 (20)
drifter ['drɪftə]: **be a drifter** sich treiben lassen *(ziellos vor sich hinleben)* V
drink [drɪŋk]:
1. Getränk I
2. drink, drank, drunk trinken I
drive [draɪv], **drove, driven:**
1. *(mit dem Auto)* fahren II
2. (an)treiben *(Tiere)* III
driven ['drɪvn] *siehe* **drive**
driver ['draɪvə] Fahrer/in III
driverless ['draɪvələs] fahrerlos, führerlos VI 3 (57)
driver's license ['draɪvəz laɪsns] *(AE)* Führerschein IV
driving licence ['draɪvɪŋ laɪsns] Führerschein III
driving test ['draɪvɪŋ test] Fahrprüfung, Führerscheinprüfung IV
drone [drəʊn] Drohne VI 3 (70)
drop [drɒp]:
1. fallen; fallen lassen VI 2 (42)
°**2.** sinken *(Flugzeug)*
drop [drɒp] Drop *(Bonbon)* III
drove [drəʊv] *siehe* **drive**
drown [draʊn] ertrinken III
drug [drʌg] Droge, Rauschgift; Arzneimittel IV
drum [drʌm] Trommel I **drums** *(pl)* Schlagzeug I
drummer ['drʌmə] Trommler/in II
drunk [drʌŋk] *siehe* **drink** **be drunk** betrunken sein IV **get drunk** sich betrinken IV
dry [draɪ]:
1. trocknen III
2. trocken IV
duck [dʌk] Ente I
dug [dʌg] *siehe* **dig**

dull [dʌl]:
1. langweilig, trist, öde IV
2. *(Farben, Licht)* stumpf, trübe VI 1 (20)
dumb [dʌm] dumm III
dump [dʌmp]:
1. (Müll-)Abladeplatz, Deponie III
2. abladen *(Müll)* III
dumper ['dʌmpə] Umweltsünder/in *(jemand, der illegal Müll entsorgt)* III
dung [dʌŋ] Dung, Mist IV
°**duration** [dju'reɪʃn] Dauer
during ['djʊərɪŋ] während III
dustbin ['dʌstbɪn] Mülleimer VI 1 (20)
Dutch [dʌtʃ] holländisch, niederländisch; Niederländisch VI 1 (10)
the Dutch die Holländer, die Niederländer VI 1 (10)
duty ['djuːti] Pflicht, Aufgabe; Dienst V
on duty im Dienst V
DVD [diːviː'diː] DVD III

E

each [iːtʃ] jede(r, s) (einzelne) II
each other einander, sich (gegenseitig) IV
eagle ['iːgl] Adler IV
ear [ɪə] Ohr II
early ['ɜːli] früh I
earn [ɜːn] verdienen *(Geld)* V
earth [ɜːθ] Erde II
earthquake ['ɜːθkweɪk] Erdbeben IV
ease [iːz]: **feel at ease** sich wohl/entspannt fühlen VI 1 (22)
east [iːst] Osten; nach Osten II
eastbound ['iːstbaʊnd] in Richtung Osten III
Easter ['iːstə] Ostern IV
eastern ['iːstən] östlich, Ost- IV
easy ['iːzi]:
1. einfach, leicht I
Take it easy. *(infml)* Reg dich nicht auf. / Bleib mal locker. III
2. take it easy sich schonen VI 2 (44)
easy-going [iːzi 'gəʊɪŋ] gelassen, locker II
eat [iːt], **ate, eaten** essen; fressen I
eaten ['iːtn] *siehe* **eat**
echo ['ekəʊ]:
1. (wider)hallen VI 1 (19)
2. *pl* **echoes** Echo VI 1 (19)
economic [iːkə'nɒmɪk] wirtschaftlich, Wirtschafts- VI 1 (11)
°**economy** [ɪ'kɒnəmi] (Volks-)Wirtschaft
°**ecosystem** ['iːkəʊsɪstəm] Ökosystem
edge [edʒ] Rand, Kante V
editor ['edɪtə] Herausgeber/in, Redakteur/in IV **letter to the editor** Leserbrief IV
education [edʒu'keɪʃn] (Schul-)Bildung V
effect [ɪ'fekt] (Aus-)Wirkung, Einfluss, Effekt VI 2 (36)
effective [ɪ'fektɪv] effektiv, wirksam VI 2 (36)

efficient [ɪ'fɪʃnt] effizient, rationell; *(Person)* tüchtig VI 3 (59)
e-friend ['i:frend] E-Mail-Freund/in II
e.g. [i: 'dʒi:] z.B. (zum Beispiel) II
egg [eg] Ei III
eight [eɪt] acht I
either ['aɪðə]: **not ... either** auch nicht II
elect sb. (to be) sth. [ɪ'lekt] jn. zu etwas wählen VI 1 (11)
election [ɪ'lekʃn] Wahl *(Abstimmung)* VI 1 (11)
electric [ɪ'lektrɪk] elektrisch, Elektro- VI 3 (56)
°**electrical** [ɪ'lektrɪkl] elektrisch, Elektro-
electricity [ɪlek'trɪsəti] Strom, Elektrizität VI 3 (56)
°**electronic** [ɪlek'trɒnɪk] elektronisch
electronics [ɪlek'trɒnɪks] Elektronik II
elephant ['elɪfənt] Elefant I
elevator ['elɪveɪtə] *(AE)* Lift, Fahrstuhl IV
eleven [ɪ'levən] elf I
else [els]: **Would you like anything else?** Möchten Sie sonst noch etwas? I
email sb./sth. ['i:meɪl] jn. anmailen/ etwas mailen IV
embankment [ɪm'bæŋkmənt] (Straßen-, Bahn-, Fluss-)Damm III
°**embarrass sb.** [ɪm'bærəs] jn. in Verlegenheit bringen
embarrassed [ɪm'bærəst] verlegen II
embarrassing [ɪm'bærəsɪŋ] peinlich IV
embrace [ɪm'breɪs] annehmen, mit offenen Armen begrüßen; (sich) umarmen VI 1 (11)
emergency [i'mɜ:dʒənsi] Notfall II
emergency services Rettungsdienste II
employee [ɪm'plɔɪi:] Arbeitnehmer/in III
°**employment** [ɪm'plɔɪmənt] Arbeit, Anstellung
empty ['empti]:
1. leer II
2. leeren II
enclose [ɪn'kləʊz] beifügen, beilegen *(einem Brief)* V
°**enclosed** [ɪn'kləʊzd] umschlossen; *(Straße)* lückenlos bebaut
encourage [ɪn'kʌrɪdʒ] ermutigen, ermuntern VI 2 (48)
end [end]:
1. (be)enden IV
end up (schließlich) gelangen, landen, enden VI 2 (38) **end up doing sth.** am Ende / schließlich etwas tun VI 2 (38)
2. Ende, Schluss I
in the end schließlich, zum Schluss II
ending ['endɪŋ] Endung; Ende *(Text, Geschichte)* II
endless ['endləs] endlos VI 3 (57)
enemy ['enəmi] Feind/in III
energetic [enə'dʒetɪk] energisch, energiereich V
energy ['enədʒi] Energie V
°**engage** [ɪn'geɪdʒ]: **it engages more than 172 countries** mehr als 172 Länder beteiligen sich daran / machen dabei mit
engine ['endʒɪn] Motor V
engineer [endʒɪ'nɪə] Ingenieur/in; Techniker/in III
engineering [endʒɪ'nɪərɪŋ] Ingenieurwesen, Maschinenbau, Technik VI (9)
England ['ɪŋglənd] England I
English ['ɪŋglɪʃ] Englisch; englisch I
°**English-speaking** ['ɪŋglɪʃ spi:kɪŋ] englischsprachig
enjoy [ɪn'dʒɔɪ] genießen II **Enjoy your meal.** Guten Appetit! III
enough [ɪ'nʌf] genug II
°**enrich** [ɪn'rɪtʃ] bereichern, anreichern
°**ensure** [ɪn'ʃʊə] sicherstellen
enter ['entə] sich anmelden, teilnehmen *(Wettbewerb)* V
entertainment [entə'teɪnmənt] Unterhaltung VI (9)
enthusiast [ɪn'θju:ziæst] Enthusiast/in, Fan VI 3 (62)
enthusiastic [ɪnθju:zi'æstɪk] begeistert V
entrance ['entrəns] Eingang; Zutritt II
entry ['entri]:
1. Eintritt, Zutritt III
2. Eintrag *(Wörterbuch)* II
environment [ɪn'vaɪrənmənt] Umwelt; Umfeld, Umgebung VI 3 (62)
°**environmental** [ɪnvaɪrən'mentl] Umwelt-
episode ['epɪsəʊd] Episode; Folge *(z.B. einer TV-Serie)* III
equal ['i:kwəl] gleich(berechtigt) V
equality [ɪ'kwɒləti] Gleichheit VI 1 (12)
equipment [ɪ'kwɪpmənt] Ausrüstung, Ausstattung III
eraser [ɪ'reɪzə] *(AE)* Radiergummi IV
e-reader ['i: ri:də] E-Book-Reader II
escalator ['eskəleɪtə] Rolltreppe III
escape [ɪ'skeɪp]:
1. Flucht VI 3 (65)
2. **escape (from)** entkommen (aus), fliehen (vor/aus) IV
especially [ɪ'speʃəli] insbesondere II
°**essential** [ɪ'senʃl] (absolut) notwendig, wesentlich
estate [ɪ'steɪt]: **housing estate** Wohnsiedlung VI 2 (43)
estimate ['estɪmeɪt] schätzen VI 2 (36)
estimate ['estɪmət] Schätzung VI 2 (36)
etc. [et'setərə] usw. (und so weiter) II
EU (= European Union) [i: 'ju:] EU (Europäische Union) III
euro (€) ['jʊərəʊ] Euro III
Europe ['jʊərəp] Europa III
European [jʊərə'pi:ən] Europäer/in; europäisch IV
European Union [jʊərəpi:ən 'ju:niən] Europäische Union III
even ['i:vn]:
1. ausgeglichen; gleich(mäßig); gerade *(Zahl)* IV
2. sogar, selbst III
even though auch wenn, obwohl *(betont)* VI 3 (62) **Do they even have streets?** Haben sie überhaupt Straßen? VI 1 (21) **not even** (noch) nicht einmal IV
evening ['i:vnɪŋ] Abend I **in the evening** abends, am Abend I
event [ɪ'vent] Ereignis II **sporting event** Sportveranstaltung VI 1 (10)
ever ['evə] jemals, schon einmal III
Have you ever ...? Hast du (schon) jemals ...? III **the most realistic game ever** das realistischste Spiel, das es je gegeben hat V
°**evergreen** ['evəgri:n] immergrün
every ['evri] jede(r, s) I **every now and again** ab und zu, von Zeit zu Zeit VI 1 (19)
everybody ['evribɒdi] jeder; alle I
everyone ['evriwʌn] jeder; alle II
everything ['evriθɪŋ] alles II
everywhere ['evriweə] überall(hin) II
°**evidence** ['evɪdəns] Nachweis(e), Beweis(e)
°**evolution** [i:və'lu:ʃn] Entwicklung
exact [ɪg'zækt] genau, exakt IV
exam [ɪg'zæm] Prüfung V **final (school) exam** (Schul-)Abschlussprüfung V **take/do an exam** eine Prüfung machen V
°**examine** [ɪg'zæmɪn] untersuchen
example [ɪg'zɑ:mpl] Beispiel II **for example** zum Beispiel II
°**exceed** [ɪk'si:d] überschreiten
excellent ['eksələnt] ausgezeichnet, hervorragend IV
except (for) [ɪk'sept] außer, bis auf IV
exchange [ɪks'tʃeɪndʒ] (Schüler-)Austausch III
excited [ɪk'saɪtɪd] aufgeregt, gespannt I
excitement [ɪk'saɪtmənt] Aufregung, Spannung, Begeisterung IV **burst with excitement** vor Aufregung ganz außer sich sein IV
exciting [ɪk'saɪtɪŋ] aufregend I
exclamation mark [eksklə'meɪʃn mɑ:k] Ausrufezeichen VI 1 (17)
°**excuse** [ɪk'skju:s]: **make excuses** sich herausreden, Ausflüchte machen
Excuse me, ... [ɪks'kju:z mi:] Entschuldigung, ... / Entschuldigen Sie, ... I
exercise ['eksəsaɪz]:
1. Übung, Aufgabe I
2. *(no pl)* Bewegung, *(körperliches)* Training VI 3 (58)
take exercise sich bewegen, trainieren VI 3 (58)
3. sich bewegen, trainieren VI 3 (58)

exercise book ['eksəsaɪz bʊk] (Schul-)Heft I
exhibition [eksɪ'bɪʃn] Messe; Ausstellung VI 3 (68)
°**exist** [ɪg'zɪst] existieren
exit ['eksɪt] Ausgang III
exoskeleton ['eksəʊskelɪtn] Exoskelett, Außenskelett VI 3 (56)
expect [ɪk'spekt] erwarten III
°**be expected to do sth.** etwas tun sollen/müssen, es wird erwartet, dass man etwas tut
expensive [ɪk'spensɪv] teuer I
experience [ɪk'spɪəriəns]:
1. Erfahrung; Erlebnis III
in my experience nach meiner Erfahrung V
2. **experience sth.** etwas erfahren, erleben II
experiment [ɪk'sperɪmənt] Experiment II
expert ['ekspɜ:t] Experte, Expertin II
explain sth. to sb. [ɪk'spleɪn] jm. etwas erklären II
°**explanation** [eksplə'neɪʃn] Erklärung
explore [ɪk'splɔ:] erforschen, erkunden V
explosion [ɪk'spləʊʒn] Explosion VI 2 (44)
express [ɪk'spres] ausdrücken, zum Ausdruck bringen V
°**expression** [ɪk'spreʃn] Ausdruck
°**extinct** [ɪk'stɪŋkt] ausgestorben
°**extinction** [ɪk'stɪŋkʃn] Ausrottung, Aussterben
extra ['ekstrə] Extra-, zusätzliche(r, s) II
extract ['ekstrækt] Auszug *(aus einem Buch, Film)* V
extreme [ɪk'stri:m] extrem IV
extremely [ɪk'stri:mli] extrem, äußerst IV
eye [aɪ] Auge II **corner of your eye** Augenwinkel IV **keep an eye on sb./sth.** jn./etwas im Auge behalten, ein (wachsames) Auge haben auf jn./etwas V

F

face [feɪs]:
1. Gesicht I
2. **face sth.** vor etwas stehen *(Problem)*; einer Sache ins Auge sehen, sich einer Sache stellen; einer Sache entgegentreten V
facing forwards/backwards nach vorn/hinten schauend; mit dem Gesicht nach vorn/hinten VI 3 (66)
facilities *(pl)* [fə'sɪlətiz] Einrichtungen, Anlage(n) VI 1 (24)
fact [fækt] Tatsache, Fakt IV **in fact** eigentlich, um genau zu sein VI 1 (18)
°**fact file** ['fækt faɪl] Informationsbogen, Steckbrief
factory ['fæktri] Fabrik VI 2 (47)
°**fairly** ['feəli] ziemlich, recht
°**fair-trade** [feə 'treɪd] Fairtrade-, aus fairem Handel
faithfully ['feɪθfəli]: **Yours faithfully** Mit freundlichen Grüßen *(Briefschluss)* V
fall [fɔ:l] *(AE)* Herbst IV
fall [fɔ:l], **fell, fallen** fallen; hinfallen I
fallen ['fɔ:lən] *siehe* **fall**
false [fɔ:ls] falsch I
°**false friend** [fɔ:ls 'frend] „falscher Freund", Übersetzungsfalle
familiar [fə'mɪliə]: **be familiar (to sb./with sth.)** (jm.) vertraut sein / (mit etwas) vertraut sein V
family ['fæməli] Familie I
family name ['fæməli neɪm] Familienname, Nachname IV
family tree [fæməli 'tri:] Familienstammbaum I
family-friendly [fæməli 'frendli] familienfreundlich III
famous ['feɪməs] berühmt II
fancy ['fænsi] ausgefallen, extravagant, schick IV
fantastic [fæn'tæstɪk] fantastisch, wunderschön V
fantasy ['fæntəsi] Fantasie II
FAQ (= frequently asked questions) [ef eɪ 'kju], [fri:kwəntli ɑ:skt 'kwestʃənz] häufig gestellte Fragen III
far [fɑ:] weit (entfernt) II **far away** weit weg II **so far** bis jetzt, bis hierher II
farm [fɑ:m]:
1. Bauernhof, Farm I
2. Landwirtschaft betreiben V
farm animal ['fɑ:m ænɪml] Nutztier; *im Plural:* Vieh III
farmer ['fɑ:mə] Bauer, Bäuerin; Landwirt/in III
farmhouse ['fɑ:mhaʊs] Bauernhaus III
farmyard ['fɑ:mjɑ:d] Hof *(eines Bauernhauses)* III
fascinate ['fæsɪneɪt] faszinieren VI 3 (62)
fashion ['fæʃn] Mode III
fast [fɑ:st] schnell I
°**fasten** ['fɑ:sn] festmachen; anlegen *(Gurt)*
fast-food restaurant [fɑ:st fu:d 'restrɒnt] Schnellimbiss V
fat [fæt] dick, fett II
fate [feɪt] Schicksal VI 2 (38)
father ['fɑ:ðə] Vater I
fault [fɔ:lt] Fehler, Schuld V
favourite ['feɪvərɪt] Lieblings- I
fear (of) [fɪə] Angst (vor) V
feather ['feðə] Feder *(eines Vogels)* IV
feature ['fi:tʃə]:
1. vorkommen, mitwirken VI 2 (48)
be featured gezeigt werden VI 2 (48)
2. Merkmal, Eigenschaft VI 1 (13)
°3. (Dokumentar-)Bericht, Feature
February ['februəri] Februar I
fed [fed] *siehe* **feed** **feel fed up** genervt sein, sauer sein; die Nase voll haben I
feed [fi:d]:
1. **feed, fed, fed** füttern I
°2. Feed *(Daten-Zufuhr; abonnierbare elektronische Nachricht im Internet)*
feel [fi:l], **felt, felt** sich fühlen; fühlen I
feeling ['fi:lɪŋ] Gefühl I
feet [fi:t] *Plural von* **foot** III
fell [fel] *siehe* **fall**
°**fellow student** ['feləʊ] Mitschüler/in
felt [felt] *siehe* **feel**
female ['fi:meɪl]:
1. weiblich III
2. weibliche Person, weibliches Tier VI 1 (15)
fence [fens] Zaun III
ferry ['feri] Fähre I
festival ['festɪvl] Fest II
few [fju:] wenige VI 1 (14) **a few** ein paar, einige II
fictional ['fɪkʃənl] erfunden, fiktiv V
field [fi:ld] Feld; Weide I **in the field** auf der Weide I
field hockey ['fi:ld hɒki] Feldhockey VI 1 (15)
fight [faɪt]:
1. Kampf; Schlägerei IV
2. **fight, fought, fought** kämpfen II
3. **fight sth.** etwas bekämpfen V
fight your way through sich durchkämpfen durch V
fighter ['faɪtə] Kämpfer/in V
figure ['fɪgə] Person *(Gestalt)*; Figur IV
fill [fɪl] füllen II **fill out** ausfüllen V
°**fill in** einsetzen; ausfüllen
film [fɪlm] filmen III
film-maker ['fɪlm meɪkə] Filmemacher/in VI 1 (27)
final ['faɪnl] Finale III
finally ['faɪnəli] schließlich, endlich II
financial [faɪ'nænʃl] finanziell VI 1 (20)
find [faɪnd], **found, found** finden I
find out herausfinden II **find out about sth.** sich über etwas informieren II
finder ['faɪndə] Finder/in V **Finders keepers, losers weepers.** Was man findet, darf man behalten. *(Redensart)* V
°**findings** *(pl)* ['faɪndɪŋz] Ergebnisse
fine [faɪn] gut, in Ordnung; schön I
I'm fine. Mir geht es gut. I
fine [faɪn]:
1. Geldstrafe IV
2. zu einer Geldstrafe verurteilen IV
finger ['fɪŋgə] Finger III
fingernail ['fɪŋgəneɪl] Fingernagel V
finish ['fɪnɪʃ]:
1. Ziel *(beim Sport)* II
2. beenden, zu Ende machen II
finish the milk die Milch alle machen, aufbrauchen IV **finish your**

drink austrinken IV **finish your meal** aufessen IV
fire ['faɪə] Feuer II
fire escape ['faɪər ɪskeɪp] Feuertreppe, Notausgang V **fire escape ladder** Feuerleiter V
fire sb. ['faɪə] jn. feuern, entlassen V **you'll get me fired** du schaffst es noch, dass ich entlassen werde V
fire station ['faɪə steɪʃn] Feuerwache I
firefighter ['faɪəfaɪtə] Feuerwehrmann, Feuerwehrfrau I
firework ['faɪəwɜːk] Feuerwerkskörper II **fireworks** *(pl)* *(ein)* Feuerwerk II
first [fɜːst]:
1. erste(r, s) I
2. zuerst, als Erstes I
at first zuerst, am Anfang II **the first morning** der erste Morgen I
first aid [fɜːst 'eɪd] Erste Hilfe II **first-aid kit** Erste-Hilfe-Set, Verbandkasten II
Firstly, ... ['fɜːstli] Erstens ... III
fish [fɪʃ]:
1. Fisch(e) I
2. fischen, angeln III
fist [fɪst] Faust II
°**fit** [fɪt] passen (zu)
fit in [fɪt 'ɪn] dazugehören; hineinpassen V
fitness tracker ['fɪtnəs trækə] Fitness-Tracker *(Gerät zur Aufzeichnung und Übertragung von gesundheitsbezogenen Daten)* VI 3 (59)
five [faɪv] fünf I **Give me five!** Gib mir fünf! *(Aufforderung zum „Abklatschen", Geste der Freude/Begrüßung)* II
fix sth. [fɪks] *(infml)* etwas in Ordnung bringen; reparieren IV
flag [flæg] Fahne, Flagge II
flash [flæʃ]:
1. *(das)* (Auf-)Blitzen V
2. blinken, leuchten VI 2 (44)
flash a torch mit einer Taschenlampe leuchten/blinken V **flash one's headlights** aufblenden, die Lichthupe betätigen VI 2 (44)
flashback ['flæʃbæk] Rückblende V
flashing lights *(pl)* [flæʃɪŋ 'laɪts] Warnlicht, Blaulicht VI 2 (44)
flashlight ['flæʃlaɪt] *(AE)* Taschenlampe IV
flat [flæt] Wohnung I **block of flats** *(pl)* Mehrfamilienhaus, Wohnblock I
flat [flæt] flach, eben V
flew [fluː] *siehe* **fly**
flexible ['fleksəbl] flexibel V
flight [flaɪt]:
1. Flug III
°2. Flucht
flight connection ['flaɪt kənekʃn] Anschlussflug III
flood [flʌd] überfluten, überschwemmen IV
floor [flɔː]:
1. Fußboden III
2. Etage, Stock(werk) IV
flour ['flaʊə] Mehl III
flower ['flaʊə] Blume; Blüte II
flown [fləʊn] *siehe* **fly**
°**fluent** ['fluːənt] fließend *(Sprache)*
flute [fluːt] (Quer-)Flöte IV
fly [flaɪ] Hosenschlitz VI 1 (22) **your fly is done up** dein Hosenschlitz ist zu VI 1 (22)
fly [flaɪ], **flew, flown:**
1. fliegen I
2. rasen *(z.B. Auto)* V
flyer ['flaɪə] Flyer *(Handzettel)* II
focus on sth. ['fəʊkəs] sich auf etwas konzentrieren IV
fog [fɒg] Nebel II
foggy ['fɒgi] nebelig II
°**folk** [fəʊk] volkstümlich, Volks-
folks *(pl)* [fəʊks] Leute IV
follow ['fɒləʊ] folgen; verfolgen I
follower ['fɒləʊə] Anhänger/in, Fan V
follow-up ['fɒləʊ ʌp] Anschluss-, Folge- VI 2 (41)
food [fuːd] Essen, Lebensmittel; Futter I
fool [fuːl] Dummkopf III
foolish ['fuːlɪʃ] töricht, dumm V
foot, *pl* **feet** [fʊt], [fiːt] Fuß III **on foot** zu Fuß III **put your foot down** Gas geben *(Auto)* VI 2 (44)
football ['fʊtbɔːl] Fußball I
footballer ['fʊtbɔːlə] Fußballspieler/in III
for [fɔː], [fə] für I **for a few minutes** ein paar Minuten (lang) II **for example** zum Beispiel II **for lots of reasons** aus vielen Gründen III **for two months** seit zwei Monaten III **great for making friends** großartig, um Freunde zu finden II **What's for homework?** Was haben wir als Hausaufgabe(n) auf? I
force sb. to do sth. [fɔːs] jn. zwingen, etwas zu tun IV **they were forced from their land** sie wurden von ihrem Land vertrieben IV
forecast ['fɔːkɑːst] Vorhersage II
foreground ['fɔːgraʊnd] Vordergrund III
foreign ['fɒrən] ausländisch, fremd VI 2 (41)
foreign language [fɒrən 'læŋgwɪdʒ] Fremdsprache VI 2 (41)
forest ['fɒrɪst] Wald III
forever, for ever [fər'evə] für immer, ewig (lange) V
forget [fə'get], **forgot, forgotten** vergessen I **forget about sth.** (etwas) vergessen, nicht mehr an etwas denken II
forgot [fə'gɒt] *siehe* **forget**
forgotten [fə'gɒtn] *siehe* **forget**
form [fɔːm]:
1. Formular V
°2. (sich) formen, bilden
formal ['fɔːml] formell IV **formal dress** formelle Kleidung, Gesellschaftskleidung IV **formal evening dress** Abendkleid, festliche Abendgarderobe IV
forth [fɔːθ]: **back and forth** hin und her V
fortunately ['fɔːtʃənətli] glücklicherweise VI 3 (64)
fortune ['fɔːtʃuːn] Vermögen IV **cost a fortune** ein Vermögen kosten IV
forward ['fɔːwəd] vorwärts, nach vorne II **look forward to** sich freuen auf II **look forward to doing sth.** sich darauf freuen, etwas zu tun IV
forwards ['fɔːwədz] nach vorne; vorwärts VI 3 (66)
fought [fɔːt] *siehe* **fight**
found [faʊnd]:
1. *siehe* **find**
°2. gründen
°**foundation** [faʊn'deɪʃn] Fundament, Grundlage
four [fɔː] vier I
fox [fɒks] Fuchs II
freak sb. out [friːk 'aʊt] *(infml)* jn. ausflippen lassen, ein Horror sein für jn. IV
free [friː]:
1. **free sb.** jn. befreien VI 1 (11)
2. frei; kostenlos I
free-time activities Freizeitaktivitäten II **run freely** frei herumlaufen III
freedom ['friːdəm] Freiheit IV
freeze [friːz], **froze, frozen:**
1. gefrieren II
2. erstarren V
freezing ['friːzɪŋ] eisig, eiskalt II
French fries *(pl)* [frentʃ 'fraɪz] *(AE)* Pommes frites IV
frequent ['friːkwənt] häufig III
fresh [freʃ] frisch I
Friday ['fraɪdeɪ], ['fraɪdi] Freitag I
fridge [frɪdʒ] Kühlschrank III
fried egg [fraɪd 'eg] Spiegelei IV
friend [frend] Freund/in I **a friend of Cindy's / of hers / of mine** ein/e Freund/in von Cindy /von ihr / von mir V **be (good) friends with sb.** mit jm. (gut) befreundet sein V
friendliness ['frendlinəs] Freundlichkeit V
friendly ['frendli] freundlich I **get friendly with sb.** sich mit jm. anfreunden IV
friendship ['frendʃɪp] Freundschaft IV
fries *(pl)* [fraɪz] **French fries** *(AE)* Pommes frites IV
frighten sb. ['fraɪtn] jm. Angst machen V
frightened ['fraɪtnd] verängstigt V **be frightened of sth.** Angst haben vor etwas V

frightening [frightening] beängstigend V
from [frɒm] von, aus I **from Monday to Friday** von Montag bis Freitag I **Where are you from?** Wo kommst du her? I
front [frʌnt]: **at the front** vorn, im vorderen Teil IV **in front of** vor I
front desk [frʌnt 'desk] Rezeption, Empfang *(z.B. Hotel)* V
front desk clerk [frʌnt 'desk klɑ:k] Empfangsmitarbeiter/in V
front garden [frʌnt 'gɑ:dn] Vorgarten V
frontier (with) ['frʌntɪə] Grenze (zu) VI 3 (62) **new frontiers** Neuland, neue Ufer VI 3 (62)
froze [frəʊz] *siehe* **freeze**
frozen ['frəʊzn] *siehe* **freeze**
fruit [fru:t] Obst I
frustrate [frʌ'streɪt] frustrieren V
frustrated [frʌ'streɪtɪd] frustriert II
frustrating [frʌ'streɪtɪŋ] frustrierend V
fry [fraɪ] braten IV
frying pan ['fraɪɪŋ pæn] Bratpfanne IV
fuel ['fju:əl] Treibstoff, Kraftstoff V
full (of) [fʊl] voll (mit, von) I
full stop [fʊl 'stɒp] Punkt *(Satzzeichen)* VI 1 (17)
full-time job [fʊl 'taɪm] Ganztagsjob, Vollzeitjob IV
fun [fʌn] Spaß I **(just) for fun** (nur) zum Spaß V **it's fun** es macht Spaß I **she's fun** es macht Spaß, mit ihr zusammenzusein I
°**function** ['fʌŋkʃn] Funktion
fund-raising ['fʌnd reɪzɪŋ] Spendenaktion; Spenden- IV **fund-raising event** Ereignis zur Beschaffung von Geld/Spenden IV
funny ['fʌni] witzig, komisch II
furious ['fjʊəriəs] wütend VI 2 (43)
furniture ['fɜ:nɪtʃə] Möbel(stücke) IV
furry ['fɜ:ri] flauschig; pelzig I
further ['fɜ:ðə] weiter; weitere V
future ['fju:tʃə] Zukunft II
°**futurologist** [fju:tʃə'rɒlədʒɪst] Zukunftsforscher/in

G

gadget ['gædʒɪt] Gerät, technischer Krimskrams VI 3 (68)
gallery ['gæləri] Galerie V
game [geɪm]:
1. Spiel I
2. Wild *(Tiere)* VI 1 (23)
gamer ['geɪmə] Gamer/in *(Computerspieler/in)* V
gaming ['geɪmɪŋ] *(das)* Spielen am Computer V
°**gap** [gæp] Lücke
garage ['gærɑ:ʒ]:
1. (Auto-)Werkstatt II
2. Garage I
garage sale Garagenflohmarkt I
garbage ['gɑ:bɪdʒ] *(AE)* Abfall, Müll IV
garbage can ['gɑ:bɪdʒ kæn] *(AE)* Abfalleimer, Mülleimer IV
garden ['gɑ:dn] Garten I
gardener ['gɑ:dnə] Gärtner/in V
gas [gæs]:
1. Gas IV
2. *(AE)* Benzin IV
gate [geɪt] Tor; Flugsteig III
gatecrash (a party) ['geɪtkræʃ] (bei einer Party) ungebeten erscheinen V
gatecrasher ['geɪtkræʃə] nicht eingeladene Person (die eine Party sprengt) V
gateway (to) ['geɪtweɪ] Tor (zu) IV
gather ['gæðə] sammeln; (sich) versammeln V
gave [geɪv] *siehe* **give**
gear [gɪə] Ausrüstung II
geek [gi:k] *jemand, der sich sehr stark für etwas begeistert (und manchmal deswegen belächelt wird)* III
gel [dʒel] Gel *(Haarstyling)* IV
gender ['dʒendə] Geschlecht *(als soziales Merkmal)* VI 2 (48)
general ['dʒenrəl] allgemein III
generally ['dʒenrəli] im Allgemeinen IV
generate ['dʒenəreɪt] erzeugen, generieren VI 3 (56)
generation [dʒenə'reɪʃn] Generation V
gentle ['dʒentl] behutsam, leicht, sanft(mütig) VI 1 (22)
gentlemen ['dʒentlmən]: **ladies and gentlemen** meine Damen und Herren VI 1 (21)
geography [dʒi'ɒgrəfi] Geografie, Erdkunde I
German ['dʒɜ:mən]:
1. deutsch; Deutsch I
2. Deutsche, Deutscher II
Germany ['dʒɜ:məni] Deutschland I
get [get], **got, got:**
1. bekommen I
2. werden II
3. **get sth.** (sich) etwas holen, (sich) etwas besorgen II
4. **get (to)** gelangen, (hin)kommen (nach) II
get around sich fortbewegen *(mobil sein)* IV **get going** in Gang kommen; sich auf den Weg machen VI 1 (22) **get into (a car)** (in ein Auto) einsteigen IV **get lost** sich verirren, sich verlaufen II **Get lost!** Verschwinde(t)! II **get off (a bus)** aussteigen (aus einem Bus) III **get off (your bike)** absteigen (vom Fahrrad) III **get on a plane/bus/train** in ein Flugzeug / einen Bus / einen Zug einsteigen III **get out (of a car)** (aus einem Auto) aussteigen IV **get out of** herauskommen aus, herausfinden aus II **get sb. to do sth.** jn. dazu bringen, etwas zu tun VI 1 (20) **get started** anfangen, loslegen III **get to do sth.** etwas tun können/dürfen; die Möglichkeit haben/bekommen, etwas zu tun IV **get up** aufstehen I **I get it.** *(infml)* Ich verstehe. / Ich kapiere. V **You got it.** *(infml)* Genau! / Du hast es! V
ghost [gəʊst] Gespenst, Geist III
giant ['dʒaɪənt] riesig; Riese/Riesin IV
°**gift** [gɪft] Geschenk
giggle ['gɪgl] kichern III
gingerbread ['dʒɪndʒəbred] Lebkuchen, Honigkuchen III
girl [gɜ:l] Mädchen I
girlfriend ['gɜ:lfrend] (feste) Freundin I
gist [dʒɪst]: **the gist** das Wesentliche; die Kernaussage(n) IV
give [gɪv], **gave, given** geben I **give a talk** einen Vortrag halten II **Give me five!** Gib mir fünf! *(Aufforderung zum „Abklatschen", Geste der Freude/Begrüßung)* II **give up** aufgeben, aufhören (mit) IV
given ['gɪvn] *siehe* **give**
glad [glæd]: **I'm glad** ich bin froh II
glamorous ['glæmərəs] glamourös V
glance [glɑ:ns] (kurzer) Blick VI 1 (22) **steal quick glances at** verstohlene Blicke werfen auf VI 1 (22)
glass [glɑ:s] Glas VI 1 (19)
glasses *(pl)* ['glɑ:sɪz] *(eine)* Brille I
glimpse [glɪmps] kurzer Blick VI 1 (19) **catch a glimpse of sth.** einen Blick von/auf etwas erhaschen; etwas nur kurz zu sehen bekommen VI 1 (19)
global warming [gləʊbl 'wɔ:mɪŋ] Erderwärmung VI 3 (65)
glove [glʌv] Handschuh II
°**glucose** ['glu:kəʊs] Traubenzucker, Glukose
go [gəʊ], **went, gone** gehen; fahren I **go after sb./sth.** hinter etwas/jm. her sein V **go crazy** verrückt werden V **Go for it!** Nichts wie ran! II **go off** klingeln *(Wecker)*; losgehen *(Alarmanlage, Waffe)* IV **go off (to a place)** (los)gehen, (los)fahren (nach/zu) IV **Go to sleep!** Schlaf jetzt! I **go with** passen zu, gehören zu I **go wrong** schiefgehen VI 3 (62) **Here we go!** *(infml)* Jetzt geht's los! II **How's it going?** Wie geht's? / Wie läuft's? I **I must go.** *(am Telefon)* Ich muss Schluss machen. I **I'm going to bring ...** ich werde ... mitbringen I °**go off** ausgehen *(z.B. Licht)*
°**goal** [gəʊl] Tor *(Sport)*
goat [gəʊt] Ziege V
God [gɒd] Gott III
gold [gəʊld] Gold III
gold mining ['gəʊld maɪnɪŋ] Goldabbau IV
golden ['gəʊldn] golden, aus Gold IV
gone [gɒn] *siehe* **go** **be gone** weg sein, nicht (mehr) da sein IV
good [gʊd] gut I **Good boy. / Good dog.** Braver Junge. / Braver Hund. II

Good morning. Guten Morgen. I **be good at sth.** etwas gut können; gut in etwas sein III **be good with sth.** gut mit etwas umgehen können III **I'm good.** *(AE)* Mir geht es gut. IV **It's good value.** Es ist sein Geld wert. / Es ist preiswert. I

Goodbye. [gʊd'baɪ] Auf Wiedersehen! I

good-looking [gʊd 'lʊkɪŋ] gut aussehend IV

goody ['gʊdi] gute Sache; leckere Sache III

got [gɒt] *siehe* **get**

government ['gʌvənmənt] Regierung; Regierungs- IV

gown [gaʊn] Robe; (Fest-)Kleid IV

GPS [dʒiː piː 'es] GPS III

grab [græb] packen, greifen (nach), ergreifen IV

grade [greɪd] *(AE)* Klasse, Jahrgang; (Schul-)Note IV

°**graduate (from)** ['grædʒueɪt] den Abschluss machen (an) *(Schule, Hochschule)*

graduation [grædʒu'eɪʃn] (Schul-, Universitäts-)Abschluss; Abschlussfeier IV

graffiti [grə'fiːti] Graffiti IV

°**gram (g)** [græm] Gramm

grand [grænd] groß(artig) III

grandad ['grændæd] Opa III

granddaughter ['grændɔːtə] Enkelin IV

grandfather ['grænfɑːðə] Großvater I

grandma ['grænmɑː] Oma I

grandmother ['grænmʌðə] Großmutter I

grandpa ['grænpɑː] Opa I

grandparents *(pl)* ['grænpeərənts] Großeltern I

grandson ['grænsʌn] Enkel IV

°**granite** ['grænɪt] Granit

granny ['græni] Oma I

graph [græf], *BE auch:* [grɑːf] Diagramm, Kurve VI 3 (61)

grass [grɑːs] Gras; Rasen II

°**grassland** ['grɑːslænd] Grasland; Steppe

grave [greɪv] Grab IV

gravestone ['greɪvstəʊn] Grabstein VI 3 (66)

graveyard ['greɪvjɑːd] Friedhof V

graveyard shift ['greɪvjɑːd ʃɪft] Nachtschicht V

°**gravity** ['grævəti] Schwerkraft

great [greɪt] toll, großartig I

Great Britain [greɪt 'brɪtn] Großbritannien II

green [griːn] grün I

greet [griːt] begrüßen V

grew [gruː] *siehe* **grow**

grey [greɪ] grau I

grill party ['grɪl] Grillparty IV

grin (at) [grɪn] (an)grinsen V

groan [grəʊn]:
1. *(das)* Stöhnen VI 3 (59)
2. stöhnen VI 3 (59)

groceries *(pl)* ['grəʊsəriz] Lebensmittel IV

grocery store ['grəʊsəri stɔː] *(AE)* Lebensmittelgeschäft IV

ground [graʊnd] (Erd-)Boden II

group [gruːp] Gruppe I

grow [grəʊ], **grew, grown:**
1. anbauen, anpflanzen IV
2. wachsen II

grow up aufwachsen; erwachsen werden IV **Money doesn't grow on trees.** Das Geld liegt nicht auf der Straße. *(Redewendung)* II

growl (at) [graʊl] (an)knurren IV

grown [grəʊn] *siehe* **grow**

growth [grəʊθ] Wachstum VI 3 (60)

°**guarantee** [gærən'tiː] garantieren

guard [gɑːd] Wärter/in; Wache III

°**guardian** ['gɑːdiən] Begleitperson

guess [ges] (er)raten I **I guess** ich nehme an, ich glaube IV

guest [gest] Gast III

guide [gaɪd]:
1. Ratgeber, Einführung III
2. Reiseführer *(Buch, Website)* IV
3. Reiseleiter/in, Fremdenführer/in III

guitar [gɪ'tɑː] Gitarre I

°**gulp sth. down** [gʌlp 'daʊn] etwas herunterschlingen, *(Getränk)* herunterstürzen

gun [gʌn] Schusswaffe IV

guy [gaɪ] Typ, Kerl I **guys** *(pl)* Leute *(Anrede)* I

gym [dʒɪm] Turnhalle, Sporthalle; Fitnessstudio III

°**gymnasium** [dʒɪm'neɪziəm] Turnhalle, Sporthalle

gymnastics [dʒɪm'næstɪks] Turnen, Gymnastik II

H

habit ['hæbɪt] (An-)Gewohnheit V

had [hæd] *siehe* **have**

hail [heɪl] Hagel VI 3 (57)

hair [heə] Haar, Haare II

hairdresser ['heədresə] Frisör/in II

hairdryer ['heədraɪə] Föhn, Haartrockner II

hairy ['heəri] behaart, haarig II

half [hɑːf] halbe(r, s) I **half an hour** eine halbe Stunde II **half past 6** halb 7 I **sixteen and a half** sechzehneinhalb V

half-brother ['hɑːf brʌðə] Halbbruder I

half-sister ['hɑːf sɪstə] Halbschwester I

°**half-time** [hɑːf 'taɪm] Halbzeit(pause)

halfway [hɑːf'weɪ] auf halbem Wege, halb(wegs) IV

hall [hɔːl]:
1. Flur, Diele I
2. Gang, Korridor II
3. Halle VI 1 (21)

hallway ['hɔːlweɪ] *(AE)* Korridor, Gang IV

ham [hæm] Schinken III **Black Forest ham** Schwarzwälder Schinken III

hammer ['hæmə]:
1. Hammer V
2. hämmern V

hamster ['hæmstə] Hamster I

hand [hænd]:
1. Hand II

back of the hand Handrücken V **know sth. like the back of one's hand** etwas wie seine Westentasche kennen; etwas in- und auswendig kennen V **on the one hand** einerseits III **on the other hand** andererseits III **put up your hand** sich melden III

2. **hand sb. sth.** jm. etwas (an)reichen, aushändigen V

handball ['hændbɔːl] Handball IV

handshake ['hændʃeɪk] Händedruck, Handschlag IV

°**handy** ['hændi] praktisch, nützlich

hang, hung, hung [hæŋ]: **hang (from)** hängen (an) IV **hang around** *(infml)* herumhängen VI 3 (65) **hang out** rumhängen, abhängen II

happen ['hæpən] geschehen, passieren I

happiness ['hæpinəs] Glück V

happy ['hæpi] glücklich, froh I **Happy birthday!** Herzlichen Glückwunsch zum Geburtstag! I **happy ending** Happy End *(glückliches Ende)* II **be happy with sth.** mit etwas zufrieden sein III

harbour ['hɑːbə] Hafen I

hard [hɑːd] schwer, schwierig; hart I **Hard luck!** Pech (gehabt)! III **rain hard** stark regnen V **try hard** sich (sehr) bemühen, sich anstrengen IV

hard-working [hɑːd 'wɜːkɪŋ] fleißig III

harmonica [hɑː'mɒnɪkə] Mundharmonika IV

has [hæz], [həz]: **it has** es (er, sie) hat I

hat [hæt] Hut, Mütze I

hate [heɪt] hassen I

haunted ['hɔːntɪd]: **a haunted castle** ein Schloss, in dem es spukt III

have [hæv], **had, had** haben I **Have a good day.** Ich wünsche dir einen schönen Tag. / Schönen Tag (noch). I **have breakfast** frühstücken I **have lunch** (zu) Mittag essen I **have to do sth.** etwas tun müssen II **I'll have …** ich nehme … *(beim Essen, im Restaurant)* II **I've lived here all my life.** Ich wohne hier schon mein ganzes Leben (lang). III °**have sth. done (by sb.)** etwas (von jm.) machen lassen

he [hiː] er I

head [hed]:
1. Kopf II
2. **head (into sth.)** sich (in etwas) hineinbegeben/-stürzen VI 3 (66)

head for sth. auf etwas zugehen/zusteuern IV **head south** Richtung Süden gehen/fahren IV

headache ['hedeɪk] Kopfschmerzen II
heading ['hedɪŋ] Überschrift III
headlight ['hedlaɪt] Scheinwerfer(licht) VI 2 (43)
headline ['hedlaɪn] Schlagzeile IV
°**headmaster** [hed'mɑ:stə] Schulleiter, Direktor
head-mounted display [hed maʊntɪd dɪ'spleɪ] Datenhelm, Datenbrille, Videobrille VI 3 (59)
headphones *(pl)* ['hedfəʊnz] *(ein)* Kopfhörer VI 3 (58)
health [helθ] Gesundheit V **Apples are good for your health.** Äpfel sind gesund. V
health care ['helθ keə] Gesundheitsversorgung V
healthy ['helθi] gesund II
hear [hɪə], **heard, heard** hören I
heard [hɜ:d] *siehe* **hear**
heart [hɑ:t] Herz III
heart rate ['hɑ:t reɪt] Herzfrequenz, Puls VI 3 (56)
°**heart-stopper** ['hɑ:t stɒpə]: **it's a heart-stopper** es ist atemberaubend
heat [hi:t]:
1. erwärmen, erhitzen VI 1 (20)
2. Hitze, Wärme V
heat stress Hitzestress, Wärmebelastung des Körpers V
heavy ['hevi] schwer III
heavyweight ['heviweɪt] Schwergewicht; Schwergewichts- V
heel [hi:l] Absatz *(Schuh)* III **(high) heels** *(pl)* hochhackige Schuhe III
°**height** [haɪt] Höhe, Größe *(bei Menschen)*
held [held] *siehe* **hold**
helicopter ['helɪkɒptə] Hubschrauber IV
hell [hel] Hölle VI 1 (20) **be scared as hell** *(infml)* höllische / furchtbare Angst haben VI 1 (23) **Where the hell is Africa?** *(infml)* Wo zum Teufel ist Afrika? VI 1 (20)
Hello. [hə'ləʊ] Hallo. I
helmet ['helmɪt] Helm I
help [help]:
1. Hilfe I
2. helfen I
Help yourselves. Bedient euch! / Greift zu! III
helpful ['helpfl] hilfsbereit; hilfreich, nützlich III
helpless ['helpləs] hilflos II
her [hɜ:], [hə] sie; ihr I
her father [hɜ:] ihr Vater I
here [hɪə] hier; hierher I **Here you are.** Bitte schön. / Hier, bitte. I
heritage ['herɪtɪdʒ] Erbe IV
hero, *pl* **heroes** ['hɪərəʊ] Held/in III
hers [hɜ:z] ihre/r, ihrs *(zu „she")* V
herself [hɜ:'self] sie/sich selbst *(zu „she")* III
°**hesitate** ['hezɪteɪt] zögern

Hi. [haɪ] Hallo. I **Say hi to everybody.** Grüß alle. I
hid [hɪd] *siehe* **hide**
hidden ['hɪdn] *siehe* **hide**
hide [haɪd], **hid, hidden** verstecken; sich verstecken I
high [haɪ] hoch II
high heels *(pl)* [haɪ 'hi:lz] hochhackige Schuhe III
high school ['haɪ sku:l] *(BE etwa:)* Gesamtschule I
high street ['haɪ stri:t] Hauptstraße *(mit vielen Geschäften)* III
Highlands ['haɪləndz]: **the Highlands** *(pl)* das schottische Hochland III
highlight ['haɪlaɪt] Höhepunkt, Schlaglicht, Highlight IV
high-rise building [haɪ raɪz 'bɪldɪŋ] Hochhaus VI 2 (43)
highway ['haɪweɪ] *(AE)* Fernstraße IV
hike [haɪk] wandern IV
°**hilarious** [hɪ'leəriəs] urkomisch, unheimlich witzig
hill [hɪl] Hügel I
him [hɪm] ihm, ihn I
himself [hɪm'self] er/sich selbst III
°**hippo**, *pl* **hippos** ['hɪpəʊ] Nilpferd
hire ['haɪə] mieten, leihen III
his [hɪz]:
1. sein/e *(zu „he")* I
2. seiner, seine, seins *(zu „he")* V
historic [hɪ'stɒrɪk] historisch *(berühmt, denkwürdig)* II
history ['hɪstri] Geschichte I
hit [hɪt], **hit, hit**:
1. schlagen, treffen IV
2. prallen/stoßen gegen/auf IV
hitchhiker ['hɪtʃhaɪkə] Anhalter/in, Tramper/in V
hi-tech [haɪ 'tek] High-Tech-, Hochleistungs- VI 3 (57)
hobby ['hɒbi] Hobby I
hockey ['hɒki] Hockey III
hold [həʊld], **held, held** halten II
hole [həʊl] Loch III
hole punch ['həʊl pʌntʃ] Locher I
holiday ['hɒlədeɪ] Urlaub I **holidays** Ferien I
home [həʊm] Heim, Zuhause I **at home** zu Hause, daheim I **dogs' home** Hundeheim II **go home** nach Hause gehen I
homecoming ['həʊmkʌmɪŋ] *(AE)* Ehemaligentreffen *(Schule)* IV
homeless ['həʊmləs] obdachlos IV
homesick ['həʊmsɪk]: **be/feel homesick** Heimweh haben II
homework ['həʊmwɜ:k] Hausaufgabe(n) I **do your homework** Hausaufgaben machen I
I forgot my homework. Ich habe meine Hausaufgaben vergessen. I
What's for homework? Was haben wir als Hausaufgabe(n) auf? I
honest ['ɒnɪst] ehrlich IV

honey ['hʌni] Honig V
hood [hʊd] Kapuze V
hooded ['hʊdɪd]: **a hooded figure** eine Person/Gestalt mit Kapuze V
hoodie ['hʊdi] Kapuzenpullover I
hoot [hu:t] hupen III
hoover ['hu:və] staubsaugen II
hope [həʊp]:
1. hoffen I
2. Hoffnung IV
hopeful ['həʊpfl] zuversichtlich, hoffnungsvoll III
hopeless ['həʊpləs] hoffnungslos VI 3 (57)
°**horn** [hɔ:n] Horn
horrible ['hɒrəbl] schrecklich V
horror ['hɒrə] Horror IV
horse [hɔ:s] Pferd II
hospital ['hɒspɪtl] Krankenhaus I
host [həʊst]:
1. Gastgeber/in III
°2. **host a party** eine Party veranstalten, feiern
host family ['həʊst fæməli] Gastfamilie III
hot [hɒt] heiß I
hot spot ['hɒt spɒt] Anziehungspunkt V **tourist hot spot** touristischer Anziehungspunkt V
hotel [həʊ'tel] Hotel III
hound [haʊnd] (Jagd-)Hund II
hour ['aʊə] Stunde II **opening hours** *(pl)* Öffnungszeiten V **working hours** *(pl)* Arbeitszeit(en) V
house [haʊs] Haus I
housework ['haʊswɜ:k] Hausarbeit *(Arbeit im Haus/Haushalt)* IV
housing estate ['haʊzɪŋ ɪsteɪt] Wohnsiedlung VI 2 (43)
how [haʊ] wie I **How are you doing?** *(AE)* Wie geht's? / Wie geht es dir/euch/Ihnen? IV **How are you?** Wie geht's? / Wie geht es dir/euch/Ihnen? I **How much are …?** Was (Wie viel) kosten? I **How much is …?** Was (Wie viel) kostet? I **how to do sth.** wie man etwas tut / tun kann / tun soll III **How's it going?** Wie geht's? / Wie läuft's? I
however [haʊ'evə] allerdings, jedoch IV
hug [hʌg] umklammern; umarmen V
huge [hju:dʒ] riesig, Riesen- III
human ['hju:mən] Mensch; menschlich V
human being [hju:mən 'bi:ɪŋ] Mensch V
humour ['hju:mə] Humor VI 1 (17) **sense of humour** (Sinn für) Humor VI 1 (17)
hump [hʌmp] Buckel, Hindernis VI 2 (43) **speed hump** Bodenschwelle, Bremsschwelle (zur Verkehrsberuhigung) VI 2 (43)
hundred ['hʌndrəd]: **a hundred, one hundred** (ein)hundert I
hung [hʌŋ] *siehe* **hang**

hunt [hʌnt] jagen IV
hurricane ['hʌrɪkən] Hurrikan, Orkan IV
hurry ['hʌri] sich beeilen; eilen I **Hurry up.** Beeil dich! / Beeilt euch! IV **be in a hurry** es eilig haben IV
hurt [hɜːt], **hurt, hurt** verletzen; wehtun II **be hurt** verletzt sein II **get hurt** sich verletzen II
hurtful ['hɜːtfl] verletzend VI 2 (36)
husband ['hʌzbənd] (Ehe-)Mann IV
hut [hʌt] Hütte VI 1 (22)
°**hyper-** ['haɪpə] Hyper-, Über-
hyphen ['haɪfn] Bindestrich, Trennstrich VI 1 (17)
hypocrisy [hɪ'pɒkrəsi] Heuchelei, Scheinheiligkeit VI 2 (38)

I

I [aɪ] ich I **I'm (= I am)** ich bin I
ice [aɪs] Eis *(gefrorenes Wasser)* III
ice cream [aɪs 'kriːm] (Speise-)Eis I
ice hockey ['aɪs hɒki] Eishockey II
ice rink ['aɪs rɪŋk] Schlittschuhbahn II
ice skates *(pl)* ['aɪs skeɪts] Schlittschuhe II
ice skating ['aɪs skeɪtɪŋ] Schlittschuhlaufen II
iced tea [aɪst 'tiː] Eistee IV
ICT (Information and Communication technology) [aɪ siː 'tiː], [ɪnfəmeɪʃn ənd kəmjuːnɪ'keɪʃn teknɒlədʒi] Informations- und Kommunikationstechnologie I
idea [aɪ'dɪə] Idee I
ideal [aɪ'dɪəl] ideal III
identify [aɪ'dentɪfaɪ] erkennen, identifizieren V
identity [aɪ'dentəti] Identität V
idiot ['ɪdiət] Idiot/in I
if [ɪf]:
 1. wenn, falls II
 2. ob II
ignore [ɪg'nɔː] nicht beachten, ignorieren IV
ill [ɪl] krank II
illegal [ɪ'liːgl] illegal; verboten III
illness ['ɪlnəs] Krankheit IV
illustrate ['ɪləstreɪt] veranschaulichen; illustrieren, bebildern V
illustration [ɪlə'streɪʃn] Abbildung, Illustration II
image ['ɪmɪdʒ] Image; Bild IV
°**imagination** [ɪmædʒɪ'neɪʃn] Fantasie, Vorstellungskraft
imaginative [ɪ'mædʒɪnətɪv] einfallsreich, kreativ V
imagine sth. [ɪ'mædʒɪn] sich etwas vorstellen III
immediate [ɪ'miːdiət] sofortige/r/s V
immediately [ɪ'miːdiətli] sofort, umgehend, unmittelbar V
immigrant ['ɪmɪgrənt] Einwanderer, Einwanderin IV
immigration [ɪmɪ'greɪʃn] Einwanderung IV
°**impact** ['ɪmpækt] Einfluss, Auswirkung
impaired [ɪm'peəd] beeinträchtigt, behindert IV **visually impaired** sehbehindert IV
impatient [ɪm'peɪʃnt] ungeduldig III
°**implant** ['ɪmplɑːnt] Implantat
°**importance** [ɪm'pɔːtns] Bedeutung, Wichtigkeit
important [ɪm'pɔːtnt] wichtig I
impossible [ɪm'pɒsəbl] unmöglich VI 2 (47)
impress [ɪm'pres] beeindrucken IV
impressed [ɪm'prest] beeindruckt IV
impression [ɪm'preʃn] Eindruck VI 1 (23)
improve [ɪm'pruːv] (sich) verbessern III
in [ɪn] in I **in English** auf Englisch I **in fact** eigentlich, um genau zu sein VI 1 (18) **in the afternoon** am Nachmittag I **in the country** auf dem Land I **in the end** schließlich, zum Schluss II **in the evening** abends, am Abend I **in the field** auf der Weide I **in the middle** in der Mitte I **in the morning** morgens, am Morgen I **in the photo** auf dem Foto I **in the picture** auf dem Bild I **in town** in der Stadt I **I haven't eaten in days.** Ich habe tagelang nichts gegessen. V **one in five** eine/r/s von fünf(en) V °**in between** dazwischen
inch [ɪntʃ] Zoll *(Längenmaß; 1 inch = 2,54 cm)* IV
°**incident** ['ɪnsɪdənt] Vorfall, Begebenheit
°**incinerate** [ɪnsɪnə'reɪt] verbrennen
include [ɪn'kluːd] (mit) einschließen VI 1 (14)
included [ɪn'kluːdɪd] inbegriffen III
including [ɪn'kluːdɪŋ] einschließlich; darunter (auch) III
increase (by) [ɪn'kriːs] steigern, (sich) erhöhen; steigen, zunehmen (um) VI 3 (57)
incredible [ɪn'kredəbl] unglaublich IV
independence (from) [ɪndɪ'pendəns] Unabhängigkeit (von) IV
independent (of/from) [ɪndɪ'pendənt] unabhängig (von) III
Indian ['ɪndiən]: **(American) Indian** Indianer/in; indianisch IV
indigenous (to) [ɪn'dɪdʒənəs] einheimisch (in) V **indigenous Australian** australische/r Ureinwohner/in V **indigenous people** Einheimische, Ureinwohner/innen V
indirect [ɪndə'rekt] indirekt V
individual [ɪndɪ'vɪdʒuəl] Einzelne/r, Individuum; Person V
°**indoor** ['ɪndɔː] im Haus/Gebäude, drinnen stattfindend
°**indoors** [ɪn'dɔːz] innen, drinnen
industry ['ɪndəstri] Industrie IV
inequality [ɪnɪ'kwɒləti] Ungleichheit VI 1 (12)
°**inexplicable** [ɪnɪk'splɪkəbl] unerklärlich
infected [ɪn'fektɪd] entzündet IV
influence ['ɪnfluəns]:
 1. beeinflussen V
 2. Einfluss V
informal [ɪn'fɔːml] informell, locker VI 3 (70)
information [ɪnfə'meɪʃn] Information(en) I
information desk [ɪnfə'meɪʃn desk] Informationsstand I
ingredient [ɪn'griːdiənt] Zutat, Bestandteil V
°**initiative** [ɪ'nɪʃətɪv] Aktion, Initiative
inland [ɪn'lænd] landeinwärts, im Landesinneren/ins Landesinnere V
inline skates *(pl)* [ɪnlaɪn 'skeɪts] Inlineskates I
inside [ɪn'saɪd]:
 1. drinnen; nach drinnen I
 2. inside a T-shirt in einem T-Shirt II
 3. the inside das Innere, die Innenseite IV
inside out [ɪnsaɪd 'aʊt] verkehrt herum, auf links *(Kleidung)* VI 2 (47)
install [ɪn'stɔːl] installieren, einbauen III
instead [ɪn'sted] stattdessen V
instead of [ɪn'sted əv] anstatt, anstelle von VI 1 (16)
°**instinctive** [ɪn'stɪŋktɪv] instinktiv
°**instruction** [ɪn'strʌkʃn] Anweisung
instructor [ɪn'strʌktə] Lehrer/in V
instrument ['ɪnstrəmənt] Instrument I
integrate ['ɪntɪgreɪt] integrieren IV
interest ['ɪntrəst]:
 1. Interesse V
 °**2. interest sb.** jn. interessieren
interested (in) ['ɪntrəstɪd] interessiert (an) II
interesting ['ɪntrəstɪŋ] interessant I
international [ɪntə'næʃnəl] international III
interrupt [ɪntə'rʌpt] unterbrechen VI 2 (41)
°**intervene (in)** [ɪntə'viːn] eingreifen, einschreiten (in, bei); sich einmischen (in)
interview ['ɪntəvjuː] Interview I **job interview** Vorstellungsgespräch V
interviewer ['ɪntəvjuːə] Interviewer/in V
°**intimate** ['ɪntɪmət] intim, eng, persönlich
intimidate [ɪn'tɪmɪdeɪt] einschüchtern IV
intimidating [ɪn'tɪmɪdeɪtɪŋ] einschüchternd, bedrohlich IV
into ['ɪntu], ['ɪntə] in (… hinein) I
introduce sb. to sb./sth. [ɪntrə'djuːs] jm. jn./etwas vorstellen, jn. mit jm./etwas bekanntmachen III
introduction (to) [ɪntrə'dʌkʃn] Einleitung, Einführung (in) IV
invention [ɪn'venʃn] Erfindung V
invisible [ɪn'vɪzəbl] unsichtbar IV
invitation (to) [ɪnvɪ'teɪʃn] Einladung (zu, nach) I
invite (to) [ɪn'vaɪt] einladen (zu, nach) I

involved [ɪn'vɒlvd]: **involved in** beteiligt an, engagiert bei VI 2 (36) **be involved (in)** sich an etwas beteiligen, sich bei etwas engagieren VI 2 (36)
Irish ['aɪrɪʃ] irisch, aus Irland III
iron ['aɪən]:
1. Bügeleisen V
2. bügeln V
°**Iron Age** ['aɪən eɪdʒ] Eisenzeit
ironing ['aɪənɪŋ]: **do the ironing** bügeln V
irritate ['ɪrɪteɪt] (ver)ärgern, irritieren V
is [ɪz] *(er/sie/es)* ist I **The calculator is £ 1.** Der Taschenrechner kostet 1 Pfund. I
island ['aɪlənd] Insel II
issue ['ɪʃu:] (Streit-)Frage, Problem, Thema VI 2 (36)
it [ɪt] er, sie, es I
item ['aɪtəm] Artikel, Gegenstand VI 2 (40) **news item** Nachrichtenmeldung, Pressemeldung VI 2 (40)
its [ɪts] sein/e, ihr/e II
itself [ɪt'self] es/sich selbst III

J

jacket ['dʒækɪt] Jacke, Jackett II
jam [dʒæm] Marmelade I
January ['dʒænjuəri] Januar I
°**jar** [dʒɑ:] Glas (z.B. für Marmelade), (Glas-/Plastik-)Gefäß
jealous ['dʒeləs] eifersüchtig, neidisch II
jeans *(pl)* [dʒi:nz] *(eine)* Jeans II
jelly ['dʒeli] *(AE)* Marmelade IV
jellyfish, *pl* **jellyfish** ['dʒelifɪʃ] Qualle V
Jewish ['dʒu:ɪʃ] jüdisch IV
job [dʒɒb] Job, (Arbeits-)stelle I **do a great/good/bad job** großartige/gute/schlechte Arbeit leisten III **Good job!** *(AE)* Gut gemacht! IV **on the job** am Arbeitsplatz IV
job interview ['dʒɒb ɪntəvju:] Vorstellungsgespräch V
join [dʒɔɪn]: **join a club** sich einem Klub anschließen; in einen Klub eintreten I **join the army** zur Armee gehen IV **Join the club.** Da bist du nicht der/die Einzige. II °**join together** sich zusammenschließen
joke [dʒəʊk]:
1. Witz, Scherz II
She can take a joke. Sie versteht Spaß. III
2. Witze machen, scherzen II
You're joking! Du machst wohl Witze! II
journal ['dʒɜ:nl] Tagebuch, Journal IV
journalist ['dʒɜ:nəlɪst] Journalist/in IV
journey ['dʒɜ:ni]:
1. Reise II
2. reisen IV
joyriding ['dʒɔɪraɪdɪŋ] Joyriding *(eine Spritztour mit einem gestohlenen Auto machen)* VI 2 (45)
judo ['dʒu:dəʊ] Judo II
juice [dʒu:s] Saft I
July [dʒu'laɪ] Juli I
jump [dʒʌmp]:
1. **jump (up)** (hoch)springen II
2. *(vor Schreck)* zusammenzucken III
junction ['dʒʌŋkʃn] (Straßen-)Kreuzung VI 2 (44)
June [dʒu:n] Juni I
°**junior** ['dʒu:niə] Junior/in
junk food ['dʒʌŋk fu:d] Junkfood *(ungesundes Essen)* II
just [dʒʌst]:
1. gerade (eben) II
2. nur, bloß; einfach III
3. **just about** so ziemlich, nahezu; (so) ungefähr VI 2 (48)
just like Berry genau wie Berry II

K

kangaroo [kæŋgə'ru:] Känguru V
keep [ki:p], **kept, kept** aufbewahren; (be)halten III **keep (on) doing sth.** etwas immer weiter/immer wieder/ständig tun VI 3 (60) **keep away from** sich fernhalten von IV **Keep it up!** Weiter so! II **Keep me posted!** Halt mich auf dem Laufenden! III **keep on** weitermachen VI 3 (60)
keeper ['ki:pə]: **Finders keepers, losers weepers.** Was man findet, darf man behalten. *(Redensart)* V
kept [kept] *siehe* **keep**
kettle ['ketl] Wasserkocher *(elektrisch)* III
key [ki:] Schlüssel; Schlüssel- V
key skills *(pl)* ['ki: skɪlz] Schlüsselqualifikationen, -kompetenzen V
kick [kɪk]:
1. Tritt, Stoß, Kick V
2. treten; *(Sport)* schießen V
3. *(infml)* *(Gewohnheit/Idee)* aufgeben, sich davon befreien V
kid [kɪd] Kind, Jugendliche/r I
kidding ['kɪdɪŋ]: **Are you kidding?** *(infml)* Machst du Witze? / Willst du mich auf den Arm nehmen? IV
kill [kɪl] töten, umbringen IV
killer ['kɪlə] Mörder/in V
kilogram, kilo ['kɪləgræm], ['ki:ləʊ] Kilo(gramm) IV
kilometre (km) ['kɪləmi:tə] Kilometer II **kilometres per hour (kph)** Kilometer pro Stunde (km/h) III
kilt [kɪlt] Kilt, Schottenrock III
kind [kaɪnd] nett, freundlich II
kind (of) [kaɪnd] Art, Sorte II **kind of glamorous** irgendwie glamourös V
king [kɪŋ] König II
Kingdom ['kɪŋdəm]: **the United Kingdom (the UK)** das Vereinigte Königreich III
kiss [kɪs]:
1. Kuss I
2. (sich) küssen III
kitchen ['kɪtʃɪn] Küche I
kitten ['kɪtn] Kätzchen, junge Katze II
knee [ni:] Knie II
knew [nju:] *siehe* **know**
knife, *pl* **knives** [naɪf], [naɪvz] Messer III
knock (on sth.) [nɒk] (an)klopfen (an etwas) III
know [nəʊ], **knew, known** wissen; kennen I **get to know** kennenlernen III
knowledge (of/about) ['nɒlɪdʒ] Wissen (von/über), Kenntnis(se) (von/in) V
known [nəʊn] *siehe* **know**
kph (kilometres per hour) [keɪ pi: 'eɪtʃ] Kilometer pro Stunde (km/h) III

L

lab [læb] Labor I
label ['leɪbl] Etikett, Schild(chen) III
lad [læd] *(infml)* Junge, junger Kerl V
ladder ['lædə] *(die)* Leiter V
ladies and gentlemen [leɪdi:z ənd 'dʒentlmən] meine Damen und Herren VI 1 (21)
lady ['leɪdi] Dame V
ladylike ['leɪdilaɪk] damenhaft IV
lain [leɪn] *siehe* **lie**
lake [leɪk] (Binnen-)See II
lamp [læmp] Lampe I
land [lænd]:
1. landen III
2. Land *(Grund und Boden)* IV
by land auf dem Landweg IV
°**landfill** ['lændfɪl] deponieren, auf einer Mülldeponie ablagern
°**landing** ['lændɪŋ] Landung
°**landmark** ['lændmɑ:k] Wahrzeichen, Sehenswürdigkeit
landscape ['lændskeɪp] Landschaft V
landscape gardener [lændskeɪp 'gɑ:dnə] Landschaftsgärtner/in V
lane [leɪn] Gasse, Weg, Sträßchen II
language ['læŋgwɪdʒ] Sprache I **official language** Amtssprache VI 1 (10)
lantern ['læntən] Laterne II
large [lɑ:dʒ] groß IV
lasagne [lə'zænjə] Lasagne II
last [lɑ:st] letzte(r, s) I **at last** schließlich, endlich III
°**last (for)** [lɑ:st] (an)dauern
late [leɪt] spät I
lately ['leɪtli] in letzter Zeit V
later ['leɪtə] später I **See you later.** Bis später. I
latest ['leɪtɪst]: **at the latest** spätestens VI 3 (62) °**the latest …** der/die/das neueste …
laugh [lɑ:f]:
1. lachen I
laugh at lachen über, sich lustig machen über III
2. *(ein)* Lachen I
with a laugh mit einem Lachen I
°**launch** [lɔ:ntʃ] starten, ins Leben rufen
law [lɔ:] Gesetz IV

lay [leɪ] *siehe* **lie**
lazy ['leɪzi] faul I
lead [liːd]:
1. (Hunde-)Leine III
2. **lead, led, led** führen, leiten V
leader ['liːdə] Leiter/in, (An-)Führer/in II
league [liːg] Liga *(Sport)* II
lean [liːn] lehnen IV
learn [lɜːn] lernen I **learn a/your lesson** eine/deine Lektion lernen V
least [liːst] *(der/die/das)* wenigste, am wenigsten IV **at least** wenigstens, zumindest II
leather ['leðə] Leder V
leave [liːv], **left, left:**
1. abfahren, losfahren II
2. *(jemanden)* verlassen; weggehen I
3. zurücklassen II
leave sb. alone jn. in Ruhe lassen V
leave sb./sth. behind etwas/jn. zurücklassen, etwas hinter sich lassen VI 3 (62)
°**LED** [el iː 'diː] Leuchtdiode
led [led] *siehe* **lead**
left [left] links; nach links I **on the left** links, auf der linken Seite I
left [left] *siehe* **leave**
leftover pizza/cake/... ['leftəʊvə] übrig gebliebene Pizza/ übrig gebliebener Kuchen/... VI 1 (20)
leg [leg] Bein I **I have a sore leg.** Mein Bein tut weh. I
legal ['liːgl]:
1. legal IV
°2. gesetzlich
legend ['ledʒənd] Legende, Sage II
lemon ['lemən] Zitrone IV
lend sb. sth. [lend], **lent, lent** jm. etwas leihen III
lent [lent] *siehe* **lend**
°**leopard** ['lepəd] Leopard
less [les] weniger II
lesson ['lesn] (Unterrichts-)Stunde I
learn a/your lesson eine/deine Lektion lernen V **teach sb. a lesson** jm. eine Lektion erteilen V
let [let], **let, let** lassen IV **Let's ...** Lass(t) uns ... I
letter ['letə]:
1. Brief I
letter to the editor Leserbrief IV
2. Buchstabe II
letter box ['letə bɒks] Briefkasten II
level ['levl] Niveau, Ebene; Grad, Stufe VI 1 (14)
library ['laɪbrəri] Bücherei, Bibliothek IV
°**licence** ['laɪsns] Lizenz, Erlaubnis
license ['laɪsns]: **driver's license** *(AE)* Führerschein IV
lie [laɪ]:
1. Lüge V
tell a lie/lies lügen V
2. **lie (to sb.)** (jn. an)lügen V
lie [laɪ], **lay, lain** liegen III **lie back** sich zurücklehnen, sich entspannen VI 2 (44)
life, *pl* **lives** [laɪf], [laɪvz] *(das)* Leben I
way of life Lebensweise V
lifeguard ['laɪfgɑːd] Rettungsschwimmer/in; Bademeister/in V
lifestyle ['laɪfstaɪl] Lebensstil V
lift [lɪft]:
1. heben, hochheben VI 3 (56)
2. Lift, Fahrstuhl IV
3. Mitfahrgelegenheit VI 2 (43)
give sb. a lift jn. (mit dem Auto) mitnehmen VI 2 (43)
light [laɪt]:
1. Licht, Lampe II
2. **light, lit, lit** anzünden V
light a fire (ein) Feuer machen V
light [laɪt] leicht; hell IV
lighthouse ['laɪthaʊs] Leuchtturm II
°**lightweight** ['laɪtweɪt] leicht, Leicht-
like [laɪk] mögen I **I don't like ...** ich mag ... nicht I **I'd (= I would) like ...** Ich hätte gern ... / Ich möchte ... I
like [laɪk]:
1. als ob, als wenn IV
2. wie I
like that so *(auf diese Art)* IV **like this** so, auf diese Art III **... like ...** *(infml)* ... irgendwie ... / ..., keine Ahnung, ... V **just like Berry** genau wie Berry II **something like this / like that** so etwas II **What's it like?** Wie ist es? / Wie sieht es aus? I
likeable ['laɪkəbl] sympathisch IV
likely ['laɪkli] wahrscheinlich V **be likely to do sth.** wahrscheinlich etwas tun (werden) V
likes and dislikes *(pl)* [laɪks ən 'dɪslaɪks] Vorlieben und Abneigungen III
°**limit** ['lɪmɪt] Grenze, Beschränkung
line [laɪn]:
1. U-Bahn-Linie III
2. Reihe; Zeile III
°**line sth.** [laɪn] etwas füttern, auskleiden, säumen
lingua franca [lɪŋgwə 'fræŋkə] Lingua Franca *(Verkehrssprache)* VI 1 (16)
link [lɪŋk] Verbindung; Link IV
lion ['laɪən] Löwe IV
lip [lɪp] Lippe V
lipstick ['lɪpstɪk] Lippenstift V
list [lɪst]:
1. Liste II
2. auflisten, aufzählen V
listen ['lɪsn]: **listen (to)** (sich etwas) anhören; zuhören I **listen for sth.** auf etwas horchen, *(beim Zuhören)* auf etwas achten VI 3 (68)
listener ['lɪsənə] Zuhörer/in III
lit [lɪt] *siehe* **light**
litre ['liːtə] Liter V
litter ['lɪtə] Abfall II
litter bin ['lɪtə bɪn] Mülleimer, Abfalleimer II
little ['lɪtl]:
1. klein I
2. wenig IV
a little ein wenig, ein bisschen III
live [lɪv] leben, wohnen I
°**live** [laɪv] live
liveable ['lɪvəbl] lebenswert V
lives [laɪvz] *Plural von* **life** I
living ['lɪvɪŋ]: **(sustainable) living** (nachhaltige) Lebensweise VI 3 (60)
°**living conditions** *(pl)* ['lɪvɪŋ kəndɪʃnz] Lebensbedingungen, Lebensumstände
living history [lɪvɪŋ 'hɪstri] *etwa:* Geschichte zum Anfassen II
living room ['lɪvɪŋ ruːm] Wohnzimmer I
°**load** [ləʊd] (ver)laden
loads (of) [ləʊdz] *(infml)* eine Menge VI 2 (36)
lobby ['lɒbi] Eingangshalle IV
local ['ləʊkl] örtlich, Orts-, Lokal- III
location [ləʊ'keɪʃn] Ort *(Standort; Einsatzort, Drehort)* VI 2 (49)
locker ['lɒkə] Spind, Schließfach IV
°**log** [lɒg] Aufzeichnungen, Protokoll
lonely ['ləʊnli] einsam I
loner ['ləʊnə] Einzelgänger/in VI 3 (65)
long [lɒŋ] lang II **no longer** nicht mehr IV
long shot ['lɒŋ ʃɒt] Totale *(Film)* VI 3 (71)
look [lʊk]:
1. sehen, schauen I
2. aussehen I
3. **Let's have a look.** Lass(t) uns mal nachschauen. II
Look, Adam. Sieh mal/Schau mal, Adam I **look after** sich kümmern um; aufpassen auf I **look at sth.** sich etwas anschauen I **look down your nose at sb.** herabblicken auf jn. IV **look for** suchen; Ausschau halten nach I **look forward to** sich freuen auf II **look forward to doing sth.** sich darauf freuen, etwas zu tun IV **look into sth.** etwas prüfen III **look up a word** ein Wort nachschlagen *(im Wörterbuch)* IV °**look out for** Ausschau halten nach, achten auf
°**lookout** ['lʊkaʊt] Aussicht
loot [luːt] plündern IV
looter ['luːtə] Plünderer/Plünderin IV
lose [luːz], **lost, lost** verlieren I **lose control** die Kontrolle verlieren I **lose the police** *(infml)* die Polizei abhängen, abschütteln VI 2 (44)
loser ['luːzə] Verlierer/in III **Finders keepers, losers weepers.** Was man findet, darf man behalten. *(Redensart)* V
lost [lɒst] *siehe* **lose** **Get lost!** Verschwinde(t)! II **I'm not lost.** Ich habe mich nicht verlaufen/verirrt. I

lot [lɒt]: **lots of** viel/e I **a lot (of)** viel/e; sehr II
loud [laʊd] laut III
love [lʌv]:
1. lieben, sehr mögen I
I'd (= I would) love to come. Ich komme sehr gern. / Ich würde sehr gern kommen. I
2. *freundliche Anrede, auch bei Unbekannten* III
3. Liebling VI 2 (44)
4. Liebe I
Give her my love. Grüß sie von mir. III **in love (with)** verliebt (in) I **Lots of love** Alles Liebe / Liebe Grüße III
lovely ['lʌvli] schön; nett, lieb II
low [ləʊ] niedrig, tief II
luck [lʌk]: **bad luck** Pech IV **Good luck.** Viel Glück! IV **Hard luck!** Pech (gehabt)! III
luckily ['lʌkɪli] glücklicherweise, zum Glück III
lucky ['lʌki]: **you're lucky** du hast Glück I
lunch [lʌntʃ] Mittagessen I **have lunch** (zu) Mittag essen I
lunch box ['lʌntʃ bɒks] Brotdose II
lunchtime ['lʌntʃtaɪm] Mittagszeit II

M

machine [mə'ʃiːn] Maschine, Gerät V **drinks machine** Getränkeautomat V
mad [mæd] wahnsinnig, verrückt VI 2 (43)
madam ['mædəm] meine Dame, gnädige Frau V **Dear Sir/Madam** Sehr geehrte Damen und Herren V
made [meɪd] *siehe* **make**
madhouse ['mædhaʊs] Irrenhaus I
magazine [mægə'ziːn] Zeitschrift II
magic ['mædʒɪk] Zauberei, Magie II
magical ['mædʒɪkl] magisch; zauberhaft II
magician [mə'dʒɪʃn] Zauberer/Zauberin II
mailman/-woman ['meɪlmən, -wʊmən] *(AE)* Briefträger/in IV
main [meɪn] hauptsächlich, Haupt- IV
mainland ['meɪnlænd] Festland VI 3 (65)
majority [mə'dʒɒrəti] Mehrheit, Mehrzahl VI 2 (39)
make [meɪk], **made, made** machen, herstellen I **make a difference** etwas bewirken, etwas ausmachen I **make friends** Freunde finden II **make money** Geld verdienen III **make sb. do sth.** jn. dazu bringen, etwas zu tun II **make sb./sth. sth.** jn./etwas zu etwas machen IV **make sure that …** darauf achten, dass …; dafür sorgen, dass … V **be made of** aus etwas (gemacht) sein IV °**make it** es schaffen, Erfolg haben

male [meɪl] männlich; männliche Person, männliches Tier VI 1 (15)
mall [mɔːl] Einkaufszentrum III
mam [mæm] *(in Irland)* Mama, Mutti III
°**mamba** ['mæmbə] Mamba *(Giftschlange)*
man, *pl* men [mæn], [men] Mann I
manage ['mænɪdʒ] verwalten, regeln V
management ['mænɪdʒmənt] Leitung, (Geschäfts-)Führung III
manager ['mænɪdʒə] Geschäftsführer/in, Manager/in III
manga ['mæŋgə] Manga II
manners *(pl)* ['mænəz] Manieren, Umgangsformen IV
many ['mæni] viele II **how many?** wie viele? II
map [mæp]:
1. Landkarte, Stadtplan I
2. kartografieren, *(Entwicklung)* verfolgen IV
March [mɑːtʃ] März I
°**margin** ['mɑːdʒɪn] Rand
mark [mɑːk]:
1. kennzeichnen, markieren III
2. (Schul-)Note, Zensur VI 1 (18)
market ['mɑːkɪt] Markt I
°**marriage** ['mærɪdʒ] Hochzeit, Ehe
married (to) ['mærid] verheiratet (mit) II **get married (to sb.)** (jn.) heiraten IV
Mars [mɑːz] *(der)* Mars VI 3 (62)
Martian ['mɑːʃn] Marsmensch VI 3 (62)
mask [mɑːsk] Maske II
match [mætʃ] Spiel, Wettkampf II
°**match (with)** [mætʃ] zuordnen
mate *(infml)* [meɪt] Freund/in, Kumpel VI 2 (43)
°**material** [mə'tɪəriəl] Material, Stoff
materials *(pl)* [mə'tɪəriəlz] Materialien, Hilfsmittel V
math [mæθ] *(AE)* Mathe(matik) IV
maths [mæθs] Mathe(matik) I
matter ['mætə]:
1. von Bedeutung sein, wichtig sein II **It doesn't matter.** Es/Das ist egal. II
2. **no matter what/how/who** (ganz) egal, was/wie/wer VI 3 (68)
What's the matter? Was ist denn? / Was ist los? II
mature [mə'tʃʊə] reif, vernünftig V
°**maximum, max.** ['mæksɪməm], [mæks] Höchst-, maximal, Maximum
May [meɪ] Mai I
maybe ['meɪbi] vielleicht I
mayonnaise [meɪə'neɪz] Majonäse III
mayor [meə] Bürgermeister/in VI 2 (35)
maze [meɪz] Irrgarten, Labyrinth II
me [miː] mich; mir I **It's me.** Ich bin's. I
meadow ['medəʊ] Wiese IV
meal [miːl] Mahlzeit, Essen III **Enjoy your meal.** Guten Appetit! III
mean [miːn]:
1. geizig II
2. gemein, fies I

mean [miːn], **meant, meant:**
1. bedeuten I
2. meinen *(sagen wollen)* I
meaning ['miːnɪŋ] Bedeutung IV
meant [ment] *siehe* **mean**
meat [miːt] Fleisch II
meatless ['miːtləs] fleischlos VI 3 (57)
mechanic [mɪ'kænɪk] Mechaniker/in III
mechanical [mɪ'kænɪkl] mechanisch VI 3 (56)
medal ['medl] Medaille III
media *(pl)* ['miːdiə] Medien V **social media** soziale Medien/Dienste V
°**mediate** ['miːdieɪt] vermitteln
°**mediation** [miːdi'eɪʃn] Vermittlung, Sprachmittlung
°**medicine** ['medsn] Medizin, Medikament(e)
medium ['miːdiəm] mittel(groß); mittlere(r, s) VI 3 (71)
medium shot ['miːdiəm ʃɒt] Halbtotale *(Film)* VI 3 (71)
meet [miːt], **met, met** kennenlernen; treffen I **Nice to meet you.** Freut mich, dich/euch/Sie kennenzulernen. I
meeting ['miːtɪŋ] Treffen; Zusammenkunft IV
member ['membə] Mitglied IV
meme [miːm] Internet-Mem, Internetphänomen VI 2 (36)
memorial (to sb./sth.) [mə'mɔːriəl] Denkmal (für jn./etwas), Gedenkstätte IV
°**memory (of)** ['meməri] Gedächtnis, Erinnerung (an)
men [men] *Plural von* **man** I
°**menacing** ['menəsɪŋ] drohend, bedrohlich
°**mend** [mend] reparieren
mention ['menʃn] erwähnen III
menu ['menjuː] Speisekarte III
mess [mes]:
1. Durcheinander, Chaos II
What a mess! Was für ein Durcheinander/Chaos! II
2. **mess with sb./sth.** herumspielen, Spielchen treiben mit jm./etwas IV
message ['mesɪdʒ]:
1. Botschaft, Aussage III
2. Nachricht, Mitteilung I
message in a bottle Flaschenpost I
leave a message eine Nachricht hinterlassen III **take a message** *(jm.)* etwas ausrichten III
3. Nachrichten schicken/austauschen V
messy ['mesi] unordentlich I
met [met] *siehe* **meet**
metal ['metl] Metall IV
°**metaphor** ['metəfə] Metapher (Stilmittel, übertragene Bedeutung)
metre ['miːtə] Meter II
mice [maɪs] *Plural von* **mouse** III
microwave ['maɪkrəweɪv] Mikrowelle VI 1 (20)

middle ['mɪdl] Mitte I **in the middle** in der Mitte I **in the middle of nowhere** am Ende der Welt III
Middle Ages *(pl)* [mɪdl 'eɪdʒɪz] Mittelalter VI 3 (60)
midnight ['mɪdnaɪt] Mitternacht III
might [maɪt]: **you might miss home** es könnte sein, dass du dein Zuhause vermisst III
migrant ['maɪgrənt] Zuwanderer/Zuwanderin III
mile [maɪl] Meile *(ca. 1,6 km)* II
°**milestone** ['maɪlstəʊn] Meilenstein, Wegmarke
milk [mɪlk]:
1. Milch II
2. melken IV
milkshake ['mɪlkʃeɪk] Milchshake II
million ['mɪljən] Million III
mind [maɪnd]:
1. aufpassen auf, achten auf IV
2. **I don't mind.** Es macht mir nichts aus. III
mind [maɪnd] Geist, Verstand; Gedanken VI 1 (20) °**change one's mind** es sich anders überlegen
mind map ['maɪnd mæp] Gedankenkarte, Wörternetz I
mind-blowing ['maɪnd bləʊɪŋ] *(infml)* irre, wahnsinnig VI 1 (22)
°**mindset** ['maɪndset] Mentalität, Denkweise
mine [maɪn] meine, meiner, meins II
minibus ['mɪnibʌs] Kleinbus VI 1 (22)
°**minimum** ['mɪnɪməm] Minimum, Mindest-, minimal
°**minimum wage** [mɪnɪməm 'weɪdʒ] Mindestlohn
mining ['maɪnɪŋ] Bergbau IV **gold mining** Goldabbau IV
minority [maɪ'nɒrəti] Minderheit VI 2 (48)
minus ['maɪnəs] minus II
minute ['mɪnɪt] Minute I
mirror ['mɪrə] Spiegel I
°**misgivings** *(pl)* [mɪs'gɪvɪŋz] Bedenken
Miss [mɪs]:
1. **Miss Borowski** Frau Borowski *(Anrede für unverheiratete Frauen)* I
2. Fräulein *(BE: Anrede für Lehrerin)* II
miss [mɪs]:
1. vermissen I
2. verpassen II
3. übersehen, überhören *(nicht mitbekommen)* II
°**mission** ['mɪʃn] Auftrag, Mission
mistake [mɪ'steɪk] Fehler II **by mistake** aus Versehen II
°**misuse** [mɪs'juːs] Missbrauch
mix [mɪks] Mix, Mischung III
mob [mɒb] Mob, Menschenmenge VI 3 (65)
mobile ['məʊbaɪl]:
1. mobil V
2. *(kurz für:* **mobile phone***)* Handy I
°**mobile home** [məʊbaɪl 'həʊm] (großer) Wohnwagen, Wohnmobil
moccasin ['mɒkəsɪn] Mokassin IV
model ['mɒdl] Fotomodell, Model V °**a model son** ein Muster-Sohn, ein vorbildlicher Sohn
moderator ['mɒdəreɪtə] Moderator/in *(z.B. bei Debatten)* V
modern ['mɒdn] modern I
modern-day [mɒdn 'deɪ] modern, von heute V
modest ['mɒdɪst] bescheiden; anständig, sittsam IV
mom [mɒm], [mɑːm] *(AE)* Mutti, Mama IV
moment ['məʊmənt] Moment I **at the moment** im Moment, gerade I
Monday ['mʌndeɪ], ['mʌndi] Montag I
money ['mʌni] Geld I **Money doesn't grow on trees.** Das Geld liegt nicht auf der Straße. *(Redewendung)* II **it's a money-saver** es spart Kosten III **make money** Geld verdienen III **pocket money** Taschengeld II
monitor ['mɒnɪtə] Monitor, Bildschirm III
monkey ['mʌŋki] Affe I
monologue ['mɒnəlɒg] Monolog, Selbstgespräch V
month [mʌnθ] Monat I
°**monument** ['mɒnjumənt] Monument, Denkmal
mood [muːd] Stimmung, Laune IV
°**moon** [muːn] Mond
more [mɔː] mehr, weitere I **more and more** immer mehr III **more popular** beliebter II
morning ['mɔːnɪŋ] Morgen I **Good morning.** Guten Morgen. I **in the morning** morgens, am Morgen I
most [məʊst]: **most popular** am beliebtesten II **(the) most sports** die meisten Sportarten II
mostly ['məʊstli] meistens; hauptsächlich II
mother ['mʌðə] Mutter I
°**motorcycle** ['məʊtəsaɪkl] Motorrad
motto ['mɒtəʊ] Motto III
mountain ['maʊntən] Berg II
mounted ['maʊntɪd]: **head-mounted display** Datenhelm, Datenbrille, Videobrille VI 3 (59)
mouse, *pl* **mice** [maʊs], [maɪs] Maus III
mouth [maʊθ] Mund I
move [muːv]:
1. (sich) bewegen III
2. **move (to)** (um)ziehen (nach) II **move house** umziehen *(an einen neuen Wohnort)* III
movement ['muːvmənt] Bewegung IV
movie ['muːvi] *(bes. AE)* Film IV
movie theater ['muːvi θɪətə] *(AE)* Kino IV
MP3 player [empiː'θriː pleɪə] MP3-Player I
Mr Brown ['mɪstə] Herr Brown I
Mrs Ford ['mɪsɪz] Frau Ford *(Anrede für verheiratete Frauen)* I
Ms Lee [mɪz], [məz] Frau Lee *(allgemeine Anrede für Frauen)* I
much [mʌtʃ] viel II **as much as ...** bis zu ...; nicht weniger als ... IV **How much is/are ...?** Was (Wie viel) kostet/kosten ...? I **How much?** Wie viel? II **miss/love sb. so much** jn. so sehr vermissen/lieben II **Thanks very much.** Vielen Dank. II
mud [mʌd] Schlamm, Matsch II
muddy ['mʌdi] matschig III
multicultural [mʌlti'kʌltʃərəl] multikulturell VI 1 (10)
multilingual [mʌlti'lɪŋgwəl] mehrsprachig VI 1 (10)
multitask [mʌlti'tɑːsk] mehrere Tätigkeiten gleichzeitig ausführen V
mum [mʌm] Mama, Mutti I
mummy ['mʌmi] Mumie II
museum [mju'ziːəm] Museum I
music ['mjuːzɪk] Musik I
musician [mju'zɪʃn] Musiker/in I
must [mʌst]:
1. müssen I
mustn't do nicht tun dürfen I
I must go. *(am Telefon)* Ich muss Schluss machen. I
2. **a must** *(infml)* ein Muss, eine Notwendigkeit IV
°**musty** ['mʌsti] muffig
mutter ['mʌtə] murmeln, brummeln IV
my [maɪ] mein/e I
myself [maɪ'self] mich, mir (selbst) I
mysterious [mɪ'stɪəriəs] geheimnisvoll II
mystery ['mɪstri] Geheimnis II

N

nail [neɪl] Nagel III
nail polish ['neɪl pɒlɪʃ] Nagellack V
name [neɪm]:
1. (be)nennen III
2. Name I
What's your name? Wie heißt du? I
narrator [nə'reɪtə] Erzähler/in VI 3 (67)
first-person narrator Ich-Erzähler/in VI 3 (67)
narrow ['nærəʊ] eng, schmal III
nation ['neɪʃn] Nation, Volk IV
national ['næʃnəl] national, National- II
national anthem [næʃnəl 'ænθəm] Nationalhymne III
national park [næʃnəl 'pɑːk] Nationalpark II
native ['neɪtɪv] einheimisch, Heimat-; Einheimische/r IV
Native American [neɪtɪv ə'merɪkən] amerikanische/r Ureinwohner/in IV
natural ['nætʃrəl] natürlich, Natur- III
natural history [nætʃrəl 'hɪstri] Naturkunde III

nature ['neɪtʃə] *(die)* Natur IV
near [nɪə] nahe (bei), in der Nähe von I **near to the city** nah am Stadtzentrum II
nearby [nɪə'baɪ] nahe gelegen, in der Nähe IV
nearest ['nɪərɪst]: **the nearest ...** der/die/das nächstgelegene ... V
nearly ['nɪəli] fast II
necessary ['nesəsəri] notwendig, nötig, erforderlich V
necklace ['nekləs] (Hals-)Kette IV
need [ni:d]:
1. brauchen, benötigen I
need to do sth. etwas tun müssen III
2. Bedürfnis V
people with special needs Menschen mit besonderen Bedürfnissen / Förderbedarf V
3. **no need for ... / no need to do sth.** kein Grund für ... / kein Grund, etwas zu tun V
needle ['ni:dl] Nadel; Kanüle VI 2 (43)
negative ['negətɪv] negativ I
neighbour ['neɪbə] Nachbar/in II
neighbourhood ['neɪbəhʊd] Nachbarschaft, Gegend, Viertel II
neighbouring ['neɪbərɪŋ] benachbart IV
neither ['naɪðə]:
1. keine/r/s *(von beiden)* V
2. **... and neither did I.** ... und ich auch nicht. VI 1 (19)
neon ['ni:ɒn] Neon; neonfarbig V
nerd [nɜ:d] *hochintelligente, aber kontaktarme Person* IV
nervous ['nɜ:vəs] nervös, aufgeregt I
net [net] *kurz für* Internet V
network ['netwɜ:k]:
1. Netz; Wortnetz I
2. Netzwerk VI 3 (58)
never ['nevə] nie, niemals I **I've never had ...** ich habe (noch) nie ... gehabt II
new [nju:] neu I
newcomer ['nju:kʌmə] Neuling IV
news [nju:z] Nachrichten I **... is bad news.** ... ist gefährlich. / ... ist (gar) nicht gut. V
news item ['nju:z aɪtəm] Nachrichtenmeldung, Pressemeldung VI 2 (40)
newsagent ['nju:zeɪdʒənt] Zeitungshändler/in II
newsletter ['nju:zletə] Mitteilungsblatt, Informationsblatt II
newspaper ['nju:zpeɪpə] (Tages-)Zeitung II
next [nekst] nächste(r, s) I **Next, please.** Der/Die Nächste, bitte. I **Next ...** Als Nächstes ... II **the next day** am anderen/nächsten Tag III
next to ['nekst tə] neben I
nice [naɪs] nett, schön I
°**nick** [nɪk] *(infml)* klauen
nickname ['nɪkneɪm] Spitzname V

night [naɪt] Nacht I **at night** nachts, in der Nacht I
nine [naɪn] neun I
nineties ['naɪnti:z]: **the 90s** die Neunzigerjahre II
no [nəʊ]:
1. nein I
2. kein, keine I
there is no doing sth. man kann etwas nicht tun VI 1 (21) **there's no such thing as ...** es gibt kein/e ... III
No./no. *pl* **Nos./nos.** ['nʌmbə] Nr. III
nobody ['nəʊbədi] niemand II
nod (to sb.) [nɒd] (jm. zu)nicken IV
noise [nɔɪz] Geräusch; Lärm I
noisy ['nɔɪzi] laut, voller Lärm I
non- [nɒn] Nicht- III
none [nʌn] keine(r, s) II
°**non-essential** [nɒn ɪ'senʃl] nicht lebensnotwendig, nicht unbedingt wichtig
normal ['nɔ:ml] normal I
north [nɔ:θ] Norden; nach Norden II
north-east Nordosten; nach Nordosten II **north-west** Nordwesten; nach Nordwesten II
northbound ['nɔ:θbaʊnd] in Richtung Norden III
northern ['nɔ:ðən] nördlich, Nord- IV
nose [nəʊz] Nase IV **look down your nose at sb.** herabblicken auf jn. IV
nosey ['nəʊzi] (auch: **nosy**) neugierig IV
not [nɒt] nicht I **I'm not a boy.** Ich bin kein Junge. I **I'm not ten.** Ich bin nicht zehn. I **She's ..., isn't she?** Sie ist ..., nicht wahr? V
°**notably** ['nəʊtəbli] insbesondere, hauptsächlich
note [nəʊt]:
1. Notiz II
make notes (sich) Notizen machen *(zur Vorbereitung)* VI 1 (21) **take notes** (sich) Notizen machen *(beim Lesen oder Zuhören)* II
°2. notieren; beachten
°**note down** aufschreiben, notieren
nothing ['nʌθɪŋ] nichts I
notice ['nəʊtɪs]:
1. (be)merken IV
2. Notiz, Aushang, Anzeige III
noticeboard ['nəʊtɪs bɔ:d] Schwarzes Brett *(Blog, Klassenraum)* IV
novel ['nɒvl] Roman V
November [nəʊ'vembə] November I
now [naʊ] nun, jetzt I **every now and again** ab und zu, von Zeit zu Zeit VI 1 (19) **from now on** von nun an, ab jetzt VI 1 (20) **right now** gerade jetzt, genau jetzt III
°**nowadays** ['naʊədeɪz] heutzutage
nowhere ['nəʊweə] nirgendwo(hin) III
in the middle of nowhere am Ende der Welt III
number ['nʌmbə] Zahl, Ziffer, Nummer I

nurse [nɜ:s] (Kranken-)Pfleger/in VI 2 (44)
nut [nʌt] Nuss I

O

oatmeal ['əʊtmi:l] Hafermehl, Haferbrei IV
object ['ɒbdʒɪkt] Objekt, Gegenstand VI 3 (56)
observer [əb'zɜ:və] Beobachter/in V
ocean ['əʊʃn] Ozean IV
o'clock [ə'klɒk]: **at 1 o'clock** um 1 Uhr / um 13 Uhr I
October [ɒk'təʊbə] Oktober I
of [ɒv], [əv] von I **(just) the two of us** (nur) wir beide V **the last day of the holidays** der letzte Tag der Ferien / der letzte Ferientag I
of course [əv 'kɔ:s] natürlich, selbstverständlich II
off [ɒf]:
1. weg von; hinunter von III
Off you go! Dann mal los! / Ab mit dir! V **get off (a bus)** aussteigen (aus einem Bus) III **get off (your bike)** absteigen (vom Fahrrad) III
go off (to a place) (los)gehen, (los) fahren (nach/zu) IV
2. **get/have a day off** einen Tag frei bekommen/haben IV
3. **go off** klingeln *(Wecker)*; losgehen *(Alarmanlage, Waffe)* IV
offer ['ɒfə]:
1. (an)bieten III
2. Angebot III
office ['ɒfɪs] Büro III
official [ə'fɪʃl] offiziell, amtlich IV
official language [əfɪʃl 'læŋgwɪdʒ] Amtssprache VI 1 (10)
°**off-road** ['ɒf rəʊd] Gelände-; abseits der Straße
often ['ɒfn], ['ɒftən] oft I
OK [əʊ'keɪ] okay, gut, in Ordnung I
old [əʊld] alt I **in the old days** früher II
old-fashioned [əʊld 'fæʃənd] altmodisch IV
olive ['ɒlɪv] Olive VI 1 (20)
Olympic [ə'lɪmpɪk] olympisch III **the Olympics** *(pl)* die olympischen Spiele III
omelette ['ɒmlət] Omelett I
on [ɒn] auf I **on 1st March** am 1. März I **on Loch Ness** am Loch Ness III **on Monday** am Montag I **on the beach** am Strand I **on the bus** im Bus I **on the job** am Arbeitsplatz IV **on the phone** am Telefon I **on the way to ...** auf dem Weg zu/nach ... I **be on** laufen, gezeigt werden *(Kino, Theater)* V **drive/run/go on** weiterfahren/-laufen/-gehen IV **Go on.** Ach, komm! / Na los, mach schon! II
once [wʌns] einmal, einst III

one [wʌn]:
1. eins I
2. man VI 3 (66)
3. the only one der/die Einzige IV
one-way ticket [wʌn 'weɪ tɪkɪt] einfache Fahrkarte VI 3 (62)
online [ɒn'laɪn] online, Online- II
only ['əʊnli]:
1. erst II
2. nur, bloß I
3. the only student der/die einzige Schüler/in I
onto the road ['ɒntu], ['ɒntə] auf die Straße III
open ['əʊpən]:
1. öffnen; aufschlagen *(Buch)* I
2. offen, geöffnet II
opening hours *(pl)* ['əʊpənɪŋ aʊəz] Öffnungszeiten V
°**open-minded** [əʊpən 'maɪndɪd] aufgeschlossen, offen
opinion [ə'pɪnjən] Meinung III **in my opinion** meiner Meinung nach III
opposite ['ɒpəzɪt] Gegenteil II
optimist ['ɒptɪmɪst] Optimist/in VI 3 (62)
optimistic [ɒptɪ'mɪstɪk] optimistisch IV
°**option** ['ɒpʃn] Wahl(möglichkeit), Option
or [ɔː] oder; sonst I
orange ['ɒrɪndʒ]:
1. orange(farben) I
2. Orange, Apfelsine I
order ['ɔːdə]:
1. bestellen III
2. Bestellung IV
3. Reihenfolge V
4. in order to um ... zu V
organic [ɔː'gænɪk] biologisch, Bio- V
organization [ɔːgənaɪ'zeɪʃn] Organisation V
organizational [ɔːgənaɪ'zeɪʃənl] organisatorisch V
organize ['ɔːgənaɪz] organisieren IV
organizer ['ɔːgənaɪzə] Organisator/in VI 3 (62)
original [ə'rɪdʒənl] original, ursprünglich, Original(-) V
orphan ['ɔːfn] Waise V
°**ostrich** ['ɒstrɪtʃ] Strauß *(Vogel)*
other ['ʌðə] andere(r, s) I **in other words** mit anderen Worten V **the other day** neulich III
our ['aʊə] unser/e I
ours [ɑːz], ['aʊəz] unsere/r, unseres V
ourselves [aʊə'selvz] wir/uns selbst III
out [aʊt]: **out of ...** aus ... (heraus/hinaus) I **go out** rausgehen, weggehen; ausgehen II **school is out** die Schule ist aus/vorbei I
outback ['aʊtbæk]: **the outback** *das Hinterland Australiens* V
outdoor ['aʊtdɔː]: **outdoor (sport)** (Sport) für draußen / im Freien II **outdoor shop** Geschäft für Outdoor-Bekleidung und -Ausrüstung III
outdoors [aʊt'dɔːz] im Freien, draußen I **the outdoors** die freie Natur V
outlaw ['aʊtlɔː] Bandit/in, Geächtete/r IV
out-of-town (shopping centre) [aʊt əv 'taʊn] (Einkaufszentrum) außerhalb der Stadt III
°**outright** ['aʊtraɪt] völlige(r, s), totale(r, s)
outside [aʊt'saɪd]:
1. außerhalb (von) III
2. draußen; nach draußen I
3. the outside das Äußere, die Außenseite IV
over ['əʊvə] über III **over 300** über / mehr als 300 III **over there** da drüben, dort drüben I **over time** im Laufe der Zeit VI 2 (44) **all over the country** überall im Land, im ganzen Land II **be over** vorbei sein, zu Ende sein I **walk over (to)** hinübergehen (zu) IV
overspend (on sth.) [əʊvə'spend], **overspent, overspent** zu viel Geld ausgeben (für etwas) V
overspent [əʊvə'spent] *siehe* **overspend**
overtake [əʊvə'teɪk], **overtook, overtaken** überholen V
overtaken [əʊvə'teɪkən] *siehe* **overtake**
overtook [əʊvə'tʊk] *siehe* **overtake**
owl [aʊl] Eule II
own [əʊn]:
1. own sth. etwas besitzen IV
2. your own lanterns deine/eure eigenen Laternen, eigene Laternen II
3. make sth. your own etwas in deinen Besitz bringen II
of one's own eigene(r, s) V **on one's own** alleine, selbstständig *(ohne Unterstützung)* V
owner ['əʊnə] Besitzer/in II
ox, *pl* **oxen** [ɒks], ['ɒksn] Ochse IV
°**oxygen** ['ɒksɪdʒən] Sauerstoff

P

p [piː]: **50p** fünfzig Pence I
pack [pæk] packen, einpacken II
packet (of) ['pækɪt] Packung, Päckchen, Tüte II
page (= p.) [peɪdʒ] (Buch-, Heft-)Seite I **What page is it?** Auf welcher Seite sind wir? / Auf welcher Seite steht das? I
paid [peɪd] *siehe* **pay**
pain [peɪn] Schmerz; Plage III **Don't be a pain.** Nerv nicht. / Geh mir/uns nicht auf die Nerven. V **What a pain!** So ein Mist! / Es nervt. III
paint [peɪnt] lackieren, (be)malen, *(mit Farbe)* streichen V
painter ['peɪntə] Maler/in V
painting ['peɪntɪŋ] Gemälde, *(gemaltes)* Bild; Malerei V **body painting** Körperbemalung V **dot painting** Punktmalerei; Punktgemälde V
pair [peə] Paar V
palace ['pæləs] Palast III
pale [peɪl] blass, bleich VI 1 (20)
pan [pæn] Pfanne IV
°**pancake** ['pænkeɪk] Pfannkuchen
panic ['pænɪk] in Panik geraten V **Don't panic.** Keine Panik. / Immer mit der Ruhe. V
pant [pænt] keuchen, hecheln VI 3 (65)
pants *(pl)* [pænts] *(AE) (eine)* Hose IV
paper ['peɪpə]:
1. Papier I
2. Zeitung II
do a paper round Zeitungen austragen II
parade [pə'reɪd] Parade, Umzug IV
paradise ['pærədaɪs] Paradies IV
paragraph ['pærəgrɑːf] Absatz *(im Text)* III
paramedic [pærə'medɪk] Rettungssanitäter/in VI 2 (44)
°**paranoid** ['pærənɔɪd] paranoid, wahnsinnig
paraphrase ['pærəfreɪz] umschreiben, mit anderen Worten sagen V
parents *(pl)* ['peərənts] Eltern I
park [pɑːk] Park I
park (a car) [pɑːk] parken III
parliament ['pɑːləmənt] Parlament III
part [pɑːt] Teil II **take part (in)** teilnehmen (an), mitmachen (bei) III
°**particular** [pə'tɪkjələ] bestimmte(r, s), spezielle(r, s)
partly ['pɑːtli] teilweise III
partner ['pɑːtnə] Partner/in I
part-time job [pɑːt 'taɪm] Teilzeitjob, Halbtagsjob IV
party ['pɑːti] Party I **have a party** eine Party feiern I
party-goer ['pɑːti gəʊə] Partygast V
pass [pɑːs]:
1. pass sb./sth. an jn./etwas vorbeigehen, vorbeifahren IV
2. pass sth. on (to sb.) etwas weitergeben (an jn.) VI 3 (57)
Pass the ball! Spiel ab! III
°**3.** vorübergehen, vorbeigehen *(Zeit, Moment, Gelegenheit)*
°**4. pass a law** ein Gesetz verabschieden
pass [pɑːs]: **visitor pass** Besucherausweis IV
°**passage** ['pæsɪdʒ] Passage *(z.B. Text, Musikstück)*
passenger ['pæsɪndʒə] Passagier/in, Fahrgast II
passenger seat ['pæsɪndʒə] Beifahrersitz VI 2 (43)
°**passive** ['pæsɪv] Passiv, passiv
passport ['pɑːspɔːt] (Reise-)Pass III

past [pɑːst]:
1. past the shop am Geschäft vorbei II
2. half past 6 halb 7 I
quarter past 6 viertel nach 6 I
past [pɑːst] Vergangenheit II
pasta ['pæstə] Pasta, Nudeln III
pasty ['pæsti] Pastete *(mit Fleisch- oder Gemüsefüllung)* II
°**pat** [pæt] tätscheln
path [pɑːθ] Weg, Pfad III
°**patience** ['peɪʃns] Geduld
patient ['peɪʃnt] geduldig III
°**patrol sth.** [pə'trəʊl] in/durch etwas patrouillieren
pattern ['pætn] *(wiederkehrendes)* Muster, Schema IV
pause [pɔːz]:
1. Pause VI 3 (66)
2. kurz innehalten, Pause machen VI 3 (66)
pause for breath kurz Pause machen, um Luft zu holen VI 3 (66)
pavement ['peɪvmənt] Gehweg, Bürgersteig IV
pay [peɪ]:
1. Bezahlung, Lohn IV
2. pay (for sth.), paid, paid (etwas be)zahlen III
it doesn't pay very well es wird nicht besonders gut bezahlt IV
PC (= police constable) [piː 'siː], [pəliːs 'kɒnstəbl] Polizeimeister/in III
PC (= personal computer) [piː 'siː], [pɜːsənl kəm'pjuːtə] PC IV
PE (physical education) [piː 'iː], [fɪzɪkl edʒu'keɪʃn] (Schul-)Sport I
°**peace** [piːs] Frieden
peaceful ['piːsfl] friedlich, friedfertig IV
peanut ['piːnʌt] Erdnuss II
peanut butter [piːnʌt 'bʌtə] Erdnussbutter II
peck sb. [pek] jm. ein Küsschen geben IV
pedestrian [pə'destriən] Fußgänger/in, Fußgänger- III
peer [pɪə] Gleichaltrige/r, Ebenbürtige/r, jemand aus derselben sozialen Gruppe V
peer pressure [pɪə 'preʃə] Gruppendruck, Gruppenzwang V
pelican ['pelɪkən] Pelikan IV
pen [pen] Kugelschreiber, Stift; Füller I
pence [pens] Pence *(Plural von Penny)* III
pencil ['pensl] Bleistift I
pencil case ['pensl keɪs] Federmäppchen I
pencil sharpener ['pensl ʃɑːpnə] Bleistiftanspitzer I
penfriend ['penfrend] Brieffreund/in II
penny ['peni] Penny II
people ['piːpl]:
1. Leute, Menschen I
2. Volk VI 1 (11)

per cent, percent [pə 'sent] Prozent IV
per hour/person [pɜː], [pə] pro Stunde/Person III
°**perception** [pə'sepʃn] Wahrnehmung
perfect ['pɜːfɪkt] perfekt II
perform [pə'fɔːm] aufführen; durchführen; auftreten *(Künstler/in)* VI 1 (12)
performance [pə'fɔːməns] Vorstellung, Aufführung VI 1 (12)
performer [pə'fɔːmə] Künstler/in, Darsteller/in VI 1 (12)
performing arts *(pl)* [pəfɔːmɪŋ 'ɑːts] darstellende Kunst VI 1 (12)
perhaps [pə'hæps] vielleicht III
period ['pɪəriəd] (Unterrichts-)Stunde IV
person ['pɜːsn] Person I
personal ['pɜːsənl] persönlich IV
personal computer [pɜːsənl kəm'pjuːtə] PC IV
personal statement [pɜːsənl 'steɪtmənt] persönliche Beschreibung, Selbstbeschreibung V
personality [pɜːsə'næləti] Persönlichkeit; Charakter II
perspective [pə'spektɪv] Perspektive IV
put sth. in perspective etwas in Beziehung setzen, relativieren IV
persuade [pə'sweɪd] überreden, überzeugen V
pessimism ['pesɪmɪzəm] Pessimismus VI 3 (61)
pessimist ['pesɪmɪst] Pessimist/in VI 3 (61)
pessimistic [pesɪ'mɪstɪk] pessimistisch VI 3 (61)
pet [pet] (Haus-)Tier I
petition [pə'tɪʃn] Petition, Unterschriftensammlung VI 2 (36)
petrol ['petrəl] Benzin IV
phone [fəʊn]:
1. Telefon I
answer the phone ans Telefon gehen V **on the phone** am Telefon I
2. anrufen I
phone call ['fəʊn kɔːl] (Telefon-)Anruf II
phone number ['fəʊn nʌmbə] Telefonnummer I
photo ['fəʊtəʊ] Foto I **take photos** Fotos machen II
photographer [fə'tɒgrəfə] Fotograf/in IV
phrase [freɪz] Ausdruck, (Rede-)Wendung I
piano [pi'ænəʊ] Klavier I
pick [pɪk] (aus)wählen, aussuchen II **pick on sb.** auf jm. herumhacken, jn. drangsalieren V **pick sb. up** jn. abholen VI 1 (22) **pick sth. up** etwas aufheben *(vom Boden)*, etwas hochheben II **pick sth. up** etwas kaufen, etwas *(aus einem Geschäft)* mitbringen V °**pick out** heraussuchen, auswählen
picnic ['pɪknɪk] Picknick I

picture ['pɪktʃə]:
1. Bild I
2. picture sth. etwas abbilden; sich etwas vorstellen IV
pie [paɪ] (gedeckter) Obstkuchen; Pastete IV
pie chart ['paɪ tʃɑːt] Tortendiagramm, Kreisdiagramm VI 2 (39)
piece [piːs] Stück IV **a piece of advice** ein Rat(schlag) IV
piercing ['pɪəsɪŋ] Piercing II
°**piezoelectric** [piːzəʊɪ'lektrɪk] piezoelektrisch *(aus Verformung Strom gewinnend)*
pig [pɪg] Schwein I
pilgrim ['pɪlgrɪm] Pilger/in II
pillow ['pɪləʊ] Kopfkissen VI 3 (57)
pineapple ['paɪnæpl] Ananas VI 1 (20)
pink [pɪŋk] rosa I
pioneer [paɪə'nɪə] Pionier/in VI 3 (62)
pirate ['paɪrət] Pirat/in II
°**piss sb. off** [pɪs 'ɒf] *(taboo)* jn. verärgern
pitch [pɪtʃ]:
1. werfen, schlagen *(Ball)* IV
°**2.** Platz, (Spiel-)Feld
pity ['pɪti]: **That's a pity.** Das ist schade. I
pizza ['piːtsə] Pizza I
place [pleɪs] Ort, Platz I **take place** stattfinden III
°**placemat** ['pleɪsmæt] Platzdeckchen
plan [plæn]:
1. Plan I
2. planen III
plane [pleɪn] Flugzeug III
planet ['plænɪt] Planet VI 2 (38)
plant [plɑːnt]:
1. Pflanze V
2. pflanzen V
plastic ['plæstɪk] Plastik, Kunststoff II
plastic bag ['plæstɪk bæg] Plastiktüte II
plate [pleɪt] Teller IV
platform ['plætfɔːm] Bahnsteig II **at platform 4** auf Gleis 4 II
°**platooning** [plə'tuːnɪŋ] Platooning *(Fahren in der Kolonne mit geringem Abstand)*
play [pleɪ] spielen I **play it cool** *(infml)* sich cool geben IV **play the guitar/the drums** Gitarre/Schlagzeug spielen I
player ['pleɪə] Spieler/in III
playground ['pleɪgraʊnd] Spielplatz IV
please [pliːz] bitte I
pleased [pliːzd] froh, erfreut, zufrieden V **Pleased to meet you.** Freut mich Sie kennenzulernen. V
plot [plɒt] Handlung(sverlauf) *(z.B. Film/Geschichte)* V
plough [plaʊ] pflügen IV
plow [plaʊ] *(AE)* pflügen IV
plus [plʌs] plus, (und) außerdem IV
pm [piː'em]: **5 pm/5 p.m.** 5 Uhr nachmittags/abends, 17 Uhr I

°**poach** [pəʊtʃ] wildern, unerlaubt jagen
°**poacher** ['pəʊtʃə] Wilderer/Wilderin, Wilddieb/in
pocket ['pɒkɪt] Tasche *(an Kleidungsstücken)* II
pocket money ['pɒkɪt mʌni] Taschengeld II
°**pod** [pɒd] Behälter, Kapsel
poem ['pəʊɪm] Gedicht I
point [pɔɪnt]:
1. Punkt III
point of view Standpunkt III
2. Argument V
make a point ein Argument vortragen V **make your point** sagen, wie du darüber denkst V
3. **2.5 million** 2,5 Millionen IV
point [pɔɪnt]: **point (at/to)** zeigen, deuten (auf) II **point a knife/gun at sb.** ein Messer/eine Waffe auf jn. richten V **point sth. out** auf etwas hinweisen, aufmerksam machen VI 2 (36). °**she pointed herself south-west** sie richtete ihren Kompass auf Südwest aus
police *(pl)* [pə'liːs] Polizei II
police officer [pə'liːs ɒfɪsə] Polizeibeamter/-beamtin III
police station [pə'liːs steɪʃn] Polizeiwache I
policy ['pɒləsi] Politik, Richtlinie(n), Bestimmung(en) III
polish ['pɒlɪʃ] Lack; Politur V
polite [pə'laɪt] höflich IV
political [pə'lɪtɪkl] politisch VI (9)
politician [pɒlə'tɪʃn] Politiker/in VI 1 (25)
politics ['pɒlətɪks] Politik VI (9)
°**pollution** [pə'luːʃn] (Umwelt-)Verschmutzung
pond [pɒnd] Teich I
pony ['pəʊni] Pony I
ponytail ['pəʊniteɪl] Pferdeschwanz *(Frisur)* V
pool [puːl] *(= swimming pool)* Schwimmbad IV
poor [pɔː], [pʊə]:
1. arm II
poor Ellie *(die)* arme Ellie II
2. schlecht, schwach, minderwertig VI 3 (69)
pop (music) ['pɒp mjuːzɪk] Pop(musik) III
popular ['pɒpjələ] beliebt, populär II
populate ['pɒpjuleɪt] bevölkern, besiedeln IV
population [pɒpju'leɪʃn] Bevölkerung, Einwohner(zahl) IV
porch [pɔːtʃ] *(AE)* Veranda IV
port [pɔːt] Hafen(stadt) III
portrait ['pɔːtreɪt] Porträt V
self-portrait Selbstporträt V
position [pə'zɪʃn] Position, (Arbeits-)Stelle, Platz IV
positive ['pɒzətɪv] positiv I
possible ['pɒsəbl] möglich IV

post [pəʊst]:
1. Post II
2. posten *(im Internet veröffentlichen)* IV
posted by gepostet von *(= in ein Blog gestellt)* IV
3. **Keep me posted!** Halt mich auf dem Laufenden! III
post office ['pəʊst ɒfɪs] Post(amt) II
°**postal** ['pəʊstl] Post-
postcard ['pəʊstkɑːd] Postkarte II
postman/-woman ['pəʊstmən, -wʊmən] Briefträger/in III
pot [pɒt] Topf III
potato, *pl* **potatoes** [pə'teɪtəʊ] Kartoffel II
potato chips *(pl)* [pə'teɪtəʊ tʃɪps] *(AE)* (Kartoffel-)Chips IV
pottery ['pɒtəri] Töpferware(n), Töpferei, Töpfer- IV
pound [paʊnd] hämmern, schlagen, pochen IV
pound (£) [paʊnd] Pfund *(britische Währung)* I
°**poverty** ['pɒvəti] Armut
power ['paʊə]:
1. Macht, Kraft, Stärke VI 2 (36)
2. Energie, Strom VI 3 (56)
powerful ['paʊəfl] kräftig, stark, mächtig IV
practice ['præktɪs]:
1. Übung; Training IV
2. Probe *(Band, Chor)* IV
practice ['præktɪs] *(AE)* üben IV
practise ['præktɪs] üben I
praise [preɪz]:
1. Lob VI 2 (40)
2. loben, rühmen VI 2 (40)
°**precise** [prɪ'saɪs] genau, präzise
predict [prɪ'dɪkt] voraussagen, vorhersagen VI 3 (62)
prediction [prɪ'dɪkʃn] Vorhersage, Voraussage VI 3 (62)
prefer sth. to sth. [prɪ'fɜː] etwas einer Sache vorziehen, etwas lieber tun/haben als etwas III **I'd prefer …** ich würde … vorziehen I
prejudice ['predʒudɪs] Vorurteil, Voreingenommenheit V
prepare (for) [prɪ'peə] vorbereiten; sich vorbereiten (auf) II
present ['preznt]:
1. Gegenwart II
2. Geschenk I
present sth. (to sb.) [prɪ'zent] (jm.) etwas präsentieren, (jm.) etwas vorstellen III
presentation [prezn'teɪʃn] Referat, Präsentation III **give a presentation** ein Referat halten III
presenter [prɪ'zentə] Referent/in V
°**presidency** ['prezɪdənsi] Präsidentschaft
president ['prezɪdənt] Präsident/in IV
press [pres] drücken V

pressure ['preʃə] Druck V **put pressure on** Druck ausüben auf VI 3 (56)
pretend (to be sth.) [prɪ'tend] so tun, als ob (man etwas wäre) V
pretty ['prɪti] hübsch III
°**previous** ['priːviəs] vorherige/r/s, vorige/r/s,
price [praɪs] (Kauf-)Preis I
pride (in) [praɪd] Stolz (auf) III
prime minister [praɪm 'mɪnɪstə] Premierminister/in III
prince [prɪns] Prinz III
princess [prɪn'ses] Prinzessin III
principal ['prɪnsəpl] Rektor/in, Schulleiter/in I
°**printer** ['prɪntə] Drucker
prison ['prɪzn] Gefängnis IV **put sb. in prison** jn. ins Gefängnis sperren V
private ['praɪvət] privat; persönlich III
prize [praɪz] Preis, Gewinn II
probable ['prɒbəbl] wahrscheinlich VI 3 (63)
probably ['prɒbəbli] wahrscheinlich III
problem ['prɒbləm] Problem I
process ['prəʊses] Verfahren, Ablauf, Prozess VI 1 (14)
product ['prɒdʌkt] Produkt III
professional [prə'feʃənl] professionell, Profi-; Profi IV
profile ['prəʊfaɪl] Profil; Beschreibung, Portrait V
profit ['prɒfɪt] Gewinn *(Profit)* III
program ['prəʊgræm] *(AE)* Programm V
programme ['prəʊgræm] (Fernseh-)Sendung I
progress ['prəʊgres]:
1. Fortschritt(e) VI 1 (14)
make progress Fortschritte erzielen/machen, vorankommen VI 1 (14)
2. **be in progress** im Gange sein VI 2 (41)
project ['prɒdʒekt] Projekt II
prom [prɒm] *(AE)* Schulball IV
promise ['prɒmɪs]:
1. Versprechen IV
2. versprechen IV
°**promote** [prə'məʊt] fördern, unterstützen
°**properly** ['prɒpəli] richtig, ordentlich, korrekt
pros *(pl)* [prəʊz]: **the pros and cons** das Pro und Kontra; das Für und Wider V
protect (from) [prə'tekt] (be)schützen (vor) IV
protest [prə'test] protestieren IV
protest ['prəʊtest] Protest(demonstration) VI 1 (13)
Protestant ['prɒtɪstənt] Protestant/in; protestantisch, evangelisch II
protester [prə'testə] Demonstrant/in VI 1 (13)
proud (of) [praʊd] stolz (auf) I

prove [pru:v] beweisen; nachweisen VI 2 (48) **prove sb. wrong** beweisen, dass jd. Unrecht hat VI 2 (48)
°**provide** [prə'vaɪd] (an)bieten, zur Verfügung stellen
°**provocative** [prə'vɒkətɪv] provozierend
°**provoke** [prə'vəʊk] provozieren
PS (= postscript) [pi: 'es] PS, Postskript *(Nachschrift unter Briefen)* IV
psychology [saɪ'kɒlədʒi] Psychologie VI 3 (57)
pub [pʌb] Kneipe III
public ['pʌblɪk] öffentlich III
public transport [pʌblɪk 'trænspɔ:t] öffentlicher Personenverkehr III
publish ['pʌblɪʃ] veröffentlichen, herausbringen VI 2 (39)
pull [pʊl] ziehen II **pull back** sich zurückziehen, zurückweichen V **pull back your hair** sich die Haare zusammenbinden V **pull in** an den Straßenrand fahren, anhalten IV **pull over** anhalten, an den Straßenrand fahren V **pull up** anhalten, an den Straßenrand fahren VI 2 (43)
pullover ['pʊləʊvə] Pullover I
pumps *(pl)* [pʌmps] Pumps *(elegante Damenschuhe)* V
punctual ['pʌŋktʃuəl] pünktlich V
punctuation [pʌŋktʃu'eɪʃn] Zeichensetzung VI 1 (17)
puppet ['pʌpɪt] Puppe *(Handpuppe, Marionette)* II
purple ['pɜ:pl] violett, lila I
°**purpose** ['pɜ:pə] Absicht, Zweck, Ziel
push [pʊʃ]:
1. schieben I
2. stoßen, schubsen IV
push sb. around jn. herumkommandieren IV
pushchair ['pʊʃtʃeə] (Kinder-)Sportwagen, Buggy II
put [pʊt], **put, put** *(etwas wohin)* tun, legen, stellen, stecken I **put down** hinlegen IV **put sth. off** etwas verschieben, hinauszögern VI 3 (65) **put sth. on** etwas anziehen *(Kleidung)*; etwas aufsetzen *(Hut)* II **put sth. on** etwas einschalten VI 2 (44) **put sth. up** etwas aufhängen *(Bild etc.)* VI 2 (48) **put sth. up (on social media)** etwas (in soziale Medien) (ein)stellen V **put up your hand** sich melden III °**put sth.** *(+ Adverb)* etwas *(auf eine bestimmte Art)* ausdrücken, formulieren
puzzled ['pʌzld] verwirrt, verwundert III
pyjamas *(pl)* [pə'dʒɑ:məz] *(ein)* Schlafanzug II

Q

qualification [kwɒlɪfɪ'keɪʃn] (Schul-)Abschluss, Qualifikation V
qualified ['kwɒlɪfaɪd] qualifiziert; ausgebildet, mit Abschluss V
qualify ['kwɒlɪfaɪ] (sich) qualifizieren V
quality ['kwɒləti] Qualität, Qualitäts-; Eigenschaft VI 2 (47) **personal qualities** persönliche Eigenschaften VI 2 (47)
°**quality (of life)** ['kwɒləti] (Lebens-)Qualität
quarter ['kwɔ:tə] Viertel I **quarter past 6** viertel nach 6 I **quarter to 7** viertel vor 7 I
queen [kwi:n] Königin III
question ['kwestʃən]:
1. Frage I
ask questions Fragen stellen I
°2. **question sb.** jn. befragen, verhören
question mark ['kwestʃən mɑ:k] Fragezeichen VI 1 (17)
queue [kju:] (Warte-)Schlange II
quick [kwɪk] schnell I
quiet ['kwaɪət] ruhig, still, leise I
quite [kwaɪt] ziemlich II
quiz [kwɪz] Quiz I
quote [kwəʊt]:
1. Zitat VI 1 (23)
2. zitieren VI 1 (23)

R

rabbit ['ræbɪt] Kaninchen I
raccoon [rə'ku:n] Waschbär IV
race [reɪs]:
1. (Wett-)Rennen V
2. rasen, schnell fahren V
race [reɪs] Rasse VI 1 (12)
racer ['reɪsə] Rennfahrer/in V
racing ['reɪsɪŋ] Rennsport V
racism ['reɪsɪzəm] Rassismus IV
racist ['reɪsɪst] Rassist/in; rassistisch V
°**radar** ['reɪdɑ:] Radar
°**radiation** [reɪdi'eɪʃn] Strahlung
radio ['reɪdiəʊ] Radio IV
rain [reɪn]:
1. Regen II
2. regnen II
rainbow ['reɪnbəʊ] Regenbogen VI 1 (10)
rainforest ['reɪnfɒrɪst] Regenwald V
rainy ['reɪni] regnerisch II
raise [reɪz]:
1. (er)heben VI 2 (36)
raise one's eyes from sth. von etwas aufschauen VI 2 (36) **raise one's voice** die Stimme erheben VI 2 (36)
2. **raise (money)** (Geld für gute Zwecke) sammeln IV
ran [ræn] *siehe* **run**
ranch [rɑ:ntʃ] Ranch, Viehfarm IV
rang [ræŋ] *siehe* **ring**
ranger ['reɪndʒə] *Aufseher/in in einem Nationalpark* II
rap [ræp] rappen I
rat [ræt] Ratte I
rate [reɪt] Quote, Rate, Tempo VI 3 (56)
°**rates** *(pl)* [reɪts] Gebühren
°**rather than** ['rɑ:ðə] anstelle von, (an) statt
reach (sb./a place) [ri:tʃ] (jn./einen Ort) erreichen V
react (to) [ri'ækt] reagieren (auf) III
reaction (to) [ri'ækʃn] Reaktion (auf) VI 1 (27)
read [red] *siehe* **read**
read [ri:d], **read, read** lesen I
reader ['ri:də] Leser/in III
ready ['redi] fertig, bereit I **get ready (for)** sich fertig machen (für), sich vorbereiten (auf) I
real [rɪəl] echt, wirklich I
realistic [ri:ə'lɪstɪk] realistisch V
reality [ri'æləti] Realität, Wirklichkeit II
reality show [ri'æləti ʃəʊ] Realityshow II
realize sth. ['ri:əlaɪz] etwas erkennen, sich einer Sache bewusst werden V
really ['ri:əli], ['rɪəli] wirklich I
reason ['ri:zn] Grund, Begründung III
for lots of reasons aus vielen Gründen III
°**reasonable** ['ri:znəbl] vernünftig, angemessen
°**reasonably (happy)** ['ri:znəbli] ziemlich/durchaus (glücklich)
receipt [rɪ'si:t] (Kauf-)Beleg, Quittung, Kassenzettel VI 3 (69)
receive [rɪ'si:v] erhalten, empfangen VI 2 (48)
recent ['ri:snt] aktuell, jüngst III
recently ['ri:sntli] in letzter Zeit; vor Kurzem III
receptionist [rɪ'sepʃənɪst] Empfangschef/in III
recharge [ri:'tʃɑ:dʒ] (wieder) aufladen VI 3 (69)
recipe ['resəpi] (Koch-)Rezept I
recommend sth. (to sb.) [rekə'mend] (jm.) etwas empfehlen VI 3 (62)
recommendation [rekəmen'deɪʃn] Empfehlung IV
°**record** [rɪ'kɔ:d] aufnehmen, aufzeichnen, dokumentieren
°**record** ['rekɔ:d] Rekord
recruitment [rɪ'kru:tmənt] Anwerbung, Einstellung *(von Personal)* VI 2 (48)
recycle [ri:'saɪkl] recyceln, wiederverwerten II
red [red] rot I
redial [ri:'daɪəl] die Wahlwiederholung betätigen V
redness ['rednəs] Rötung, Röte V
reduce (by) [rɪ'dju:s] reduzieren, verringern (um) V
reef [ri:f] Riff V
°**refer to** [rɪ'fɜ:] sich beziehen auf, Bezug nehmen auf
reference ['refrəns] Referenz, Empfehlung; jd., der eine Referenz erteilt V
°**referendum (on sth.)** [refə'rendəm] Volksentscheid (über etwas)
refugee [refju'dʒi:] Flüchtling VI 2 (40)

refund [rɪ'fʌnd] *(Kosten)* (rück)erstatten VI 3 (69)
refund ['riːfʌnd] Rückzahlung, (Kosten-)Erstattung VI 3 (69)
reggae ['regeɪ] Reggae(musik) II
region ['riːdʒən] Region, Gegend VI 3 (57)
°**register to vote** [redʒɪstə tə 'vəʊt] sich in die Wählerlisten eintragen lassen
regular ['regjələ] regelmäßig, normal V
relationship [rɪ'leɪʃnʃɪp] Beziehung, Verhältnis IV
relative ['relətɪv]:
1. Verwandte/r IV
2. relativ VI 2 (36)
relax [rɪ'læks] sich entspannen II
relaxing [rɪ'læksɪŋ] entspannend, beruhigend II
relevant ['reləvənt] relevant, wichtig VI 2 (48)
reliable [rɪ'laɪəbl] zuverlässig, verlässlich V
religion [rɪ'lɪdʒən] Religion VI 1 (10)
remarkable [rɪ'mɑːkəbl] bemerkenswert VI 2 (40)
remember [rɪ'membə]:
1. sich erinnern (an) I
2. daran denken, nicht vergessen I
remind sb. of sth. [rɪ'maɪnd] jn. an etwas erinnern IV
remote [rɪ'məʊt] entlegen, abgelegen V
°**remote control** [rɪməʊt kən'trəʊl] Fernbedienung
rent [rent] mieten, leihen IV
repair [rɪ'peə]:
1. reparieren IV
°2. Reparatur
repeat [rɪ'piːt] wiederholen V
°**repetition** [repə'tɪʃn] Wiederholung
replace (with) [rɪ'pleɪs] ersetzen (durch), austauschen (gegen) VI 2 (36)
reply [rɪ'plaɪ]:
1. Antwort VI 1 (15)
2. antworten VI 1 (15)
report [rɪ'pɔːt]:
1. Bericht IV
2. **report (on)** berichten (über) IV
report sth./sb. (to) etwas/jn. melden, anzeigen (bei) *(z.B. bei der Polizei)* VI 2 (40)
reporter [rɪ'pɔːtə] Reporter/in III
request [rɪ'kwest] Wunsch, Bitte; Anfrage V
require [rɪ'kwaɪə] erfordern, benötigen VI 1 (27)
requirement [rɪ'kwaɪəmənt] Voraussetzung, Anforderung V
rescue ['reskjuː]:
1. Rettung(sdienst) IV
2. retten VI 2 (49)
research [rɪ'sɜːtʃ]:
1. erforschen, untersuchen, recherchieren II
°2. Forschung(en), Recherche(n)
°**do research** recherchieren

reservation [rezə'veɪʃn]:
1. Reservierung, Buchung III
2. Reservat *(Gebiet)* IV
reserve [rɪ'zɜːv] Schutzgebiet V
resident ['rezɪdənt] Anwohner/in, Bewohner/in III
resort [rɪ'zɔːt] Urlaubsort V
respect [rɪ'spekt]:
1. Respekt III
2. respektieren, achten III
respectable [rɪ'spektəbl] anständig, angesehen, ehrbar V
respectful (to) [rɪ'spektfl] respektvoll (gegenüber) V
respond [rɪ'spɒnd] reagieren, antworten VI 1 (23)
response (to) [rɪ'spɒns] Reaktion, Antwort (auf) VI 1 (23)
responsibility [rɪspɒnsə'bɪləti]:
1. Aufgabe, Zuständigkeit V
2. Verantwortung VI 1 (12)
responsible (for) [rɪ'spɒnsəbl] verantwortlich (für); verantwortungsbewusst IV
rest [rest]:
1. sich ausruhen III
2. Pause, Rast I
restaurant ['restrɒnt] Restaurant I
restroom ['restruːm] *(AE)* Toilette *(in öffentlichen Gebäuden)* IV
result [rɪ'zʌlt] Ergebnis, Resultat III
as a result folglich, demzufolge VI 1 (16)
°**retake** ['riːteɪk] Nachdrehen einer Szene *(Film)*
°**retreat** [rɪ'triːt] sich zurückziehen
return [rɪ'tɜːn]:
1. zurückkehren, zurückkommen V
2. **return (ticket)** Rückfahrkarte VI 3 (62)
°**reuse** [riː'juːz] wiederverwenden
review [rɪ'vjuː] Besprechung, Rezension, Kritik IV
reviewer [rɪ'vjuːə] Rezensent/in, Kritiker/in IV
°**revision** [rɪ'vɪʒn] Wiederholung *(von Lernstoff)*
revolution [revə'luːʃn] Revolution VI 2 (47)
°**rewrite** [riː'raɪt], **rewrote, rewritten** neu schreiben, umschreiben
°**rewritten** [riː'rɪtn] *siehe* **rewrite**
°**rewrote** [riː'rəʊt] *siehe* **rewrite**
°**rhetorical question** [rɪtɒrɪkl 'kwestʃən] rhetorische Frage
°**rhino,** *pl* **rhinos** ['raɪnəʊ] *(infml)* Nashorn
rhyme [raɪm]:
1. (sich) reimen II
2. Reim II
°**rhythm** ['rɪðəm] Rhythmus
rice [raɪs] Reis III
rich [rɪtʃ] reich V
rid [rɪd]: **get rid of sth.** etwas loswerden II

ridden ['rɪdn] *siehe* **ride**
ride [raɪd] Fahrt; Fahrgeschäft *(auf Volksfest, in Vergnügungspark)* III
ride [raɪd], **rode, ridden:**
1. reiten I
2. fahren I
ride a bike Rad fahren I
right [raɪt]:
1. richtig I
be right Recht haben I
2. rechts; nach rechts I
on the right rechts, auf der rechten Seite I
3. **right** *(adverb)* genau, direkt VI 2 (44)
right behind him direkt hinter ihm VI 2 (44) **right now** gerade jetzt, genau jetzt III
right [raɪt] Recht IV **civil rights** *(pl)* Bürgerrechte IV **have every right to do sth.** guten Grund / das Recht haben, etwas zu tun V
ring [rɪŋ] Ring VI 1 (20)
ring [rɪŋ], **rang, rung:**
1. läuten, klingeln I
2. anrufen III
ringtone ['rɪŋtəʊn] Klingelton III
rise (by) [raɪz], **rose, risen** (an)steigen (um) IV
risen ['rɪzən] *siehe* **rise**
risk [rɪsk]:
1. riskieren, wagen V
2. Risiko IV
take a risk ein Risiko eingehen IV
risky ['rɪski] riskant VI 3 (57)
river ['rɪvə] Fluss II
road [rəʊd] Straße *(Landstraße zwischen Orten; Straße in Orten)* I
road trip ['rəʊd trɪp] Autoreise V
robber ['rɒbə] Räuber/in VI 2 (40)
robot ['rəʊbɒt]:
1. Roboter VI 3 (68)
°2. Ampel *(südafrikanisches Englisch)*
rock [rɒk]:
1. Fels(en) I
2. **Sydney rocks.** *(infml)* Sydney bringt's. / In Sydney geht die Post ab. V
rock climbing ['rɒk klaɪmɪŋ] Felsklettern II
rocking chair ['rɒkɪŋ tʃeə] Schaukelstuhl IV
rode [rəʊd] *siehe* **ride**
role [rəʊl] Rolle IV
role model ['rəʊl mɒdl] Vorbild III
role-play ['rəʊl pleɪ] Rollenspiel IV
roll [rəʊl]:
1. rollen; (sich) verdrehen *(Augen)* III
roll over sich überschlagen VI 2 (44)
2. schaukeln, schwanken *(Schiff)* IV
Roman ['rəʊmən] Römer/in; römisch II
romance [rəʊ'mæns] Romanze; Romantik IV
romantic [rəʊ'mæntɪk] romantisch IV
roof [ruːf] Dach IV

room [ruːm], [rʊm] Raum, Zimmer I
°**root** [ruːt] Wurzel
rose [rəʊz] *siehe* **rise**
round [raʊnd]:
1. rund II
2. **do a paper round** Zeitungen austragen II

route [ruːt] Route, Weg III
routine [ruːˈtiːn] Routine IV
row [rəʊ] rudern VI 3 (65)
rowing boat [ˈrəʊɪŋ bəʊt] Ruderboot VI 3 (65)
rubber [ˈrʌbə]:
1. Radiergummi I
2. Gummi IV

rubbish [ˈrʌbɪʃ]:
1. (Haus-)Müll, Abfall II
2. *(infml)* Unsinn, Quatsch III **That's rubbish.** Das ist Unsinn. / Das ist Quatsch. III

rucksack [ˈrʌksæk] Rucksack II
rude [ruːd] unhöflich, frech III
rug [rʌg] Teppich, Läufer I
ruins *(pl)* [ˈruːɪnz] *(eine)* Ruine II
rule [ruːl] Regel II
ruler [ˈruːlə] Lineal I
run [rʌn], **ran, run** rennen, laufen II **run a business/a hotel** eine Firma/ein Hotel leiten, führen III **run a campaign** eine Kampagne durchführen VI 2 (48) **run out** knapp werden V **I often run out of money.** Mir geht oft das Geld aus. / Bei mir wird oft das Geld knapp. V
rung [rʌŋ] *siehe* **ring**
runner [ˈrʌnə] Läufer/in III
rural [ˈrʊərəl] ländlich IV
rush sb. to … [rʌʃ] jn. auf dem schnellsten Weg nach …/zu … bringen VI 2 (44)
rustler [ˈrʌslə] Viehdieb/in IV

S

sad [sæd] traurig I
sadness [ˈsædnəs] Traurigkeit V
safe [seɪf] sicher *(gefahrlos)* IV
safety [ˈseɪfti] Sicherheit II
said [sed] *siehe* **say**
sail [seɪl] segeln, *(mit dem Schiff)* fahren II
sailor [ˈseɪlə] Seemann; Matrose/Matrosin II
salad [ˈsæləd] Salat *(als Gericht oder Beilage)* I
salami [səˈlɑːmi] Salami II
salary [ˈsæləri] Lohn, Gehalt V
sale [seɪl] Verkauf; Schlussverkauf I
salesperson [ˈseɪlzpɜːsn] Verkäufer/in III
salt [sɔːlt] Salz III
same [seɪm]: **the same** derselbe/dieselbe/dasselbe; dieselben I
sample [ˈsɑːmpl] Muster, Probe(exemplar) V
sand [sænd] Sand I
sandals *(pl)* [ˈsændlz] Sandalen V
sang [sæŋ] *siehe* **sing**
sank [sæŋk] *siehe* **sink**
sat [sæt] *siehe* **sit**
Saturday [ˈsætədeɪ], [ˈsætədi] Samstag I
sauce [sɔːs] Sauce V
sausage [ˈsɒsɪdʒ] Wurst, Würstchen I
save [seɪv]:
1. retten III
2. sparen *(Geld, Zeit)* II
3. **God save the Queen.** Gott (be)schütze die Königin. III

saving [ˈseɪvɪŋ] Einsparung, Ersparnis VI 3 (57)
savvy [ˈsævi] *(infml)* versiert, gewieft, erfahren V
saw [sɔː] *siehe* **see**
saw [sɔː] Säge IV
say [seɪ], **said, said** sagen I **Say hi to everybody.** Grüß alle. I **say sorry** sich entschuldigen V
°**scale** [skeɪl] Skala **internet-scale security** Internet-Sicherheit
scan (a text for) [skæn] (einen Text) überfliegen (nach), absuchen (nach) IV
scanner [ˈskænə] Scanner, Lesegerät VI 3 (59)
scar [skɑː]:
1. Narbe VI 2 (43)
2. **scar sb.** bei jm. Narben hinterlassen VI 2 (43)
scarred von Narben bedeckt VI 2 (43)

scarecrow [ˈskeəkrəʊ] Vogelscheuche II
scared [skeəd]: **be scared (of)** Angst haben (vor) II
scarf, *pl* **scarves** [skɑːf], [skɑːvz] Schal II
scary [ˈskeəri] unheimlich, beängstigend, gruselig I
scene [siːn] Szene I
scenery [ˈsiːnəri] Landschaft VI 1 (21)
schedule sth. for (a time) [ˈʃedjuːl] etwas (für eine Uhrzeit) ansetzen VI 1 (24) **the train was scheduled to leave at 14.18** der Zug sollte planmäßig um 14.18 (ab)fahren VI 1 (24)
school [skuːl] Schule I **school is out** die Schule ist aus/vorbei I **at school** in der Schule I
school bag [ˈskuːl bæg] Schultasche I
school yard [ˈskuːl jɑːd] Schulhof II
science [ˈsaɪəns] Naturwissenschaft I
science fiction, *infml auch* **sci-fi** [saɪəns ˈfɪkʃn], [ˈsaɪ faɪ] Sciencefiction III
scientist [ˈsaɪəntɪst] (Natur-)Wissenschaftler/in VI 3 (57)
scissors *(pl)* [ˈsɪzəz] *(eine)* Schere I
scone [skɒn] *Milchbrötchen (leicht süß, oft mit Rosinen)* I
score [skɔː] *(Punkt/Tor/Treffer)* erzielen IV
Scot [skɒt] Schotte/Schottin III
Scotland [ˈskɒtlənd] Schottland III
Scottish [ˈskɒtɪʃ] schottisch, aus Schottland III
scrambled eggs *(pl)* [skræmbld ˈegz] Rühreier IV
scream [skriːm] schreien II
screech [skriːtʃ] kreischen; *(Reifen, Bremsen)* quietschen VI 2 (43)
screen [skriːn] Leinwand; Bildschirm V
script [skrɪpt] Drehbuch VI 2 (49)
sea [siː] Meer, *(die)* See I **the sea's coming in** die Flut kommt; das Wasser steigt I
sea lion [ˈsiː laɪən] Seelöwe IV
seagull [ˈsiːgʌl] Möwe I
search [sɜːtʃ]:
1. Suche IV
2. **search (for sth.)** (etwas/nach etwas) suchen IV

seasick [ˈsiːsɪk] seekrank IV
season [ˈsiːzn] Jahreszeit II
seat [siːt] (Sitz-)Platz I **take a seat** Platz nehmen VI 1 (31)
seat belt [ˈsiːt belt] Sicherheitsgurt VI 1 (21)
second [ˈsekənd] zweite(r, s) I
second [ˈsekənd] Sekunde IV
second-hand [sekənd ˈhænd] second-hand, aus zweiter Hand II **second-hand shop** Second-Hand-Laden II
Secondly, … [ˈsekəndli] Zweitens … III
secret [ˈsiːkrət]:
1. Geheimnis II
2. geheim II

security [sɪˈkjʊərəti] Sicherheit VI 1 (22) °**internet-scale security** Internet-Sicherheit
security guard [sɪˈkjʊərəti gɑːd] Sicherheitsbedienstete/r VI 1 (22)
see [siː], **saw, seen** sehen I **See for yourself.** Sieh selbst! / Sehen Sie selbst! V **See you around.** Bis dann. V **See you later.** Bis später. I **I see.** Ach so. / Aha. / Verstehe. II
seed sth. [siːd] etwas säen VI 3 (57)
seem (to be/do) [siːm] erscheinen; (zu sein/zu tun) scheinen IV
seen [siːn] *siehe* **see**
segregate [ˈsegrɪgeɪt] trennen IV
segregation [segrɪˈgeɪʃn] Trennung *(nach Rasse/Religion/Geschlecht)* IV
self-portrait [self ˈpɔːtreɪt] Selbstporträt V
sell [sel], **sold, sold** verkaufen III
send [send], **sent, sent** senden, schicken I
°**senior** [ˈsiːniə]:
1. für Fortgeschrittene; für Erwachsene *(bei Sport-Teams)*
2. *Schüler/in im letzten Schuljahr*

°**sense** [sens]: **make sense** Sinn ergeben, sinnvoll sein
sense of humour [sens əv ˈhjuːmə] (Sinn für) Humor VI 1 (17)
°**sensible** [ˈsensəbl] vernünftig
sent [sent] *siehe* **send**
sentence [ˈsentəns] Satz II
separate [ˈseprət] getrennt, separat IV

September [sep'tembə] September I
series, *pl* series ['sɪəri:z] Serie; (Sende-)Reihe VI 2 (36)
serious ['sɪəriəs] ernst(haft) III **be serious about** es ernst meinen mit VI 1 (14)
seriously ['sɪəriəsli] im Ernst III
servant ['sɜ:vənt] Diener/in, Bedienstete/r IV
serve [sɜ:v] servieren *(Essen, Getränke)*; bedienen *(Kundschaft)* III **serve sb. (with sth.)** jn. betreuen, (mit etwas) versorgen, jm. behilflich sein V
service ['sɜ:vɪs] Dienst II **emergency services** *(pl)* Rettungsdienste II
set [set]: **(film) set** Bühnenbild, (Film-)Kulisse IV
set, set, set [set]: **set the table** den Tisch decken I **°set off** aufbrechen, losfahren/-fliegen **°set sth. up** etwas einrichten, aufbauen **°be set (in)** spielen (in) *(Film, Geschichte)*
setting ['setɪŋ] Schauplatz *(z.B. Film/Geschichte)* V
settler ['setlə] Siedler/in IV
seven ['sevn] sieben I
several ['sevrəl] mehrere, einige IV
shack [ʃæk] Baracke, Hütte IV
shade [ʃeɪd] Schatten *(vor der Sonne geschützt)* V
shadow ['ʃædəʊ] Schatten *(Umriss)* V
shake [ʃeɪk], **shook, shaken:**
1. schütteln III
shake sb.'s hand jm. die Hand schütteln III
2. zittern VI 1 (20)
shaken ['ʃeɪkən] *siehe* **shake**
Shall I ...? [ʃæl], [ʃəl] Soll ich ...? IV
shame [ʃeɪm] **a shame** eine Schande; schade V
°shameful ['ʃeɪmfl] schändlich, beschämend
share [ʃeə] teilen I **share a room with sb.** sich ein Zimmer mit jm. teilen I
shark [ʃɑ:k] Hai V
°shark spotter ['ʃɑ:k spɒtə] Hai-Beobachter/in; jemand, der nach Haien Ausschau hält
sharpener ['ʃɑ:pnə] Anspitzer I
shatter (into) ['ʃætə] zerbrechen (in) VI 3 (59)
she [ʃi:] sie *(weibliche Person)* I
shed [ʃed] Schuppen *(Hütte, Lagerraum)* VI 3 (65)
sheep, *pl* sheep [ʃi:p] Schaf I
sheepdog ['ʃi:pdɒg] Hütehund *(zum Hüten von Schafen)* III
sheet [ʃi:t] Blatt *(Papier)* V
shelf, *pl* shelves [ʃelf], [ʃelvz] Regal I
sheriff ['ʃerɪf] *(AE)* Sheriff IV
shift [ʃɪft] Schicht *(bei der Arbeit)* V
work shifts im Schichtdienst arbeiten V
shine [ʃaɪn], **shone, shone** scheinen *(Sonne)*; leuchten, strahlen, glänzen III **°shine a light on ...** die Aufmerksamkeit lenken auf ...
ship [ʃɪp] Schiff II
shipbuilder ['ʃɪpbɪldə] Schiffbauer/in, Schiffbaufirma VI 3 (56)
shirt [ʃɜ:t] Hemd I
shock [ʃɒk]:
1. Schock III
2. schockieren V
shocked [ʃɒkt] schockiert III
shocking ['ʃɒkɪŋ] schockierend V
shoe [ʃu:] Schuh I
shoestring ['ʃu:strɪŋ]: **on a shoestring** *(infml)* mit ganz wenig Geld IV
shone [ʃɒn] *siehe* **shine**
shook [ʃʊk] *siehe* **shake**
shoot [ʃu:t], **shot, shot** schießen; anschießen, erschießen IV
shop [ʃɒp]:
1. Laden, Geschäft I
2. einkaufen, „shoppen" III
shop for sth. etwas kaufen (gehen) VI 3 (68)
shop window [ʃɒp 'wɪndəʊ] Schaufenster VI 1 (19)
shopper ['ʃɒpə] Käufer/in IV
shopping ['ʃɒpɪŋ]: **shopping centre** Einkaufszentrum I **shopping list** Einkaufsliste V **shopping mall** Einkaufszentrum III **do the shopping** Einkäufe erledigen, einkaufen gehen V **go shopping** einkaufen gehen I
shore [ʃɔ:] Ufer *(eines Sees)* VI 3 (66)
short [ʃɔ:t]:
1. kurz II
2. klein *(Person)* II
short cut [ʃɔ:t 'kʌt] Abkürzung V
short story [ʃɔ:t 'stɔ:ri] Kurzgeschichte V
shorts *(pl)* [ʃɔ:ts] *(eine)* kurze Hose I
shot [ʃɒt]:
1. Schuss III
2. Aufnahme, Foto; *(Film)* Einstellung VI 3 (71)
3. *siehe* **shoot**
should [ʃʊd]: **What should I do?** Was sollte ich tun? II **You shouldn't have.** Das wäre doch nicht nötig gewesen. III
shoulder ['ʃəʊldə] Schulter I
shout [ʃaʊt]:
1. rufen II
2. Ruf VI 3 (65)
show [ʃəʊ] Show, Vorführung, Aufführung II
show [ʃəʊ], **showed, shown:**
1. zeigen I
show up *(infml)* erscheinen, kommen, sich zeigen VI 2 (38) **°show sb. (a)round (your town)** jn. (in deiner Stadt) herumführen
2. sich zeigen, sichtbar sein V
shower ['ʃaʊə] Dusche; Schauer III
shown [ʃəʊn] *siehe* **show**
shut, shut, shut [ʃʌt]: **Shut up!** *(infml)* Halt den Mund! I **°shut sb./sth. off from** jn./etwas abschneiden, abkapseln von
shy [ʃaɪ] scheu, schüchtern II
sick [sɪk] krank IV **I'm/I feel sick.** Mir ist schlecht/übel. IV
side [saɪd] Seite *(z.B. Straßenseite)* III **side by side** Seite an Seite IV
sidewalk ['saɪdwɔ:k] *(AE)* Gehweg, Bürgersteig IV
sigh [saɪ] seufzen VI 1 (20)
sight [saɪt]:
1. Anblick, Bild I
2. Sehenswürdigkeit III
sign [saɪn]:
1. Schild; Zeichen I
2. unterschreiben IV
sign up (for) sich anmelden (für) VI 3 (62)
°sign language ['saɪn læŋgwɪdʒ] Zeichensprache, Gebärdensprache
signal ['sɪgnəl] Signal III
signature ['sɪgnətʃə] Unterschrift VI 2 (36)
silence ['saɪləns] Stille IV
silent ['saɪlənt] still, ruhig; lautlos VI 1 (20) **fall silent** still werden, verstummen VI 1 (20)
silly ['sɪli] dumm, blöd; albern II
silver ['sɪlvə] Silber; silberfarben VI 1 (21)
similar (to sb./sth.) ['sɪmələ] (jm./einer Sache) ähnlich IV
°simile ['sɪməli] Vergleich *(Stilmittel)*
simple ['sɪmpl] einfach, simpel V
°simplicity [sɪm'plɪsəti] Einfachheit, Schlichtheit
since [sɪns]:
1. **since August** seit August III
since then seitdem VI 2 (41)
°2. weil, da
sincerely [sɪn'sɪəli]: **Sincerely ...** *(AE)* Mit freundlichen Grüßen *(Briefschluss)* IV **Sincerely yours** *(AE)* Mit freundlichen Grüßen *(Briefschluss)* V **Yours sincerely** Mit freundlichen Grüßen *(Briefschluss)* III
sing [sɪŋ], **sang, sung** singen I
singer ['sɪŋə] Sänger/in I
single ['sɪŋgl] ledig, alleinstehend II
single parent [sɪŋgl 'peərənt] Alleinerziehende/r IV
sink [sɪŋk], **sank, sunk** sinken V
sink down in your seat auf dem Sitz zusammensinken, nach unten rutschen V
sir [sɜ:]:
1. mein Herr *(höfliche Anrede z.B. für einen Kunden oder Vorgesetzten)* II
2. (gnädiger) Herr V
Dear Sir/Madam Sehr geehrte Damen und Herren V
siren ['saɪrən] Sirene VI 2 (44)
sister ['sɪstə] Schwester I

sit [sɪt], **sat, sat** sitzen; sich setzen I
sit up sich aufsetzen, sich gerade hinsetzen V
site [saɪt] Stelle, Platz, Stätte III
situation [sɪtʃu'eɪʃn] Situation II
six [sɪks] sechs I
size [saɪz] Größe IV **What size do you take?** Welche Größe hast du? IV
skateboard ['skeɪtbɔːd] Skateboard fahren I
skating ['skeɪtɪŋ] *(= ice skating)* Schlittschuhlaufen; *(= roller skating)* Rollschuhlaufen V
skeleton ['skelɪtn] Skelett VI 3 (56)
skewer ['skjuːə] (Grill-)Spieß IV
ski [skiː]:
1. Ski laufen, Ski fahren II
2. Ski(-) V
skier ['skiːə] Skiläufer/in III
skill [skɪl] Fähigkeit, Fertigkeit V
skim a text [skɪm] einen Text überfliegen *(um den Inhalt grob zu erfassen)* III
skin [skɪn]:
1. Haut; Schale *(z.B. Banane)* IV
2. häuten IV
skinny ['skɪni] *(infml)* mager, dürr III
skipping ['skɪpɪŋ] Seilspringen III
skirt [skɜːt] Rock I
skive [skaɪv] *(infml) (Schule)* schwänzen II
sky [skaɪ] Himmel II
skyscraper ['skaɪskreɪpə] Wolkenkratzer IV
slam [slæm] (zu-, hin)knallen V **slam down the phone** den Hörer aufknallen V
slave [sleɪv] Sklave, Sklavin IV
slavery ['sleɪvəri] Sklaverei III
sleep [sliːp]:
1. Schlaf II
Go to sleep! Schlaf jetzt! I
2. **sleep, slept, slept** schlafen I
sleeping bag ['sliːpɪŋ bæg] Schlafsack I
sleepless ['sliːpləs] schlaflos VI 2 (44)
sleepover ['sliːpəʊvə] Schlafparty I
sleepy ['sliːpi] müde, verschlafen III
slept [slept] *siehe* **sleep**
°**slide** [slaɪd]:
1. Dia(-); Folie *(bei Präsentation m. Computerprogramm)*
2. Rutsche, Rutschbahn
slip [slɪp] (aus)rutschen VI 3 (65)
°**slippery** ['slɪpəri] rutschig, glatt
slogan ['sləʊgən] Slogan V
slow [sləʊ]:
1. langsam I
2. **slow down** (sich) verlangsamen, langsamer werden VI 3 (65)
small [smɔːl] klein I
smart [smɑːt] schick, smart; schlau, clever IV
smell [smel]:
1. riechen II
2. Geruch IV
smelly ['smeli]: **be smelly** stinken II

smile [smaɪl]:
1. lächeln II
2. *(ein)* Lächeln II
smoke [sməʊk] rauchen IV
smoothie ['smuːði] Smoothie *(Getränk aus Fruchtpüree, evtl. mit Milchprodukten)* II
smuggler ['smʌglə] Schmuggler/in I
snack [snæk] Snack, kleine Mahlzeit II
snake [sneɪk] Schlange I
sneakers *(pl)* ['sniːkəz] *(AE)* Sportschuhe IV
sniff (at) [snɪf] schnüffeln, schnuppern (an) II
snow [snəʊ] Schnee II
snowy ['snəʊi] schneebedeckt; verschneit II
so [səʊ]:
1. also, daher I
2. so II
so far bis jetzt, bis hierher II **so that** sodass, damit IV **and so on** und so weiter VI 3 (68)
3. **I don't think so.** Das glaube/denke ich nicht. III
I think so. Ich glaube ja. III
soap [səʊp] Seife; *infml auch* Seifenoper II
soccer ['sɒkə] Fußball IV
social ['səʊʃl] gesellschaftlich, sozial; gesellig V
social media *(pl)* [səʊʃl 'miːdiə] soziale Medien/Dienste V
social skills *(pl)* [səʊʃl 'skɪlz] Sozialkompetenz V
°**society** [sə'saɪəti] *(die)* Gesellschaft
sock [sɒk] Socke I
sofa ['səʊfə] Sofa I
software engineer ['sɒftweə endʒɪnɪə] Softwareentwickler/in VI 2 (48)
°**solar panel** [səʊlə 'pænl] Sonnenkollektor
sold [səʊld] *siehe* **sell**
soldier ['səʊldʒə] Soldat/in IV
solution (to a problem) [sə'luːʃn] Lösung (eines Problems) V
solve [sɒlv] lösen *(Rätsel, Problem)*, lüften *(Geheimnis)* III
some [sʌm], [səm] einige, ein paar; etwas, ein wenig I **Would you like some tea/chips?** Möchtest du (etwas) Tee / (ein paar) Pommes frites? II
somebody ['sʌmbədi] jemand II
somehow ['sʌmhaʊ] irgendwie VI 1 (19)
someone ['sʌmwʌn] jemand II
someplace ['sʌmpleɪs] *(AE)* irgendwo(hin) IV
something ['sʌmθɪŋ] etwas I **… or something** … oder so was III
sometime ['sʌmtaɪm] irgendwann V
sometimes ['sʌmtaɪmz] manchmal I
somewhere ['sʌmweə] irgendwo(hin) III
son [sʌn] Sohn III
song [sɒŋ] Lied I

soon [suːn] bald I **as soon as** sobald; so bald wie V
sore [sɔː] schmerzhaft II **a sore throat** Halsschmerzen II **I have a sore leg.** Mein Bein tut weh. I
Sorry. / I'm sorry. ['sɒri] Tut mir leid. / Entschuldigung. I **say sorry** sich entschuldigen V
°**sort** [sɔːt]: **that sort of thing** so etwas; dergleichen
sound [saʊnd]:
1. klingen III
2. Geräusch; Klang, Laut I
soup [suːp] Suppe I
°**source** [sɔːs] Quelle *(z.B. Text)*
south [saʊθ] Süden; nach Süden II
south-east Südosten; nach Südosten II **south-west** Südwesten; nach Südwesten II
southbound ['saʊθbaʊnd] in Richtung Süden III
southern ['sʌðən] südlich, Süd- IV
souvenir [suːvə'nɪə] Souvenir III
space [speɪs]:
1. Platz I
2. Raum, Fläche VI 1 (22)
°**spacecraft**, *pl* **spacecraft** [speɪskrɑːft] Raumfahrzeug, Raumschiff
speak [spiːk], **spoke, spoken** sprechen I **speak to sb.** sprechen mit jm. III
speaker ['spiːkə]:
1. Lautsprecher I
2. Sprecher/in; Redner/in V
special ['speʃl]:
1. besondere(r, s) I
2. Special; Sondersendung; besonderes Angebot V
special effects *(pl)* [speʃl ɪ'fekts] Special Effects *(in Filmen)* IV
special offer [speʃl 'ɒfə] Sonderangebot I
°**specialist** ['speʃəlɪst] Spezialist/in, Fachmann/-frau
°**speciality** [speʃi'æləti] Spezialität
°**speculate** ['spekjuleɪt] spekulieren
sped [sped] *siehe* **speed**
speech [spiːtʃ] Rede, Ansprache III
°**deliver a speech** eine Rede halten
speed [spiːd]:
1. Geschwindigkeit VI 2 (43)
2. **speed, sped, sped** rasen, zu schnell fahren VI 2 (43)
speed hump ['spiːd hʌmp] Bodenschwelle, Bremsschwelle *(zur Verkehrsberuhigung)* VI 2 (43)
spell [spel] buchstabieren I
spelling ['spelɪŋ] Rechtschreibung, Schreibweise IV
spend time/money (on) [spend], **spent, spent** Geld ausgeben (für); Zeit verbringen (mit) II
spent [spent] *siehe* **spend**
spider ['spaɪdə] Spinne V
spinach ['spɪnɪtʃ], ['spɪnɪdʒ] Spinat III

spirit ['spɪrɪt] Geist, Stimmung IV **spirit of the times** Zeitgeist IV **be in good spirits** in guter Stimmung sein, guter Dinge sein IV **community spirit** Gemeinschaftssinn IV **school spirit** Schulklima, Gemeinschaftsgefühl IV **team spirit** Teamgeist IV
spite [spaɪt]: **in spite of** trotz VI 3 (62)
splash [splæʃ]:
1. spritzen, platschen VI 3 (66)
°2. Fleck, Spritzer
spoke [spəʊk] *siehe* **speak**
spoken ['spəʊkən] *siehe* **speak**
°**spokesperson**, *pl* **spokespersons** *or* **spokespeople** ['spəʊkspɜːsn] Sprecher/in
sponsor ['spɒnsə]:
1. sponsern V
2. Sponsor/in *(Geldgeber/in)* V
spook [spuːk] *(infml)* Gespenst, Geist V
spooky ['spuːki] unheimlich, gruselig V
sport [spɔːt] Sport; Sportart I **do sport** Sport treiben I
sporting event ['spɔːtɪŋ ɪvent] Sportveranstaltung VI 1 (10)
sports hall ['spɔːts hɔːl] Sporthalle I
sportsman/-woman ['spɔːtsmən, -wʊmən] Sportler/in III
sporty ['spɔːti] sportlich II
spot [spɒt]:
1. entdecken IV
2. Fleck, Pickel IV
3. Stelle, Ort V
°**spotter** ['spɒtə]: **shark spotter** Hai-Beobachter/in; jemand, der nach Haien Ausschau hält
spray-paint ['spreɪ peɪnt] mit Farbe besprühen IV
spread (sth.) [spred], **spread, spread** etwas verbreiten *(Virus, Krankheit)*; sich ausbreiten V
spring [sprɪŋ] Frühling II
spy on sb. ['spaɪ ɒn] jm. nachspionieren, jn. bespitzeln VI 3 (59)
square [skweə] Platz *(in der Stadt)* I
squat [skwɒt] (ein Haus/Grundstück) besetzen V
squatter ['skwɒtə] Hausbesetzer/in V
stadium ['steɪdiəm] Stadion III
staff [stɑːf] Personal, Belegschaft III
stage [steɪdʒ] Bühne VI 2 (40)
stairs *(pl)* [steəz] *(eine)* Treppe; (Treppen-)Stufen II
stall [stɔːl] (Markt-)Stand, Bude III
stamp [stæmp] Stempel; Briefmarke II
stand [stænd]:
1. **stand, stood, stood** stehen; sich (hin)stellen II
stand up aufstehen IV °**stand up for** eintreten für, sich einsetzen für
2. Standpunkt, Haltung VI 2 (34)
take a stand (on/against sth.) Stellung beziehen (zu/gegen etwas) VI 2 (34)
standard ['stændəd]:
1. Norm, Standard V
2. normal, üblich, Standard- V
stank [stæŋk] *siehe* **stink**
star [stɑː] Stern IV
stare (at) [steə] (an)starren IV
start [stɑːt]:
1. Anfang, Start II
2. beginnen, anfangen I
start off (as) anfangen (als) IV
start out (zunächst) beginnen; am Anfang stehen VI 1 (14) **To start with, …** Erstens …, Zuerst (mal) …, Zunächst … IV
state [steɪt]:
1. (Bundes-)Staat IV
°2. Zustand
statement ['steɪtmənt] Aussage(satz) III **personal statement** persönliche Beschreibung, Selbstbeschreibung V
station ['steɪʃn] Bahnhof II
statue ['stætʃuː] Statue II
°**status update** ['steɪtəs ʌpdeɪt] Statusaktualisierung *(bei sozialen Netzwerken)*
stay [steɪ]:
1. bleiben I
2. Aufenthalt III
steal [stiːl], **stole, stolen** stehlen IV
step [step]:
1. Schritt; Stufe II
step by step Schritt für Schritt V
2. treten *(einen Schritt tun)* V
step closer näher treten, näher (heran)kommen IV
stepbrother ['stepbrʌðə] Stiefbruder I
stepdad ['stepdæd] Stiefvater I
step-dancing ['step dɑːnsɪŋ] Step Dancing *(irischer Tanz)* IV
stepfather ['stepfɑːðə] Stiefvater I
stepmother ['stepmʌðə] Stiefmutter I
stepmum ['stepmʌm] Stiefmutter I
stepsister ['stepsɪstə] Stiefschwester I
stereotype ['steriətaɪp] Stereotyp, Klischee(vorstellung) VI 2 (48)
stick [stɪk] Stock IV
stick [stɪk], **stuck, stuck** (haften) bleiben VI 1 (27) **stick together** zusammenhalten III **stick with sth.** bei etwas bleiben V
still [stɪl] (immer) noch; trotzdem II
°**still** [stɪl]: **(film) still** Standbild *(Film)*
sting [stɪŋ]:
1. (Insekten-)Stich V
2. **sting, stung, stung** stechen *(Insekt)*; brennen V
stink [stɪŋk], **stank, stunk** stinken IV
stole [stəʊl] *siehe* **steal**
stolen ['stəʊlən] *siehe* **steal**
stomach ['stʌmək] Bauch; Magen II
stomach ache Bauchschmerzen II
stone [stəʊn] Stein II
°**Stone Age** ['stəʊn eɪdʒ] Steinzeit
stood [stʊd] *siehe* **stand**
stoop [stuːp] *(AE)* kleine Terrasse vor der Tür, Treppe/Aufgang zum Hauseingang IV
stop [stɒp]:
1. Haltestelle II
2. Halt, Haltepunkt VI 1 (24)
make (three) stops (dreimal) anhalten VI 1 (24)
3. (an)halten; stoppen; aufhören (mit) I
stop by vorbeischauen (in/bei/an) II
store [stɔː] Geschäft, Laden III
storey ['stɔːri] *(BE)* Stock, Stockwerk, Etage V
storm [stɔːm]:
1. Sturm; Gewitter IV
2. stürmen VI 3 (66)
story ['stɔːri]:
1. Geschichte I
2. *(AE)* Stock, Stockwerk, Etage V
storyline ['stɔːrilaɪn] Handlung *(z.B. eines Films/einer Geschichte)* VI 2 (49)
°**stow** [stəʊ] verstauen
straight [streɪt]:
1. gerade; *(Haare)* glatt II
2. direkt, gleich VI 1 (19)
straight on [streɪt 'ɒn] geradeaus (weiter) II
strange [streɪndʒ] seltsam, sonderbar II
stranger ['streɪndʒə] Fremde/r VI 1 (19)
strawberry ['strɔːbəri] Erdbeere IV
stream [striːm]:
1. Bach VI 1 (20)
2. strömen VI 1 (20)
street [striːt] Straße *(in Ortschaften)* I
streetball ['striːtbɔːl] Streetball *(Variante des Basketballs)* IV
streetballer ['striːtbɔːlə] Streetball-Spieler/in IV
strength [streŋθ] Stärke, Kraft V
stress [stres]:
1. Stress, Belastung V
heat stress Hitzestress, Wärmebelastung des Körpers V
°2. betonen
stressed [strest] gestresst III
°**stretch** [stretʃ] sich erstrecken
stretcher ['stretʃə] Trage, (Trag-)Bahre VI 2 (44)
strict [strɪkt] streng I
°**strike** [straɪk] Streik
stripe [straɪp] Streifen V
stroke [strəʊk] streicheln I
strong [strɒŋ] stark III
structure ['strʌktʃə]:
1. strukturieren, gliedern III
2. Struktur V
struggle ['strʌgl]:
1. kämpfen, sich abmühen VI 1 (20)
2. Kampf VI 1 (20)
stuck [stʌk] *siehe* **stick**
stud [stʌd] (Ohr-/Nasen-)Stecker V
student ['stjuːdnt] Schüler/in; Student/in I
studio ['stjuːdiəʊ] Studio I
study ['stʌdi] studieren; lernen V

stuff [stʌf] *(infml)* Zeug, Kram II
stung [stʌŋ] *siehe* **sting**
stunk [stʌŋk] *siehe* **stink**
stupid ['stju:pɪd] dumm, blöd I
style [staɪl] Stil(richtung); Art IV
stylist ['staɪlɪst] Friseur/in; (Mode-) Stylist/in V
°**stylistic** [staɪ'lɪstɪk] stilistisch, Stil-
°**stylistic device** [staɪlɪstɪk dɪ'vaɪs] Stilmittel
subject ['sʌbdʒɪkt]:
1. Thema; *(in E-Mails)* Betreff II
°**2.** Gegenstand, *(Film)* Hauptperson
suburb ['sʌbɜ:b] Vorstadt, Vorort VI 1 (12)
subway ['sʌbweɪ] *(AE)* U-Bahn IV
success [sək'ses] Erfolg IV
successful [sək'sesfl] erfolgreich III
°**successively** [sək'sesɪvli] hintereinander, nacheinander
such (a) [sʌtʃ] so(lch) (ein/e) III
there's no such thing as … es gibt kein/e … III
suck [sʌk]: **It sucks!** Es nervt! / Es ist Mist! III
sudden ['sʌdn] plötzliche(r, s) VI 1 (19)
suddenly ['sʌdənli] plötzlich, auf einmal II
suffer (from) ['sʌfə] leiden (an), erleiden V
sugar ['ʃʊgə] Zucker II
sugary ['ʃʊgəri] süß(lich), zuckerhaltig II
suggest sth. (to sb.) [sə'dʒest] (jm.) etwas vorschlagen III
suggestion [sə'dʒestʃən] Vorschlag V
°**suit** [su:t] (Herren-)Anzug; (Damen-) Kostüm
suitable ['su:təbl] geeignet, passend V
sum sth. up [sʌm 'ʌp] etwas zusammenfassen III
summarize ['sʌməraɪz] zusammenfassen III
summary ['sʌməri] Zusammenfassung III
summer ['sʌmə] Sommer I
summer camp ['sʌmə kæmp] (Sommer-)Ferienlager II
sun [sʌn] Sonne I
suncream ['sʌnkri:m] Sonnencreme I
Sunday ['sʌndeɪ], ['sʌndi] Sonntag I
sung [sʌŋ] *siehe* **sing**
sunglasses *(pl)* ['sʌnglɑ:sɪz] *(eine)* Sonnenbrille I
sunk [sʌŋk] *siehe* **sink**
sunlight ['sʌnlaɪt] Sonnenlicht IV
sunny ['sʌni] sonnig II
sunshine ['sʌnʃaɪn] Sonnenschein IV
superhero, *pl* **superheroes** ['su:pəhɪərəʊ] Superheld/in VI 3 (71)
supermarket ['su:pəmɑ:kɪt] Supermarkt I
supply [sə'plaɪ] Versorgung, Lieferung; Vorrat VI 3 (66) **supplies** *(pl)* Verbrauchsgüter, Vorrat/Vorräte IV
support [sə'pɔ:t]:
1. unterstützen V
2. Unterstützung V
supposed [sə'pəʊzd]: **be supposed to be/do sth.** etwas sein sollen/ etwas tun sollen VI 2 (43)
sure [ʃʊə], [ʃɔ:] sicher I **for sure** ganz sicher, ganz bestimmt V **make sure that …** darauf achten, dass …; dafür sorgen, dass … V
surf [sɜ:f] surfen (über) IV
surprise [sə'praɪz]:
1. überraschen IV
2. Überraschung I
surprised [sə'praɪzd] überrascht II
surprising [sə'praɪzɪŋ] überraschend IV
surprisingly überraschenderweise IV
°**surround** [sə'raʊnd] umgeben
survey ['sɜ:veɪ] Umfrage II
survival [sə'vaɪvl] *(das)* Überleben VI 2 (40)
survive [sə'vaɪv] überleben VI 2 (40)
survivor [sə'vaɪvə] Überlebende/r IV
suspend (sb. from sth.) [sə'spend] (jn. von etwas) suspendieren, zwangsbeurlauben III
suspension bridge [sə'spenʃn brɪdʒ] Hängebrücke IV
suspicious (of) [sə'spɪʃəs] verdächtig; misstrauisch (gegenüber) IV
sustainable [sə'steɪnəbl] nachhaltig, umweltverträglich; zukunftsfähig VI 3 (60)
swam [swæm] *siehe* **swim**
swamp [swɒmp] Sumpf IV
swap (for) [swɒp] (aus-, um)tauschen (gegen) IV
sweat [swet] Schweiß IV
sweatshop ['swetʃɒp] Ausbeutungsbetrieb VI 2 (47)
sweets *(pl)* [swi:ts] Bonbons, Süßigkeiten I
swerve [swɜ:v] *(das Auto/Steuer)* herumreißen, *(mit dem Auto)* ausweichen V
swim [swɪm], **swam, swum** schwimmen I **go swimming** schwimmen gehen I
swimmer ['swɪmə] Schwimmer/in III
swimming pool ['swɪmɪŋ pu:l] Schwimmbad I
swimming trunks *(pl)* ['swɪmɪŋ trʌŋks] *(eine)* Badehose I
swimsuit ['swɪmsu:t] Badeanzug I
swing [swɪŋ], **swung, swung** schwingen; *(zum Schlag)* ausholen IV
switch sth. on/off [swɪtʃ 'ɒn], [swɪtʃ 'ɒf] etwas einschalten / ausschalten II
sword [sɔ:d] Schwert II
swum [swʌm] *siehe* **swim**
swung [swʌŋ] *siehe* **swing**
symbol ['sɪmbl] Symbol III
°**symbolic (of)** [sɪm'bɒlɪk] symbolisch (für)
system ['sɪstəm] System V

T

table ['teɪbl]:
1. Tisch I
set the table den Tisch decken I
°**2.** Tabelle
°**tackle** ['tækl] *(Problem)* angehen; angreifen
tae kwon do [taɪ kwɒn 'dəʊ] Taekwondo I
tag line ['tæg laɪn] (Werbe-)Slogan IV
tail [teɪl] Schwanz II
take [teɪk], **took, taken:**
1. (mit)nehmen; bringen II
2. dauern, *(Zeit)* brauchen, in Anspruch nehmen III
take it easy sich schonen VI 2 (44)
Take it easy. Reg dich nicht auf. / Bleib mal locker. III **take me to the theatre** mit mir ins Theater gehen I
take over die Macht übernehmen V
take photos Fotos machen II **take place** stattfinden III **take sth. off** etwas abnehmen, ausziehen *(Kleidung)* VI 3 (69) **take sth. on** etwas annehmen, übernehmen V **take sth. up** mit etwas (neu) anfangen III
take the time to do sth. sich die Zeit nehmen, etwas zu tun IV **take the train** den Zug nehmen II **I'll take it.** Ich nehme es (ihn, sie). *(beim Einkaufen)* I **She can take a joke.** Sie versteht Spaß. III °**take to sth.** sich flüchten zu/an *(einen Ort)*
takeaway ['teɪkəweɪ] Essen zum Mitnehmen V
taken ['teɪkən] *siehe* **take**
°**take-off** ['teɪk ɒf] Start *(Flugzeug)*
talent ['tælənt] Talent, Begabung III
talk [tɔ:k]:
1. talk (to) sprechen, reden (mit) I
talk sth. over (with sb.) etwas (mit jm.) besprechen VI 1 (20)
2. Vortrag, Rede; Gespräch II
give a talk einen Vortrag halten II
talker ['tɔ:kə] Redner/in III
tall [tɔ:l] groß *(Person)*; hoch *(Gebäude)* II
tan [tæn] bräunen; braun werden *(in der Sonne)* IV
tap sth. [tæp] (leise) klopfen, tippen an etwas IV
target ['tɑ:gɪt]:
1. Ziel V
2. target sb. auf jn. zielen *(jn. als Zielgruppe haben/wählen)*, jn. ins Visier nehmen V
tart [tɑ:t] (Obst-)Törtchen III
task [tɑ:sk] Aufgabe II
taste [teɪst] schmecken; kosten *(probieren)* III
tattoo [tə'tu:] Tattoo, Tätowierung II
taught [tɔ:t] *siehe* **teach**
taxi ['tæksi] Taxi II
tea [ti:] Tee I

teach [tiːtʃ], **taught, taught** jn. unterrichten; jm. etwas beibringen III
teach sb. a lesson jm. eine Lektion erteilen V
teacher ['tiːtʃə] Lehrer/in I
team [tiːm] Team, Mannschaft I
teammate ['tiːmmeɪt] Mannschaftskamerad/in V
teamwork ['tiːmwɜːk] Teamwork, Teamarbeit III
tear [tɪə] Träne IV
tease sb. [tiːz] jn. hänseln, sich über jn. lustig machen V
tech [tek] *(infml)* Technik VI 3 (68)
technician [tek'nɪʃn] Techniker/in II
technique [tek'niːk] Methode, Technik VI 1 (27)
technology [tek'nɒlədʒi] Technik(unterricht); Technologie I
teen [tiːn] Teenager II
teen talk ['tiːn tɔːk] Teenagergespräche II
teenage kids ['tiːneɪdʒ] Kinder im Teenageralter III
teeth [tiːθ] *Plural von* tooth IV
telephone ['telɪfəʊn] Telefon III
television ['telɪvɪʒn] Fernsehen VI 1 (21)
tell (about) [tel], **told, told** erzählen (von), berichten (über) II **tell sb. (not) to do sth.** jn. auffordern, etwas (nicht) zu tun; jm. sagen, dass er/sie etwas (nicht) tun soll IV
temperature ['temprətʃə] Temperatur; Fieber II **have a temperature** Fieber haben II **take sb.'s temperature** (bei jm.) Fieber messen V
ten [ten] zehn I
tense [tens]:
1. sich anspannen, sich verkrampfen VI 3 (59)
2. angespannt, verkrampft VI 3 (59)
tent [tent] Zelt II
term [tɜːm] Trimester III
terrible ['terəbl] schrecklich, fürchterlich I
territory ['terətri] Gebiet, Territorium IV
terror ['terə] (panische) Angst VI 1 (20)
test [test]:
1. testen III
2. Klassenarbeit, Test II
3. **(***kurz für:* **driving test)** Fahrprüfung, Führerscheinprüfung IV
text [tekst]:
1. SMS; Text I
2. **text sb.** jm. eine SMS schicken I
text message ['tekst mesɪdʒ] SMS I
textbook ['tekstbʊk] Schulbuch, Lehrbuch I
than [ðən]: **older than me** älter als ich II
thank sb. [θæŋk] sich bei jm. bedanken II
thank you ['θæŋk juː] danke (schön) I
thanks [θæŋks] danke (schön) I
°**thanks to** ['θæŋks tə] dank
Thanksgiving [θæŋks'gɪvɪŋ] Erntedankfest *(amerikanischer Feiertag am vierten Donnerstag im November)* IV
that [ðæt]:
1. das (dort) I
that field das Feld (dort), jenes Feld I **That's £ 159.** Das macht 159 Pfund. I
2. **that bad** so schlecht/schlimm V
3. der, die, das *(Relativpronomen)* II
a dog that could be Buster ein Hund, der Buster sein könnte II
4. dass II
the good news is that ... die gute Nachricht ist, dass ... II
the [ðə] der, die, das I
theatre ['θɪətə] Theater I
their [ðeə] ihr/e *(Plural)* I
theirs [ðeəz] ihre/r, ihrs *(zu „they")* V
them [ðem], [ðəm] sie, ihnen I **It wasn't them.** Sie waren es nicht. II
°**theme** [θiːm] Thema
theme park ['θiːm pɑːk] Themenpark *(Freizeitpark mit Attraktionen zu einem bestimmten Thema)* I
themselves [ðəm'selvz] sie/sich selbst *(Plural)* III
then [ðen]:
1. dann, danach I
2. **(back) then** damals VI 1 (12)
there [ðeə] da, dort; dahin, dorthin I
there are es sind / es gibt I **there's (= there is)** es ist / es gibt I
°**therefore** ['ðeəfɔː] daher, deshalb
these [ðiːz] die, diese (hier) I
these days ['ðiːz deɪz] heutzutage VI 2 (36)
they [ðeɪ]:
1. sie *(Plural)* I
2. man *(die Leute)* VI 3 (66)
thin [θɪn] dünn IV
thing [θɪŋ] Ding, Sache I
think [θɪŋk], **thought, thought** denken, meinen, glauben I **think about** nachdenken über V **think of sth.** denken an etwas; sich etwas überlegen, ausdenken III **What do you think?** Was meinst du? / Was denkst du? I
thinker ['θɪŋkə] Denker/in V
third [θɜːd] dritte(r, s) I
Thirdly, ... ['θɜːdli] Drittens ... III
thirsty ['θɜːsti]: **be thirsty** durstig sein, Durst haben II
this [ðɪs]:
1. dies; diese(r, s) I
This is Rob Blake. Hier spricht Rob Blake. *(am Telefon)* III **this morning/afternoon/evening** heute Morgen/Nachmittag/Abend II
2. **this bad** so schlecht/schlimm V
those boys [ðəʊz] die Jungen dort, jene Jungen II
though [ðəʊ]:
1. obwohl V
even though auch wenn, obwohl *(betont)* VI 3 (62)
2. **... though.** ... aber ..., ... trotzdem ... V
thought [θɔːt]:
1. *siehe* **think**
°2. Gedanke
thousand ['θaʊznd] tausend III
threaten ['θretn] (be)drohen V
three [θriː] drei I
threw [θruː] *siehe* **throw**
°**thrill sb.** [θrɪl] jn. begeistern, überwältigen
°**thrilling** ['θrɪlɪŋ] aufregend, spannend
throat [θrəʊt] Hals II **a sore throat** Halsschmerzen II
through [θruː] durch I
throw [θrəʊ], **threw, thrown** werfen III
thrown [θrəʊn] *siehe* **throw**
thumb [θʌm] Daumen IV **give sb. the thumbs down** jm. Ablehnung zeigen IV **give sb. the thumbs up** jm. Zustimmung zeigen IV
°**thump** [θʌmp] (heftig) schlagen, klopfen
thunder ['θʌndə] Donner VI 3 (71)
thunderstorm ['θʌndəstɔːm] Gewitter IV
Thursday ['θɜːzdeɪ], ['θɜːzdi] Donnerstag I
°**tick** [tɪk] ticken *(Uhr)*
ticket ['tɪkɪt] Eintrittskarte, Fahrkarte I **one-way ticket** einfache Fahrkarte VI 3 (62)
ticket office ['tɪkɪt ɒfɪs] Kartenschalter II
tidy ['taɪdi]:
1. aufräumen II
2. ordentlich II
tie [taɪ] Krawatte I
tiger ['taɪgə] Tiger I
tights *(pl)* [taɪts] *(eine)* Strumpfhose I
till [tɪl] bis V
time [taɪm]:
1. Zeit; Uhrzeit I
at all times jederzeit, ständig V **on time** pünktlich II **over time** im Lauf der Zeit VI 2 (44) **take the time to do sth.** sich die Zeit nehmen, etwas zu tun IV **What's the time?** Wie spät ist es? I °**in time** rechtzeitig
2. Mal I
this time dieses Mal I °**at a time** jeweils, ununterbrochen
timeline ['taɪmlaɪn] Zeitstrahl, Zeitachse, Chronik IV
timetable ['taɪmteɪbl] Stundenplan I
tiny ['taɪni] winzig VI 1 (21)
tip [tɪp] Tipp II
tired ['taɪəd] müde I **be tired of sth.** die Nase voll haben von etwas VI 1 (20)
title ['taɪtl] Titel, Überschrift IV
to [tu], [tə]:
1. zu, nach I

to the cinema ins Kino I **Have you ever been to …?** Bist du schon mal in … gewesen? III **the most interesting information to me** die interessanteste Information für mich II
2. (um) zu I
how to do sth. wie man etwas tut / tun kann / tun soll III **she didn't know what to say** sie wusste nicht, was sie sagen sollte II **things to do** Dinge, die man tun kann III **time to eat** Zeit zu essen I
3. bis I
from Monday to Friday von Montag bis Freitag I
4. vor *(Uhrzeiten)* I
quarter to 7 viertel vor 7 I

toast [təʊst] toasten IV
today [tə'deɪ] heute I
together [tə'geðə] zusammen I
toilet ['tɔɪlət] Toilette I
toilet roll ['tɔɪlət rəʊl] Rolle Toilettenpapier II
told [təʊld] *siehe* **tell**
°**tolerant** ['tɒlərənt] tolerant
tomato, *pl* tomatoes [tə'mɑːtəʊ] Tomate III
tomorrow [tə'mɒrəʊ] morgen II
tongue [tʌŋ] Zunge; Sprache IV **Has the cat got his tongue?** Hat's ihm die Sprache verschlagen? IV
tonight [tə'naɪt] heute Nacht, heute Abend III
°**tonne** [tʌn] Tonne *(= 1.000 kg)*
too [tuː]:
1. auch I
from Berlin too auch aus Berlin I
2. too old zu alt I
took [tʊk] *siehe* **take**
tool [tuːl] Werkzeug IV
tooth, *pl* teeth [tuːθ], [tiːθ] Zahn IV **through my teeth** mit zusammengebissenen Zähnen IV
toothpaste ['tuːθpeɪst] Zahnpasta IV
top [tɒp] Spitze, oberes Ende I **at the top** oben, am oberen Ende; an der Spitze I
topic ['tɒpɪk] Thema II
torch [tɔːtʃ] Taschenlampe; Fackel V **flash a torch** mit einer Taschenlampe leuchten/blinken V
tornado, *pl* tornadoes [tɔː'neɪdəʊ] Tornado *(Wirbelsturm)* IV
torture ['tɔːtʃə]:
1. Folter V
2. foltern V
total ['təʊtl] total II
touch [tʌtʃ]:
1. anfassen, berühren III
°**2. get in touch with** (sich) in Verbindung setzen mit
tough [tʌf] (knall-)hart; zäh, robust IV
tour [tʊə] Tour, Reise III **a tour of the school** ein Rundgang durch die Schule I
tour guide ['tʊə gaɪd] Reiseleiter/in, Fremdenführer/in III
tour operator ['tʊər ɒpəreɪtə] Reiseveranstalter/in VI 1 (22)
tourism ['tʊərɪzəm] Tourismus V
tourist ['tʊərɪst] Tourist/in I
tourist office ['tʊərɪst ɒfɪs] Touristeninformation, Fremdenverkehrsbüro III
toward(s) [tə'wɔːdz] nach, auf … zu, in Richtung (von) IV
towel ['taʊəl] Handtuch I
tower ['taʊə] Turm III
town [taʊn] Stadt I
°**townhouse** ['taʊn haʊs] *(AE)* Reihenhaus
township ['taʊnʃɪp] Township *(überwiegend von Schwarzen bewohnte Siedlung in Südafrika)* VI 1 (11)
toy [tɔɪ] Spielzeug II
track [træk]:
1. Pfad, (Feld-)Weg III
°**2.** (zurück-, nach)verfolgen, beobachten
tractor ['træktə] Traktor III
trade [treɪd] Handel V
tradition [trə'dɪʃn] Tradition IV
traditional [trə'dɪʃənl] traditionell III
traffic ['træfɪk] (Straßen-)Verkehr III
traffic lights *(pl)* ['træfɪk laɪts] *(eine)* Ampel II
trail [treɪl] Weg, Pfad IV
train [treɪn] Zug, Eisenbahn II
train sb. [treɪn]:
1. jn. trainieren, ausbilden III
2. train as eine Ausbildung machen als/zu VI 3 (63)
train station ['treɪn steɪʃn] Bahnhof II
trainee [treɪ'niː] Auszubildende/r, Trainee V
trainers *(pl)* ['treɪnəz] Sportschuhe I
training ['treɪnɪŋ]:
1. Training III
2. Ausbildung V
tramp [træmp] Obdachlose/r, Stadtstreicher/in V
trampoline ['træmpəliːn] Trampolin I
transform [træns'fɔːm] umwandeln, verändern, umgestalten VI 1 (14)
transformation [trænsfə'meɪʃn] Umwandlung, Veränderung, Umgestaltung VI 1 (14)
°**translate** [træns'leɪt] übersetzen
°**translator** [træns'leɪtə] Übersetzer/in
transport ['trænspɔːt] *(no pl)* Fortbewegungsmittel; Beförderung II
trap [træp] einschließen, fangen *(mit einer Falle)* IV **be trapped** gefangen sein, in der Falle sitzen IV
trash [træʃ] *(AE)* Abfall, Müll IV
travel ['trævl] *(das)* Reisen V
travel costs *(pl)* ['trævl kɒsts] Reisekosten V
Travelcard ['trævlkɑːd] *Ein- oder Mehrtagesfahrkarte (London)* III
°**traveller** ['trævələ] Reisende/r
°**tray table** ['treɪ teɪbl] Klapptisch *(im Flugzeug)*
treasure ['treʒə] Schatz IV
tree [triː] Baum I **Money doesn't grow on trees.** Das Geld liegt nicht auf der Straße. *(Redewendung)* II
°**treetop** ['triːtɒp] Baumwipfel
trek [trek] Wanderung, Treck V
trendy ['trendi] modisch, „angesagt" III
tribal ['traɪbl] Stammes- VI 1 (11)
tribe [traɪb] (Volks-)Stamm IV
trick [trɪk] Trick, Kunststück V
trip [trɪp] Ausflug; Reise I
troll [trəʊl] Troll, Kobold; *(in Online-Medien)* Provokateur/in VI 2 (36)
tropical ['trɒpɪkl] tropisch, Tropen- V
trouble ['trʌbl] Ärger, Schwierigkeiten I **be in trouble** Ärger haben, in Schwierigkeiten sein I
trousers *(pl)* ['traʊzəz] *(eine)* Hose I
truck [trʌk] Last(kraft)wagen, LKW IV
true [truː] wahr, richtig I **come true** wahr werden V
truly ['truːli]: **Yours truly** *(AE)* Mit freundlichen Grüßen *(Briefschluss)* IV
trust [trʌst] (ver)trauen IV
truth [truːθ] Wahrheit IV
try [traɪ] probieren, ausprobieren I **try hard** sich (sehr) bemühen, sich anstrengen IV **try to do sth.** versuchen, etwas zu tun III
tube [tjuːb] Schwimmreifen I **the Tube** *(infml)* die Londoner U-Bahn III
tuck your shirt in [tʌk 'ɪn] das/dein Hemd in den Rock/die Hose stecken IV
Tuesday ['tjuːzdeɪ], ['tjuːzdi] Dienstag I
tuition [tju'ɪʃn] Unterricht, Anleitung; Studiengebühren VI 2 (38)
tuition fees *(pl)* [tju'ɪʃn fiːz] Studiengebühren VI 2 (38)
tunnel ['tʌnl] Tunnel VI 1 (19)
turn [tɜːn] sich umdrehen IV **turn around** sich umdrehen IV **turn away** sich abwenden, sich wegdrehen V **turn back** umkehren VI 1 (21) **turn over** (sich) umdrehen III **turn right/left** (nach) rechts/links abbiegen II **turn sth.** etwas umdrehen V **turn to** sich wenden an, gehen zu VI 2 (36) **turn up** auftauchen, erscheinen V **turn yellow** gelb werden VI 1 (20) **There was no turning back.** Es gab kein Zurück (mehr) VI 1 (21) °**turn sth. off** etwas ausschalten °**turn sth. on** etwas einschalten
turn [tɜːn]: **It's your turn.** Du bist dran. / Du bist an der Reihe. I °**take turns** sich abwechseln
TV [tiː'viː] Fernseher I
twelve [twelv] zwölf I
twice [twaɪs] zweimal III
twig [twɪg] (kleiner) Zweig IV

twin [twɪn]: **twin sister/brother** Zwillingsschwester/-bruder IV **twins** *(pl)* Zwillinge IV
twin room [twɪn 'ru:m] Zweibettzimmer III
two [tu:] zwei I
type (of) [taɪp] Art, Sorte, Typ (von) V
typical (of) ['tɪpɪkl] typisch (für) III
tyre ['taɪə] Reifen V

U

ugly ['ʌgli] hässlich I
umbrella [ʌm'brelə] (Regen-)Schirm I
unable to do sth. [ʌn'eɪbl] unfähig / nicht in der Lage, etwas zu tun III
unattractive [ʌnə'træktɪv] unattraktiv V
unbeatable [ʌn'bi:təbl] unschlagbar; unübertrefflich VI 1 (15)
uncle ['ʌŋkl] Onkel I
uncomfortable [ʌn'kʌmftəbl] unbequem, ungemütlich III
unconscious [ʌn'kɒnʃəs] bewusstlos VI 2 (44)
uncool [ʌn'ku:l] uncool II
under ['ʌndə] unter I
underage disco [ʌndər'eɪdʒ] Disco für Minderjährige III
underground ['ʌndəgraʊnd] U-Bahn III
°**underline** [ʌndə'laɪn] unterstreichen
understand [ʌndə'stænd], **understood, understood** verstehen I
understood [ʌndə'stʊd] *siehe* **understand**
unemployed [ʌnɪm'plɔɪd] arbeitslos III
°**unemployment** [ʌnɪm'plɔɪmənt] Arbeitslosigkeit
unequal [ʌn'i:kwəl] ungleich VI 1 (12)
unfair [ʌn'feə] unfair III
unfit [ʌn'fɪt] nicht fit II
°**unforgettable** [ʌnfə'getəbl] unvergesslich
unfortunately [ʌn'fɔ:tʃənətli] unglücklicherweise, leider VI 3 (64)
unfriendly [ʌn'frendli] unfreundlich II
unhappy [ʌn'hæpi] unglücklich I
unhealthy [ʌn'helθi] ungesund II
uniform ['ju:nɪfɔ:m] Uniform I
unimportant [ʌnɪm'pɔ:tnt] unwichtig, unbedeutend VI 1 (15)
uninteresting [ʌn'ɪntrəstɪŋ] uninteressant II
unit ['ju:nɪt]:
1. Lektion, Kapitel I
2. Abteilung *(z.B. im Krankenhaus)* VI 2 (44)
United [ju'naɪtɪd]: **United Nations, UN** Vereinte Nationen V **the United Kingdom (the UK)** das Vereinigte Königreich III
university [ju:nɪ'vɜ:səti] Universität V
unknown [ʌn'nəʊn] unbekannt VI 1 (22)
unless [ən'les] es sei denn; außer (wenn) IV
unlike [ʌn'laɪk] anders als, im Gegensatz zu V
unlikely [ʌn'laɪkli] unwahrscheinlich VI 3 (62)
unnatural [ʌn'nætʃrəl] unnatürlich V
unsure [ʌn'ʃʊə], [ʌn'ʃɔ:] unsicher II
untidy [ʌn'taɪdi] unordentlich, unaufgeräumt VI 1 (20)
until [ən'tɪl] bis *(zeitlich)* II
untuck your shirt [ʌn'tʌk] das/dein Hemd aus dem Rock/der Hose (heraus)ziehen IV
unusual [ʌn'ju:ʒʊəl] ungewöhnlich III
unwanted [ʌn'wɒntɪd] unerwünscht V
unwelcome [ʌn'welkəm] unerwünscht, unwillkommen II
unwell [ʌn'wel] unwohl, krank III
up [ʌp] hinauf, hoch II **be up for sth.** *(infml)* bei etwas dabei sein, mitmachen V
up to ['ʌp tə] bis (zu) V
upside ['ʌpsaɪd] Vorteil, gute Seite III
upside down [ʌpsaɪd 'daʊn] verkehrt herum, auf dem/den Kopf V
upstairs [ʌp'steəz] (nach) oben *(die Treppe hoch)* I
uptown [ʌp'taʊn] *(AE)* außerhalb des (Stadt-)Zentrums, am Stadtrand IV
us [ʌs], [əs] uns I
use [ju:z] benutzen, verwenden I
use [ju:s] Gebrauch, Verwendung VI 3 (56) **make use of** Gebrauch machen von, nutzen VI 3 (56)
used to [ju:st]:
1. **be used to** gewöhnt sein an IV **get used to** sich gewöhnen an IV
2. **where he used to play** wo er früher (immer) gespielt hat IV
useful ['ju:sfl] nützlich, hilfreich II
user ['ju:zə] (Be-)Nutzer/in V
usual ['ju:ʒʊəl] üblich, gewöhnlich III
usually ['ju:ʒuəli] normalerweise, meistens I

V

vacation [və'keɪʃn] *(AE)* Urlaub IV
vacuum cleaner ['vækjuəm kli:nə] Staubsauger V
vain [veɪn] eitel V
valid ['vælɪd] aktuell, gültig V
valley ['væli] Tal IV
value ['vælju:] Wert I **It's good value.** Es ist sein Geld wert. / Es ist preiswert. I
vamping ['væmpɪŋ] *spät in der Nacht noch aktiv sein* V
vampire ['væmpaɪə] Vampir V
van [væn] Transporter, Lieferwagen III
vegetables, *infml auch* **veg** ['vedʒtəblz], [vedʒ] Gemüse I
°**vegetarian** [vedʒə'teəriən] vegetarisch; Vegetarier/in
vegetation [vedʒə'teɪʃn] Vegetation VI 1 (10)
vehicle ['vi:əkl] Fahrzeug V
°**vérité** [verɪ'teɪ]: **(cinema) vérité** Cinéma vérité *(bestimmte Technik des Dokumentarfilmens)*
°**verse** [vɜ:s] Vers, Strophe *(Lied)*
°**version** ['vɜ:ʃn] Version
very ['veri] sehr I **Thanks very much.** Vielen Dank. II
victim ['vɪktɪm] Opfer V
video ['vɪdiəʊ] Video II
video chat ['vɪdiəʊ tʃæt] Videochat *(Telefongespräch per Videokonferenz)* II
video-chat ['vɪdiəʊ tʃæt] sich per Videokonferenz unterhalten V
view [vju:] (An-)Blick, (Aus-)Sicht II **in my/your/... view** meiner/deiner/... Ansicht nach VI 2 (38) **point of view** Standpunkt III
°**viewer** ['vju:ə] Zuschauer/in
village ['vɪlɪdʒ] Dorf I
vinegar ['vɪnɪgə] Essig III
violence ['vaɪələns] Gewalt; Gewalttätigkeit IV
violent ['vaɪələnt] gewalttätig; gewaltsam III
virtual ['vɜ:tʃʊəl] virtuell V
virus, *pl* **viruses** ['vaɪrəs], ['vaɪrəsɪz] Virus V
visa ['vi:zə] Visum IV
vision ['vɪʒn] Vision; Vorstellung VI 3 (56)
visit ['vɪzɪt] besuchen I
visitor ['vɪzɪtə] Besucher/in; Gast I
visitor pass ['vɪzɪtə pɑ:s] Besucherausweis IV
visual ['vɪʒuəl] optisch, Seh- IV
visually impaired [vɪʒuəli ɪm'peəd] sehbehindert IV
visuals *(pl)* *(kurz für:* **visual materials**) ['vɪʒuəlz] visuelle Materialien/Hilfsmittel V
°**vital** ['vaɪtl] wichtig, wesentlich, unerlässlich
vitamin ['vɪtəmɪn] Vitamin II
vocabulary [və'kæbjələri] Wortschatz, Vokabular; Vokabelverzeichnis VI 3 (58)
voice [vɔɪs] Stimme II
°**voice-over** ['vɔɪs əʊvə] Filmkommentar, Off-Stimme
volleyball ['vɒlibɔ:l] Volleyball II
volunteer [vɒlən'tɪə]:
1. freiwillig/ehrenamtlich arbeiten *(unbezahlt)* IV
2. Freiwillige/r, Ehrenamtliche/r IV **volunteer work** freiwillige/ehrenamtliche Arbeit IV
volunteering [vɒlən'tɪərɪŋ] Freiwilligentätigkeit, ehrenamtliches Arbeiten IV
vote [vəʊt]:
1. abstimmen V
2. wählen, zur Wahl gehen VI 2 (38) **vote for sb.** für jn. stimmen II °**register to vote** sich in die Wählerlisten eintragen lassen
voyage ['vɔɪɪdʒ] (See-)Reise IV

W

wage, *oft auch:* **wages** *(pl)* [weɪdʒ] Lohn, Gehalt VI 2 (47) **°minimum wage** Mindestlohn
wagon ['wæɡən] Planwagen, (Pferde-) Fuhrwerk IV
waistcoat ['weɪskəʊt] Weste V
wait (for) [weɪt] warten (auf) I **wait and see** abwarten I **you can't wait** du kannst es kaum erwarten III
waiter ['weɪtə] Kellner III
waitress ['weɪtrəs] Kellnerin III
wake [weɪk], **woke, woken** wecken I **wake up** aufwachen I
walk [wɔːk]:
1. wandern, (zu Fuß) gehen I **walk around** umhergehen II **walk sb. home** jn. zu Fuß nach Hause begleiten V
2. Spaziergang II **go for a walk** einen Spaziergang machen, spazieren gehen II
walker ['wɔːkə] Wanderer/Wanderin, Spaziergänger/in III
walking boots *(pl)* ['wɔːkɪŋ buːts] Wanderstiefel II
°walkway ['wɔːkweɪ] Fußweg, Laufgang
wall [wɔːl] Wand, Mauer III
want [wɒnt] wollen I **want sb. to do sth.** wollen, dass jd. etwas tut III **want to be** *(etwas)* sein wollen I
war [wɔː] Krieg IV
wardrobe ['wɔːdrəʊb] Kleiderschrank I
warm [wɔːm] warm II
warn sb. (about/against/of sth.) [wɔːn] jn. warnen (vor etwas) V
warning (of/against) ['wɔːnɪŋ] Warnung (vor) IV
was [wɒz], [wəz]: **I/he/she/it was** *siehe* **be**
wash [wɒʃ] waschen; sauber machen II **wash up** abwaschen I
washing machine ['wɒʃɪŋ məʃiːn] Waschmaschine V
waste [weɪst]:
1. Verschwendung V
°2. Müll, Abfall
°waste management ['weɪst mænɪdʒmənt] Abfallwirtschaft
watch [wɒtʃ] Armbanduhr VI 3 (58)
watch sth. [wɒtʃ] sich etwas anschauen; etwas beobachten I **watch for** Ausschau halten nach III **watch sb. do sth.** (zu)sehen, wie jemand etwas tut II **watch TV** fernsehen I
water ['wɔːtə]:
1. Wasser I
°2. gießen, (be)wässern
°waterless ['wɔːtələs] wasserlos, ohne Wasser
waterproof ['wɔːtəpruːf] wasserdicht, wasserfest, wasserundurchlässig V
wave [weɪv] Welle IV
wave (to sb.) [weɪv] (jm. zu)winken I
way [weɪ]:
1. Weg I
ask sb. the way jn. nach dem Weg fragen II **on the way to ...** auf dem Weg zu/nach ... I **one-way ticket** einfache Fahrkarte VI 3 (62) **tell sb. the way** jm. den Weg beschreiben II **°a long way (from)** weit (entfernt) (von)
2. Art und Weise II
way of life Lebensweise V **by the way** übrigens V **in some ways** in mancher Hinsicht IV **It's the way you do it.** So macht man das. VI 3 (66) **No way!** Auf keinen Fall! III **the way you live** deine Lebensweise (die Art, wie du lebst) II
3. Richtung VI 2 (43)
come sb.'s way auf jn. zu kommen VI 2 (43) **the wrong way** (in) die falsche Richtung VI 2 (43) **this way** hier entlang/in diese Richtung VI 2 (43)
4. **way cooler** *(infml)* viel cooler, weit(aus) cooler IV
we [wi], [wiː] wir I
weak [wiːk] schwach III
weakness ['wiːknəs] Schwäche V
weapon ['wepən] Waffe V
wear [weə], **wore, worn** tragen, anhaben *(Kleidung)* II
wearable ['weərəbl] tragbar *(Kleidung)* VI 3 (58)
weather ['weðə] Wetter II
weather forecast ['fɔːkɑːst] Wettervorhersage II
website ['websaɪt] Website II
wedding ['wedɪŋ] Hochzeit IV **wedding present** Hochzeitsgeschenk IV
Wednesday ['wenzdeɪ], ['wenzdi] Mittwoch I
°wee [wiː] *(infml, Kindersprache)* Pipi machen
weed [wiːd] (Un-)Kraut V
week [wiːk] Woche I
weekday ['wiːkdeɪ] Werktag, Wochentag III
weekend [wiːk'end] Wochenende I **at the weekend** am Wochenende I
weeper ['wiːpə]: **Finders keepers, losers weepers.** Was man findet, darf man behalten. *(Redensart)* V
weigh [weɪ] wiegen V
weight [weɪt] Gewicht V **lose weight** abnehmen *(Gewicht)*, dünner werden V
weird [wɪəd] seltsam, komisch III
welcome ['welkəm]:
1. **welcome sb. (to)** jn. begrüßen (in), jn. willkommen heißen (in) III **Welcome to Plymouth.** Willkommen in Plymouth. I
2. **You're welcome.** Bitte, gern geschehen. / Nichts zu danken. I
°welfare ['welfeə] Wohl, Wohlergehen
Well, ... [wel] Nun, ... / Also, ... / Na ja, ... I
well [wel]: **Well done.** Gut gemacht! I **as well** auch VI 1 (22) **do well** es gut machen; gut abschneiden, erfolgreich sein VI 1 (14) **I hope you are well.** Ich hoffe, es geht euch gut. / Ich hoffe, ihr seid gesund/wohlauf. IV **I'm not feeling well.** Ich fühle mich nicht gut. II **it doesn't pay very well** es wird nicht besonders gut bezahlt IV **work/speak well** gut funktionieren/sprechen I
°well heeled [wel 'hiːld] *(infml)* gut betucht, wohlhabend
well-built [wel 'bɪlt] gut gebaut, kräftig IV
well-known [wel 'nəʊn] bekannt V
went [went] *siehe* **go**
were [wɜː], [wə]: **we/you/they were** *siehe* **be** **°If he were to ...** Wenn/Falls er ...
west [west] Westen; nach Westen II
westbound ['westbaʊnd] in Richtung Westen III
western ['westən] westlich, West- IV
wet [wet] nass I
whale [weɪl] Wal IV
what [wɒt]:
1. was I
2. welche(r, s) I
What about you? Und du? / Was ist mit dir? I **What are ...?** Was sind ...? I **What is it?** Was ist los? I **What page is it?** Auf welcher Seite sind wir? / Auf welcher Seite steht das? I **What's the time?** Wie spät ist es? I **What's your name?** Wie heißt du? I
Whatever. [wɒt'evə] *(infml)* Ach, egal. / Was soll's. IV
wheel [wiːl] Rad I **°wheels** *(pl, infml)* fahrbarer Untersatz, Auto
wheelchair ['wiːltʃeə] Rollstuhl I
when [wen]:
1. als II
2. wann I
When's your birthday? Wann hast du Geburtstag? I
3. wenn I
where [weə] wo; wohin I **Where are you from?** Wo kommst du her? I
°wherever [weər'evə] wo(hin) (auch) immer; überall, wo(hin)
°whether ['weðə] ob
which [wɪtʃ]:
1. **Which club?** Welcher Klub? II
2. der, die, das; die *(Relativpronomen)* V
while [waɪl]:
1. Weile IV
2. während IV
whisper ['wɪspə]:
1. flüstern II
2. Flüstern VI 2 (38)
whistle ['wɪsl] (Triller-)Pfeife II
white [waɪt] weiß I

°**whizz (by)** [wɪz] (vorbei)sausen, (vorbei)zischen
who [huː]:
1. wer I
Who are you? Wer bist du? / Wer seid ihr? I
2. wen; wem II
Who did Adam meet? Wen hat Adam getroffen? / Wen traf Adam? II
3. der, die *(Relativpronomen, Person)* I
a person who … eine Person, die … I
whole [həʊl] ganze(r, s) II
whom [huːm]:
1. wem; wen *(Fragewort)* VI 3 (65)
… whom you could trust. *(fml)* …, wem man trauen konnte. VI 3 (65)
2. den/dem/die/denen *(Relativpronomen)* VI 3 (65)
whose [huːz]:
1. wessen V
Whose are these? Wem gehören die (hier)? V
°2. dessen, deren *(Relativpronomen)*
why [waɪ] warum I **that's why** deshalb, darum II
wide [waɪd] breit, weit V
wife, *pl* **wives** [waɪf], [waɪvz] (Ehe-)Frau IV
Wi-fi ['waɪ faɪ] WLAN, kabellose Datenübertragung III
wild [waɪld] wild I
wildlife ['waɪldlaɪf] Tiere *(in freier Wildbahn)*, Tierwelt VI 1 (10)
will [wɪl]: **it won't rain (= it will not rain)** es wird nicht regnen II **the weather will be good** das Wetter wird gut sein II **We'll (= we will) find him.** Wir werden ihn finden. II
win [wɪn], **won, won** gewinnen I
wind [wɪnd] Wind II
winding ['waɪndɪŋ] kurvenreich III
window ['wɪndəʊ] Fenster I
windscreen ['wɪndskriːn] Windschutzscheibe *(Auto)* III
windscreen wipers *(pl)* ['wɪndskriːn waɪpəz] Scheibenwischer III
windy ['wɪndi] windig II
winner ['wɪnə] Gewinner/in II
winter ['wɪntə] Winter II
wireless ['waɪələs] drahtlos, Funk- VI 3 (57)
wish [wɪʃ] wünschen IV **I wish I could tell you …** Ich wünschte, ich könnte dir erzählen, … IV
wishes ['wɪʃɪz]: **Best wishes** Viele Grüße … *(Briefschluss)* I
witch [wɪtʃ] Hexe II
with [wɪð] mit I **with Ellie** bei Ellie I
within [wɪ'ðɪn] innerhalb (von), in VI 3 (69)
without [wɪ'ðaʊt] ohne II
woke [wəʊk] *siehe* **wake**
woken ['wəʊkən] *siehe* **wake**
woman, *pl* **women** ['wʊmən], ['wɪmɪn] Frau I
won [wʌn] *siehe* **win**
wonder ['wʌndə] sich fragen; gern wissen wollen III
wonderful ['wʌndəfl] wunderbar III
won't [wəʊnt]: **it won't rain (= it will not rain)** es wird nicht regnen II
wood [wʊd] Holz; Wald III
wooden ['wʊdn] hölzern, Holz- IV
woodwork(ing) ['wʊdwɜːk] Holzbearbeitung IV **woodworking tools** *(pl)* Holzbearbeitungswerkzeuge IV
word [wɜːd] Wort I **word building** das Bilden von Wörtern II
°**wordbank** ['wɜːdbæŋk] *Sammlung von Wörtern zu einem Thema*
wore [wɔː] *siehe* **wear**
work [wɜːk]:
1. Arbeit I
at work bei der Arbeit, am Arbeitsplatz I
2. arbeiten; funktionieren I
work on sth. arbeiten an etwas V
work sth. out etwas herausfinden, etwas herausarbeiten IV
work experience ['wɜːk ɪkspɪəriəns] Praktikum/Praktika; Arbeitserfahrung(en) V
workday ['wɜːkdeɪ] Arbeitstag I
worker ['wɜːkə] Arbeiter/in III
working hours *(pl)* [wɜːkɪŋ 'aʊəz] Arbeitszeit(en) V
world [wɜːld] Welt I **the best of both worlds** das Beste von beidem I
°**worldly** ['wɜːldli] welterfahren, weltgewandt
worldwide ['wɜːldwaɪd] weltweit VI 1 (11)
worn [wɔːn] *siehe* **wear**
worried (about) ['wʌrid] beunruhigt, besorgt (wegen) I
worry (about) ['wʌri] sich Sorgen machen (wegen, um) I **Don't worry.** Mach dir keine Sorgen. I
worse [wɜːs] schlechter, schlimmer II
worst [wɜːst] der/die/das schlechteste, schlimmste; am schlechtesten, am schlimmsten II
worth [wɜːθ] wert IV **The film is worth watching.** Es lohnt sich, den Film anzuschauen. IV
would [wʊd]: **I'd (= I would) like …** Ich hätte gern … / Ich möchte … I **I'd (= I would) love to come.** Ich komme sehr gern. / Ich würde sehr gern kommen. I **they would sit …** sie saßen (früher) immer … VI 3 (66)
would-be ['wʊd biː] künftige(r, s), angehende(r, s); Möchtegern- VI 3 (62)
wrestling ['reslɪŋ] Ringen IV
write [raɪt], **wrote, written** schreiben I
write sth. down etwas aufschreiben III
writer ['raɪtə] Autor/in, Verfasser/in III
written ['rɪtn] *siehe* **write**
wrong [rɒŋ] falsch I **be wrong** Unrecht haben I **go wrong** schiefgehen VI 3 (62) **prove sb. wrong** beweisen, dass jd. Unrecht hat VI 2 (48)
wrote [rəʊt] *siehe* **write**

Y

yard [jɑːd]:
1. Gelände III
2. *(AE)* Garten IV
3. Hof *(Innenhof)* III
school yard Schulhof II
yeah [jeə] *(infml)* ja I
year [jɪə] Jahr(gang) I **a 16-year-old** ein/e Sechzehnjährige/r III
yellow ['jeləʊ] gelb I
yes [jes] ja I
yesterday ['jestədeɪ] gestern II
yet [jet]: **… yet?** … schon …? IV
not … yet noch nicht II
Yippee! [jɪ'piː] Hurra! I
you [ju], [juː]:
1. du; dich; dir; ihr; euch; Sie; Ihnen I
2. man VI 3 (66)
young [jʌŋ] jung I
your [jɔː], [jə] dein/e; euer/eure; Ihr/e I
yours [jɔːz] deine, deiner, deins I
yourself [jɔː'self], [jə'self] du/dir/dich selbst I **See for yourself.** Sieh selbst! / Sehen Sie selbst! V
yourselves [jɔː'selvz], [jə'selvz] ihr/euch selbst III
youth [juːθ] Jugend, Jugend- III
Yuck! [jʌk] Igitt! III
yum [jʌm] *(infml)* lecker I
yummy ['jʌmi] *(infml)* lecker II

Z

zip up sth. [zɪp 'ʌp] den Reißverschluss von etwas zumachen IV
zip wire ['zɪp waɪə] Seilrutsche I
zone [zəʊn] Zone III
zoo [zuː] Zoo I

How to start	Wie man beginnt
I want to tell you about ...	Ich möchte euch/Ihnen etwas über ... erzählen.
I'm going to talk about ...	Ich werde über ... sprechen.
In this talk, I'm going to look at ...	In diesem Vortrag werde ich mich mit ... befassen.
My presentation is about ...	Mein Referat ist über ...
How to link ideas	**Wie man Gedanken verbindet**
Firstly .../Secondly .../Thirdly ...	Erstens .../Zweitens .../Drittens ...
Next ...	Als Nächstes ...
In addition ...	Außerdem/Zusätzlich ...
So ...	Also/Daher ...
For example ...	Zum Beispiel ...
How to explain things	**Wie man Dinge erklärt**
Look at the screen/transparency, please.	Schaut bitte auf den Bildschirm/die Folie.
This picture/photo shows ...	Dieses Bild/Foto zeigt ...
Look, here it is on the map.	Schaut, hier ist es auf der Karte.
It's on the board.	Es steht an der Tafel.
The word ... means ...	Das Wort ... bedeutet ...
I picked this because ...	Ich habe mich dafür entschieden, weil ...
I learned/found out that ...	Ich habe herausgefunden, dass ...
Did you know that ...	Wusstet ihr, dass ...
When you're stuck	**Wenn man nicht weiter weiß**
Just a minute.	Einen Augenblick.
What's the word?	Wie heißt das Wort?
What I'm trying to say is ...	Was ich versuche zu sagen, ist ...
It's something like ...	Es ist so etwas Ähnliches wie ...
Sorry, I mean ...	Entschuldigung, ich meine ...
How to end	**Wie man zum Schluss kommt**
So on the whole I'd say ...	Im Großen und Ganzen würde ich sagen, ...
So to finish I'd like to say ...	Zum Abschluss möchte ich sagen, ...
That's the end of my talk.	Das ist das Ende meines Referats.
Thank you for listening.	Danke fürs Zuhören.
I hope you enjoyed my talk.	Ich hoffe, mein Referat hat euch/Ihnen gefallen.
Do you have any questions?	Habt ihr/Haben Sie irgendwelche Fragen?
Giving feedback	**Wie man Feedback gibt**
I think your talk had a clear structure.	Ich denke, dein Vortrag war gut aufgebaut.
You explained unknown words.	Du hast unbekannte Wörter erklärt.
You spoke slowly and clearly.	Du hast langsam und deutlich gesprochen.
You looked at the class.	Du hast die Klasse angeschaut.
You didn't just read from your notes.	Du hast nicht nur von deinen Notizen abgelesen.
Your pictures were very helpful.	Deine Bilder waren sehr hilfreich.

IRREGULAR VERBS

infinitive	simple past	past participle	
be	*I/he/she/it* **was**; *you/we/you/they* **were**	**been**	sein
beat	**beat**	**beaten**	schlagen, besiegen
become	**became**	**become**	werden
begin	**began**	**begun**	beginnen, anfangen
bite [aɪ]	**bit** [ɪ]	**bitten** [ɪ]	beißen
bleed	**bled**	**bled**	bluten
blow	**blew**	**blown**	blasen (in); wehen *(Wind)*
break	**broke**	**broken**	brechen; zerbrechen
bring	**brought**	**brought**	bringen, mitbringen
build	**built**	**built**	bauen
buy	**bought**	**bought**	kaufen
catch	**caught**	**caught**	fangen, erwischen
choose [uː]	**chose** [əʊ]	**chosen** [əʊ]	(sich) aussuchen, (aus)wählen
come	**came**	**come**	kommen
cost	**cost**	**cost**	kosten
creep up (on)	**crept**	**crept**	sich heranschleichen (an)
cut	**cut**	**cut**	schneiden; *(Rasen)* mähen
deal with	**dealt** [e]	**dealt** [e]	umgehen mit, fertigwerden/klarkommen mit
dig	**dug**	**dug**	graben
do	**did**	**done** [ʌ]	tun, machen
draw	**drew**	**drawn**	zeichnen; ziehen
drink	**drank**	**drunk**	trinken
drive [aɪ]	**drove**	**driven** [ɪ]	*(mit dem Auto)* fahren; (an)treiben
eat	**ate** [et, eɪt]	**eaten**	essen
fall	**fell**	**fallen**	fallen, hinfallen
feed	**fed**	**fed**	füttern
feel	**felt**	**felt**	fühlen; sich fühlen
fight	**fought**	**fought**	kämpfen; bekämpfen
find	**found**	**found**	finden
fly	**flew**	**flown**	fliegen
forget	**forgot**	**forgotten**	vergessen
freeze	**froze** [əʊ]	**frozen** [əʊ]	(ge)frieren; erstarren
get	**got**	**got**	bekommen; holen, besorgen; werden; gelangen, (hin)kommen
give	**gave**	**given**	geben
go	**went**	**gone** [ɒ]	gehen
grow	**grew**	**grown**	wachsen; anbauen, anpflanzen; (allmählich) werden
hang	**hung**	**hung**	hängen
have	**had**	**had**	haben
hear [ɪə]	**heard** [ɜː]	**heard** [ɜː]	hören
hide [aɪ]	**hid** [ɪ]	**hidden** [ɪ]	verstecken; sich verstecken
hit	**hit**	**hit**	schlagen; treffen; prallen/stoßen gegen/auf
hold	**held**	**held**	halten
hurt	**hurt**	**hurt**	verletzen; wehtun
keep	**kept**	**kept**	behalten; halten; aufbewahren
know [nəʊ]	**knew** [njuː]	**known** [nəʊn]	wissen; kennen
lay	**laid**	**laid**	legen
lead	**led**	**led**	führen, leiten
leave	**left**	**left**	abfahren; (weg)gehen; verlassen; zurücklassen

infinitive	simple past	past participle	
lend sb. sth.	**lent**	**lent**	jm. etwas leihen
let	**let**	**let**	lassen
lie [aɪ]	**lay**	**lain**	liegen
light	**lit**	**lit**	anzünden
lose [uː]	**lost** [ɒ]	**lost** [ɒ]	verlieren
make	**made**	**made**	machen
mean [iː]	**meant** [e]	**meant** [e]	bedeuten; meinen, sagen wollen
meet	**met**	**met**	treffen; sich treffen; kennenlernen
overspend (on)	**overspent**	**overspent**	zu viel Geld ausgeben (für)
overtake	**overtook**	**overtaken**	überholen
pay	**paid**	**paid**	bezahlen
put	**put**	**put**	*(etwas wohin)* tun, legen, stellen
read [iː]	**read** [e]	**read** [e]	lesen
retell	**retold**	**retold**	nacherzählen
ride [aɪ]	**rode**	**ridden** [ɪ]	reiten; *(Rad)* fahren
ring	**rang**	**rung**	läuten, klingeln; anrufen
run	**ran**	**run**	rennen, laufen
say [eɪ]	**said** [e]	**said** [e]	sagen
see	**saw**	**seen**	sehen
sell	**sold**	**sold**	verkaufen
send	**sent**	**sent**	schicken, senden
set the table	**set**	**set**	den Tisch decken
shake	**shook**	**shaken** [eɪ]	schütteln
shine	**shone** [ɒ]	**shone** [ɒ]	scheinen *(Sonne)*
show	**showed**	**shown**	zeigen
shut up	**shut**	**shut**	den Mund halten
sing	**sang**	**sung**	singen
sink	**sank**	**sunk**	sinken
sit	**sat**	**sat**	sitzen
sleep	**slept**	**slept**	schlafen
speak	**spoke**	**spoken**	sprechen
speed	**sped**	**sped**	rasen, zu schnell fahren
spend	**spent**	**spent**	ausgeben *(Geld)*; verbringen *(Zeit)*
spread	**spread**	**spread**	verbreiten *(z.B. Krankheit)*
stand	**stood**	**stood**	stehen; sich (hin)stellen
steal	**stole**	**stolen**	stehlen
stick	**stuck**	**stuck**	(haften) bleiben
sting	**stung**	**stung**	stechen *(Insekt)*; brennen
stink	**stank**	**stunk**	stinken
swim	**swam**	**swum**	schwimmen
take	**took**	**taken**	nehmen; mitnehmen; (weg-, hin)bringen; dauern, *(Zeit)* brauchen
teach	**taught**	**taught**	unterrichten, lehren
tell	**told**	**told**	erzählen, berichten
think	**thought**	**thought**	denken
throw	**threw**	**thrown**	werfen
understand	**understood**	**understood**	verstehen
wake	**woke**	**woken**	wecken
wear [eə]	**wore** [ɔː]	**worn** [ɔː]	tragen, anhaben *(Kleidung)*
win	**won** [ʌ]	**won** [ʌ]	gewinnen
write	**wrote**	**written**	schreiben

First names (Vornamen)

Akhia [æ'kiə]
Alex ['ælɪks]
Alice ['ælɪs]
Allan ['ælən]
Alma ['ælmə]
Amar [ə'mɑː]
Amy ['eɪmi]
Andre ['ɒndreɪ]
Andrew ['ændruː]
Anita [ə'niːtə]
Apache [ə'pætʃi]
Asandiswa [ʌ'sʌndɪswʌ]
Avril ['ævrɪl]
Bafana [bə'fɑːnə]
Barack [bə'ræk]
Benjamin ['bendʒəmɪn]
Beth [beθ]
Brode ['brəʊdə]
Bryan ['braɪən]
Buyi ['buːɪ]
Buyisiwe [bʊjɪ'siːwə]
Cathy ['kæθi]
Chris [krɪs]
Cooper ['kuːpə]
Dan [dæn]
Daniel ['dænjəl]
Danny ['dæni]
David ['deɪvɪd]
Ea [iː]
Elizabeth [i'lɪzəbəθ]
Emma ['emə]
Fanie ['fʌni]
Gary ['gæri]
Hannah ['hænə]
Iris ['aɪrɪs]
Jake [dʒeɪk]
James [dʒeɪmz]
Jamilia [dʒə'mɪliə]
Janine [dʒə'niːn]
Jeff [dʒef]
John [dʒɒn]
Johnny ['dʒɒni]
Jon [dʒɒn]
Jonathan ['dʒɒnəθən]
Julia ['dʒuːliə]
Kate [keɪt]
Katy ['keɪti]
Leitah ['laɪtə]
Lindokuhle [lɪndəʊ'kuːlə]
Louis ['luːi]
Lucy ['luːsi]
Luke [luːk]
Lukie ['luːki]
Lwazi [lə'wɑːzi]
Lyca ['laɪkə]
Marcus ['mɑːkəs]
Marsha ['mɑːʃə]
Martin ['mɑːtɪn]
Matthew ['mæθjuː]
Maya ['maɪə]
Meg [meg]
Murray ['mʌri]
Naomi ['neɪəmi], [neɪ'əʊmi]
Natalie ['nætəli]
Natasha [nə'tæʃə]
Nate [neɪt]
Nazma [nʌz'mɑː]
Nelson ['nelsn]
Paula [pɔːlə]
Pete [piːt]
Peter ['piːtə]
Pule [pjuːl]
Ravi ['rʌvi]
Richart ['rɪtʃət]
Rory ['rɔːri]
Sarah ['seərə]
Serena [se'riːnə]
Shane [ʃɑːn], [ʃeɪn]
Sharon ['ʃærən]
Shiva ['ʃiːvə]
Sienna [si'enə]
Simon ['saɪmən]
Simoshile [sɪ'məʊʃɪleɪ]
Siseko [si'seɪkəʊ]
Tahiat ['tɑːhiət]
Tariq ['tærɪk]
Tess [tes]
Vanessa [və'nesə]
Vince [vins]
Vincent ['vɪnsnt]
Vulu ['vuːluː]
Winnie ['wɪni]
Zoe ['zəʊi]
Zola ['zəʊlə]

Family names / Surnames (Familiennamen)

Begum ['beɪgəm]
Bluhm [bluːm]
Bond [bɒnd]
Budd [bʌd]
Callebaut ['kʌləbaʊt]
Connolly ['kɒnəli]
Cox [kɒks]
De Klerk [də 'kleək]
Donald ['dɒnld]
Fletcher ['fletʃə]
Gunther ['gʌntə]
Habana [hə'bɑːnə]
Heyns [heɪnz]
Hinton ['hɪntən]
Ingram ['ɪŋgrəm]
Mahboob [mə'buːb]
Mandela [mæn'delə]
Mosley ['məʊzli]
Ntsoelengoe [ntsəʊ'leng]
O'Ferrall [əʊ'ferəl]
Obama [əʊ'bæmə]
Radcliffe ['rædklɪf]
Sedgwick ['sedʒwɪk]
Smith [smɪθ]
Sowa ['səʊə]
Tambo ['tæmbəʊ]
Thun [tuːn]
Turk [tɜːk]
Viljoen [fi'jɜːn]
Wenger ['veŋə]
Williams ['wɪljəmz]
Wills [wɪlz]
Zephaniah [zefə'naɪə]

Place names (Ortsnamen)

Alabama [ælə'bæmə]
Amazon ['æməzən]
Balule [bel'juːl]
Birmingham ['bɜːmɪŋəm]
Brussels ['brʌslz]
Cambridge ['keɪmbrɪdʒ]
Camden ['kæmdən]
Cape Town ['keɪp taʊn]
Capilano River [kæpɪlɑːnəʊ 'rɪvə]
Heathrow ['hiːθrəʊ]
Huntsville ['hʌntsvɪl]
Jamshedpur [dʒɑːm'ʃedpə]
Jersey ['dʒɜːzi]
Johannesburg [dʒəʊ'hænəzbɜːg]
Joyxee Island [dʒɔɪgsiː 'aɪlənd]
Khayelitsha [kaɪə'liːtʃə]
Kruger National Park [kruːgə næʃnəl 'pɑːk]
Maine [meɪn]
Melbourne ['melbən], ['melbɔːn]
Mvezo [m'vezɒ]
Norwich ['nɒrɪdʒ]
Rana Plaza [rænə 'plɑːzə]
Robben Island [rɒbən 'aɪlənd]
San Francisco [sæn frən'sɪskəʊ]
Sharpeville ['ʃɑːpvɪl]
Stansted ['stænsted]
Sydney ['sɪdni]
Transvaal [trænz'vɑːl]
Vancouver [væn'kuːvə]
Washington ['wɒʃɪŋtən]
Waterberg Mountain ['wɔːtəbɜːg maʊntən]
Waterworld ['wɔːtəwɜːld]
Westphalia [west'feɪliə]

Other names (Andere Namen)
Afrikaans [æfrɪ'kɑːns]
Blue Moon Hostel [bluː 'muːn hɒstl]
Brexit ['breksɪt]
Chatwin ['tʃætwɪn]
Floodland ['flʌdlənd]
Fly-Hi [flaɪ 'haɪ]
Ford [fɔːd]
isiNdebele [ɪsin'debələ]
isiXhosa [ɪsi'kɔːsə]
isiZulu [ɪsi'zuːluː]
Lilypad ['lɪlipæd]
Mandarin ['mændərɪn]
NASA ['næsə]
Ndebele [n'debələ]
Ngiyabonga [nəgiə'bɒŋgaː]
Nobel Peace Prize [nəʊbel 'piːs praɪz]
ROBOTECH ['rəʊbəʊtek]
Sawubona [saʊ'bəʊnə]
Sepedi [sə'pedi]
Sesotho [sɪ'suːtuː]
Setswana [sət'swɑːnə]
siSwati [si'swɑːti]
Springboks ['sprɪŋbɒk]
Tshivenda [tʃiː'vendə]
UNICEF ['juːnɪsef]
Xitsonga [ʃi'tsɒŋgʌ]
Zulu ['zuːluː]

ENGLISH SOUNDS AND ALPHABET

English sounds

[iː]	**green**, **he**, **sea**
[ɑː]	**ask**, **class**, **car**, **park**
[ɔː]	**or**, **ball**, **door**, **four**, **morning**
[uː]	**ruler**, **blue**, **too**, **two**, **you**
[ɜː]	**early**, **her**, **girl**, **work**, **T-shirt**
[ɪ]	**in**, **big**, **expensive**
[e]	**yes**, **bed**, **again**, **breakfast**
[æ]	**animal**, **apple**, **black**, **cat**
[ʌ]	**mum**, **bus**, **colour**
[ɒ]	**song**, **on**, **dog**, **what**
[ʊ]	**book**, **good**, **pullover**
[ə]	**again**, **today**, **a sister**
[i]	**happy**, **monkey**
[eɪ]	**name**, **eight**, **play**, **great**
[aɪ]	**I**, **time**, **right**, **my**
[ɔɪ]	**boy**, **toilet**, **noise**
[əʊ]	**old**, **no**, **road**, **yellow**
[aʊ]	**now**, **house**
[eə]	**where**, **pair**, **share**, **their**
[ɪə]	**here**, **dear**
[ʊə]	**tour**
[b]	**bike**, **table**, **verb**
[p]	**pen**, **paper**, **shop**
[d]	**day**, **window**, **good**
[t]	**ten**, **letter**, **at**
[g]	**go**, **again**, **bag**
[k]	**kitchen**, **car**, **back**
[m]	**man**, **remember**, **mum**
[n]	**no**, **one**, **ten**
[ŋ]	**wrong**, **young**, **uncle**, **thanks**
[l]	**like**, **old**, **small**
[r]	**ruler**, **friend**, **sorry**
[w]	**we**, **where**, **one**
[j]	**yes**, **you**, **uniform**
[f]	**family**, **after**, **laugh**
[v]	**very**, **seven**, **have**
[s]	**six**, **poster**, **yes**
[z]	**zoo**, **quiz**, **his**, **music**, **please**
[ʃ]	**she**, **station**, **English**
[ʒ]	**usually**, **revision**, **garage**
[tʃ]	**child**, **teacher**, **watch**
[dʒ]	**job**, **German**, **project**, **orange**
[θ]	**thing**, **three**, **bathroom**, **both**
[ð]	**the**, **father**, **with**
[h]	**house**, **who**, **behind**
[x]	*ach*, *doch*

The English alphabet

a [eɪ]	**e** [iː]	**i** [aɪ]	**m** [em]	**q** [kjuː]	**u** [juː]	**y** [waɪ]
b [biː]	**f** [ef]	**j** [dʒeɪ]	**n** [en]	**r** [ɑː]	**v** [viː]	**z** [zed]
c [siː]	**g** [dʒiː]	**k** [keɪ]	**o** [əʊ]	**s** [es]	**w** ['dʌbljuː]	
d [diː]	**h** [eɪtʃ]	**l** [el]	**p** [piː]	**t** [tiː]	**x** [eks]	

General	Allgemein
Read the tasks carefully.	Lies die Aufgaben sorgfältig.
You now have 60 seconds to read the tasks.	Du hast ab jetzt 60 Sekunden zum Lesen der Aufgaben.
Now do the tasks.	Nun bearbeite die Aufgaben.
Tick the correct box / the correct boxes.	Setze ein Häkchen (✓) in das / die richtige(n) Kästchen.
Tick the right statements. (There's only one possible answer per statement.)	Setze ein ✓ bei den korrekten Aussagen. (Pro Aussage ist nur eine Antwort möglich.)
Complete the sentences (with not more than three words per gap / … than two words each).	Vervollständige die Sätze (mit bis zu drei Wörtern pro Lücke / mit je bis zu zwei Wörtern).
Fill in the information / the missing words.	Füge die Information / die fehlenden Wörter ein.
Fill in suitable words / the correct numbers.	Füge passende Wörter / die korrekten Zahlen ein.
Fill in only one detail per box.	Füge nur ein Detail pro Kästchen ein.
Complete these sentences.	Vervollständige diese Sätze.
There is only one possible answer.	Es gibt nur eine mögliche Antwort.
There are two more words than you need.	Es gibt zwei Wörter mehr als du benötigst.
Choose the correct options and fill in the blanks.	Wähle die korrekten Varianten und fülle die Lücken aus.
Mark *true* or *false*.	Markiere (z.B. mit einem ✗) *wahr* oder *falsch*.
There is an example at the beginning.	Am Anfang steht ein Beispiel.
You have a choice here. Choose one of the following tasks: …	Hier hast du die Wahl. Wähle eine der folgenden Aufgaben aus: …

Listening	Hörverstehen
You are going to hear a story / an interview about …	Du wirst eine Geschichte / ein Interview über … hören.
Listen to the interview.	Höre dir das Interview an.
Listen to these people talking about … Who thinks what? Tick the correct letters.	Höre dem Gespräch dieser Personen über … zu. Wer denkt was? Setze ein ✓ bei den korrekten Buchstaben.
You will hear five short conversations.	Du wirst fünf kurze Gespräche hören.
You will hear each conversation twice.	Du wirst jedes Gespräch zweimal hören.
While you are listening, tick the correct box.	Während du zuhörst, setze ein ✓ in das richtige Kästchen.
At the end you will hear the story / interview again.	Am Ende hörst du die Story / das Interview nochmal.
Now listen to the story and do the tasks.	Höre dir jetzt die Geschichte an und löse die Aufgaben.
Which word group completes the sentence best?	Welche Wortgruppe vervollständigt den Satz am besten?
Mark the correct option to complete the sentences.	Markiere die jeweils korrekte Vervollständigung der Sätze.
Complete the table using two to five words.	Vervollständige die Tabelle mit zwei bis fünf Wörtern.

Reading and writing	Leseverstehen und Schreiben
First read the text. Then read the sentence beginnings and tick the correct ending.	Lies zuerst den Text. Dann lies die Satzanfänge und setze ein ✓ beim jeweils korrekten Satzende.
First read the information about the people, then look at the job / holiday / … offers. In each case find two options the person could choose.	Lies zuerst die Informationen über die Personen, dann schau dir die Job-/ Ferien-/ …-Angebote an. Finde für jede Person zwei Möglichkeiten, die sie wählen könnte.
You need not write complete sentences.	Du musst keine vollständigen Sätze schreiben.
Quote from the text.	Zitiere aus dem Text.
Find the correct parts of Mr Miller's quote.	Finde die korrekten Teile aus Mr. Millers Zitat.
Match each of these headings with a suitable paragraph from the text. (Some paragraphs don't match.)	Ordne jede dieser Überschriften einem passenden Textabsatz zu. (Zu einigen Absätzen passt keine Überschrift.)
Match the correct sentence parts. (Write down the letter in the box.)	Ordne die passenden Satzteile einander zu. (Schreibe den Buchstaben in das Kästchen.)
Match 1–4 to the information given in A–G. Some information doesn't fit.	Ordne 1–4 den Informationen in A–G zu. Einige Informationen lassen sich nicht zuordnen.
Answer the questions below. Give short answers.	Beantworte die unten stehenden Fragen kurz.
Answer the questions in complete sentences.	Beantworte die Fragen mit vollständigen Sätzen.
You can't find the answers to the following questions directly in the text.	Du wirst auf die folgenden Fragen keine direkten Antworten im Text finden.
The following words have more than one meaning. Which of the meanings is the one used in the text?	Die folgenden Wörter haben mehr als eine Bedeutung. Welche Bedeutung ist im Text gemeint?
Write down the German meaning as used in the text.	Schreibe die im Text gemeinte deutsche Bedeutung auf.
Complete the following sentences with suitable phrases from the text (with not more than five to seven words per gap).	Vervollständige die folgenden Sätze mit passenden Wendungen aus dem Text (max. fünf bis sieben Wörter pro Lücke).
Finish the sentences using information from the text.	Beende die Sätze mit Informationen aus dem Text.
Decide whether the following statements are right or wrong.	Entscheide, ob die folgenden Aussagen wahr oder falsch sind.
Find out whether the following statements are true, false or not given in the text. Tick the correct box.	Sind die folgenden Aussagen wahr, falsch oder nicht im Text gegeben? Setze ein ✓ in das korrekte Kästchen.
Scan paragraph A. Name two examples …	Scanne Absatz A. Nenne zwei Beispiele …

Find the opposites in the text.	Finde im Text die Gegensätze.
Find words or expressions that mean more or less the same.	Finde bedeutungsähnliche Wörter oder Wendungen.
Complete the text with words from the box.	Vervollständige den Text mit Wörtern aus dem Kasten.
Fill in suitable words or tick the correct box.	Trage passende Wörter ein oder setze ein ✓ beim korrekten Kästchen.
Complete the text with the correct form of the verbs.	Vervollständige den Text mit den korrekten Verbformen.
Use each word only once.	Verwende jedes Wort nur einmal.
Write complete sentences.	Schreibe vollständige Sätze.
Include the following points: ...	Berücksichtige die folgenden Punkte: ...
Make sure to write about all the aspects presented in each task.	Achte darauf, dass du über alle Aspekte jeder Aufgabe schreibst.
Write at least 80 words.	Schreibe mindestens 80 Wörter.
Write your introductory letter.	Schreibe einen Brief, in dem du dich vorstellst.
Describe what you get to know about ...	Beschreibe, was du über ... erfährst.
Explain Susan's opinion of ... and how she feels about ...	Erkläre Susans Meinung über ... und wie sie zu ... steht.
Comment on the statement (from your point of view).	Kommentiere die Aussage (aus deiner Sicht).
Write about your own experience.	Schreibe über deine eigenen Erfahrungen.
Give your personal opinion about / of / on ...	Schreibe deine persönliche Meinung über / zu ...
Give reasons for your opinion.	Begründe deine Meinung.
Write a conclusion and state ...	Schreibe eine Schlussfolgerung und lege ... dar.
Write a diary entry / a letter of complaint / a suitable ending (in the way the story is told).	Schreibe einen Tagebucheintrag / eine Beschwerde / ein passendes Ende (im Stil der Geschichte).
Read what the blogger has written. Then write back, answering all of her questions. Write 100–160 words.	Lies den Blog-Eintrag. Dann antworte und berücksichtige alle Fragen der Bloggerin. Schreibe 100–160 Wörter.
Write a reply to the blog entry / email and include at least four of these aspects: ...	Schreibe eine Antwort auf den Blog-Eintrag / die E-Mail und berücksichtige mindestens vier dieser Aspekte: ...
Continue the dialogue / conversation.	Setze den Dialog / die Konversation fort.
Write a structured text in which you show ...	Schreibe einen gegliederten Text, in dem du ... zeigst.
Choose one topic and mark it. Write a text of about 180 words. Count your words and write the number at the end of the text.	Wähle ein Thema aus und markiere es. Schreibe etwa 180 Wörter. Zähle die Wörter und schreibe die Summe ans Ende deines Texts.
Explain two of the following words in complete sentences.	Erkläre zwei der folgenden Wörter in vollständigen Sätzen.
Complete the questionnaire below. Write keywords or short sentences.	Vervollständige den untenstehenden Fragebogen. Schreibe Stichwörter oder kurze Sätze.
You want to sell ... Write an advert. Include: a headline / a slogan, information on the ... and its condition, on price and transport.	Du möchtest ... verkaufen. Schreibe eine Anzeige: mit einer Überschrift / einem Slogan, Informationen über ..., seinen Zustand, über den Preis und den Transport.
Choose one of the following tasks and write about 150 words.	Wähle eine der folgenden Aufgaben aus und schreibe ca. 150 Wörter.
What is the story behind the picture? Imagine you're one of the people. Write a text and include at least four of the following aspects: ...	Was ist die Geschichte hinter dem Bild? Stell dir vor, eine der abgebildeten Personen zu sein. Schreibe einen Text und berücksichtige mindestens vier dieser Aspekte: ...

Speaking / Sprechen

Describe the picture.	Beschreibe das Bild.
Look at the role card and act out the conversation.	Sieh dir die Rollenkarte an und führe das Gespräch vor.
Talk about what you think of ...	Sprich darüber, was du über ... denkst.
Give reasons.	Begründe.
Give (more) examples.	Gib (mehr) Beispiele an.
Discuss the advantages and disadvantages of ...	Erörtere / Diskutiere die Vor- und Nachteile von ...
Name other possibilities.	Nenne andere Möglichkeiten.
Explain which ... you would choose and why.	Erläutere, welche/n/s ... du wählen würdest und warum.
Explain the positive and negative aspects / the pros and cons of ...	Erläutere die positiven und negativen Aspekte von / die Pro- und Contra-Argumente zu ...
Ask four different questions about ... Use four different question forms.	Stelle vier verschiedene Fragen zu ... Verwende vier unterschiedliche Frageformen.

Mediation / Sprachmittlung

Read the information and write down the main ideas in German.	Lies die Informationen und notiere die Hauptgedanken auf Deutsch.
Read the text and write down five tips in German that are important when ...	Lies den Text und notiere fünf Tipps auf Deutsch, die wichtig bei ... sind.
Summarize the article in complete German sentences.	Fasse den Artikel in vollständigen deutschen Sätzen zusammen.
Pass on the information.	Gib die Informationen (auf Deutsch) weiter.

Titelbild
Shutterstock/Dudarev Mikhail

Illustrationen
Carlos Borrell Eiköter, Berlin (Umschlaginnenseite 2; S. 8/9 *Hintergrund*; S. 87 *unten* (u. S. 99 *unten*); **Michael Fleischmann**, Waldegg (S. 17 *oben*; S. 32 *(3b)*; S. 94); **Jeongsook Lee**, Heidelberg (S. 212; S. 213); **Klein & Halm, Berlin (S. 16; S. 31** *Flaggen; S. 55 Zug, Flugzeug; S. 55 Mitte li. u. re.)*; **David Norman**, Meerbusch (S. 45; S. 47; S. 53; S. 65; S. 66; S. 67; S. 150; S. 155); **Dorina Teßmann**, Berlin (*alle Hantel-Icons*; S. 83 u. S. 98).

Bildquellen
action press (S. 75 *oben: REX FEATURES LTD./Vincent Callebaut Architectures)*; **akg-images (S. 11** *Mitte: africanpictures; S. 13 re.: africanpictures)*; **CartoonStock (S. 176** *oben: Richard Dall, unten li.: Kresten Forsman, unten re.: Ralph Hagen)*; **www.colourbox.de (S. 68** *(2); S. 74 oben: JuNiArt)*; **Connect Community Development (S. 4** *oben re.; S. 14)*; **Corbis (S. 33** *re.: Frederic Soltan)*; **ddp images (S. 11** *oben: CAMERA PRESS/Martine Velon; S. 31 oben: 360°/CAMERA PRESS/Chad Chapman/Gallo Images; S. 50: CAMERA PRESS/Felix Clay; S. 62 oben: Capital Pictures)*; **epd-bild (S. 13** *li.: Keystone/Bandphoto Agency; S. 111: Henner Frankenfeld)*; **F1online (S. 105:** *re. UpperCut Images/B)*; **Fotolia (S. 4 oben li.: reif,** *unten re.: Alexander Raths; S. 6 oben li. großes Bild: ra2 studio, oben Mitte: Artur Marciniec, oben re.: destina, unten: jannoon028; S. 8 (A): Jacob Lund Photography; S. 9 (D): micromonkey, (E): michaeljung, Janine: Mayer Riccardo; S. 10 unten: demerzel21; S. 15 jozigirl: István Hájas; S. 17 unten: zooco; S. 24 oben: Jacques PALUT, unten: IRStone; S. 25 unten: Samuel Borges; S. 30 buffalo: VOLODYMYR BURDYAK, elephant: gallas, tiger: Michael Wick; S. 39: Alexander Raths; S. 53 oben: milosducati, unten Tablet: koosen; S. 55 oben: Zffoto; S. 56 (A) li.: ra2 studio, (A) re.: Artur Marciniec; S. 60 (A): destina; S. 62 Mars: Vadim Sadovski, DrSpock: photo-nuke; S. 68 oben re.: Sergey Nivens, (4): ZakS Photography; S. 70: Oleksandr Delyk; S. 72: Tom Wang; S. 77: romvo; S. 78 (1A): andrej pol, (1B): shaunwilkinson, (1C): vinbergv, (3B): aruba2000, (3C): Elnur, unten: WavebreakmediaMicro; S. 81 (u. S. 96): Maridav; S. 84 oben: Serj Siz`kov; S. 85 Bus: zmiter, Schule: trokerr; S. 87 oben: IEGOR LIASHENKO; S. 88: didecs; S. 91 unten: Dan Race; S. 92 oben li.: Felix Pergande, beach holiday (u. S. 101): Romolo Tavani, city visit: vitaliyvill; S. 93 (5) oben li.: highwaystarz, (5) oben Mitte: Sachs500, (5) oben re.: Dan Race, (5) unten li.: Lisa F. Young, (5) unten 2. von li.: Delphotostock, (5) unten re.: Klaus Eppele; S. 96 (u. S. 81) Maridav; S. 101 oben Mitte: Romolo Tavani, unten Mitte: Dan Race, unten re.: highwaystarz; S. 104 Werkzeug: romvo; S. 119 oben Mitte (u. S. 92): Romolo Tavani, unten re.: floya7; S. 127 Bundesverfassungsgericht: Klaus Eppele; S. 129 rubbish: Oleg Zhukov, pesticides: Dusan Kostic, wasting water: studioDG, industry: Ralf Geithe; S. 135 unten: VOLODYMYR BURDYAK; S. 140: Andrey Kuzmin; S. 149: Chris Hinkley; S. 150 li.: Daniel Ernst; S. 151 unten; S. 152: Daniel Ernst; S. 154 re.: Marina Lohrbach; S. 155 unten: Dirk Vonten; S. 161: Monkey Business; S. 165: jesadaphorn; S. 167: JPC-PROD; S. 179 unten: www.miriamdoerr.com)*; **GlowImages (S. 68** *oben li. u. oben Mitte: BlendRFBlendRF; S. 57 (D): ScienceFaction)*; **Julia Gunther (S. 29)**; **Image Source (S. 40** *re.: Brock Jones; S. 64 (u. S. 123): Petra Weitz; S. 134 oben: Craig Robinson; S. 166 unten: J. Geoffrey Canon)*; **interfilm (S. 27 u. S. 180: Amar/Pilgrim Films Production; S. 49: Walk or Fly/It's My Shout Productions LTD; S. 71 u. S. 126: The Red Thunder/Seariders Entertainment)**; **laif (S. 54: Polaris; S. 60** *(C): Le Figaro Magazine/Gladieu;* **S. 76: Reporters/Merlin Meuris ; S. 102: hemis.fr/Emmanuel Berthier); S. 130** *unten: Le Figaro Magazine/Martin)*; **mauritius images (S. 9** *(C) li.: mauritius images/robertharding/Gavin Hellier; S. 19: mauritius images/Alamy Stock Photo/Alex Segre; S. 32 (3a): age/Melba; S. 33 li.: Alamy/Naomi Bailey; S. 36 re. oben u. unten: Alamy/Wendy White; S. 47 oben: Alamy/zakir hossain chowdhury zakir; S. 55 (3): Alamy/Jochen Tack; S. 75 unten: Alamy/classic/Roger Cracknell 01; S. 93 (5) unten 2. von re.: Juice Images/Ian Lishman; S. 95 unten: Alamy/Angela Hampton Picture Library; S. 119 unten li.: Alamy/PE Forsberg; S. 131 oben: Alamy/TRVL/Horizons WWP; S. 134 unten: Alamy/Richard Smith; S. 175: Onoky/Eric Audras; S. 178 oben: UrbanImages/Alamy; S. 101 unten li.: Juice Images/Ian Lishman)*; **One Login (S. 48** *Mitte: Isis Wenger Ashalee, oben)*; **PantherMedia (S. 48** *(C): justtscott; S. 57 (F): Harvepino; S. 78 (2A): GeoImages; S. 79 unten: iophoto, S. 82 oben (u. S. 97 unten): kjpargeter; S. 97: kipargeter (u. S. 82))*; **Picture-Alliance (S. 36** *li.: AP, S. 56 (B): dpa, (C): AP Photo; S. 57 (E): dpa; S. 60 (D); S. 84 unten: dpa; S. 131 2. von oben abaca)*; **Prince EA (S. 61: "Sorry" Still from "Dear Future Generations")**; **Shutterstock (S. 4** *2. v. oben li.: michaeljung, unten li.: abeadev; S. 8 (B): Dragon Images; S. 9: David imtmphoto; S. 10/11 unten Hintergrund: Andrzej Kubik; S. 10 oben li.: Don Pablo, linker Rand: wikki, S. 11 unten: Nicole Gordine, rechter Rand: wikki; S. 15 Siseko: ibrandify gallery, Nate: Andre Valadao, Bafana: michaeljung, Suri: anekoho; S. 20: Monkey Business Images; S. 23: Anna Om; S. 25 Daniel Radcliffe: Featureflash, Queen Elizabeth: Joseph Sohm, Serena Williams: Leonard Zhukovsky, Barack Obama: Frederic Legrand - COMEO; S. 30 rhinoceros: Anton_Ivanov, lion: Deborah Kolb; S. 31 unten: Shane Gross; S. 37: Akhenaton Images; S. 40 li.: jtairat; Mitte: Armin Staudt; S. 42 oben: Claudia Paulussen, unten: Doin Oakenhelm; S. 46 oben: LianeM, unten: abeadev; S. 48 (A): Blend Images, (B): CURAphotography (D): RobinE; S. 53 Mitte: Shutterstock/symbiot; S. 55 (1): Kzenon, (2): Christian Draghici; S. 56/57 Hintergrund: Willyam Bradberry; S. 58 oben: Kostsov, unten: Ralwel; S. 59: Aleksandra Suzi; S. 62 Spacecadet: Reginast777; S. 68 (1): Pavel Ignatov, (3): Eric Isselee; S. 69: PathDoc; S. 74 unten ZouZou; S. 78 (2B): Matej Kastelic, (2C): kurhan, (3A): Patricia Hofmeester; S. 79 oben: Avatar_023; S. 82 unten (u. S. 97): SpeedKingz; S. 90 (u. S. 100): Martin Novak; S. 91 oben li.: Yulia Grigoryeva, oben re.: John Gomez; S. 92 hiking (u. S. 101): Sharon Freeman, boat trip: NEILRAS cycling tour: Gabi Wolf; S. 93 (6) li.: Reno Martin; S. 95 oben: Avatar_023; S. 97 oben (u. S. 82): SpeedKingz; S. 100 (u. S. 90): Martin Novak; S. 101 oben li. (u. S. 92): Sharon Freeman; S. 104 li.: Sebastian Duda, oben Mitte: Axel Bueckert, S. 105 li.: Monkey Business Images; S. 127 oben li.: XiXinXing, oben re.: Bobb Klissourski, Bundestag: Sergey Kelin, Bellevue: bofotolux, Bundesrat: Elpisterra, Kanzleramt: Sergey*

Kohl; S. 128: Photographee.eu; S. 129 chemicals: Victor Rotaru, sewage: keantian, mineral resource: abutyrin, nuclear waste: cromic, expanding cities: gyn9037, more deserts: Galyna Andrushko, cars: Juergen Faelchle; S. 130 oben: Dolimac, Mitte: GUDKOV ANDREY, Hintergrund Karte: Sergey Pomogayev; S. 131 2. von unten: Becky Stares, unten: satori.artwork; S. 132: LU-STOCKPHOTO; S. 133 oben li.: saiko3p, oben re.: ChameleonsEye, unten li.: Susan Santa Maria, unten re.: Bill Kret; S. 135 oben: niall dunne; S. 136 li.: J Main, Mitte: Zack Frank, re.: Adam Parent; S. 145: art4all; S. 146: Constantin Stanciu; S. 147: Pinar Ince; S. 150 re.: Robert Kneschke; S. 151 oben: Robert Kneschke; S. 153: Robert Kneschke; S. 154 li.: Daniel M Ernst; S. 155 oben: Frolphy; S. 159: dotshock; S. 160: Lorelyn Medina; S. 163: Blend Images; S. 166 oben: Jesus Sanz; S. 168: Tharakorn; S. 171: Monkey Business Images; S. 174: l i g h t p o e t; S. 178 (u. S. 199)Flaggen: Christopher Poliquin; S. 179 oben: Artisticco; S. 206: Solaie; S. 208: Blan-k; S. 209: Nightman1965; S. 210 li.: Victoria Kurylo, re.: saknakorn; S. 211 oben: suwatpatt, Mitte li.: Gouraud Studio, Mitte re.: Misha Beliy, unten: Camilo Torres; S. 212: Feng Yu; S. 215: Elena Noeva; S. 216 oben: faithie, Mitte: Vertes Edmond Mihai, unten li.: Arcady, unten re.: phoelixDE; S. 217 oben li.: Neil Mitchell, oben re.: StockCube, Mitte li.: Dja65, Mitte re.: Early Spring, unten: STILLFX; S. 218 oben: nulinukas, Mitte: ArtStudia Group, unten li.: AlexRoz, unten re.: Petr Malyshev; S. 219 oben: Weenee, 2. von oben: Tyler Olson, 2. von unten: Minerva Studio, unten li.: Hriana, unten re.: Fer Gregory; S. 220 oben: Blablo101, unten: wavebreakmedia; S. 221: Christopher Elwell; S. 222: Rob Byron; S. 223 oben: AlexRoz, unten: Maksym Bondarchuk; S. 224: Liudmyla Marykon; S. 225: grace21; S. 226 oben: Marbury, Mitte: CTR Photos, unten: Microgen; S. 227 oben: tektur, 2. von oben: Punyaruk Baingern, 2. von unten: Ints Vikmanis, unten: Zadiraka Evgenii; S. 228 li.: Patrick Foto, re.: pavel dudek; S. 229: Slavoljub Pantelic; S. 230 oben: gualtiero boffi, Mitte: Ricardo Reitmeyer, unten: BPTU; S. 231 li.: Tabby Mittins, Mitte: Anan Kaewkhammul, re.: Eric Isselee; S. 232: Rafal Kulik); **The Independent (S. 28: Julia Gunther 2015); TopicMedia (S. 92** *oben re.: imageBROKER/hkp);* **Trócaire (S. 86 (u. S. 99: Trócaire); Gary Turk (from „It's your future": S. 38); © UNICEF (S. 34, S. 35); Vincent Callebaut Architectures (S. 60** *(E)); Unschlaginnenseite 3: Angela Jones);* **Visum, Hannover (S. 104** *oben re.: A. Vossberg);* **Alexia Webster (S. 12); WILDLIFE, Hamburg (S. 93** *(6): re.* S. Muller); **YourPhotoToday** (S. 84 *Mitte*)

Textquellen

S. 12 "South Africa – then and now". Berichte von Akhia und Lindokuhle aus: "Born Frees and the Confidence of Youth". Alexia Webster 2014;
S. 19-23 "Returned". Aus: Fanie Viljoen: "Scarred Lions". Ransom Publishing, Winchester 2013. S. 10-57;
S. 28 "The Lion Queens". Aus: Kate Wills: "Power Rangers – The Lion Queens" The New Review. 27.09.2015. S. 20-21;
S. 38 Auszug aus "It's Your Future", Gary Turk (2015);
S. 43-44 "No turning back". Aus: Benjamin Zephaniah: "Face". © 1999 by Benjamin Zephaniah. Published by Bloomsbury Publishing Children's Books, U.S.A., New York 2004. S. 45-65;
S. 50 Jon Snow: "My shameful dilemma". http://blogs.channel4.com/snowblog/my-shameful-dilemma/1715 (25.06.2009);
S. 65-66 Marcus Sedgwick: "Floodland". Orion children's books (imprint of Hodder & Stoughton, reissue 2010). First published in Great Britain as a Dolphin paperback (2000). S. 3-8;
S. 81 u. S. 96 "I'm a European". Aus: „I am European" Wettbewerb 2013/youthreporter.eu;
S. 82-83 u. S. 97 Ann Angel: "The Bracelet". Aus: "Sudden Flash Youth". 65 Short-short stories, ed. by Christine Perkins et al. Persea Books Inc, New York 2011. S. 154-157;
S. 86 u. S. 99 "Climate change challenge weekend". Trócaire 2015;
S. 88 Daniel Handler: "Principals and principles". Aus: "Guys write for guys read". Edited by Jon Scieszka. Viking 2005. S. 112-113;
S. 110 "Interview with Film-maker Andrew Hilton". Tahiat Mahboob. Asia Society 2012;
S. 120 Auszug aus: "Dear Future Generations: Sorry", Prince Ea, 2015;
S. 142-145 Malorie Blackman: "Searching for a two-way street". Aus: "Stories celebrating Human Rights". Amnesty International. Walker Books Ltd, London 2009. S. 136-142;
S. 148 Hanna Bottomy Voskuil: "Currents". Aus: "Sudden Flash Youth". 65 Short-short stories, ed. by Christine Perkins et. al. Persea Books Inc, New York 2011. S. 28-29.

COUNTRIES AND CONTINENTS

Country/Continent	Adjective	Person	People
Florence is from **Canada**.	*Hockey is* **Canadian**.	*Florence is* **a Canadian**.	**Canadians love** *Hockey.*
Afghanistan [æf'gænɪstæn] *Afghanistan*	**Afghan** ['æfgæn]	**an Afghan**	**the Afghans**
Africa ['æfrɪkə] *Afrika*	**African** ['æfrɪkən]	**an African**	**the Africans**
Albania [æl'beɪniə] *Albanien*	**Albanian** [æl'beɪniən]	**an Albanian**	**the Albanians**
America [ə'merɪkə] *Amerika*	**American** [ə'merɪkən]	**an American**	**the Americans**
Asia ['eɪʃə, 'eɪʒə] *Asien*	**Asian** ['eɪʃn, 'eɪʒn]	**an Asian**	**the Asians**
Australia [ɒ'streɪliə] *Australien*	**Australian** [ɒ'streɪliən]	**an Australian**	**the Australians**
Austria ['ɒstriə] *Österreich*	**Austrian** ['ɒstriən]	**an Austrian**	**the Austrians**
Belarus [ˌbel'ruːs] *Weißrussland*	**Belarusian** [ˌbel'ruːsiən]	**a Belarusian**	**the Belarusians**
Belgium ['beldʒəm] *Belgien*	**Belgian** ['beldʒən]	**a Belgian**	**the Belgians**
Bosnia and Herzegovina ['bɒzniə ən ˌhɜːtsəgə'viːnə] *Bosnien und Herzegowina*	**Bosnian** ['bɒzniən]; **Herzegovinian** [ˌhɜːtsəgə'vɪniən]	**a Bosnian; a Herzegovinian**	**the Bosnians; the Herzegovinians**
Botswana ['bɒtswɑːnə] *Botswana*	**Botswanan** ['bɒtswɑːnən]	**a Motswana**	**the Batswana**
Brazil [brə'zɪl] *Brasilien*	**Brasilian** [brə'zɪliən]	**a Brasilian**	**the Brasilians**
Bulgaria [bʌl'geəriə] *Bulgarien*	**Bulgarian** [bʌl'geəriən]	**a Bulgarian**	**the Bulgarians**
Canada ['kænədə] *Kanada*	**Canadian** [kə'neɪdiən]	**a Canadian**	**the Canadians**
China ['tʃaɪnə] *China*	**Chinese** [tʃaɪ'niːz]	**a Chinese**	**the Chinese**
Croatia [krəʊ'eɪʃə] *Kroatien*	**Croatian** [krəʊ'eɪʃn]	**a Croatian**	**the Croatians**
the Czech Republic [tʃek rɪ'pʌblɪk] *Tschechien, die Tschechische Republik*	**Czech** [tʃek]	**a Czech**	**the Czechs**
Denmark ['denmɑːk] *Dänemark*	**Danish** ['deɪnɪʃ]	**a Dane** [deɪn]	**the Danes**
England ['ɪŋglənd] *England*	**English** ['ɪŋglɪʃ]	**an Englishman/-woman**	**the English**
Estonia [e'stəʊniə] *Estland*	**Estonian** [e'stəʊniən]	**an Estonian**	**the Estonians**
Europe ['jʊərəp] *Europa*	**European** [jʊərə'piːən]	**a European**	**the Europeans**
Finland ['fɪnlənd] *Finnland*	**Finnish** ['fɪnɪʃ]	**a Finn** [fɪn]	**the Finns**
France [frɑːns] *Frankreich*	**French** [frentʃ]	**a Frenchman/-woman**	**the French**
Germany ['dʒɜːməni] *Deutschland*	**German** ['dʒɜːmən]	**a German**	**the Germans**
(Great) Britain ['brɪtn] *Großbritannien*	**British** ['brɪtɪʃ]	**a Briton** ['brɪtn]	**the British**
Greece [griːs] *Griechenland*	**Greek** [griːk]	**a Greek**	**the Greeks**
Holland ['hɒlənd] *Holland, die Niederlande*	**Dutch** [dʌtʃ]	**a Dutchman/-woman**	**the Dutch**
Hungary ['hʌŋgəri] *Ungarn*	**Hungarian** [hʌŋ'geəriən]	**a Hungarian**	**the Hungarians**
Iceland ['aɪslənd] *Island*	**Icelandic** [aɪs'lændɪk]	**an Icelander** ['aɪsləndə]	**the Icelanders**
India ['ɪndiə] *Indien*	**Indian** ['ɪndiən]	**an Indian**	**the Indians**
Iran [ɪ'rɑːn] *Iran*	**Iranian** [ɪ'reɪniən]	**an Iranian**	**the Iranians**
Ireland ['aɪələnd] *Irland*	**Irish** ['aɪrɪʃ]	**an Irishman/-woman**	**the Irish**
Italy ['ɪtəli] *Italien*	**Italian** [ɪ'tæliən]	**an Italian**	**the Italians**
Jamaica [dʒəmeɪkə] *Jamaika*	**Jamaican** [dʒəmeɪkən]	**a Jamaican**	**the Jamaicans**
Japan [dʒə'pæn] *Japan*	**Japanese** [dʒæpə'niːz]	**a Japanese**	**the Japanese**
Kosovo ['kɒsəvəʊ] *Kosovo*	**Kosovan** ['kɒsəvən]	**a Kosovan**	**the Kosovans**
Latvia ['lætviə] *Lettland*	**Latvian** ['lætviən]	**a Latvian**	**the Latvians**
Lebanon ['lebənən] *Libanon*	**Lebanese** [lebə'niːz]	**a Lebanese**	**the Lebanese**
Lesotho [lə'suːtuː] *Lesotho*	**Basotho** [bə'suːtuː]	**a Mosotho**	**the Basotho**
Lithuania [ˌlɪθju'eɪniə] *Litauen*	**Lithuanian** [ˌlɪθju'eɪniə]	**a Lithuanian**	**the Lithuanians**
Luxembourg ['lʌksəmbɜːg] *Luxemburg*	**Luxembourg**	**a Luxembourger** ['lʌksəmbɜːgə]	**the Luxembourgers**
Malta ['mɔːltə] *Malta*	**Maltese** [mɔːl'tiːz]	**a Maltese**	**the Maltese**

Mexico ['meksɪkəʊ] *Mexiko*	**Mexican** ['meksɪkən]	**a Mexican**	**the Mexicans**
Moldova [mɒl'dəʊvə] *Moldawien*	**Moldovan** [mɒl'dəʊvən]	**a Moldovan**	**the Moldovans**
Montenegro [ˌmɒntɪ'ni:grəʊ] *Montenegro*	**Montenegrin** [ˌmɒntɪ'ni:grɪn]	**a Montenegrin**	**the Montenegrins**
Mozambique [məʊzæm'bi:k] *Mosambik*	**Mozambican** [məʊzæm'bi:kən]	**a Mozambican**	**the Mozambicans**
Namibia [nə'mɪbiə] *Namibia*	**Namibian** [nə'mɪbiən]	**a Namibian**	**the Namibians**
the Netherlands ['neðələndz] *die Niederlande, Holland*	**Dutch** [dʌtʃ]	**a Dutchman/-woman**	**the Dutch**
New Zealand [nju: 'zi:lənd] *Neuseeland*	**New Zealand** [nju: 'zi:lənd]	**a New Zealander**	**the New Zealanders**
North America [ˌnɔ:θ‿ə'merɪkə] *Nordamerika*	**North American** [ˌnɔ:θ‿ə'merɪkən]	**a North American**	**the North Americans**
Northern Ireland [ˌnɔ:ðən‿'aɪələnd] *Nordirland*	**Northern Irish** [ˌnɔ:ðən‿'aɪrɪʃ]	**a Northern Irishman / a Northern Irishwoman**	**the Northern Irish**
Norway ['nɔ:weɪ] *Norwegen*	**Norwegian** [nɔ:'wi:dʒən]	**a Norwegian**	**the Norwegians**
Pakistan [pækɪ'stæn] *Pakistan*	**Pakistani** [pækɪ'stæni]	**a Pakistani**	**the Pakistani**
Poland ['pəʊlənd] *Polen*	**Polish** ['pəʊlɪʃ]	**a Pole** [pəʊl]	**the Poles**
Portugal ['pɔ:tʃʊgl] *Portugal*	**Portuguese** [pɔ:tʃu'gi:z]	**a Portuguese**	**the Portuguese**
Republic of North Macedonia [ˌmæsə'dəʊniə] *Republik Nordmazedonien*	**Macedonian** [ˌmæsə'dəʊniən]	**a Macedonian**	**the Macedonians**
Romania [ru'meɪniə] *Rumänien*	**Romanian** [ru'meɪniən]	**a Romanian**	**the Romanians**
Russia ['rʌʃə] *Russland*	**Russian** ['rʌʃn]	**a Russian**	**the Russians**
Scotland ['skɒtlənd] *Schottland*	**Scottish** ['skɒtɪʃ]	**a Scotsman/-woman, a Scot** [skɒt]	**the Scots, the Scottish**
Serbia ['sɜ:biə] *Serbien*	**Serbian** ['sɜ:biən]	**a Serb** [sɜ:b]	**the Serbs**
Slovakia [slə'vækiə] *die Slowakei*	**Slovak** ['sləʊvæk]	**a Slovakian** [slə'vækiən]	**the Slovakians**
Slovenia [slə'vi:niə] *Slowenien*	**Slovene** ['sləʊvi:n]	**a Slovenian** [slə'vi:niən]	**the Slovenians**
Somalia [sə'mɑ:liə] *Somalien*	**Somali** [sə'mɑ:li]	**a Somali**	**the Somali**
South America [ˌsaʊθ‿ə'merɪkə] *Südamerika*	**South American** [ˌsaʊθ‿ə'merɪkən]	**a South American**	**the South Americans**
Spain [speɪn] *Spanien*	**Spanish** ['spænɪʃ]	**a Spaniard** ['spænɪəd]	**the Spaniards**
Swaziland [swɑ:zilænd] *Swasiland*	**Swazi** [swɑ:zi]	**a Swazi**	**the Swazis**
Sweden ['swi:dn] *Schweden*	**Swedish** ['swi:dɪʃ]	**a Swede** [swi:d]	**the Swedes**
Switzerland ['swɪtsələnd] *die Schweiz*	**Swiss** [swɪs]	**a Swiss**	**the Swiss**
Syria ['sɪriə] *Syrien*	**Syrian** ['sɪriən]	**a Syrian**	**the Syrians**
Tunisia [tju'nɪziə] *Tunesien*	**Tunisian** [tju'nɪziən]	**a Tunisian**	**the Tunisians**
Turkey ['tɜ:ki] *die Türkei*	**Turkish** ['tɜ:kɪʃ]	**a Turk** [tɜ:k]	**the Turks**
Ukraine [ju:'kreɪn] *die Ukraine*	**Ukrainian** [ju:'kreɪniən]	**a Ukrainian**	**the Ukrainians**
the United Kingdom (the UK) [junaɪtɪd 'kɪŋdəm, ju:'keɪ] *das Vereinigte Königreich (Großbritannien und Nordirland)*	**British** ['brɪtɪʃ]	**a Briton** ['brɪtn]	**the British**
the United States of America (the USA) [junaɪtɪd steɪts‿əv‿ə'merɪkə, ju:‿es‿'eɪ] *die Vereinigten Staaten von Amerika*	**American** [ə'merɪkən]	**an American**	**the Americans**
Vietnam [ˌvi:et'næm], [ˌvi:et'nɑ:m] *Vietnam*	**Vietnamese** [vi:ˌetnə'mi:z]	**a Vietnamese**	**the Vietnamese**
Wales [weɪlz] *Wales*	**Welsh** [welʃ]	**a Welshman/-woman**	**the Welsh**
Zimbabwe [zɪm'bɑ:bwi] *Zimbabwe*	**Zimbabwean** [zɪm'bɑ:bwiən]	**a Zimbabwean**	**the Zimbabweans**